CHARRED LULLABIES

E D I T O R S

Sherry B. Ortner, Nicholas B. Dirks, Geoff Eley

A LIST OF TITLES

IN THIS SERIES APPEARS

AT THE BACK OF

THE BOOK

PRINCETON STUDIES IN

CULTURE / POWER / HISTORY

CHARRED LULLABIES

CHAPTERS IN AN ANTHROPOGRAPHY OF VIOLENCE

E. Valentine Daniel

PRINCETON UNIVERSITY PRESS
PRINCETON, NEW JERSEY

PUBLISHED BY PRINCETON UNIVERSITY PRESS, 41 WILLIAM STREET,
PRINCETON, NEW JERSEY 08540
IN THE UNITED KINGDOM: PRINCETON UNIVERSITY PRESS,
CHICHESTER, WEST SUSSEX

LIBRARY OF CONGRESS CATALOGING-IN-PUBLICATION DATA

DANIEL, E. VALENTINE.
CHARRED LULLABIES : CHAPTERS IN AN ANTHROPOGRAPHY
OF VIOLENCE / E. VALENTINE DANIEL.
P. CM. — (PRINCETON STUDIES IN CULTURE/POWER/HISTORY)
INCLUDES BIBLIOGRAPHICAL REFERENCES AND INDEX.
ISBN 0-691-02774-9 (CLOTH : ALK. PAPER)
ISBN 0-691-02773-0 (PBK. : ALK. PAPER)
1. ETHNOLOGY—SRI LANKA—FIELD WORK.
2. ETHNOLOGY—SRI LANKA—PHILOSOPHY.
3. VIOLENCE—SRI LANKA. 4. SRI LANKA—ETHNIC RELATIONS.
5. SRI LANKA—SOCIAL CONDITIONS.
6. SRI LANKA—POLITICS AND GOVERNMENT—1978–
I. TITLE. II. SERIES.
GN635.S72D36 1996
303.6'095493—DC20 96-20275 CIP

THIS BOOK HAS BEEN COMPOSED IN BERKELEY BOOK

PRINCETON UNIVERSITY PRESS BOOKS ARE PRINTED
ON ACID-FREE PAPER AND MEET THE GUIDELINES FOR
PERMANENCE AND DURABILITY OF THE COMMITTEE ON
PRODUCTION GUIDELINES FOR BOOK LONGEVITY
OF THE COUNCIL ON LIBRARY RESOURCES

PRINTED IN THE UNITED STATES OF AMERICA

1 3 5 7 9 10 8 6 4 2

Dedicated to the Memory of
Rajani Rajasingam Thiranagama

CONTENTS

ACKNOWLEDGMENTS

IT HAS TAKEN me more than a decade to write this book. Over this period I have acquired many debts, more than I can number. I will name only a few. Among colleagues, students, and friends, the following have given me helpful comments on various parts and versions of *Charred Lullabies*: Fr. Amilraj, Ben Anderson, Arjun Appadurai, Ben Bavink, Susan Bean, John Comaroff, Bernard Cohn, Veena Das, Jaysingh David, Piyal de Silva, A. Devadas, Nicholas Dirks, Carol Eastman, Clifford Geertz, Kumari Jayawardena, Arthur Kleinman, John Knudsen, Riyad Koya, Richard Kurin, David Ludden, David Pederson, Harry Powers, Franklin Pressler, Nirmala Rajasingam, Lee Schlesinger, David Spain, and Anne Stoler. My brother, George Daniel, was an invaluable consultant during my writing of chapter 3. Stephanie Hoelscher was of enormous help in tracking down references and helping me with the index. The four readers whom I wish to separate out in order to express to them my special gratitude for their critical input are Allen Feldman, Webb Kean, Gananath Obeyesekere, and, especially, Susan Reed. I, however, am solely responsible for any and all of the book's shortcomings.

Grants from the following institutions have enabled me to carry out the research necessary for the completion of this book: The Social Science Research Council and the American Council of Learned Societies, the American Institute of Indian Studies, the World Institute for Development and Economic Research, in Helsinki. A grant from the National Endowment for the Humanities was made available to me the academic year of 1985–1986, during which I was able to transcribe the bulk of my field interviews. Several awards from the University of Michigan's Faculty Research Fund enabled me to make brief trips back to Sri Lanka and India during the later stages of the writing of this book in order to recheck some details with informants and in archives, and clear up some eleventh-hour doubts. I thank them all.

Grateful acknowledgment is also made to the publishers for permission to reproduce, in highly revised forms, the following chapters:

Chapter 1 is a revised version of "Three Dispositions towards the Past: One Sinhala, Two Tamil." In *Identity, Consciousness and the Past*, ed. H. L. Seneviratne. Special issue of *Social Analysis* (1989).

Chapter 2 is a revised version of "Sacred Places and Violent Spaces." In *Sri Lanka: History and the Roots of Conflict*, ed. Jonathan Spencer. London: Routledge, 1990.

Chapter 3 is a revised version of "Tea Talk: Violent Measures in the Discursive Practices of Sri Lanka's Estate Tamils." *Comparative Studies in Society and History* 15(3) (1993)

Chapter 5 is a revised version of "The Individual in Terror." In *Embodi-*

ment and Experience: The Existential Ground of Culture and Self, ed. Thomas Csordas. Cambridge: Cambridge University Press, 1994.

Chapter 6 is a revised version of "Suffering Nation and Alienation." In *Questioning Otherness: An Interdisciplinary Exchange. Papers from the 1995 Distinguished International Lecture Series*, ed. Virginia R. Dominguez and Catherine M. Lewis, 1995.

Chapter 7 is a revised version of "Crushed Glass, or, Is There a Counterpoint to Culture?" In *Culture/Contexture*, ed. E. Valentine Daniel and Jeffrey Peck. Berkeley and Los Angeles: University of California Press, 1996.

I must thank my wife Peg Hoey-Daniel and my sons, Naren and Sateesh, who have endured much during the writing of this book. I thank them for their patience and understanding.

Above all, I thank the more than one thousand informants who made this book both necessary and possible, and who must, alas, remain unnamed.

I dedicate this book to the memory of Dr. Rajani Rajasingam Thiranagama, a Tamil, married to a Sinhala, Professor of Anatomy at the University of Jaffna, a fearless fighter for human rights, daughter of my favorite math teacher, and whom I remember best as a sparkling little girl with the brightest and biggest eyes you would have ever seen. She was shot to death, in full view of her children, by a fellow Tamil whose only claim to glory was to follow orders.

NOTES ON TRANSLITERATION

Tamil

Short Vowels

a	as in English *u*p
i	as in English s*i*t
u	as in English p*u*t
e	as in English g*e*t
o	as in English l*oo*k

Long Vowels

ā	as in English p*a*lm
ī	as in English l*ea*d
ū	as in English p*oo*l
ē	as in English w*a*de
ō	as in English r*o*be

Consonants

k (initial position)	as in English *c*over
k (other positions)	as in English *h*ut
kk	as in English bu*cc*aneer
c	as in English *s*un
cc	as in English ca*tch*
ṭ (retroflex)	as in English lar*d*er (approximately)
ṭṭ (retroflex)	as in English ho*t-d*og
t	as in English ra*th*er (with no aspiration)
tt	as in English pa*th* (with no aspiration)
p (initial position)	as in English *p*unt
p (other positions)	as in English ru*bb*er
pp	as in English ru*p*ture
r	as in English (British) b*r*ook
rr	as in English *tr*y
ṅ (before k)	as in English pu*n*k
ñ	as in Spanish se*ñ*or
ṇ (retroflex)	as in English (American) cair*n* (approximately)
ṇ (dental; before t)	as in English a*n*them

m	as in English *m*other
l	as in English *lill*y
ṛ (retroflex)	As in English (American) hu*rr*ah (aproximately)
ḷ (retroflex)	no equivalent in English; an "l" made with the tip of the tongue on the roof of the mouth

Sinhala (in Addition to the Tamil Equivalents Above)

ä	as in English h*a*t
ə	as in English *a*nnounce
ṁ	as in Latin su*mm*um (stressed nasalized bilabial)
ś	between *sh*am and *s*and (also occurs in Tamil)
d	as in English *the* (no aspiration)

CHARRED LULLABIES

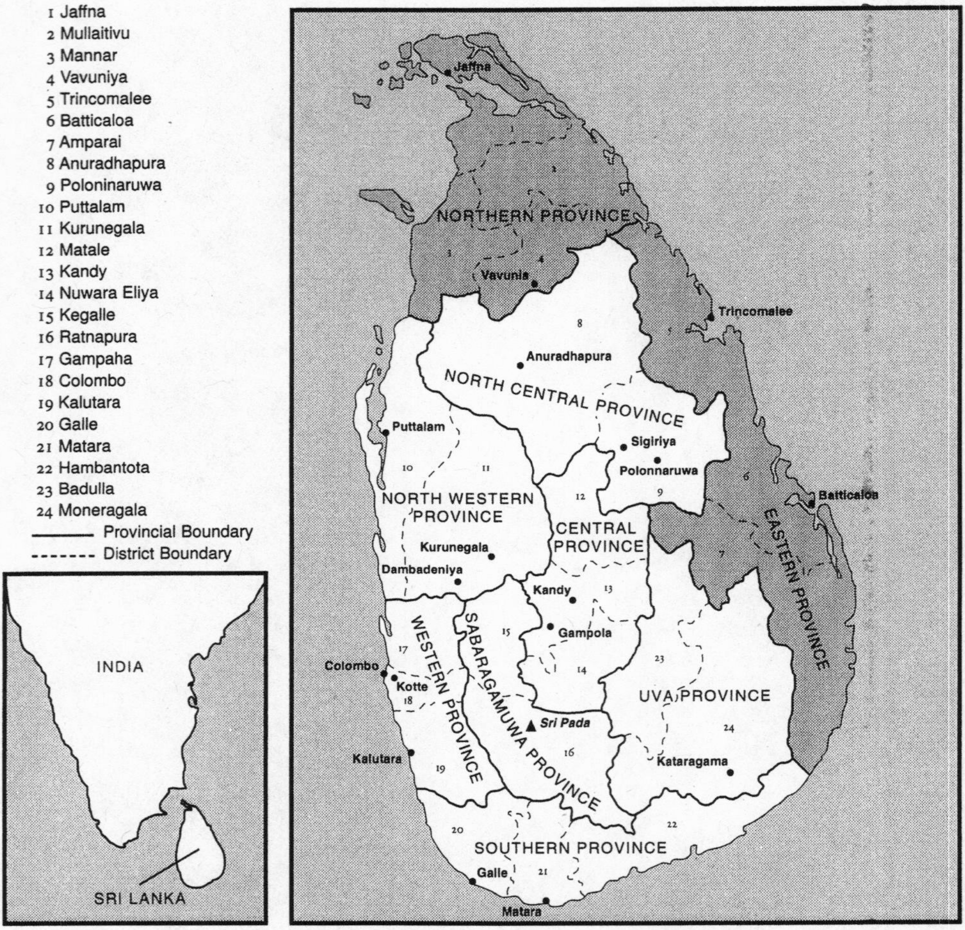
1 Jaffna
2 Mullaitivu
3 Mannar
4 Vavuniya
5 Trincomalee
6 Batticaloa
7 Amparai
8 Anuradhapura
9 Poloninaruwa
10 Puttalam
11 Kurunegala
12 Matale
13 Kandy
14 Nuwara Eliya
15 Kegalle
16 Ratnapura
17 Gampaha
18 Colombo
19 Kalutara
20 Galle
21 Matara
22 Hambantota
23 Badulla
24 Moneragala
Provincial Boundary
District Boundary
INDIA
SRI LANKA
Jaffna
NORTHERN PROVINCE
Vavunia
Trincomalee
Anuradhapura
NORTH CENTRAL PROVINCE
Puttalam
Sigiriya
Polonnaruwa
Batticaloa
NORTH WESTERN PROVINCE
CENTRAL PROVINCE
EASTERN PROVINCE
Kurunegala
Dambadeniya
Kandy
Gampola
WESTERN PROVINCE
SABARAGAMUWA PROVINCE
Colombo
Kotte
UVA PROVINCE
Sri Pada
Kalutara
Kataragama
SOUTHERN PROVINCE
Galle
Matara

Map 1. Sri Lanka

INTRODUCTION

MANY have died. To say more is to simplify, but to fathom the statement is also to make the fact bearable. Tellipalai, Nilaveli, Manippay, Boosa, Dollar Farm, Kokkadicholai—mere place-names of another time—have been transformed into names of places spattered with blood and mortal residue. Kelani Ganga and Kalu Ganga, Sri Lankan rivers of exquisite beauty, for a shudderingly brief period in 1989, were clogged with bodies and foamed with blood. Many have died. How to give an account of these shocking events without giving in to a desire to shock? And more important, what does it mean to give such an account? That is the burden of this book.

Background

In the spring of 1982 I applied to the Social Science Research Council for a grant to enable me to go to Sri Lanka the following year. My project was a benign one: to collect folk songs sung by Tamil women who worked on that country's tea estates. Based on a sample, which I had collected on previous visits, of lamentations, work songs, nuptial songs, devotional songs, and especially lullabies, I hypothesized that in the lyrics of such songs one could discover an ethnohistory that was different from the "master narratives" found in the official histories of tea plantations and of plantation workers.

When I wrote my proposal, I was on a quest for an alternative narrative, one that would serve as a counterpoint to the official one about the history of labor and displacement. Little did I expect to find *another alternative* narrative, one that defied my expectations and plans. I had no idea that by the time I reached Sri Lanka the following year, I would arrive on the heels of the worst anti-Tamil riots known in that island paradise to find that none of my singers were in a mood to sing, and to find my best singer rummaging for what she might salvage from the shell of her fire-gorged home.[1] What greeted me was an outpouring of reports of men's (mainly) inhumanity to their fellowmen, women, and children. Before I knew it, defying all research designs and disciplinary preparations, I was entangled in a project that had me rather than I it. The very words "project," "informants," "information," "interview," "evidence," "description" took on new and terrifying meanings. Those anthropological methodologies and theories designed to enhance the understanding and explanations of coherent social units, be they called castes, tribes, villages, street corners, or neighborhoods, all defined by a certain measure of concordance of thought and practice, had suddenly become inappropriate. The challenge was to understand a state of utter discordance that had begun to be sustained by the relentless presence—now exploding, then simmering—of violence. That method of fieldwork, made famous by Bronislaw Malinowski and now a standard practice in anthropology, of staying put in one location for a certain length of time in order to study a place or a problem, had become impossible. I was urged to move on, partly by my informants and partly by the information: to move away from where my continued presence could have spelled trouble for both my informants and me, and to move after stories, not so much to find newer and greater horror tales as to confirm, by "positive means" (a rather bizarre method for a hermeneutically inclined anthropologist such as myself), the truth—preferably the untruths—of the rumors I had heard; and then to understand. Between the latter part of 1983 and the end of June 1984 I traveled thousands of miles all over Sri Lanka and southern India engaged in such a quest. I returned to Sri Lanka and South India in the spring of 1986 and again in the summer of 1987. I also spent parts of the summers of 1987, 1990, 1992, and 1994 in Europe—mainly in the United Kingdom. All this to follow trails, to confirm and confute rumors, to understand if and why what I had heard was true, and also to act as a courier for family members and friends who were separated by violence, terror, and death. Stories, stories, stories! I have never known for sure if I am their prisoner or their jailer.

Leading Questions

Ever since my first return to the United States in 1984[2] I have also been burdened with the problem of what to do with all the material I had gathered, how to understand the hundreds of hours of taped interviews, transcripts, and field notes. The problem posed itself in the form of five leading questions:

1. Accounts of violence, especially of the kind of collective violence that occurred in Sri Lanka in 1983 (or far more horrendously in Nazi Germany in World War II), are vulnerable to taking on a prurient form. How does an anthropologist write an ethnography or—to borrow a more apt term from Jean-Paul Dumont—an anthropography of violence (1986), without its becoming a pornography of violence?

2. When faced with the risk of an account's being fattened up into prurience, flattening it down into theory presents itself as an easy alternative to the scholar. This escape route, however, comes at a price: the price of betraying those victims of violence (and, in at least one instance, a perpetrator of violence) who wished to communicate with the anthropologist and through him to the outside world some part of the experience of the passion and the pain of violence in its brutal immediacy. To call an experience "immediate" is not to say that it is unmediatable in principle, but to acknowledge the enormous difficulty entailed in mediating or communicating it in fact and the impotency one feels in trying to do so. To complicate one's charge further,

what must be conveyed is not only the experience of violence as an event but complex agendas and already begun mediations such as demands for justice, revenge, forgiveness, freedom, and relief. How to be true, then, to these charges as well?

3. One may avoid both of the above problems by doing nothing. This has been the alternative by which I have, over the past twelve years, been most frequently tempted. But the discomfort that I would be condemned to live in for the rest of my life were I to have chosen such an alternative would have been an ethical one. In opening up my tape recorder and notebook to my informants, I took upon myself the responsibility of telling a wider world stories that they told me, some at grave risks to their lives, only because they believed that there was a wider world that cared about the difference between good and evil. The charge to tell a wider world also betrays these victims' despair over their own narrow world that has lost its capacity to tell the difference between good and evil and their hope in a wider world that has not. How are these victims and informants constructing this wider world in general and its agent, me, in particular? Or conversely, how do they construct the wider world through their construction of me?

4. Many of those who were informants from my perspective were informers from the perspective of organizations in whose hands lay the power to punish, to torture, to kill. These included the various "law-enforcing organizations" of two nation-states (Sri Lanka and India) and the various Tamil militant groups. How could I assure the anonymity of my informants?

5. Last but not least was my concern for my own safety and my desire to safeguard the possibility of my returning to Sri Lanka, to a country and a people I cannot help but love.

Were this book to be judged on the basis of how I have managed these five leading problems, on prima facie evidence, the book is a failure. But I cannot even imagine what it would mean to have succeeded. For the ingenuity required for success—even if I were capable of such ingenuity—could have only distracted us from this anthropography's burden. The prurience of violence has leaked in. How else could the average reader, living in an antiseptic even if not an uncaring world, have an inkling of the foul scent that he or she has been spared. Theory too I have admitted, neither surreptitiously nor sparingly but with a vengeance. However, the dominant theory that I have employed serves my purpose by paradox, as it were. There are those theories which, by virtue of their long-standing naturalization in the social sciences as well as their partial integration into common sense (e.g., Marxism, psychoanalysis, functionalism, and most pervasively, Cartesianism), can be mistaken for descriptivism: "being true to the facts," along the positivist criteria of an Ernst Mach or a J. S. Mill. Because of the easy sense they make, their distinctiveness as theory—providing a way of *seeing* the world—becomes blurred and fades into appearing to be one with what is discovered in reality. The theory I have chosen is relatively unknown, saddled with awkward terminology, apparently irrelevant and even inappropriate, from a man who knew much about everything but almost nothing about power and politics. I am referring to the semeiotic of C. S. Peirce, which I have bent even further to suit the purpose at hand.[3] It should, if it works as intended, cause the kind reader nervous embarrassment on the author's behalf at certain moments when theory and event are jarringly juxtaposed in the text. Whatever else it may be taken to be, theory cannot and should never be mistaken for the reality of violence I wish to represent. Granted, theory, any theory, is a way of understanding reality and not a collection of observations about reality. To the extent that it enhances one's understanding of the real, it literally "stands under" observations and gives form to these observations. But violence is such a reality that a theory which purports to inform it with significance must not merely "stand under" but conspicuously "stand apart" from it as a gesture of open admission to its inadequacy to measure up to its task. I do not mean to valorize violence hereby, but to foreground it so as to make the more general point regarding theory: that it is often forgotten that even ordinary life is not transparent to theory. Violence just brings this point home. There is much more that can be explicitly said about the relationship of theory to event, but I must choose restraint at this point and allow this relationship to work itself out in the body of the text itself.

Leading questions four and five, in addition to the first two, endure in the chapters of this book as an undercurrent. The flow of events in Sri Lanka, its unpredictable turns, and the magnitude of its meaninglessness have made some of these concerns lose their earlier force and urgency. Some of my informants have since been killed, and there are others whose whereabouts I do not know. Some of the earlier brutalities appear as gestures of kindness in comparison to the more recent acts of violence, seriously compromising my own desire to be able to return to that land and its people. Yet I assemble these chapters, knowing full well that a manageable undercurrent can in an instant become an unmanageable undertow. And I write this book mainly because I know of no other way to get around the third leading question.

I call this book a collection of chapters. Unlike the chapters of a conventional book, however, they do not march toward a single point; they barely sustain a consistent thesis. Taken as a whole, they are juxtaposed in mutual discordance so as to echo the discordance of the phenomenon being studied—violence and its effects—albeit in a different register. Their discordance is not one constituted of oppositions and contradictions, for that would, in its own way, have given the book a form of Hegelian, even if not a Cartesian, coherence. Rather, the discordance is one akin to a rescuer whose capacities are overwhelmed by the task he faces and who engages in a set of disparate and desperate forays into the roughest of waters in order to recover meaning. Some of these chapters have been published in different forms elsewhere and at different times. All of them, however, even in their earliest drafts, shared a common struggle, which I hoped to make clearer in their eventual gathering in a book. And in the forms in which they have been gathered, revised, and arranged here, they are no longer a collection of distinct essays. In some instances the most minute of changes—minute from a mechanical point of view, not unlike the changes on the computer screen—have sent words tumbling across the text altering the argument or the conclusion of a chapter quite radically. These chapters may not march toward a single point, but they register movement. The first movement they register is the movement of time itself. This movement is from the relative confidence in the intellect's and this intellectual's capacity to make sense of the events before, during, and since the summer of 1983 to a far less gallant stance of hoping to leave behind a testament to the memory of the fallen, the unfallen, and the fall itself. One may never understand, but one must never forget.

I have called this an anthropography of violence rather than an ethnography of violence because to have called it the latter would have been to parochialize violence, to attribute and limit violence to a particular people and place. Granted, the events described and discussed in the body of this work pertain to a particular people: Sri Lankans, Sinhalas and Tamils. But to see the ultimate significant effects of this work as ethnographic would exculpate other peoples in other places whose participation in collective violence is of the same sort; even more dangerously, it could tranquilize those of us who live self-congratulatory lives in times and countries apparently free of the kind of violence that has seized Sri Lanka recently, could lull us into believing that we or our country or our people were above such brutalities. This kind of conceit is most evident in editorials and field reports that appear regularly in the Western press. A bomb explodes in Paris and two Frenchmen are slightly injured. The incident makes the front page of the *New York Times* as if it were a potential threat to Western civilization—implying that violence is essentially outside the scope of Western civilization. More circumspect writers wring their hands in anxious fear over a much smaller cultural area that they consider precious: Western Europe or North America. A few years ago when I taught a course on ethnic violence in South Asia, a student wrote the following in her term paper:

> In these parts of the world, violence is endemic, almost instinctual. The values of the enlightenment that have made civil society possible in Europe and North America are yet to take root in Africa and Asia. Sri Lanka is a particularly striking example in this regard. Tribal animosities prevail over citizenship (etymologically related to civil and civilization).

When it was pointed out to this student that one was less likely to be killed in the middle of the civil war in Lebanon or northern Sri Lanka than on the streets of Washington, D.C., or New York, she blamed these cases on immigrants. Germany had already been forgotten; that the history of Europe—more than any other part of the world—is a history of belligerence was also forgotten; white South Africa was not mentioned. Bosnia was yet to come when this student wrote her paper. What this student has so unguardedly expressed and revealed with a certain measure of refreshing innocence is nothing more than what is urbanely concealed in high journalism, in the pronouncements in parliaments and houses of elected representatives, and even in academic prejudices of the West.

The sad irony is that Sri Lankans too had come to identify with this conceit of the West: the conceit of being civilized in contradistinction to those others who were not. There were several important ingredients in this state of civilization, as understood by Sri Lankans: an ancient and noble past to which they were entitled to lay claim; a written language—a language that belonged to the noble Indo-European family of languages; an ancient literature; their land's role as protector of one of the "world religions"—Buddhism—and as a home to another three; a cultivated body of manners and customs; and above all a democratic polity, thanks to which regular elections were held and parties were voted into and out of power with relative calm and decorum. When Sri Lankans spoke of Latin America, Africa, or even Southeast Asia, they spoke of the countries of these regions as tyrannical, antidemocratic, dictatorial, bloody, and barbaric. Names such as Marcos, Suharto, Idi Amin, institutions such as the Latin American juntas and the Chilean death squads, and countries that ranged from Saudi Arabia to China were invoked so as to implicitly throw into clear relief the more civilized nations and to tacitly highlight Sri Lanka's membership in this group of nations. How many times have I heard Sri Lankans abroad describe their country by proudly quoting or paraphrasing the American political scientist Howard Wriggins on how Ceylon was the most successful democracy in Asia? When July 1983 happened and Sri Lankans, especially the Sinhala majority, were forced to see themselves as the international press saw them—as a people capable of much atrocity—they writhed in embarrassment and anxiously searched for good reasons and excuses, while pleading for understanding. In no other country and among no other people that I have known has the sensitivity to what others would think of them been so tender as in Sri Lanka right after 1983. Tamil groups that engaged in public relations and propaganda for their cause detected and exploited this vulnerability of the Sinhala people to the fullest, enticing and generating the most desperate and absurd of defenses from the Sri Lankan state and statesmen. In the waning years of the United National Party government of Presidents Premadasa and Wijetunga, the concern for world opinion became increasingly linked to the prospects of financial aid and imminent meetings of the various aid-giving consortia and banks. Peace talks became a better guarantor of aid than peace. The Tamil militants and their growing reputation for violence have in their turn made the Sri Lankan government and many more Sinhalas less sensitive to world opinion. The point is not to decide whether the hypersensitivity to what others think or the increasing callousness toward world opinion is good or bad, nor solely to trace the decline in the valorization of nonviolence among the Tamils or the Sinhalas. Rather, it is to point out that changes in disposition toward violence on the part of a given people are every bit as possible among other peoples as well. Thus every ethnography of violence is also its anthropography. Violence is not peculiar to a given people or culture; violence is far more ubiquitous and universally human, a dark wellspring of signs with which, to be true to ourselves, we must communicate, and also as a force we must hold at bay. But having said this, I must hasten to add that I write of the human condition, not its nature.

If the *anthropos* part of the titular word is important, so is the *graphien*. Others have written more eloquently on the problems of writing than I ever could. To the extent that there is a recurrent and irresistible undertow of writing-centered reflexivity, it has been exacerbated by the subject of this book: violence. I have not tamed violence by and into the representations of writing. Indeed one cannot. But neither can one overcome the will to try nor forget the fact of one's trials in so willing. When and where I have paused to ponder about the difficulties in writing on violence (especially in chapter 6), it is only to make explicit in places the far more pervasive hidden heavings that sustain the book in the hope of both sharing with others and learning from others how one might better come to terms with such a struggle.

And finally, anyone who reads this book to find causes and their corollary, solutions, to what has come to be called the ethnic conflict, reads in vain. If there be solutions, they may well rest in forgetting the causes and remembering the carnage in "paradise."

Point of View

In Gadamer's formulation, "the standpoint that is beyond any standpoint . . . is pure illusion" (1975:339). Obviously, the standpoint in this book is my own but, alas, a very complicated one, which I sketch not because I like being autobiographical but because I have chosen to write on a subject upon which who I am has a bearing of more than passing significance. I am a trained anthropologist. It would have been simple if the matter ended there. I am also a naturalized American, born to Sri Lankan parents, and lived the first twenty years of my life in that country. The violence I have chosen to write about is mainly (even if not exclusively) the violence between Sri Lanka's two major ethnic groups, the Sinhalas and the Tamils. It is of more than sociobiological interest, then, that my father is a Tamil, my mother part Sinhala and part European. I grew up mainly in the Sinhala-speaking south of the island on and off a tea plantation where 99 percent of the population was Tamil. These

Tamils were set apart from the Sri Lankan or indigenous Tamils as being Tamils of relatively recent Indian origin, whose ancestors came to the island from the villages of South India in the nineteenth and early part of the twentieth centuries to labor on the island's coffee, rubber, and tea plantations. My father, though not a laborer himself, belongs to this group of Tamils and spoke their dialect of Tamil. When we were not living on a plantation, we interacted with as many Sinhalas as Tamils. As children we were in and out of their houses as they were in and out of ours. For reasons I could only speculate on but will not at this time, the traffic between our home and the homes of Sinhala friends was greater than that between ours and Tamil homes. When it was time for me to attend high school, I was sent to boarding school in Jaffna, the "center" of the current separatist movement. My stay in Jaffna lasted four years, not counting three months' holidays each year. Though relatively brief, my interaction with the Tamils of Jaffna was intense, heightened by hectic hormonal activity becoming of a teenager. Jaffna was also where the schools were reputed to be among the best on the island. There I learned a different dialect of Tamil and with it the art of dialect switching, which I needed when I came home south to the hills for holidays. As is well known, dialect and dialect switching have more to do with social relations than with linguistics. This is certainly true in the case of Tamil in Sri Lanka. Thus for me, in metonymic fashion, Tamil and Tamils were complicated in a way that Sinhala and the Sinhalas were not. As far as I knew, there was only one Sinhala dialect and one kind of Sinhala people. I spoke this language with reasonable fluency and interacted with the Sinhalas with far greater ease than I did with the Tamils.

Because of the anomalous position carved out for me by the reasons I have outlined, I have had an access to the dynamics of interethnic relations not available to most Sri Lankans. I have been taken into the confidence of the prejudices of all three ethnic (sub)groups, sometimes in full knowledge that I did not belong to the group whose confidence I shared and sometimes in the mistaken belief that I did belong to the said group, or to a fourth (that is, that I was a Burgher).

I am left, then, with the classic hermeneutic problem: How can I accept my prejudicial condition as integral to my being and yet critically rise above *particular* prejudices? The fact that I have now lived more than half my life in the West, most of it as an academic anthropologist, has thrown into clear relief for me the absurdities of the particular concatenation of prejudices, from grubby to bloody, that have constituted Sri Lanka's recent history. Nevertheless, readers should be forewarned that they would be correct in detecting a gentle prejudicial tilt, self-confessedly willed, in favor of the point of view of Sri Lanka's Estate Tamils. If the reason for such a tilt is biographical, so be it. But I would rather hold that I tilt thus, privileging the world as seen by this group of Tamils, because theirs is a point of view that gets little or no recognition in writings on ethnic relations in Sri Lanka, be it in the arguments between indigenous Tamils and the Sinhalas about the objectivity of their respective stances or in the writings of outside scholars who write "disinterested" commentaries on these arguments. It is hoped that this privileging of a "neglected viewpoint" in the manner of a comparative anthropology will place the other points of view, including the "disinterested" analyst's, in a more enlightening relation to one another.

Some Cautionary Notes

1. After much deliberation as to whether to follow the ethnographic convention of substituting pseudonyms for real names or to use real names only, I have decided upon the following compromise. I have used real names to refer to all political and public figures, with a very few exceptions where the individual(s) in question gave me information under conditions of anonymity. In several instances I have not mentioned real place names because in 1983 and 1984 the informants involved in the reported incidents did not want me to be too specific lest they be identified and bring harm upon themselves, their families, and in some instances their local communities. In some such cases, even though the events described to me have subsequently become public knowledge, for a whole complex of reasons—disappearance, death, emigration, and the like—I have not been able to locate the original informants in order to obtain release from my original commitment to them.

2. The name Ceylon was changed to Sri Lanka in 1972. In the text you will find me using Ceylon and Sri Lanka almost interchangeably. Closer scrutiny will reveal that in general, when I describe events and sentiments prior to the name change, I use Ceylon or Ceylonese, and for those after 1972, Sri Lanka or Sri Lankans.

3. Since I began writing this book, which has taken me almost seven years, the spuriousness of the "ethnographic present" that has characterized so much of anthropological writing has taken on new meaning. Such canonized ethnographers as Malinowski and Evans-Pritchard, and a whole generation of anthropologists since then, have been criticized for writing about the Trobrianders, the Nuer, or whoever else in a manner that seemed to convey the impression that "this is how it has always been and always will be" with regard to the people among whom they studied. This tradition has been rightly criticized, and some efforts have been made to correct this tendency in the ethnographic writings practiced today. Despite our recent attempts to historicize what we write about, our choices tend to settle on relatively stable objects of study: objects that will look more or less the same at least from the time of the ethnographic encounter until the time of its publication and a few years beyond. What needs to be acknowledged, however, is that what really matters to

the anthropologist-ethnographer is not the relative stability of the ethnographic object but rather the relative stability of the theoretical claims made upon the object of study. Can our theories—ways of seeing an object—survive into a second edition? Will our books be read for more than their value as period pieces? These are the questions which seek for a response that assures relative stability. Often forgotten are (a) that ethnographic objects are, by definition, theorized objects, and (b) that insofar as theory and object can be separated from each other by an abstract mental activity called "prescinding,"[4] we must also remember that the two are dialectically, if not dialogically, codeterminant.

In the Sri Lankan situation, events have changed and continue to change so rapidly that one does not need a span of fifty or even twenty-five years to relegate something to "history." Concerns and issues that were characterized as burning become irrelevant within months or even weeks. For example, "race" was of considerable concern to the debates of the late seventies and early eighties. To many ardent racists among Sinhalas and Tamils of yesteryear, race has become a fairy tale not worthy of serious attention. In the early eighties (as you will see in chapter 1), Tamils who themselves or whose ancestors worked on the tea plantations debated as to whether they should be called Estate Tamils, or Tamils of Indian descent, or Tamils of recent Indian origin, or New Tamils. Within the few intervening years, this group has come to terms with both the formal appellation of Hill-Country Tamils and the informal one of Estate Tamils, with the latter, gradually and without any fuss, giving way to the former in daily use. Likewise, on my side, observations that moved me to theorize an event explicitly or implicitly (i.e., descriptively), sometimes with passion, seem misplaced in hindsight. The Sinhala-speaking tour guide of chapter 2, whom I trailed in 1984, was nowhere to be found in my latest visit to the same pilgrimage sites in 1994; the phenomenon of "tourism for the locals" that I then expected to become a new wave has failed to persist even as a ripple, undermining some of my theoretical speculations regarding the growing new middle and upper middle classes. There are many more such instances. It took me ten years to abandon the exercise of "updating," to realize that the world—especially the contemporary Sri Lankan world—does not hold still for the theorist to finish his or her sketch. Since beginning to write this book almost thirteen years ago, I have come to realize that concerns which dominated Sri Lankans and the theoretical stances or inquiries that they motivated at one time are replaced by others, even as the civil war continues to provide the backdrop for these changes. I have come to realize the value of the periodicism of even the best-theorized descriptions. Even if all they do is continue to serve us as period pieces in that they preserve the concerns, values, and prejudices of certain times and places, they will have served us and future generations well. In that spirit, I have let stand many of the traces of previous years' concerns and contours unmodified.

1

OF HERITAGE AND HISTORY

Already a fictitious past occupies a place in our memories,
the place of another, a past of which we know nothing
with certainty—not even that it is false.
(Jorge Luis Borges)

ESSENTIALISM has come to be the bad word of late modernity. The human sciences have rushed to embrace and expound upon the doctrine of the constructedness of practically everything. Among these, gender, race, ethnicity, culture, and nation are the best known. These are not essential identities but constructed ones, we are told. Much good has come out of these constructivist exercises, some so brilliant as to deserve the adulation of generations to come. The scholarship that most obviously merits such adulation is of course that of Michel Foucault and a few who have followed (and preceded) his example by showing, with meticulous attention to detail, how something that has been constructed—be it an institution, an ideology, a habit, or a discourse—has been seamlessly put together. But there are to be found in some constructivist scholarship at least two unintended, not so very salubrious, effects. Both concern the uncanny resemblance that certain schools of constructivism bear to the essentializing impulses operating in the ethnicism, racism, and culturalism which they critique. In other words, constructivists themselves become definers of their own identity much as racists, ethnicists, and culturalists become definers of theirs. This mechanism of identity consolidation operates on the principle that one defines one's self by not being the Other. Constructivism's Other, of course, is essentialism. In the first instance, such an identity quest paradoxically begins to habitualize (essentialize?) the practices and perspectives of the constructivists themselves. Second, if such an Other does not figure exactly as some would please, they are wont to construct him, her, or it, at least as a caricature. This tendency has been most apparent in a relatively recent movement bent on dispensing with the concept of culture as being essentialized and essentializing even as race and (to a lesser extent) ethnicity are. In anthropology, one of the most assertive in this regard has been Lila Abu-Lughod (1991), whose main inspiration comes

This chapter is based, with respect to tea estate workers in particular, on fieldwork carried out in the years 1971, 1974, 1976, 1983–1984, and 1987. The *oral histories* I employ herein are biased toward the pre-1983 years and toward older informants. Much has changed since 1983, as will be explored in the latter part of this book.

from three major cultural critiques: Pierre Bourdieu (1977 and 1985), Edward Said (1978), and James Clifford (1986 and 1988).[1] Despite the great insights these scholars have brought to bear upon the practice of anthropology and cultural studies, the cultural essentialists they attack are more apparent than real. The best students of culture had never assumed that cultures were anything but constructed. But in the excitement to find nothing but constructions, there has been a flattening down of culture to a single dimension and a loss of perspective on the relative differences in resilience among the various cultural constructions as well as their relative latency (or depth, as some would prefer to call it). Some cultural constructions are sturdy but obvious, and others obvious but fragile—both sorts revealing their constructedness on the slightest reflection even to those who live in and with them. Some constructions, though inconspicuous (or latent), may be either quite impermanent or quite resilient, both concealing not only their constructedness but possibly even their very presence.

Let it be declared quite early and clearly that in Sri Lanka ethnic identities are constructed. But it is equally important to know that some of these constructions' constructedness, whether fleeting or resilient, is easily revealed, whereas that of some others persists in its inconspicuousness. In this chapter I wish to make conspicuous one of these latent cultural constructions in Sri Lanka that has endured through the greater part of its history. This construction concerns two distinctive dispositions toward the past, each identified with one of the two ethnic groups in Sri Lanka, the Sinhalas and the Tamils. I call these "history" and "heritage." The chapter ends with the study of a third ethnic (sub)group, the Estate Tamils, whose disposition toward the past, I argue, is a hybrid of history and heritage. Before turning my focus on history, heritage, and their hybrid, I would like to present some of the more obvious features that make up ethnic identities in Sri Lanka, identities that, even if far more readily deconstructable, contribute to the complex and vexing character of ethnicity.

In this my contribution to the question of identity and difference, in highlighting two (and a hybrid third) discursive constructions of a reality that have thus far remained largely politically subliminal but persistent, in contradistinction to the politically manifest differences of language, religion, and even race, I hope to shed some new light upon the question of identity and difference. My purpose is not merely to show the manner in which a reality (a disposition, in this instance) is culturally and historically constituted, but how deeply so; and in so doing, to draw the reader, especially if he or she is a Sinhala or Tamil who believes in essential differences, away from some of the more impassioned but silly questions to be encountered below about relative dumbness and smartness and nosiness, to ponder over the constructedness of our world and ourselves more generally and more profoundly. The appeal is not to deny difference "but to understand identity as a site of multiple disjunctions in need of politicization as well as unities that enable life" (Connolly 1991:163).

Ethnicity and Its Vicissitudes

Every story in the press has somewhere buried in it a key sentence, intended to provide a fundamental bit of information, without which, it would seem, the story as a whole will not be adequately understood. In press reports concerning the crisis in Sri Lanka this sentence takes the following typical form: Ethnic Tamils speak the Tamil language and are Hindus, and ethnic Sinhalas speak the Sinhala language and are Buddhists. The worldly-wise in Sri Lanka too, when called upon to describe the current turmoil in their island nation, do so by calling it an interethnic conflict. They may refine this bit of fundamental information by adding: Sinhala is a language that belongs to the Indo-Aryan family of languages, its speakers, mostly Buddhists, making up the island's majority; Tamil is a language belonging to the Dravidian family of languages and is spoken by the island's most populous minority, who are most likely to be Hindus. One immediately senses the mighty hand of nineteenth-century Orientalist scholarship beginning to cast its long shadow of the classification of languages on the political and demographic landscape. Can the classification of "races" be far behind? In fact, not. In Sri Lanka, race, religion, and language have formed an unholy alliance that is charged by its claimants, adherents, and speakers, respectively, with the mission of dividing the nation's citizens. Of the three, however, language—or, more exactly, linguistic nationalism—leads with its banner.[2] "Race," at least among the enlightened, has an ugly face, even for battle, and is granted open season only when things get really nasty. And religion, especially Buddhism, is not supposed to be the harbinger of violence and death but of life and liberation. In my interviews with religious zealots—Buddhists, Hindus, and a few Muslims—who were ready to resort to violence to "protect" their religion, I would attempt to startle their frame of mind by paraphrasing Walter Colton to the effect that men will wrangle for, write for, fight for, and die for religion—anything but live it. It would invariably shock them into varying degrees of embarrassment that would take the forms of denial, defense, or reflection.[3] Race and religion, though present in ethnic conflict, cause embarrassment to many. Not so with language. It is gallantly unembarrassing.

If the world press does not have the time and patience to be thoughtful on matters of ethnicity and its complexities, neither do most Sri Lankans, even though they live in and live out such complexities in their daily lives. Even for those within the very thicket of crosscutting and ever-shifting identities and differences, the description of the conflict as the Sinhala-Tamil conflict comes easily, with the implication that the parties to the conflict are a monolithic Sinhala ethnic group on the one hand and an equally monolithic Tamil ethnic group on the other. In coming to believe in this great and sole divide, many Sri Lankans have either forgotten or do not know that there was a time in Sri Lanka when where one lived mattered more than what language one spoke or what one's religion was. The Sinhalas, who now make up 71 percent of the island's population, had, in the nineteenth and first half of the twentieth centuries, self-consciously divided and defined themselves as either Low Country Sinhalas or Kandyan Sinhalas.[4] The Low Country Sinhalas lived in the island's southern and southwestern coastal regions, which were the earliest regions of the island to come under European rule, consolidated under the Portuguese by 1600 and the Dutch by 1656. The Kandyans lived in the southern hinterland; their kingdom came under foreign rule only in 1815 when the British defeated the last Kandyan king, took over the colony from the Dutch, and brought the entire island under a single imperial rule. The Kandyans were distinguishable from their Low Country counterparts by their manner of dress and deportment, their names, and the dialect of Sinhala they spoke. The relatively recent linguistic nationalism[5] has displaced the importance of locality, thereby making linguistic identity primary, such that all speakers of Sinhala define themselves against those who speak Tamil.

The fissures, however, are by no means triggered only by language, race (whatever that might be), and the two major South Asian religions. What of the Christian Sinhalas and Christian Tamils? As Christians, are they as "Sinhala" as Buddhist Sinhalas are or as "Tamil" as Hindu Tamils are? Are these Christians more Sinhala or Tamil, as the case may be, today than they were forty years ago? To the outsider, these questions may seem puzzling. The world press typically loses interest at this point. The thoughtful Sri Lankan who has followed the flux within categories knows that these are categories in flux. The complexities thicken. Questions of identity and difference have a way of neither coming to a close nor always taking a predictable path. We define who we are by defining who we are not. Time was when it was the Sinhala Anglican Christian or the Roman Catholic in whom difference was identified and converted into otherness; by this means was secured the certainty of one's Sinhala-Buddhist self. The schoolboy in the island's leading Buddhist schools of Ananda and Nalanda did not consider the Tamil boy in Jaffna Hindu College as his nemesis but rather the Sinhala Christian who was attending St. Thomas's or St. Joseph's. There was a time when a Tamil Veḷḷāḷa would have considered marrying off his daughter to a Sinhala Goyigama, or a Goyigama marrying off his daughter to a Tamil Veḷḷāḷa, before either one of them would have contemplated marrying their daughters into the fishing castes of their own linguistic group (a Sinhala Karāva or a Tamil Karayār).

Even to this day, the patrilineal Tamils of the north are loath to marry the matrilineal Tamils of the east, and vice versa.

Whereas, at least since the 1930s, despite fault lines in its political geography, the Sinhala-speaking people of the island have moved toward consolidating their identity, the plural identities of the Tamils have been far more openly articulated, not only by the state, but also, until the early eighties, by the various Tamil groups as well. In fact, the Sinhala state likes to have it both ways. On the one hand, faced with the threat of a Tamil separatist movement, the state, in whose interest it is to emphasize that there is no single Tamil interest and therefore cannot be a single Tamil state, does like to highlight the differences among Tamils. In this mode, it differentiates the Tamils of the Jaffna Peninsula from those who live along the east coast, from those who live along the northwest coast, from those who work on the tea estates in the island's south-central hills, and so on. On the other hand, the state, at various times and to various degrees, fuels the more general Sinhala sentiment that holds all Tamils (including the Tamils of South India) to constitute the monolithic Other against whom the Sinhala people, along with the Sinhala state, can define its identity. The blueprint for this construction is to be found in linguistic nationalism.

In the climate of linguistic nationalism that prevails in Sri Lanka, real choices made within the context of real communities have taken on perverse forms. In the west-coast town of Puttalam, I met monolingual Tamil-speaking grandparents who had raised bilingual, Sinhala- and Tamil-speaking children, who in their turn raised monolingual Sinhala-speaking sons who were among the arsonists who burned down Tamil-owned shops in the riots of 1983. Then follow even more contentious identity-claims such as who came first to the island and which group has more unfair advantages over the other; and silly ones such as who is fairer and who is dumber, who can and cannot add and subtract, and whose character is fundamentally flawed.

Tamils Divided in Unity

Despite recent attempts on the part of the island's Tamils at consolidating their own identity in the face of the consolidation of Sinhala identity, there remains one relatively deep dividing line that runs through the Tamil community. On one side of this line are those Tamils whose contribution to linguistic nationalism has been almost as energetic as that of the Sinhalas. These Tamils have been variously called "Ceylon," "Sri Lankan," or "Indigenous" Tamils. This group now constitutes 12.6 percent of the nation's population. For reasons to be explained below, I call this group, somewhat imprecisely, Jaffna Tamils. On the other side of this line are those Tamil-speakers whose ancestors came to the island from South India in the nineteenth and first half of the twentieth centuries mostly to labor on the island's coffee and (subsequently) tea plantations. They speak a slightly different dialect of Tamil which, in the Sri Lankan context, is seen as less prestigious than that spoken by the island's Jaffna Tamils. According to the 1981 census this group made up 5.6 percent of the population. At its peak (1953) this group constituted 12 percent of the island's population, 1 percent more than the number of Jaffna Tamils at that time. They also exceeded the Jaffna Tamil total in the 1946 census. In fact, their number is likely to have been higher, since fears of being accused of illicit residence on the island prompted many of these Tamils to duck the census takers. Deportation and voluntary emigration have depleted their numbers. I shall, for reasons that will soon be made clear, call this group Estate Tamils. Moreover, as indicated in the introduction, in order to tilt the book's tone in favor of this group's prejudices, I will provide below a somewhat extended treatment of this (neglected) group's identity formation.

Most of these Estate Tamils live in the tea plantations located in the island's south-central hills of the old Kandyan kingdom. The contempt shown toward these hill-country Tamils by the Jaffna Tamils and the incorrigible distrust that the former have for the latter is too well known among both groups to even require mention. The non-Estate Tamils call the hill-country Tamils *vaṭakkattayān* ("Northerner") to indicate their recent arrival from the foreign country north of them, India; and the hill-country Tamils call all non-Estate Tamils, regardless of whether they come from Jaffna or elsewhere, by the deprecatory epithet *panankoṭṭai cūppis* ("suckers of palmyra seeds"). These two groups of Tamils make fun of each other's dialects of spoken Tamil. The issue, however, is not language at all, except negatively: that is, proving the inability of language alone to sustain an imagined community that linguistic nationalism needs.

What about the once Tamil-speaking but increasingly Sinhala-speaking Muslims? The mostly Tamil-speaking Muslims have, since the mid-fifties, conspicuously resisted their being unequivocally identified as Tamils. The Sri Lankan Sinhala historian K. M. de Silva finds this resistance commendable, serving the interest of a modern, pluri-ethnic nation-state.[6] The Tamils consider such a commendation as being nothing more than the expedient remark of a Sinhala nationalist. The Tamils who stand to lose the most by the Muslims' renouncing of their Tamil-linguistic identity consider such shiftings of identities—characteristic, they would add, of the Muslims since the late-colonial and particularly the postindependence period—as shameless opportunism. Most Sinhalas would cynically agree. Alternatively it may be argued that such "Muslim-strategies" represent the vestige of a common precolonial practice when neither linguistic chauvinism nor linguistic nationalism prevailed, the practice of a time when communities were less imagined (in Anderson's sense) and more real—that is, when communities were not made up of those whom we might meet and in whom we recognized "sameness" only in principle, but of those whom we met in fact and with whom we were compelled to realize common interests, in which we identified likeness and difference and the necessary contingencies of change. National languages and official languages, be they Tamil, Sinhala, or English, need and create imagined communities, communities of people who never meet and are unlikely to do so. From this point of view, for example, the colonizer's language first transformed real communities of "likeness" in order to create those imagined communities of difference so that it might then live up to its role as a "link language." Thus, and contrary to the prevailing perspective, English did not unite the various language groups in South Asia but initiated their abstraction into mutually antagonistic enclaves. This phenomenon may be more clearly seen in several regions of India. The case of the breakup of the former Madras Presidency into Tamil Nadu and Telangana is such a revealing example. Formerly there were many more Tamil- and Telugu-speaking bilinguals in what was called the Madras Presidency of South India than there are now in the two divided linguistic states, and intermarriage between the two linguistic groups was quite common. Not so since the arrival of English, the "link language." The same has become true of other "official" and "national" languages that have entered people's worlds in order to link but in so doing have only divided. Thus insofar as the Sri Lankan Muslims drift between two languages, they may be seen as enacting a precolonial pattern in which Sinhalas and Tamils too (and no less than Muslims) participated. It is only in the contemporary climate of linguistic nationalism that such shifts are perceived as indicative of the propensity to change with the shift of every political wind—as betraying an imagined community. Keenly aware of this perspective on their choices, Muslims who in times past have identified themselves now with the one and then with the other, depending on the real community of their interactions, nowadays consider themselves neither as Tamils nor as Sinhalas but have substituted the more overarchingly imagined community of Islam.

The Estate Tamils

The identity of the Estate Tamil, more than that of any of the others, is caught in the throes of change, a change that implicates both history and heritage. I shall enter into the problem of history, heritage, identity, and change by considering the nomenclatural discomfiture that these Tamils find themselves in. The reason for my choosing such an entry point is as follows. Gottlob Frege taught us that in addition to their ordinary *reference*, referring terms have *sense* (1960:56–78). A name is such a term. A referring term is presumed to mean what it does merely by virtue of what it refers to. "That is, their contribution to the meaning of sentences they occur in is entirely to 'tie' these sentences to the things (or sets of things) they name" (Martin 1987:143). Built into a theory of reference is the conceit of the *objectivity* of meaning, the realization of an external objective thing. A theory of *sense*, by contrast, implicates an expression and certain circumstances of its use in people's habits of thought and action. In the prevailing political and historical discourse in and about Sri Lanka, the presumption is that what matters ultimately is *reference*. While some terms are argued over (for example, who came first to the island, the Sinhalas or the Tamils), others are taken to be beyond referential doubt (for example, that the name "Sinhala" or "Tamil" refers to an unambiguous "set of animate objects"—to resort to language philosophers' manner of phrasing the matter). In concerning myself with names and naming as they pertain to the Estate Tamils' quest for the "right name" by which they would like to be called, I hope to show more generally how and why *sense* matters more than reference and also how a sense of history and heritage are folded in.

What's in a Name?

In discussions on ethnicity, the Estate Tamils are characteristically denied a distinct identity and lumped together with the rest of Sri Lanka's Tamils. Most Estate Tamils I have interviewed resent such a simple identification extended to them by the Sinhalas on the one hand and the Jaffna Tamils on the other, an identification seen as serving the latter two groups' respective political agendas. As these Estate Tamils see it, the Jaffna Tamils choose to include them under a single Tamil rubric only in times of crisis in order to force Indian state intervention during the periodic anti-Tamil riots, since among these Estate Tamils are some actual or potential Indian citizens, which has justified such interventions in the past. And when such interventions occur, they have served the Jaffna Tamils' interests as well.[7]

For the Sinhalas, viewing these two groups of Tamils as a single one helps sustain in unity two opposed but complementary stereotypical characterizations of all Tamils. The Jaffna Tamils take care of the one stereotype: Tamils are privileged, caste-conscious, calculating, given to usury, intelligent but crafty, rich and miserly. Estate Tamils on their part believe this to be true, but true only of Jaffna Tamils. Tamils in general (for the Sinhalas) and Jaffna Tamils in particular (for the Estate Tamils) are the ones who hold the best jobs, monopolize the professions, control the economy, have huge bank accounts, and whose women wear the most gold jewelry and expensive silk saris. When government pamphlets proclaim that "in the economic sphere, . . . ranging from the largest industrial ventures to the smallest entrepreneurial enterprise, the Tamils have achieved signal success,"[8] this is the stereotype they promote. On their part, the Estate Tamils hold that this is true of the Jaffna Tamils but not of themselves. Not all or even most Jaffna Tamils fit this simple stereotype. But then popular perceptions are popular precisely because they do not entertain complexity. The very label "Jaffna Tamil" is itself another mark of this simplification, deriving from the northern peninsula of Jaffna, which is seen as the cultural center or capital of all these other Tamils.[9] The Tamils of Trincomalee, Batticaloa, Mannar, and Vavuniya, who would not wish to be so easily equated with the Tamils of Jaffna, and who resent the cultural "hegemony" of the peninsular Tamils over them, are not, from the Sinhala and Estate Tamil points of view, any different. For the Estate Tamils, all the island's Tamils, excepting themselves, are "Jaffna Tamils." Indeed, the perception of who these non-Estate Tamils are tends to be skewed by the fact that the non-Estate Tamils who may be encountered in the tea-growing areas of the central highlands tend to be English-educated Tamils from Jaffna. And since many of these Tamils from Jaffna are professionals and white-collar workers, they are seen as belonging to "management," be it as part of the state, schools, or offices—belonging, that is, to the side of power. And indeed, when there is dispute between estate workers and the superintendent, the Jaffna Tamils along with the rest of the white-collar staff have tended to curry favor with management. The second pole of the Sinhala stereotype of Tamils is embodied by the Estate Tamil. According to this stereotype, Tamils are wretchedly poor, live in filth, are uneducated, wear rags, are good coolies, and "like rabbits" breed children who have the virtue of being trainable into docile domestic servants. Estate Tamils are aware of these stereotypes that are extended toward them and occasionally find poetic justice in instances such as the following, fondly and repeatedly recalled for my benefit by laborers on a certain estate. When Mr. May, a Burgher, became the manager of this estate, he is supposed to have declared that the coolies were a fine people but they "bred like rabbits." At that time he had fathered only one child, a daughter. In the next fifteen years, however, he sired fifteen more children and then died of mouth cancer.

If Estate Tamils resent the failure of the Sinhalas and the other Tamils to provide them with a distinct identity, they resent equally the names by which they are called when the others do choose to differentiate them from non-Estate Tamils. I shall bring out the nature of this resentment by briefly reviewing some of the names by which this ethnic group is called and also calls itself, considering these names against the Fregian distinction of *sense* and *reference*. What are some of these other names? There are the few openly derogatory names such as *kaḷḷattōni* ("illicit boat-person") and *tōṭṭakkāṭṭān* ("plantation-jungle-man"). But my concern here is with the more "proper" names. "Indian Tamil" was used until recently as the official, and remains the most popular unofficial, designation. But one needs to distinguish these Tamils from the fifty million Tamils of southern India. The former, and their ancestors two to five generations deep, had never left this island of their birth; the latter had never left India, the land of their birth. Therefore, the expansion "Tamils of Indian Origin" was tried. But this failed to differentiate these Tamils from the other Tamils of the island who also (even as the Sinhalas do) claim to have come to the island from the mainland, albeit "a *very* long time ago." As a solution to this problem the even lengthier "Tamils of Recent Indian Origin" was substituted and subsequently contracted to the less cumbersome "New Tamils." This, reflexively, gave the other Tamils the appellation "Old Tamils." In my interviews with Tamils, mostly Estate Tamils and some Jaffna Tamils, I was struck by their resistance to and dissatisfaction with such nuanced labels. But their objections to these names, even if impelled initially by an apparent concern on their part for greater referential accuracy, unfolded to reveal a deeper concern with the adequacy of sense. Moreover, it was with the last choice—"New" versus "Old" Tamils—that this underlying concern with sense began to separate itself out from the more superficial concern with reference.

I found it intriguing that whereas the contrastive label which troubled several of the Jaffna Tamils was "Old," most of my Estate Tamil informants were bothered by the label "New." Of course, the point of significance is that the Jaffna Tamils in question were English educated and were evaluating the words "old" and "new" as English words. My Estate Tamil informants, by contrast, were reacting to the various connotations of the Tamil glosses for "old" and "new." Here is a Jaffna Tamil schoolteacher, Mr. Mylvaganam:

> We are a new and vibrant people. Our ideas are up-to-date. Our thinking is modern. We are not old-fashioned. Our people are not old and weary like the estate workers. . . . The future is ours. That is why we must be called "New Tamils."

Other informants were not as articulate as this schoolteacher but seemed to be troubled by the same connotation of "Old."[10] The Estate Tamils I interviewed, almost all of them monolingual Tamil-speakers, did not like the Tamil word for "new," *putiya* (*tamiṛar*). The nature of their objections may be abstracted from the following sample of quotations:

> Tamil is always called *panṭaittamiṛ* [which means Tamil (language) of old]. To call one a Tamil is to call him a *panṭaittamiṛan* (a Tamil of antiquity or the member of an ancient race).

> How can one call them [Jaffna Tamils] "Old Tamils?" We who come from *tamiṛakam* [the heart of Tamil country or Tamil Nadu] are the ones who are the true Old Tamils. Jaffna is a place that was a gift to a lutenist in the king's palace. We can say of him, "He came but yesterday."

I shall spare you my attempts at explaining to my informants the meanings of "new" and "old" as pertaining to political matters of a nation-state rather than denoting these Tamils' antiquity or lack thereof. I shall also spare you their responses, which opened with, "Yes, but . . ." and then returned to sentiments similar to the ones represented in the last two quotations. What became evident is Tamils' valorization of "antiquity" and their pride in their (presumed) ancient heritage. It is interesting that the sense of "old and spent," which happened to be the primary connotation of the English word "old" for several of the English-speaking Jaffna Tamils, is not foregrounded in the Tamil gloss, *paṛam*. Rather, it is the sense of "antiquity" that becomes salient. I shall return to this fondness for the antiquarian identity in connection with Tamils' general disposition toward the past, a disposition that I shall describe as a comportment with *heritage*.

Continuing our quest for the name that makes the most perfect *sense* to these Tamils, we may ask, what of the name "Estate Tamils" (*tōṭṭattu tamiṛar*), or its equivalent, "Hill-Country Tamils" (*malai akat tamiṛar*), the very names that these Tamils kept using when they talked about themselves. (For most of these Tamils, "Hill-Country" and "Estate" are seen as semantic equivalents, since most estates are to be found in the hilly parts of Sri Lanka.) Whenever it was suggested to some of the very men and women who employed this name most naturally in ordinary conversation that "Estate Tamils" be the official name by which they identify themselves, many of them, as if alerted to referential correctness, objected. "Not all of us are estate workers, and not all of us live in the hilly tea country," they said. Needless to say, there was much ambiguity about this name. On the one hand it suggested the historic and social stigmatization they hoped to escape; on the other it admitted to the fact that they had "developed [loyalty] towards the estates in which they and their families had worked for generations . . . despite the humiliation, oppression and deplorable condition of living that they have suffered from within the plantation system" (Bastian 1987:172).

To be sure, objections to the name "Estate Tamils" were raised only when it was discussed under the somewhat specialized rubric of appropriate nomenclature. However, it was clear that these Tamils' experience-fraught identities were defined by life on the estates. This was true even in conversations with Estate Tamils who were merchants or clerks in metropolitan towns far removed from the plantations. For this reason, I concluded that "Estate Tamil," the objections notwithstanding, was the name that made the greatest *sense* and, as will become clear, is especially appropriate with regard to the topic of this chapter, dispositions toward the past.[11]

Finding a named identity that makes the greatest *sense*, regardless of referential accuracy, is not an end in itself. It reveals something further. It is this very identity that constitutes one-half of these Estate Tamils' orientation toward the past, *history*. The other half is to be found in the reasons for their objections to the adjective "new" in the name "New Tamils." The "new," as already indicated, undermines something that all ethnic Tamils value deeply, *heritage*.

The polar, albeit ideal-typical, orientations a people may assume toward the past I call history and heritage. I shall argue that in a specifiable Sri Lankan ethnohistorical context, the Sinhalas have privileged history, whereas the non-

Estate Tamils have privileged heritage. The second and the more extensive section of the chapter will be concerned with the third ethnic subgroup, which I have already introduced, the "Estate Tamils," who may be seen to combine both stances toward the past in the process of defining who they are. The dispositions under consideration are held to be, with slight variations over time, integral markers of the identities of the groups in question. I cannot sufficiently emphasize the fact that I am not claiming the Sinhalas to be exclusively given to history and the Tamils to heritage. Rather, what I am claiming is that for specifiable historical reasons, Sinhala Buddhists more readily privilege history in their disposition toward the past than do Tamils, and that Tamil Hindus more easily privilege heritage in their disposition toward the past.

Alberuni's Complaint

It has been observed by several scholars that Hindu India is niggardly in yielding to the "objectivist historian" the raw material needed for his craft. Alberuni put it this way: "Unfortunately the Hindus do not pay much attention to the historical order of things, they are very careless in relating the chronological succession of kings, and when they are pressed for information are at a loss, not knowing what to say, they invariably take to tale-telling."[12]

History, as a function of linear time, marked by those distinct, nonrepeating "events," eludes the typical[13] historian. Events qua events are swallowed up by mythology, and tokens subsumed by types. Richard Salomon (1980) remarks that the "General Indian Historical Traditions" are indifferent to chronology and in this respect stand in contrast to India's peripheral cultural traditions such as those of Nepal, Sri Lanka, Tibet, Assam, and even Kashmir.[14] In the heartland of India, chronology becomes significant only with the advent of Islam.

What of Buddhist Sri Lanka? Buddhism, like Islam and Christianity, is a historical religion, marked by time, by the events of Buddha's birth and enlightenment. Consequently, Sinhala Sri Lanka has developed the kind of historical consciousness not found in Hindu India or in Hindu (Tamil) Sri Lanka. In the Hindu-Tamil and Sinhala-Buddhist cases of Sri Lanka one would be hard pressed to deny that, from an "objectivist" historian's point of view, there are no chronicles among the Hindu Tamils that are as compendious as the Buddhist *Mahāvaṁsa*, *Cūlavaṁsa*, and *Dīpavaṁsa*. It is not the historical verity of these chronicles that concerns me but the insistence on the part of the culture that has produced and nurtured these documents that their content is true in the sense that it can be actually or potentially verified (or falsified). This stance characterizes the entirety of Sri Lankan historical scholarship, spanning the whole range, from the most sophisticated academic scholarship of a Gananath Obeyesekere (1984 and 1991) or a K. M. de Silva (1981) to the writings of historians of the folk such as the late member of parliament Cyril Mathew and former Prime Minister (and late President) Premadasa, or an E. T. Kannangara (1984). Scholars such as R.A.L.H. Gunawardana (1990) and W. I. Siriweera (1985) who foreground the "merely mythic" or "hermeneutically" constructed aspects of these chronicles in their finely argued papers are participants in the same discourse as are their nemeses.[15] One needs, then, to ask the further question as to whether this difference has any correspondence, causal or otherwise, in the consciousness of the past of contemporary Tamils and Sinhalas of Sri Lanka.

History versus Heritage

Any student of Sri Lankan scholarship will be struck by the fact that the social sciences in general and the disciplines of history and archaeology in particular are overwhelmingly represented by Sinhalas, in contrast to the natural sciences, which are disproportionately represented by Jaffna Tamils.[16] This historical consciousness is not limited to Sinhala academics writing in English and directing their writings to scholarship that extends to readers beyond Sri Lanka. The Sinhala-Buddhist nationalist hero of the early part of this century Anagarika Dharmapala is the best known in a line of folk-scholars whose audience and readership were largely if not exclusively Sinhalas. The ex-minister Mr. Cyril Mathew was a figure of considerable prominence in the 1980s who belonged to this cadre of nationalistic historians. The late President Premadasa was another. Whether or not the chauvinism of many of these "historians of the folk" constitutes "disciplined" history is quite beside the point. What is true is that there is, among these men, a faith that their view of the past will be supported by the past. Or even more forcefully stated, their faith is that their view of the past exists only because an objective past—and, in the best of all possible worlds, an archaeologically unearthable or documented past—exists.

During my fieldwork in Sri Lanka in 1983–1984 following the major ethnic riots of the summer of 1983, I came upon a new historian of the folk in the person of the Sinhala-speaking tour guide, a figure and a phenomenon we shall encounter in greater detail in the following chapter. In the early eighties, internal tourism had grown alongside foreign tourism. The English-, German-, Italian-, or French-speaking tour guide had his Sinhala-speaking counterpart who guided local tourists to the island's tour-worthy places, mainly the ruins of once great kingdoms. In 1983–1984, I spent several days with local groups of tourist-pilgrims who were guided around the ancient cities of Anuradhapura and Polonnaruwa by Sinhala-speaking tour guides. Over and over again, the guide would point to a ruin, a once great palace, temple, or dagoba, describe its past glory, and then describe the circumstances of its ruin. And time and time again, the destroyers were identified as Tamil invaders from India. A certain university professor's textbook was cited as the source upon the authority of which the information was based. "This is not what *I* am saying. It is thus written in the book of the great professor, K. M. de Silva,"[17] he would punctuate his often lengthy and animated accounts. The effect on the tourist-pilgrims was to confirm with archaeological and documentary evidence what they had suspected all along. The Tamils were the enemy of the glorious past of the Sinhala people, and the Tamil is the enemy of the present as well. There is also an increasing number of Sinhala-language newspapers and Sinhala pamphlets that are intensely engaged in (if not obsessed with) issues pertaining to the history of the Sinhala-Buddhist people and nation.

Nothing comparable had developed among the Tamils. In their call for Eeḷam, a separate Tamil state, Jaffna Tamil separatists have spawned publications that attempt to raise a distinctly Tamil historic consciousness with respect to a historical Tamil nation which needs to be reestablished. But the call rings hollow and is often contradicted by Marxist hopes for a *new* nation. Whether Tamils choose to establish Eeḷam has little to do with the fact that there was once a Tamil kingdom in the island's north. The Jaffna Tamils, the Eeḷamists included, did not have a strongly cultivated sense of their political history. In 1983, I asked several randomly selected high school classes in the heart of Jaffna Tamil country, Jaffna, how many of them could write down the names of two Tamil kings of their own historic past. From a total of about a hundred students, only twelve were able to name even one king. Furthermore, many of these students recalled the name of Elara (who, of course, was not a king of the Jaffna kingdom), the just Tamil king who was defeated by the Sinhala Duttugamunu. Others named the South Indian dynasties of the Chērās, Chōḷās, and Pāṇḍyans. I was unable to carry out a similar experiment with Sinhala schoolchildren. But in 1987, informal and random questioning of about twenty Sinhala children in the island's south revealed that all of them were able to name at least three Sinhala kings. And as I had expected, the kings who were recalled most frequently were Duttugamunu (the king of the Sinhala people's "charter myth," the one who defeated the Tamil Elara and united the island under Sinhala-Buddhist rule, according to the Sinhala chronicles), Parakramabahu the Great (the builder of the great irrigation tanks and channels that are so often recalled as the glorious past that is being reclaimed now in Sri Lanka's ambitious multimillion-dollar Mahāwāli hydroelectric project), and Devanampiya Tissa (the first Sri Lankan king to embrace Buddhism), in that order. The Tamils' lack of awareness of their own historical past is, to be sure, partly due to the content of the history textbooks assigned by the government, which has consistently slighted the Tamil side of Ceylonese and Sri Lankan history. However, it must be noted that even at the height of the nineteenth- and early-twentieth-century cultural renaissance (long before the postindependent Ceylon started assigning textbooks), historical consciousness among the Tamils in general remained subdued (see Kailasapathy

1985). This was not so on the Sinhala-Buddhist side of the same renaissance. When compared to the linguistic consciousness and the awareness of the literary and religious *heritage* of the Tamils, the consciousness of their political *history* is as dim as a candle before the sun.

In the many days that I spent with Tamil militants who were fighting for the separate state of Eeḷam, only once did they invoke the Tamil *historic* past, and then only to yoke it to the romanticism of bourgeois Tamil politicians of the (then) outlawed Tamil United Liberation Front. These militants claimed that the TULF and its ilk had only recently found it expedient to recall the existence of a Jaffna kingdom merely in reaction to Sinhala hyperbole about their ancient kingdoms. The militants were right, at least to the extent that most Jaffna Tamils are not deeply concerned about their ancient kings, kingdoms, and dates. They were indifferent to such a history, especially to its chronology. By contrast, the invocation of Hindu religious and Tamil cultural heritage of dance, literature, architecture, and sculpture was not considered bourgeois even by these revolutionaries.

There are other ways of formulating this distinction between the Sinhala and Tamil views of the past. It may be seen as one between political history and cultural history, or objectivist history and transcendental history. To the extent that such formulations appear reasonable, they do so only because they are underwritten, as it were, by two distinct orientations to the past. What these Tamils and the greater Indian cultural traditions share is more a consciousness of the present, one's present heritage of the past, than of the past as past. "History" is one thing, "heritage" another. The one is sharply defined and clearly instantiated, even if only in the imagination; the other is a vague,[18] though rich, potentiality.

A Semeiosic Formulation of the Distinction

In formal semeiosic[19] terms, the Peircean distinction between dicisigns (or dicent signs) and a rheme (or rhematic signs) may help us see the difference being drawn here with greater clarity. Dicisigns are signs whose effects are seen to have been *actualized* in some "here and now." Signs of the Sinhala past—the Buddha's visit to the island, for instance—are seen as actualized events, quite literally in his footprint on the mountain of Sri Pada. The reality of King Parakramâbahu the Great is found in his irrigation tanks. Heritage, by contrast, is a semeiosic rheme. Whereas dicisigns are, to the community of interpreters, signs of actual fact (the factitiousness of these facts notwithstanding; that is a separate issue, which I shall not take up here), a rheme is not a sign of actuality but one of possibility; or more exactly, it is a sign that has a qualitative possibility as its significant effect. Peirce compares a rheme (he also calls it a *term* or a *rhema*) to a proposition with a blank for its subject (2.95). "If parts of a proposition be erased so as to leave *blanks* in their places, and if these blanks are of such a nature that if each of them be filled by a proper name the result will be a proposition, then the blank form of proposition which was first produced by the erasure is termed a *rheme*" (2.272). Or again, "A [rheme] is a sign which leaves its Object, and a fortiori its Interpretant, to be what it *may*" (emphasis added; 2.95). As a semeiosic rheme, "heritage" is a sign of possibility that needs no actualization to make it real and that no number of actualizations can exhaust. With history as a dicisign, one begins with the idea that without a past to realize there would not be a consciousness of a past; with heritage as a rheme, one begins with the idea that without a consciousness of the past there would not be a past to be conscious of. The former describes a Sinhala disposition toward the past, the latter, that of the Tamils.

Furthermore, dicisigns strive to particularize or concretize;[20] rhemes tend to synthesize and primordialize. Both are activities of making real, *real*ization. Particularization sets apart. What is set apart is a person, place, or event that marks a breach in the unfolding fabric of time. But particularization, true to its dual meanings of "part" (as opposed to whole) and "particle" (as in *concrete* particle), entails a search for objects in which "meanings" can be incarnated and the world fragmented at one and the same time. Bruce Kapferer (1988) holds that "fragmentation" in a Buddhist state is threatening, is fraught with evil, and is the antithesis of a hierarchical and holistic (Buddhist) state. By its very nature, then, historiography is ironic. In its very quest for the whole, it admits its lack. In being a "particularizing" (potentially or actually fragmenting) activity it runs counter to the constitution of a sound Buddhist state. In other words, if Kapferer is correct, in the Buddhist state's very *historicity* lie the seeds of its own contradiction. History, in its particularizing endeavor, is built on the assumption that the whole is yet not-at-hand, and that it has to be recovered, piece by piece, particle by particle, particular by particular.

It is in this sense that historiography has been burdened with the need to concretize. Its objects are documents and monuments, both of which are amply "discoverable" in Buddhist Sri Lanka. The historian and the historically minded people become the subjects who *see* these objects. Primordialization, in the rhematic sense in which I use the word, is both holistic and nondualistic; its verity is affirmed, not in any particular object or objectivity, but in a lived experience of intersubjective *being*.

Heritage with History

To be sure, when I say that history constitutes a Sinhala disposition toward the past and heritage a Tamil disposition toward the past, I overstate the case for emphasis. The foregoing discussion and distinction between what I have called history on the one hand and heritage on the other should not be taken as meaning that a people who hold to one view of the past are incapable of the other. The Tamil-Sinhala contrasts are to be taken as general and strong propensities rather than as mutual exclusivities. A sense of heritage does have a place in Sinhala consciousness, as does a sense of history in the consciousness of Tamils. However, the biases are real and are to be recognized. In my opinion, Bruce Kapferer's claim that "for Sinhalas the past is always in the present and the person is inseparable from history, the person and history [forming] a cosmic unity" (1988:213) is only partly correct or, rather, is truer of the Hindu-Tamil disposition toward the past than that of the Sinhala Buddhist. What makes the Buddhist-Sinhala disposition different from the Hindu-Indian one and similar to the European one is what I have chosen to emphasize here. For the Sinhala Buddhist, the past qua past is the independent variable, and its presence in the present is the dependent variable. In this respect, the Sinhalas are more like Kapferer's Australians ("given to placing history outside themselves" [1988:214]) than are the Tamils. For their part, some Tamils have entered the debate on the historical verity of this or the other fact pertaining both to Sinhala claims of a Sinhala past and to their own past (see Ponnambalam 1983 and Satyendra 1985). The debate is carried out in discursive terms that are identical to those employed by the other side (see Coomaraswamy 1987).

While the Jaffna Tamil, following the general Indian pattern, favors "heritage" and the Sinhalas favor "history," the Estate Tamils' view of the past can be apperceived at dead center of a palpable dialectic entailing heritage and history. Like their Jaffna Tamil counterparts, and as revealed in their objection to being called "New Tamils," Estate Tamils think of themselves as an ancient people belonging to an ancient civilization, with an ancient heritage. However, these Tamils see their claim to this great heritage as being openly monopolized by the Jaffna Tamils. The agents who remind them of this monopoly are the schoolteachers, who have been (until recently) predominantly these "other Tamils." These teachers are the ones who introduced the Estate Tamil child to classical Tamil literature, in a modern dialect of Tamil. This dialect of Tamil, which is alien to the student, is called *centamiṛ* (elegant or pure Tamil) by the teacher while he or she simultaneously brands the Tamil spoken by Estate Tamil students *koṭuntamiṛ* (coarse or corrupt Tamil).[21]

In Sri Lankan schools, religion is a mandatory subject. Here too it is the Jaffna Tamil teacher who teaches and prepares the Estate Tamil schoolchildren for their examination in Hinduism. The brand of Hinduism taught is Śaiva Siddhānta, which Jaffna Tamils claim to have preserved and nurtured in its purity and prevented from going the way of Saivism in Tamil Nadu. Estate Hinduism is coarse: a "little tradition," according one Jaffna Tamil informant, who has read some anthropology.[22] Here again the sacred trust of the great tradition is a matter of heritage, not mere history.

In this regard we may note that the Jaffna Tamils' conceit about their dialect of Tamil or about Śaiva Siddhānta is comparable to Sinhala Buddhists' belief that they have been entrusted by the Buddha to preserve and defend Buddhism in its pristine form against all threats of latter-day corruption. The difference, however, is a significant one. Sinhala Buddhists hold the entrusting of Buddhism in their hands to have been an actualized event; the Jaffna Tamils see themselves as living embodiments of a tradition (linguistic and religious) that no mere event initiated and no mere event could end. They, as a people, like the dialect of Tamil they speak and the religion they practice, are timeless, with neither beginning nor end.

There is one aspect of the Estate Tamils' heritage that has not been alienated from them, an aspect that they feel has not been colonized by the Jaffna Tamil. This consists of poetry, song, drumming, and the art of storytelling. I shall call this the bardic heritage. This bardic heritage has two extensions: one in time, and the other in space. The temporal extension goes back to the great Tamil poet of the early Christian era, Tiruvalluvar. While all Tamils proudly lay claim to Tiruvalluvar as *their* poet, and many love citing the Reverend G. U. Pope (1886), who introduced his English translation of the *Tirukkuraḷ* by describing its greatness as having no parallel in any other language, it is the Parayans, the untouchable caste of drummers, who lay special claim to this famous poet. They consider Tiruvalluvar as their very own ancestor. To this day, the priests of Parayans are called *Vaḷḷuvars*. And as any fieldworker is bound to find out in short order, estate life owes its musicality—its songs of work and wailing, its rhythms of drums and dance, its tales of ups and downs—to the Parayans (see, for example, Egnor 1986:294–344). In the words of a popular quatrain sung by a Parayan:

Kaḷḷans have power
Veḷḷāḷans have wealth
Paḷḷans have revenge
Parayans have song.[23]

(kaḷḷanukku pavarirukku
veḷḷāḷanukkuppaṇamirukku
paḷḷanukkuppaliirukku
parayanuukkuppāṭṭirukku)

If the temporal line of this bardic heritage extends to Tiruvalluvar, its spatial extension moves inward, touching each individual's innermost being with the clarity of felt immediacy. And what is more, in this inward extension, *heritage* intersects with *history*, to be nourished by a common experience.

This history is not a history of "long ago"; it is a history of "just yesterday." It is not a finished chapter that may be reopened at will, looked at, reexperienced if so wished, and reclosed. It is still being "written." It is not an abstract history or a history of abstractions; it is anchored in experience, the experience of suffering. And this history is constituted by a "root metaphor" (Pepper 1942; Turner 1974), the metaphor of labor (*uṛaippu*) (see Velupillai 1970).

In the following two sections I shall attempt to illustrate this dialectical play between the elements of heritage and those of history as they are constituted in labor and pain. In the first section, I provide a synoptic sketch in the voice of a *typical* oral historian.[24] In the second section I provide a self-consciously constructed *people's legend* by one of the best-known Estate Tamil writers, the late C. V. Velupillai. On the face of it the first section may appear to carry the flag of history and the second that of heritage. But within each of them, as within the discourses that bear them, the dialectical play between historical consciousness and the consciousness of heritage is densely enacted.

Suffering: A Catalog

This is how the typical account runs:

> Two years after Sri Wickrama Rajasingam,[25] the last Kandyan king, was deposed by the British (in 1815),[26] the first group of laborers were brought to Kaṇṭi from India. The first to come were all men. They came not to work on plantations but to build roads and railroads.[27] These were the men who built the Colombo-Kandy road. These men were hired by the British government. They were hired not from India's villages but from her towns. Unlike villagers, these men were without kin; mere drifters; without discipline (*kaṭṭuppāṭu*; from the root, *kaṭṭu*-to bind or restrain, and *pāṭu*—suffering. Thus, to voluntarily suffer or subject one's self to restraint). It is said that many of them died from diseases in those early days. But they were free to return to India whenever they liked. And many who survived did. Some stayed on. The British government also brought Indians who could read, could write, and knew arithmetic to work in the civil service. They too came from towns and cities. They came mainly from Madras and Cochin. Many of these people brought their families and stayed. Their descendants became the *Kolombə Koccis*. Some of these Colombo Kochchis deny that they are Indian and have, in recent riots, burned Tamil businesses and homes.[28]
>
> A few years after Sri Wickrama Rajasingam was banished to India to live there in exile, there were many famines in India.[29] In those days, English planters gave *kaṅkāṇis*[30] money to take laborers from our villages to clear the jungles of Sri Lanka and plant coffee. That is how our forefathers came to Sri Lanka to clear the jungle and plant coffee. In the beginning those who came here were mostly men. Later, especially when tea replaced coffee, entire families came to the island together. Many died of disease before they even reached the mountains. Some died in the sea when their boats capsized in monsoon storms. Others died en route in the dense jungles of the North Western and North Central Provinces. While

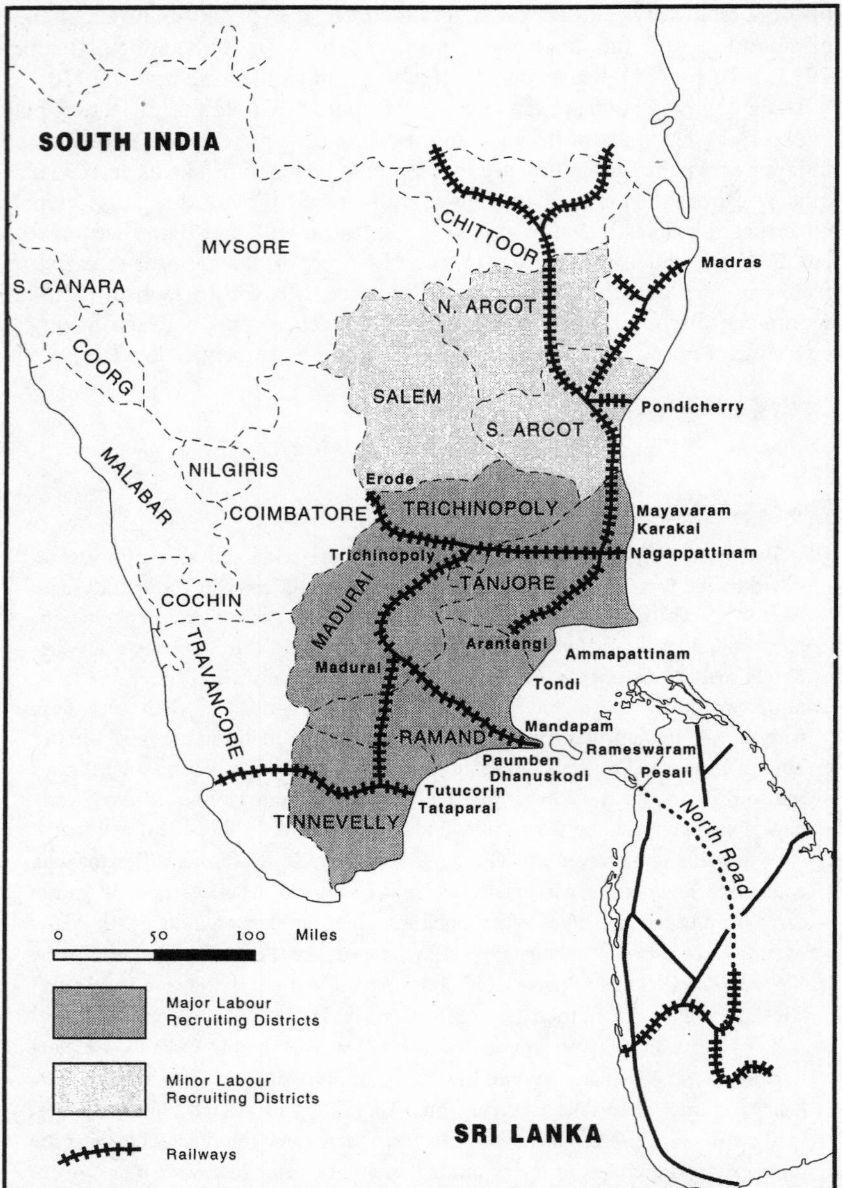

Map 2. South Indian districts from which labor was recruited for plantations in Sri Lanka (adapted from D. Wesumperuma)

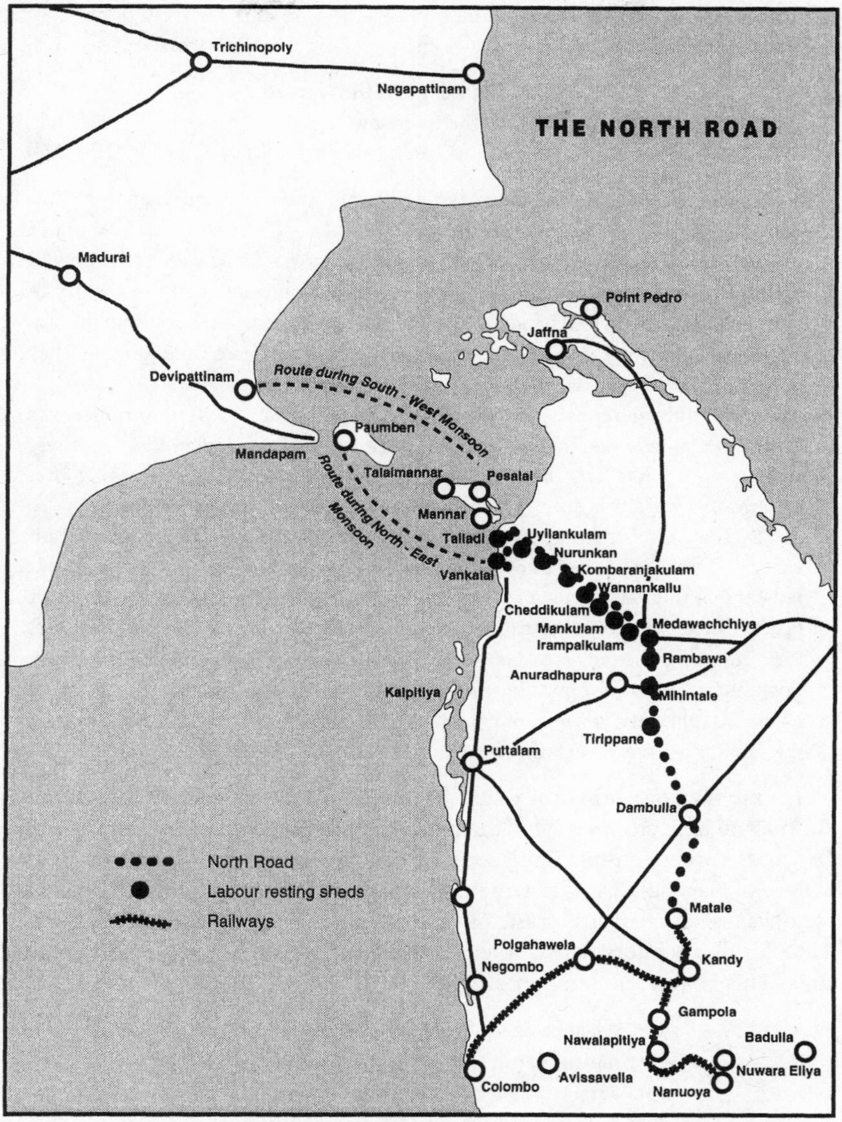

Map 3. The North Road (adapted from D. Wesumperuma)

Parayan musicians beat their drums to keep the wild animals away, a few bold men went ahead to survey the jungles and plan how, when, and where to set fires.

> The wild boar and the leopard
> Died in the forest fire.
>
> *(From a ballad recorded by Velupillai [1970:35])*

The others cut down the jungle, making a road all the way from Mannar to Anuradhapura, and from there to Kandy.

Some died of cholera, typhoid, smallpox, and malaria. Some were eaten by wild animals. They cut more roads through the jungle from Kandy all the way up to Nuwara Eliya and then to Bandarawela, Badulla, and down to the south to the sea. The Sinhalas did not work on these roads because they feared the jungles. They stuck to their villages. Furthermore, they were lazy.[31]

In 1827 the white man planted coffee. That was when most of our ancestors came.[32] First, only men came. Since in coffee growing the demand for labor was seasonal, our forefathers thought that they could return to India every year after the seasonal work was done. The kaṅkāṇis and the white *dorais* (bosses) led us to believe that this was how it was going to be. At first we were given a small "advance" by the kaṅkāṇi. He got this money from the white man. But he told our fathers that this was his own money, advanced to them out of the kindness of his heart, which they could return, whenever convenient, with a small interest. But they devised a ruse to force us to stay. After the season was over and the work done, they delayed our payment. The dorai did this to save himself the trouble of having to look for a new set of laborers the following year. The dorai's story was the same, every year, year after year.

Let me now parenthetically shift from our *typical narrator's voice* to my own in order to expand upon what the narrator has called the *dorai's story* by turning to its expression in a work song. This song was sung for me in the Indian village of Naganallur in the Tiruchchirappalli District of Tamil Nadu by a man who was repatriated under the Sirimavo-Shastri Indo-Ceylon Pact of 1964.[33] He and his ancestors had worked on Blackwater Estate in the Ambagamuwa area. This is how the song goes:

> Mr. Mackenzie, Mr. Mackenzie, where is our pay?
> Marimuttu, Marimuttu, have you seen the prices fall?
> Mr. Wright, Mr. Wright, where is our pay?
> Rengamuttu, Rengamuttu, I have to buy
> another coffee estate.
> Mr. Smith, Mr. Smith, where is our pay?
> Sinnasamy, Sinnasamy, come back next year.
> Mr. Kaṅkāṇi, Mr. Kaṅkāṇi, where is our pay?
> O *karmam*, o *karmam*, the first half the bugs ate.
> The second is paying up the interest you owe.

This little song, which I collected in 1975, I had relegated to a box labeled "Fieldnotes: miscellaneous scraps" until ten years later when I came across the following note in an appendix in K. M. de Silva (1965):

> In his evidence before the Parliamentary Committee on Ceylon, 2nd report on Ceylon 1850 (p. 303) the Ceylon planter George Ackland showed that on a single day in 1840 the following Civil Servants bought 13,275 acres (5376 ha) of land in the Ambagamuwa District (Central Province).

The Rt. Hon. J. S. Mackenzie, Governor	1,120 acres
The Hon. W. O. Carr (Puisne Justice) and Captain Skinner (Commissioner of Roads)	862 acres
F. B. Norris (Survey-General) and others	762 acres
G. Turnour (Governor Agent, Central Province, and at that time Acting Colonial Secretary)	2,217 acres
H. Wright (District Judge, Kandy) and G. Bird	1,751 acres
Sir R. Arbuthnot (Commander of the Forces) and Capt. Winslow (A.D.C.)	855 acres
T. Oswin, Esq. (District Judge)	545 acres
C. R. Buller (later Government Agent, Central Prov.)	764 acres
Capt. Layard and others	2,204 acres
P. E. Wodehous (Government Agent and Assistant Colonial Secretary)	2,135 acres
Total	13,275 acres

It is most intriguing that two of the names which appear in the song also appear in the above list, and that these purchases were in the Ambagamuwa District, the district within which Blackwater Estate is located. My research in the Public Records Office in London and in the archives in Colombo has not turned up any evidence directly implicating Governor Mackenzie and District Judge Wright in the nonpayment or delayed payment of wages to the laborers who worked on their estates. Nor have I been able to find any songs that include other names from the above list. "Smith" is in the song and not on this list. Perhaps he was too minor a figure for George Ackland's purposes. There also seems to be a chronological problem in the songs. If the reference to the bugs that had eaten the coffee plants is an allusion to the great and final coffee blight of the late 1870s, that would place all these events, with their charges and excuses, forty-odd years after the massive purchases of land described in Ackland's list. Then again, the reference could have been to an earlier minor crop disease. However, if indeed the song speaks the truth about these highest of officials in colonial Ceylon, it would be one of the severest indictments of British colonial exploitation of Estate Tamil laborers. In any case, it remains true that planters of that period reaped several benefits from these irregular, delayed, and infrequent payments of wages. As Wesumperuma notes, "the underlying factor for the planters' preference for infrequent payment was the shortage of working capital which the coffee planters experienced" (1986:194). Mackenzie's excuse does have some basis in fact. Coffee prices were notorious for their dips and rises. But if "working capital" extended to entail investment capital as well, as the charge against "Mr. Wright" in the song seems to indicate, then it is clear that white planters expanded their landholdings on the backs of unpaid laborers; the wages due them went directly into the purchase of more estates.

Returning to the voice of our narrator, we find that the kaṅkāṇi supported this policy of delayed payments for even more diabolical reasons.

> It forced us to turn again to the kaṅkāṇi for the means of our livelihood. So the first year's payment would be paid only at the beginning of the next year's work season. By then our forefathers were so deep in debt that they never even saw the color of these wages. It was directly deducted from their accounts by the kaṅkāṇi. They continued to work the next season so that they could go back home with some earnings. But that never happened. What happened at the end of the first year was repeated after the second, the third, and the fourth year. Then it became the custom. Each year, our forefathers got themselves deeper and deeper into debt; and each year our forefathers' entire annual wages had to be used to repay loans and interest to the kaṅkāṇi.

Thus the following song:

> Speak not of Kandy to me;
> Nor repeat its name.
> For in that casteless Kandy
> The cobbler is the kaṅkāṇi.[34]
>
> *(Velupillai 1970:34)*

To this day, many of us are in debt to those kaṅkāṇis and their children, some of us continuing the old debt-obligation in village India where we have returned under the various repatriation schemes. Some managed to break this vicious cycle early on by determinedly returning to India empty-handed, along the same treacherous route. Others went further into debt to bring their wives and children to join them and their labor.

Then in 1878 the coffee blight happened in Sri Lanka. Many white planters abandoned their land and their debts to us and left. For three years our people died of starvation.

> In yonder field
> Strung with pegs
> Where coffee plants sprout
> I lost my beloved brother.
>
> *(Velupillai 1970:35)*

Then came tea. We were rehired. More of our people were brought from India. More people came to Kandy from India in the year Queen Victoria died than in any other year.[35] This time as many women and children as men were brought to the hills, since plucking tea is a woman's job, weeding around the tea bushes a child's job, and both women and children were paid less than were men.

The Sinhalas in the villages bordering the estates where we worked brought us breadfruit, honey, jaggery, and arrack. We shared our rations of rice and dhal with them. We also paid them in rupees and cents. They did not understand money and preferred payment in kind. When it comes to money, the (Kandyan) Sinhala villager is easily cheated, even to this day. Small traders from the low country set up shops in the hill towns alongside those set up by our Vellalas, Chettiars, and goldsmiths. These low-country Sinhalas cheated Kandyan Sinhalas whenever an exchange in money was involved. Some of our people laughed at their simpleness, behind their backs, along with the low-country Sinhala merchant; others taught the Kandyan villager how not to be cheated and how to count his change. In those days, fights between Sinhalas and us were rare. You will hear an occasional story of how one of our men was threatened by a group of Sinhala villagers. Sometimes it was a Kandyan Sinhala attacking us for not warning them against the low-country cheaters; and at others it was a low-country Sinhala merchant or his hired thugs attacking us for informing the Kandyan peasant that this *mudalāli* (shop owner) or that was cheating them.

Of course the peasants laughed at us, and we at them. They at our language; we at how they sowed their rice paddy fields without plan or purpose. But on the whole we had little to do with them, except when some of our people went with some of theirs to Kadirgamam (Kataragama in Sinhala). It was the white man and the kaṅkāṇis that we either liked or hated. They are the ones who worked us, beat us, underfed, underpaid, and underhoused us, and cheated us; and sometimes were kind to us. And if ours was a good kaṅkāṇi or a kind dorai we were proud of him.

> Of all the dorais in the land
> OUR dorai is the court dorai.
> The court dorai is a tough man,
> Get off the road, here he comes.[36]
>
> *(Velupillai 1970:38)*

After one hundred years, the white man gave all the people of this land the right to vote, including us. The others did not like this. "They are foreigners," they said of us. "They earn money here and send it back to their villages in India." Only the Cheṭṭiārs and some Moṭṭa Veḷḷāḷa kaṅkāṇis had enough money to send back to India. They, along with the Boras and the Bhais,[37] had enough money to buy the right to vote and the right to be a citizen. They bankrolled the politicians and the white planters.[38]

In 1920 all the people of Sri Lanka, including the Estate Tamils, were given the right to vote. Ten years later they took that right from many of us by introducing newer and stricter eligibility requirements. Now only those who possessed a Certificate of Permanent Settlement were allowed to vote. And anyone who had gone back to India within the previous five years for a visit was not allowed to be a citizen. In spite of this there were 100,000 Estate Tamils who voted. This the Sinhalas did not like. So they made the requirement stricter. A voter had to be literate in Sinhala, Tamil, or English. But they would not allow our children the privilege of schools. They did not even provide a crèche where our women could leave their infants and toddlers when they went to the fields. Nowadays there are crèches, but the "teacher" at these crèches is a Sinhala woman who does not even know Tamil. A voter had to own more than Rs.500 of immovable property or he had to earn Rs.50 or more per month. These requirements were made only of us Estate Tamils. Then they said that we had to prove that we had a permanent interest in this country. So in 1936 they made the rule tighter for us while at the same time allowing white men, who came and went as they pleased and always returned to England, to vote. And all the Burghers[39] who eventually went to Australia were allowed to vote. We, who did not even have money to buy a train ticket to Talai Mannar to take the ferry to India if we wanted to, were deemed not to have a permanent interest in the island. In spite of this, more and more of us qualified to vote.[40] So they made the rules tighter yet in 1940. And still there were one and a half lakhs (one hundred thousand) among us who were qualified to vote.[41] And what did the Jaffna Tamils do? They did not care about us most of the time. C. Suntharalingam[42] was the brain behind everything that D. S. Senanayake did, including our eventual disenfranchisement after independence. G. G. Ponnambalam briefly showed interest in our problem only when he thought that it might help his Tamils too.[43] Then came the elections after the war. We elected seven Indian Congress members and seven leftist members to Parliament.[44] This scared the Sinhala capitalists, the Jaffna Tamil capitalists, and the British capitalists. So they took away our citizenship and then our right to vote. This was planned with the British. People who know about these matters more than we do tell us that every word that was uttered during the independence negotiations between Senanayake and the British was written down. If this be so they must surely have talked about us who made up 13 percent of this country's population. But they tell us that there is no record of a single word about us. How is it that we who mattered so much before every election since 1920 didn't even warrant mention when independence was discussed? The records are either hidden or destroyed. For if they are found it will reveal a conspiracy: a conspiracy in 1947 to prevent a democratically elected leftist party from coming to power. Then in 1964, the prime ministers of Ceylon and India, Sirimavo Bandaranaike and Lal Bhadhur Shastri, decided, without consulting us, how India and Ceylon were going to divide us. They arbitrarily decided that 525,000 of us were to be sent back to India, whence we had come 150 years earlier, and 300,000 were to be given Ceylonese citizenship but their names would appear on a separate registry. We were to be marked. This left 150,000 whose fate was undecided.

The horror tales that we hear from those who went to India are worse than anything we could tell you about our sojourn in Sri Lanka. We are cheated of our meager possessions even before we leave the estates. The estate office clerks and some Sinhala superintendents extract bribes from us in exchange for the release of our papers and provident funds. But this is usually minor. These people know how poor we are. But matters get really bad at the Indian High Commission in Kandy or Colombo. There the clerks try to relieve us of as much jewelry and cash as they possibly can. But nothing is as bad as when we land in India. Here there is justice. Over there there is only injustice. The Sinhalas attack us only during the periodic riots. Jaffna Tamils look to us only to see if we can be used for their purposes. Our own Tamils in India attack us every day in countless ways. From the customs officers who treat us like cattle, to the porters, the *tasildars*, the bank clerks, and finally our own relatives—of whom we have only heard vague stories from our grandparents—all exploit us, not just our material wealth but even our labor. Many of us have become bonded laborers;[45] many others have become beggars in the cities of Madurai and Madras. It is said that some of our women have even turned to prostitution.

The whole of the above account, especially that of the postdisenfranchisement and postrepatriation years, is a highly abbreviated one. But what may be keenly felt in this account is a historical consciousness: history in the making, as it were.

Now let us turn to an account that emphasizes heritage, but heritage with a uniquely historical twist.

Born of Labor

What follows is the sketch of a story obtained from the late C. V. Velupillai—a poet and trade union leader whose roots went back to the tea estates—in my last interview with him, in 1984, two years before his death.[46] He wished to call it *malayakattamiṛar purāṇam* (The Legend of the Hill-Country Tamils).[47]

"Her name was Tamil.[48] She was the most beautiful woman (*pen*) in the world. Her other name was Mother Tamil (*tamiṛ tāi*)."[49] She was the only daughter of Siva, "the apple of his eye (*Sivamaṇi*)." One day when she was thirsty, she came to a sea of milk. Delighted, she quenched her thirst in it. It was the sea that Lord Vishnu had churned. She did not know this. And she became pregnant. Lord Siva, filled with rage at his daughter, cursed her to go into painful labor. And her children and their children's children were also cursed to labor all their lives. After much anguish and pain she gave birth to a daughter and then died as many of our women die during labor to this very day. Sivaperuman (Lord Siva) was deeply saddened. He held out to his granddaughter one of the spears left behind by his son, Murugan (also called Skanda), and told her to give it to her sons. "It belongs to your mother's brother (*tāi māman*). Tell your sons to follow him to the land that he has gone to.[50] And let your daughters follow your sons. In that land there will be a bush. It will have spread so as to cover much of that land. Tell your sons to use this *āyutam* (weapon; also instrument or tool) and your daughters their bare hands to harvest every last leaf from this bush and thereby make that land prosper. After the last leaf has been harvested, my son Murugan will come to claim his āyutam. Then your curse shall be lifted." As soon as his granddaughter received the spear, its tip bent, and one of its sides became the sharpest of blades, changing the whole into a *kavvāttukkatti* (the curved knife used for pruning tea bushes).

"This is our symbol (*cinnam*): a kavvāttukkatti and the *koṛuntu* (the two tea leaves and a bud from which tea is manufactured). [At this point Mr. Velupillai showed me a sketch of the symbol.]" But of course there is that curse where the pain of labor in childbirth (*prasava vētanai*) continues in the pain of labor (*uṛaippu vētanai*) among the bushes on the mountains of the tea estates.[51] But that, as Sivaperuman said, will end only when every last tea leaf has been plucked. But the kavvāttukkatti prunes a bush, and the more one prunes a bush the more luxuriantly leaves grow. "This is the crux of our life's problem. How will this end? How will the curse be lifted? How will every last leaf be nipped off? That is our secret. It *will* happen. And when it does, we will go to Kadirgamam. And there we will give Murugan his knife. And what do you think will happen?"

Expecting Siva's boon to be fulfilled according to plan, I said, "It will turn back into a spear!" Mr. Velupillai laughed and picked up the picture of the symbol of Estate Tamils he had sketched. "No! It will turn into this." And he sketched over the outlines of the knife, extending it into the shape of a sickle, in whose arc remained three leaves and a bud.

I must restrain myself for now from the temptation to subject this purāṇam to the variety of mythological analyses it invites, including the one that perennially fascinates anthropologists, the subject of "incest." But I cannot resist raising at least several small points of curious significance. The ancestress, Mother Tamil, is called a woman (presumably human). But she turns out to be the daughter of Siva and the sister of Skanda (therefore, a goddess?). But if she is a goddess, she does not fit either one of the two types of South Indian Saiva goddesses, Consort Goddesses and Virgin Goddesses, who remain unimpregnatable virgins (see Ramanujan 1986:55–64). Her death is described in human terms. (Perhaps this was a function of the narrative's having been but a sketch.) Giving birth vaginally, though known in Hinduism (especially Vaishnavism), is not the most common form of divine delivery. Mr. Velupillai was educated in a Christian school. Could that have had some bearing on his purāṇam? Could this, combined with his leftist politics, also have made him end the myth in the somewhat "sacrilegious" manner in which he did end it: with the last word not going to Siva or the spear to Murugan; rather, to an implied revolutionary struggle and/or victory by and for his people? Then

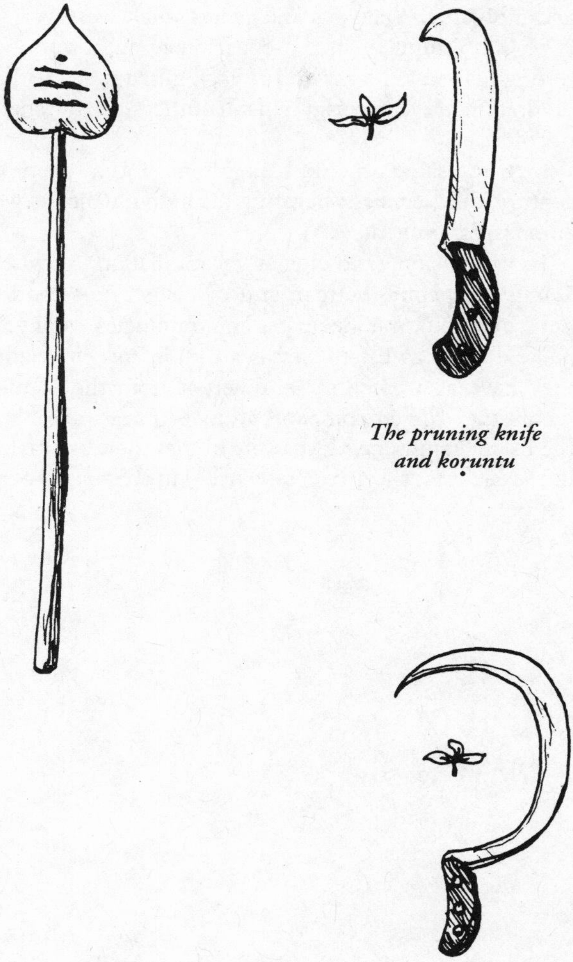

Figure 1. The emblem of Estate Tamils (based on C. V. Velupillai's drawings)

there is always that question of the typicality of a tale and the idiosyncrasy of an informant such as this. Despite these unanswered questions we may close this chapter with the following observations:

a. Mr. Velupillai saw himself as a descendent of Tiruvalluvar. Both belong to the Vaḷḷuvan subcaste of Parayans. Tiruvalluvar is seen as a *historical* figure, and an *individual*. The two are complementary since history makes individuals and individuals (persons and events) make history.

b. Mr. Velupillai, in self-consciously authoring a purāṇam, was both asserting his individuality and engaging in a practice that runs against the grain of Brahmanic Hinduism where authors of purāṇams are never historical individuals.

c. At the same time, in seeing himself as a token of a type, as a twentieth-century Valluvar, he is negating his individuality as well as his historicity. The emphasis is on *heritage*.

In conclusion (and not as recapitulation), I wish to suggest that Estate Tamils are people both in and of history, not condemned to be moored to permanent cultural ideologies and ontologies, or any such Durkheimian *moral order*.[52] Even as Estate Tamils are different from Jaffna Tamils and Sinhalas, they have also come to be different from the Tamils of the mainland with whom they parted company 50 to 150 years ago. Of all three ethnic groups, the Estate Tamils are most aware of their nonessentialness, that they are beings in the making, sheer concrescence[53] in the meeting of history and heritage.

2

HISTORY'S ENTAILMENTS IN THE VIOLENCE OF A NATION

In actuality, its true goal—even in utilizing general knowledge—
is to understand an historical phenomenon in its singularity,
in its uniqueness. Historical consciousness is interested in
knowing, not how men, people, or states develop *in general*,
but, quite on the contrary, how *this* man, *this* people, or *this* state
became what it is; how each of these *particulars* could come to pass
and end up specifically *there*.
(H. G. Gadamer)

THERE is more to be said about the status of history in Sri Lanka than to call it a disposition toward the past, cultivated by a monastic scholarly tradition concerned with chronology and chronicles, and favored by Sinhala Buddhists. There is a shade to history that was introduced into South Asia as part and parcel of European colonialism which has had its different and differentiating effects on South Asians. Most significantly, I believe, colonialism hybridized what I shall now qualify as traditional historic consciousness, which was part of "a way of being in" the world, with a modern[1] European historical consciousness that presumed to provide its adepts a superior way, "a way of seeing the world." The dialectical workings of history and heritage under the impress of certain modern historical and historicizing conditions can be better appreciated if we look deeper into this dichotomy of "seeing" and "being." What I wish to argue is that traditional historic consciousness has, since colonization, been goaded by a characteristically European historical consciousness into moving toward a "way of seeing" with the concurrent denial of a "way of being" in the world. The historic consciousness that found its place of germination in Buddhist monasteries and among monkish chroniclers had not denied that theirs was a mode of being. The new, largely European-induced, modern historic consciousness, however, lays claim to transcending being. In order to better elucidate this new, compounded sense of history, and its bearing on the politics of identity and ethnicity, I shall shortly resort to three further analytic concepts that I hold will be helpful. These are "the mythic," "the ontic," and the "epistemic." "The mythic" I shall contrast with "history," whereas "the ontic" and "the epistemic" constitute a further contrasting pair. Before I do this, however, I wish to review and refine, as economically as possible, some of the essential arguments of the previous chapter.

In charting the distinctiveness of a historical consciousness by contrasting it with the consciousness of heritage, I had argued that Sinhala-Buddhist consciousness of the past has privileged history in a manner that Tamil-Hindu pride in heritage has not. Would this have been true throughout the almost two millennia that these two groups have lived in proximity to each other? Certainly not. Even to speak of two groups as spanning two millennia, as if their essences and features were fixed, is misleading. Speakers of Tamil, speakers of Sinhala, speakers of Sinhala and Tamil, Buddhist Tamils, non-Buddhist Tamils, Buddhist Sinhalas and non-Buddhist Sinhalas, Shaivites—Tamil-speakers and possibly Sinhala-speakers—drifted with relative ease, at different times for different purposes and conveniences, from one sociological formation into another. This is not to argue that there were no symbolic totem poles around which one group or another rallied whenever in need of a sense of community. For the Sinhala Buddhists, the remarkably ancient *vaṁsa* literary tradition of chronicles, begun around the sixth century A.D., provided a distinct rallying point. For Tamils, the literary traditions that provided such centers were quite different, centering on poetic, epic, and bardic traditions. But these groups did not form closed circles as they have today. Neither Tamils nor Sinhalas were essentialized—let alone racialized—in this manner. But were there Hindus, in the contemporary sense of Hinduism as an organized set of religious beliefs and practices? Unlikely. The Tamil Hindu represents a very recent category. There were Tamil-speaking Vaishnavites or Shaivites or Jains or Buddhists. But "Hindu" was a term applied to those people who lived east of the Indus River by those who lived west of it, including the Arabs and the Greeks. How these shifting sociological formations did or did not coincide with epistemologies, ideologies, ontologies are matters that are mostly lost to us or await future historical research of a kind that has barely begun.[2] What we know best is the present and perhaps the recent past, and the essentializing drift of two linguistic-cum-religious groups and their recent crystalization of identity. But we also know that the greater part of the island's past and the semeiosic predisposition to, or elective affinity for, modern historical consciousness was preserved, nurtured, and protected largely by a Buddhist monastic tradition. Furthermore, except in times and places that spawned theological and doctrinal debates, the line dividing the Buddhist-Sinhala historical consciousness from the Tamil-Hindu consciousness of heritage was a very fuzzy one at best. This is true in some quarters of the Sinhala population up to this very day.

The careful reader will have noticed that in the last chapter, I coupled "history" and "heritage" with three interchangeable nouns: disposition, orientation, and consciousness. In fact, these nouns are graded along a continuum of awareness that spans from "being" to "seeing." Even if consciousness need not necessarily employ one's actual eyes, it invokes the notion of the "mind's eye" and by extension brings us to the threshhold of an "optic" understanding of whatever we claim to be conscious of. More important, consciousness also brings us to the point where subject and object are precipitated out against each other: that which is conscious against that which one is conscious of. "Disposition," by contrast, does not privilege the optic even figuratively; it is unambiguously a way of being in the world. "Orientation" falls in between, sharing both in the being of "disposition" and the seeing (one is oriented toward something only if one's eyes are pointing in that direction) of "consciousness." Insofar as I have applied these terms to both historic consciousness and heritage, I have done so because both the consciousness of heritage and the historic consciousness of precolonial times provide one with ways of being in the world as well as ways of seeing the world, with shifting emphases on seeing or being that vary in time, place, and occasion. A hint of this nontranscendent accommodation between history and heritage may be found in Obeyesekere's (1991) essay with respect to chronology. He shows us how chronology in the Sinhala-Buddhist chronicle, the *Mahāvaṁsa*, cannot be read as a simple system of dating as chronologies are treated in much of Western historiography, a practice that has recently been emulated by Sri Lankan historians. Minimally, Obeyesekere argues that the *Mahāvaṁsa*'s chronology cannot be appreciated independent of a system of numerology on the one hand and folk understandings of events on the other. In my reading of Obeyesekere's essay we see "history"—or even chronology—as participating in the onticity of a people rather than laying claim to being a purely epistemic exercise, as it has subsequently come to do. In the texts Obeyesekere dealt with, when chronology was found wanting, numerology filled in the lacuna; and when the choice was between chronology and numerology, the latter, which more thoroughly pervaded folk life, prevailed. Numerology was thoroughly constitutive of what it meant to be a Sinhala Buddhist (or, for that matter, a Saivite Tamil).

In the contrast between being and seeing, neither the image of transcendence nor that of polarity is adequate, because the relationship is nontranscendentally hierarchic: seeing is but one form, or a selective form, of being; whereas being is not fully subsumable under seeing. (This would be true of the status of modern historic consciousness or of traditional historic consciousness, except that, as we shall soon see, modern historic consciousness is uncomfortable with any such form of diffuse nondualism.) At times, being and seeing may take apparently polarized positions or forms. Let me illustrate this possibility with an analogy from a homey example: a toy *tabla* that my twin sons played with (more than played on) when they were younger. The tympanum of the drum was made of rubber rather than animal skin, but it did have a dark spot near the center mimicking the off-center black spot that all real tablas have. In time, this rubber tympanum was cut loose from the body of the drum and the boys converted it into a rubber band in the following manner. One of them held onto the dark center spot by pinching it between his thumb and forefinger, and the other scrunched up the edges in his fist. Then, as they pulled, the tympanum would take on the appearance (and even the function) of a rubber band, with two polar ends. But in fact an insect crawling from the fist-held end to the fingers-held end would not be moving from one pole to the other as much as it would be be gradually moving from the outermost, all-containing circle through a series of less-containing concentric circles to the innermost, least-containing center. This is what, I would like to propose (and will elaborate upon below), the relationship between being and seeing is like, with seeing positioned in the least-containing (but most-selective) center.

What is it that in recent times has goaded a monastically cultivated historic consciousness from being part of being-in-the-world into joining those exclusive claims to having risen above mere being to seeing-the-world? Among the Sinhala Buddhists of contemporary Sri Lanka the traditional (mainly monkish) historical consciousness has been transformed into a far more intense and less diffuse form as a result of two nineteenth-century events: (a) the introduction of modern history[3] as a disciplinary epistemology by the agencies of nineteenth-century Europe into its colonies, and (b) the concept of the nation-state. During the late nineteenth and twentieth centuries, the discourse of modern history and the discourse of nation-state made "historical consciousness" into an even more distinctive and more context-free insignia of Sinhala-Buddhist identity. And, in its turn, violence has found much of its raison d'être in the discourses of history and nation that have come to constitute the identity of the Sinhalas. In analyzing this violence, then, I shall not be as interested in its causes as in the conditions of its possibility, history being one of them.

Modern history—quite apart from the historicity of the event—is in its origins and development a largely European discursive practice. History partakes of a discourse that provides one with a distinctive disposition toward the world in general and the past in particular. Even though its most obvious manifestation is to be found in the subject of history, which occupies a place in the curricula of schools and universities, its effect on the Sinhalas' consciousness of the past has been far more pervasive. Prima facie, history is a reportorial exercise, a telling of what *really* happened. But at a deeper level, its being is epistemic. The ground of history is densely spun with questions about what it is to know and what it is that is known. Thus traditional historic consciousness becomes, under the new regime of history, epistemic; that is, it becomes emphatically a way of seeing the world. In societies where the dominant discourse is historic—in the sense we have introduced in this chapter—heritage too turns to history for support and sustenance. This is only too clear if one picks up an issue, say, of the magazine *American Heritage*—where the common sense of heritage can be encountered. It is instantly remarkable that heritage chases after history for approval and its raison d'être. In a country or among a people where the historical discourse does not dominate or claim preeminence—as has been the case in India (arguably until quite recently) or among the Tamils of Sri Lanka—heritage is not subservient to history. Rather, its ground[4] is mythic, its being ontic.[5]

The argument thus far is as follows: From the depths of the ontic—being-in-the-world—in which the consciousness of heritage and history had distinguishable dispositions and orientations toward the past, traditional historic consciousness was goaded by modern history to renounce being and enter the domain of knowing, of epistemology, of seeing. (This is not to deny that a being-free seeing is only an epistemic conceit.) This is also to acknowledge that in traditional historic consciousness lay an elective affinity to the European tradition of history that was to come to Sri Lanka along with colonialization. Heritage too has already been tempted by traditional history's success in courting power and prestige that comes from the recognition traditional history (as embodied in the *Mahāvaṁsa*, for instance) has received from the dominant discourse of modern epistemic history. We have seen this change in the consciousness of heritage even though it lags far behind traditional history for want of a positive event comparable to the birth of Siddhartha Gautama and the enlightenment of Gautama the Buddha. The erosion of heritage's ontic moorings in its quest after an epistemic history is best illustrated by what has come to be known as the Ayodhya-Babri Masjid crisis, in which a section of India's Hindu right destroyed a sixteenth-century mosque in trying to establish that it was the birthplace of Lord Rama. Thus heritage too has to a certain extent been compromised by modern epistemic history. What persists and is unabashedly and unapologetically displayed in the ontic world of being is what I call the mythic.

In what is to follow, "heritage" will not drop out of the equation as much as yield to an understanding of its ground, the mythic. Heritage, historic consciousness, history, the epistemic, the ontic, and now the mythic! I beg your indulgence for the proliferation of terms and then for asking you further to rethink these terms, and in the case of one of them, the mythic, to radically revise its conventional usage. There is a purpose. These terms will become clearer as we go along, less in the abstract and more in the context of the dynamic interplay of the mythic and the historic in the focused ethnographies of six pilgrimage sites in Sri Lanka, as well as in the manner in which identities are constructed by these discourses. These pilgrimage sites have been chosen because of their situatedness within the larger context of a nation-state, a context in which the dynamic interplay between the mythic and the historic entails violence. In preparation, let us briefly examine the significant effects that Sri Lanka's colonization by European powers has bequeathed this island nation, especially through the discipline and discourse of history.

Europeanization: A Sketch of a Discursive Formation and History's Place in It

If we were to set aside the erstwhile settler-colonies such as Australia, Canada, and the United States, Sri Lanka arguably remains one of the most extensively and intensively Europeanized former colonies. Its Europeanization, which was formally inaugurated by the Portuguese (who subjugated the island's low country by 1600), continued even after the last European power, the British, formally left the island in 1948. It is not merely the length of time spanned by European occupation but also the island's size (compared to India) that accounts for the degree of its European traces. Marks of such Europeanization are many, some of which are thinly and yet significantly distributed among the country's elite, some more deeply among the same class, and some widely among the population at large. In the case of the elite, a partial list would include a Latin Club in Colombo that meets regularly to read Cicero or St. Jerome's letters, a bookstore in the capital that sells issues of the *Times Literary Supplement*, the collecting of antiques, the connoisseurship of Western classical music and jazz, the organization of space in homes (especially living rooms and kitchens), and the unabashed Anglophilia or its acute opposite among Sri Lankans. With respect to the organization of space, my comparison is specifically with middle-class homes in South India, where, rather than filling a living room with furniture, people opt for more free floor space. For a Sri Lankan, the Indian living room may seem "empty" or spartan, the pictures on the wall hung in too straight a line, whereas to an Indian, the Sri Lankan living room might seem cluttered and crowded. Potted plants inside the house would, for a South Indian, be only an invitation to snakes. Not so for Sri Lankans of a comparable class. Among the many contrasts that strike an observer of these two regions' kitchens, the most noticeable aspect would be the preference for elevated counters and tables over the use of an unfailingly cleanly swept floor or low tables and stools. More generally distributed among the population are the ease with which young women wear short skirts and dresses (called "frocks") with neither apology nor embarrassment (a stark contrast with South Indian villagers and even townsfolk); the tacit hierarchy established between those who wear trousers and are therefore assumed to speak English and those who wear sarongs or the national dress;[6] and the popularity of a genre of music of Iberian origin called *bailā* and the accompanying taste for harmony (in contradistinction to Indians' general appreciation for the melodic and tonal). Other distinctly European traces that have become part of the sociocultural topography are so thoroughly naturalized as to escape most observers' attention—excepting possibly those who travel between South India and Sri Lanka—and still others we shall encounter further along in this chapter. But at this point I wish to insert into the list, at the more explicitly intellectual level, two more traces that have been written into the island's sensibilities by Europe. These are the disciplines and, more generally, the discourses, of anthropology and history. The greater part of these two discourses may be considered as subsets of a larger process of Europeanization called Orientalism.

With respect to anthropology, I shall be brief. The puzzle of why Sri Lanka has produced such a disproportionate number of internationally known anthropologists, I hypothesize, finds its resolution in the measure of the island's Europeanization and the colonial sentiments that accompanied it. The knowledge of anthropology's colonialist origins is by now commonplace and its kinship to Orientalism undeniable. Thus to adopt with appropriate amendments what R. G. Collingwood said of the historian some fifty years ago, "it need hardly be added that since the [anthropologist] is a son [or daughter] of his [or her] time, there is a general likelihood that what interests him [or her] will interest his [or her] contemporaries" (1946:305).

The "time" referred to in the Collingwood quotation above pertains to its moral tenor, which was Europeanist, colonialist, and Orientalist. To be sure, contemporary Sri Lankan anthropologists do write their respective anthropologies against the shadow of that time and temper, but it is still against *that* time and temper that they write. "Contemporaries," in the same quotation, refers to a largely Euro-American (or Europeanized) readership that has been raised in a climate in which the anthropological idiom of expression and interests does not go unappreciated.

What is true of anthropology in Sri Lanka is even more deeply true of history. Today, history is not unitary in form or purpose. It is fractured into a complex of complementary and contradictory sets of postulates about subject, object, and method.[7] One may, as Paul Ricoeur has done, draw a major dividing line between French and Anglo-Saxon historiography[8] and place the greater part of history in Sri Lanka under the aegis and concerns of analytic philosophy, a largely Anglo-Saxon brand of historical preoccupation and prejudice. To the extent that the practice of history in this tradition is theorized, it is explicitly or tacitly concerned more with historical knowledge as the art of bringing particulars under Hempelian "covering laws," however loosely defined (Hempel 1959), than with a concern about the nature of narratives (Gallie 1964 or Ricoeur 1984) or tropes (White 1973 and 1987). More pertinently, two historical works by a couple of Victorian gentlemen, William Knighton (1845) and James Tennent (1859), provided the ideological framework within which the greater part of Sri Lanka's historiography continues to be written. "Both of these books . . . sought to place the events they described in the context of human progress" (Rogers 1990:90). What is held in common, however, by all of European history since Herodotus and Thucydides, continental or otherwise, is its preoccupation with the epistemology and ontology of the "event." This is as true of the poststructuralists and deconstructionists of today as it was of Romantic and Victorian historicists of yesteryear, or of the pre-Socratic Thales and Parmenides.[9] To the satisfaction of the European historian and the delight of his Europeanized counterpart, in Sri Lanka (unlike India) it was possible to hold up an event that was to serve as the nourishing ground and constituting kernel from which the discourse of history was to bud forth as a fully naturalized genus of knowledge on the island. If the sheer command of the idiom of this discourse were the only measure, the best of Sri Lankan history was (and is) second to none.[10] The event inaugurates the possibility of a chronicle. And the chronicle, though it may not be history,[11] provides the template upon which the historical narrative (and even a nonnarrative history) could be written. This event was the Buddha.[12] Even though the Buddha was born in what is now Nepal and attained enlightenment in India, the event has been fully appropriated by and for Sri Lanka, dwarfing thereby all uncertainties and ambiguities about its people's past.

Discordance in Mythic and Historic Realities

The principal argument of this chapter takes the form of an informed hypothesis, namely, that one of the structural conditions for collective violence is to be found in the discordance that obtains between what I call the epistemic and ontic discursive practices and the subsequent plea for recognition of identities constituted of these practices. The particular instances of the epistemic and ontic that are at issue in this chapter concern a people's dispositions toward the past, dispositions that I have further characterized as being mythic on the one hand and historic on the other. To be sure, neither history nor the mythic exhausts the epistemic and ontological realities respectively, but they constitute an important part of these respective realities. As dispositions toward the past, the mythic—as an ontic discursive practice—provides a people with a way of *being in the world*; history—as an epistemic discourse—provides a way of *seeing the world*. The former is an *embodied* discursive practice that is fundamentally ontological, and the latter is a *theoretical* discursive practice that is fundamentally epistemological.

As already noted, being and seeing, though fundamentally different, are not mutually exclusive, and the relationship is hierarchical in that seeing is a way of being but being is not a way of seeing. Recall the model of the tabla. Epistemology is parasitic upon and derived from a more basic onticity—a way of being-in-the-world—that provides a people the very condition of its possibility of knowing, seeing, theorizing, and even doubting.

The discordance we speak of is not assured merely by the existence of a history that is antithetical to a people's mythic reality, but is to be found in those moments and contexts in which such a history comes face to face with and demands to be incorporated into an unobliging ontic reality, a reality that has heretofore determined a people's comportment toward the world in general and a past in particular. By examining the dynamic interplay between historic and mythic discursive practices in the context of six places of pilgrimage in Sri Lanka, I hope to submit evidence that makes such a hypothesis reasonable. But let us first take a closer look at history, this time against the exposition of what I have called the mythic.

The Mythic and the Historical/Theoretical

In order to appreciate my interpretation of what the mythic is, the reader must hold in abeyance some of the more familiar understandings of this human creation, especially the one that aligns history and myth with that prejudicial pair known as "true" and "false." An element of the mythic is inherent in all our intellectual activities, not only in what is commonly called myth. My use thus far of the adjectival form "mythic" over the nominal form "myth" was intentional to prevent the reduction of the mythic to mere myth. In fact, stories that we ordinarily identify as myths by virtue of their necessary (though not sufficient) narrative structure are not the best embodiments of the mythic available to us. That honor goes to ritual, particularly to rituals that are not readily available for reflective scrutiny. To be sure, myth as narrative—let us mark it as myth^n (where *n* stands for narrative)—does intersect with what I have called the mythic; but unlike ritual, myth^n is not encompassed by the mythic. Now that I am done with cautioning the reader against an easy collapse of the mythic into the customary myth^n, I shall henceforth use "myth" only in the sense of the "mythic" just specified.

What then is the relationship of myth to history?[13] There are many commonalities between myth and history, the most salient of which is that neither is factual but both are factitious. That is, their concern is fundamentally not with what can be found in reality but with how one comes to terms with reality. In this respect, in the Sri Lankan context, Mahānāma's *Mahāvaṁsa*—the founding chronicle of the Sinhala people first composed around the sixth century A.D. (called a "mythohistory" by Tambiah [1986:70])—and the "multiple [oral] histories" collected by anthropologists such as Mark Whitaker (1990) in eastern Sri Lanka are equally factitious. But so are the writings of the most perspicacious of contemporary mythoclasts, R.A.L.H. Gunawardana (1990). And what of President J. R. Jayewardene's claim to President Reagan during a state visit to Washington, D.C., in 1984 that he was the 193d head of state of Sri Lanka (Kemper 1990:193)? Again, factitious. Whether it is "history" or "myth"—as we commonly understand this contrasting pair—is a question whose answer must be determined at another level.

There are differences, however. Important ones. The assertions of history are logically future-oriented even though they may be about the past. The structure of these assertions, more explicit in the natural sciences, is implicitly present in the human sciences as well, including history. These assertions relate to actualities as potentialities; they take the form of subjunctives, dispositionals, and contrary-to-fact conditionals. That is, they are concerned with what would be the case were certain conditions to be actualized. History, like all theoretical discourses, is in principle verificationist. To say that history is verificationist, however, does not mean that its truth is about a strict correspondence between what is written and what is written about—even though there may be some historians who continue to define their inquiry in these terms. History is not so much about *finding* truth as it is about *making* true. Insofar as it is future-oriented, it nurtures the hope that when inquiry is pursued long enough, a picture will have been painted in whose truth a community of inquirers will have concurred. The assertions of myth, by contrast, insist that past actualities be contemporaneous, that what is now is what was then and what was then is what is now. It is this collapse of time, where past becomes present enactment, that characterizes myth. In a mythic world, the very same conditions that made past events possible still prevail.

A second feature that distinguishes history from myth is the "aboutness" of the former and the "participatoriness" of the latter. (This is why it is so easy to appreciate the mythic aspect of ritual.) History is a theoretical discourse, and as with any theoretical discourse its "aboutness" is basic. Theory, true to its etymological origins in the Greek root *thea* (to see), provides us with a way of *seeing* the world. Hence my contention that history provides one with a way of seeing the world. In myth we find a way of *being* in the world, where participation is fundamental. The classical Malinowskian notion of "myth as charter" fails to capture this important feature of myth's essence. In the sense being developed here, a charter myth is less myth and more history to the extent that it provides one with a way of *seeing* the world. To repeat, history (including charter myths) is theoretical and therefore largely epistemic, whereas myth, as I have defined it, is essentially ontic.

There is a third difference that may be stated only in the fashion of a parenthetical prolegomenon. History is a theoretical discourse that is in the main, and in Sri Lanka in particular, simplex. It is underwritten by chronology and a logic of cause and effect.[14] Furthermore, this kind of history, seen in its fullest bloom in the nineteenth century—call it Hegelian, Rankeian, Michelетian, or Marxian (and think how exceptional Foucault is!)—is endogenous to European culture and civilization in a manner and to an extent that it is not to South Asia, especially to Hindu South Asia. Hindu India appears to confound the craft of the event-and-chronology-centered historiographer by the manner in which it "records" (if that be the word) events. More than one European historian, mostly in keeping with the nineteenth century's understanding of history, has expressed his frustration with the "Indian historical record" when attempting to write "The History of India." Perhaps, as Bernard Cohn (1985) points out, the Europeans' attempts at writing the history of India, rather than the histories of India, may have been the real problem. But according to the then dominant (and still alive) understanding of what "history" is all about, anything but a simplex history would not have been history. Rather, it would qualify as a mélange of fact and fancy, a collection of contradictory legends; and this indeed has been European historians' dominant view of the Indian historical record. To quote from S. R. Lushington on the matter, "From the little attention given by the natives of India to History, or tradition, historical subjects are generally involved in dark obscurity or embellished with unintelligible fables" (cited in Dirks 1987:55).

Thanks to the *Mahāvaṁsa*, as John Rogers (1990) and Steven Kemper (1991) have so finely demonstrated, the Sri Lankan past presents itself to epistemic history with an élan worthy of the European historiographer's tastes, and as superior to anything Hindu India had to offer. For this reason it is easier to write "The History of Sri Lanka" than "The History of India." By homologous extension, it is much easier to write "The History of the Sinhalas" than it is to write "The History of the Tamils," given the Tamils' cultural identification with Hindu South India rather than with Buddhist Sri Lanka. The Tamils do not have a simplex document or a great uncontested event comparable to the birth of Gautama Buddha. As Hellmann-Rajanayagam (1990) and Whitaker (1990) have shown, their "history" is multiple and multiplex. It is only recently, and mainly in social history, that European historiography assimilated multiplexity into its craft. On the Indian scene we see similar acknowledgment and accommodation of the multiplex especially since the historiographies of the historians of the Subaltern Collective. In the greater tradition of historiography, both in the West and in South Asia, it is the simplex narrative that remains normative. In India, as Thapar (1989) has shown us, in history's very thinning out of the multiplex in the record of the past, in the reduction of its manifold forms to a single strand, communal violence finds its raison d'être.

If myth, as a way of being in the world, is multiplex, then on structural grounds alone the likelihood of its striking up a discordant relationship with a "single-minded"[15] simplex history is greater than that of its generating discordance with a multiplex history. Multiplex histories are more easily accommodated within the multiplexity of lived experience. A simplex history is more likely to assert, with impetuosity, its independence, shrilly proclaiming its exclusive claim to truth. Its story tends to be unitary. This is not to deny the violence that has emerged among the Tamils of Sri Lanka. Rather, it is to argue that the conditions which generate violence by and among Tamils ought to be sought elsewhere, not in these Tamils' views of their past; at least not yet. A cruder way of (over)stating the same point is that no Tamil is likely to die or kill for history.[16] But Sinhalas do die and do kill because of and for their history, and especially when such a history contradicts the lived experience of myth.

Participation in myth is one of degree. A full participant in a myth is a participant in its ritual enactment as well. The range of ritual extends from a single performative utterance to an elaborate set of actions.[17] Let us take President J. R. Jayewardene's claim to President Reagan, mentioned above, that he was Sri Lanka's 193d head of state. Contextualized by the general tenor of pronouncements he made between his election in 1977 and the beginning of his serious disenchantment, leading to his retirement in 1988, this claim would qualify as mythic. As one source who was close to President Jayewardena during these years put it to me in a 1987 interview, "The President believes this [that he was the 193d "king" of Sri Lanka] to be true in his very bones." This is not to say that these bones did not rattle at times, and with increasing frequency toward the later years of his presidency. Some of this could be seen in the almost schizoid pronouncements he made when under stress. Within a span of a few days one finds him claiming that he was Aśoka, the Prince of Peace, and also that he could, if he wished to (and implying that he might choose to), wipe out the Tamils within a few minutes if he only so decided. On another occasion, while claiming to be a vessel of Buddha's compassion, he urged his supporters among Sri Lanka's Estate Tamils to use whatever work instruments were at their disposal as weapons to attack any outsider who tried to enter the plantations to "create trouble." He called India his "first love" because it was the land of the Buddha; he also called India "our archenemy," owing to the many battles fought between the kings of the two geographic units. Such are instances of myth under stress. On the elaborate side, the many "rituals of development" described to us by the late Serena Tennekoon (1988) were, for at least some of the ministers intimately involved in them, more than mere strategies or ploys to dupe the masses. The discourse of developmentalism in Sri Lanka, with its many rituals, doctrines, speeches, exhortations, offices, landscapings, and macro- and micro-politics, is not so much about development of something new as about the recovery of something lost, a return to another noonday. A close study of the speeches of Gamini Dissanayake when he was minister of lands and land development and minister of Mahāwāli development will show that he deeply believed that he was engaged in the restoration of Sri Lanka to the glory days of King Parakramabahu the Great, a twelfth-century monarch who ruled over the greater part of the island. These rituals are mythic in our sense, where, to use Evans-Pritchard's felicitous expression, "meanings are imprisoned in action" (1937: 81); or, in Peirce's pragmaticist phrase, "mind [becomes] hide-bound with habits" (6.158).

In 1984 I interviewed two young brothers who had participated in the riots against the Tamils. They had been displaced from the town of Kotmale by the new hydroelectric dam and resettled in the dry zone in the north-central part of the island, where they were supposed to reap the benefits of the diverted Mahawäli River. Resettled at the tail end of an irrigation canal beyond the reach of the sweet waters of the Mahāwäli, they were deprived of the promised green revolution of Parakramabahu the Great's reign. The excuse given to them by the minister's minions was that even as the Tamil Chōḷās of the tenth century had frustrated and destroyed the flourishing glory of the Sinhala people's hydroagricultural past, the Tamil Tigers[18] of today were frustrating and destroying the hydroagricultural projects of the present and future. They were told that funds which had been set aside for building dams, sluices, and dikes had to be diverted to finance the Sri Lankan army's war in the north. The emphasis was not so much on an unbroken history as on the past become present and a present become past.

One may participate in a ritual without participating in its enunciatory myth.[19] That is when a ritual becomes a *mere* ritual. Such nonparticipation is often one of degree. In a recent study of a village in Sri Lanka's North-Central Province, James Brow found that its residents who identified themselves as Veddas[20] could not be full participants in nationalist rituals that were introduced in their midst. These rituals, as far as these villagers were concerned, were mere rituals, distant and difficult (1988). Only slightly less removed from participation were the residents of another Sinhala-Buddhist village, studied by the anthropologist Michael Woost (1990). If, in the village Brow studied, residents found it difficult to see and even more difficult to experience the community imagined *for* them by the state in the speeches of its representatives, in the village studied by Woost, nationalism and a national past were staged in "mere rituals" of developmentalism in what Woost calls the "theater of the past." In both cases, the rituals and the accompanying narratives produced by the official political culture lacked the centripetal force of myth's enunciatory modality.

A narrative, even an imported one, that begins as theory, providing a people with a way of seeing the world, can, however, in time, become embodied in practice, as when the nineteenth-century European scientific racism outlined for us by Siriweera (1985), Rogers (1990), Gunawardana (1990), and Kemper (1991) instantiated itself in 1983, with Sinhala "Aryans" killing Tamil "non-Aryans." This is an instance of epistemic theory's becoming ontic myth. Spencer (1990) is correct when he argues against the view that ideas about identity are primordial givens. Indeed, they are, in Spencer's words, "painstakingly constructed, asserted, and argued about within specific historical and social conditions" (1989:14). To this extent they remain epistemic realities. But when thought sinks below the threshold of reflection, and ideas rise above the possibility of argument, then narrative history as well as myth as narrative become onticized, which brings them in line with their mythic essence.

Before turning to look at the interplay between history and myth in six places of pilgrimage, I wish to insert a few words on the nature of my own fieldwork, upon which part of this chapter is based.

In late 1983 and again in early 1984, when it was not clear whether the biggest storm of violence was behind or before us, and at a time when the state and private machines of ideological overproduction were operating at full and anxious throttle, I visited Anuradhapura, Polonnaruwa, Sigiriya, and Adam's Peak. All these places, still vaguely sacred for me, I had visited many times before, mostly in my youth. In this chapter I shall also write about two other places, or rather place-events, that I did not visit in 1983–1984 but am acquainted with from previous visits: the Kandy Äsələ Perəhärə and Kataragama.

Given the unusual state of affairs in Sri Lanka during 1983–1984, my fieldwork was not harnessed to the planned, systematic, long-term, informant-centered, statistical sample-sensitive (even if not sample-bound), stay-put-in-one-place methodology that is the characterizing privilege of most conventional anthropological research. In my previous anthropological field research stints information, or "data" (for those who prefer), came in controlled trickles toward the basically sedentary anthropologist. In 1983–1984, even though I was (I had to be) constantly on the move, I was deluged with information on the ethnic conflict. The peripatetic genre of pilgrimage around which this chapter is built is metonymic in several respects to my entire fieldwork during this period. In my travels to and through the island's historic cities and sacred places, my informants were many, all on the move—fellow pilgrims, tourists, tourist guides, hoteliers, tour bus and tourist car drivers—and were mostly strangers. I, the anthropologist, was also a fellow pilgrim-tourist, at times a voyeur, an eavesdropper, and an interloper.

The Ontic and Epistemic in Sacred Places

In my study of a South Indian village in *Fluid Signs* (1984), I attempted to bring to light the sense concealed in the term *ūr*, a term that has been used, interchangeably with *kirāmam*, to mean "village." There I showed that unlike the referential equivalent "kirāmam," "ūr" is a place for which a people have a deep, even if diffuse, affinity. It is a place to which one "belongs," in the full, affective sense of the term. An ur is defined through its center. I went on to argue that the affinity which holds a people and their ūr is a sense of shared substance. In the terminology of the current chapter, I might have added that an ūr and its people are bound together by ontic forces. Kirāmam, by contrast, was a space, defined and demarcated by a boundary, and primarily served outsiders' interests, principally that of the revenue officer and other agents of the law and the state. It was an epistemic space that provided the outsider a way of seeing a part of the world rather than an ontic place in which a people sought and found a way of being in the world. I am obliged to direct the reader's attention in more than passing to the difference between the premodern South Asian state and the modern nation-state, the one center-focused and the other boundary-focused. In this chapter, when I use the term "place" in contradistinction to space, I do so to connote essentially what ūr connotes in Tamil Nadu. A "space," by contrast, is an epistemic unit, marked by primarily non-ontic sentiments, be they those of the revenue officer, the archaeologist, the museologist, or the historian.

Polonnaruwa, where a medieval kingdom once stood, was a locale that until recently, for all except most of its long-term residents, occupied the epistemic end in our proposed scheme. The story of Polonnaruwa was thoroughly historicized and epistemicized in Sinhala consciousness at large, made into an object of knowledge, available to be inquired into. It was a museum-town that provided the Sinhala people with a story about the past. For the residents of Polonnaruwa, the town was a place constituted of sentiments and experiences other than those which were beginning to constitute the "imagined community" of growing Sinhala nationalism—the nationalism that rose to a violent pitch in 1983. The residents of Polonnaruwa lived in its ontic center. The tourists and pilgrims, from within and from without Sri Lanka, came to look at it. With the arrival of the Mahawäli waters in its environs and the attendant nationalistic rhetoric and settlers, Polonnaruwa has felt a certain rumble in its ontic core. A keeper of the Polonnaruwa Rest House, whom I first interviewed in 1974 and then ten years later, embodied the change: in the earlier interview he spoke as a citizen of the city who had no interest in its medieval monuments beyond their potential for supporting his livelihood; in the later one he claimed to be able to trace his ancestry to the courtiers of King Parakramabahu the Great. By and large, however, Polonnaruwa still (as of 1984) remained a space in the epistemic landscape of Sinhala awareness, a place in history, providing the Sinhalas and non-Sinhalas a way of seeing the past.

The same holds true for Sigiriya, the famous realm of refuge upon a rock where there once lived a king who had passion enough to kill his father for a kingdom and then to paint frescoes of his many women, all beautiful, all bare-breasted, and all carp-eyed. Contemporary Sri Lankans' reactions to these bare-breasted women are varied. Some, with Victorian sensibilities, titter with embarrassment behind cupped hands. Some condemn with puritanical self-righteousness the decadence they represent (Ponnambalam 1983:24). But a well-educated English-speaking tourist guide I met called upon the guided to admire "the lines of face, the sharp angles, and the sharp noses." His often repeated refrain was, "Look at the 'lines of face and the shades of color.'" Of these paintings R.A.L.H. Gunawardana observes: "The complexions of the ladies depicted in the paintings vary from a light yellow-brown to a deep blue or black color. These ladies are richly adorned with jewelry including tiaras, earrings, necklaces, and bangles. The paintings certainly depict members of the highest social strata. The variety of physical types that they represent clearly indicates that the dominant social group at the time was not physically homogeneous" (1990:60). Our guide (let me call him Mr. Senaratne rather than by his real name, which he did not want me to use when I revealed my plan of writing a book) did not draw our attention to the dark women. He focused on the fair ones instead, remarking to his group how well the colors had been preserved, retaining their resemblance to the skin color of the ancient Sinhalas.

Polonnaruwa and Sigiriya, like many other places and objects in India and Sri Lanka, "became victim to the major interpretive strategy by which South Asia was to become known to Europeans in the seventeenth, eighteenth and nineteenth centuries," namely, through a construction of the histories of India (and Ceylon). "The interpretive interests of Europe varied over these centuries, but they established an enduring structural relationship between South Asia and the West. Europe was progressive and changing, India [and Ceylon were] static. Here could be found a kind of living fossil bed for the European past, a museum which was to provide for the next hundred years a chance to impose Europe's own vision of history" (Cohn 1985:13).

Polonnaruwa and Sigiriya, like Anuradhapura, are nineteenth-century phenomena, subjects of "discovery," first by British troops, then by British colonial officers and amateur archaeologists. Fortresses, palaces, bathing pools, gardens, stupas, and temples, all of which had been rendered secure but irrelevant to the local inhabitants by the overgrowth of forests and time, were found, "unearthed, and rescued from the jungle's snarl, surveyed, mapped, and prepared for labeling."[21]

The historicization of place by its transformation into space is accompanied by the historicization of a people through their transformation into a race. The sketch given us by Gunawardna (1990) on the "Aryanization" of the Sinhala people in the eighteenth and nineteenth centuries, in the context of the spread of scientific racism to the colonies, can hardly be bettered. Among those implicated—even if unwittingly—in this endeavor were the great Orientalists Sir William Jones (1746–1794), Max Muller (1825–1900), and the missionary Robert Caldwell (1913); the lesser known historians H. W. Codrington (1926) and William Knighton (1845); and the still lesser known ethnologists C. F. and B. P. Sarasin (1886) and Rudolph Virchow (1886). And what is more, as Bernard Cohn (1985:7) has written of India (it is equally apt for Ceylon), "The classification of languages and race, along with 'surveys,' 'maps,' 'histories,' 'dictionaries,' 'reports,' and 'recommendations,' were part of a massive production of texts in the nineteenth century which continued the establishment of discursive formations, the defining of an epistemological space, the creation of a discourse (Orientalism), and the conversion of Indian experiences (and also forms of knowledge) into European objects."

Anthropometry is alive and well in South Asia. How lasting are the contributions of such pioneering physical anthropologists as the Sarasins and Virchow is attested to by the existence to this day of an official museum monograph called *The Physical Anthropology of Ceylon*, which repeats the same anthropometric nonsense on race that served nineteenth-century European interests so well. This epistemicized history was picked up by Sinhala nationalism in the first half of this century and Sinhala chauvinism more recently and was used to bludgeon first "the decadence of the West" and then the "alien Tamils from the North." In late 1983, a Sinhala politician commented on the similarity of the Aryan noses of J. R. Jayewardene and the Kashmiri Brahmin Mrs. Indira Gandhi, and contrasted these with the Dravidian nose of Mr. A. Amirdhalingam, the then leader of the Tamil United Liberation Front.[22] The little episode in Parliament cited by Serena Tennekoon (1990) about Jayewardene's Aryan nose and Amirdhalingam's non-Aryan nose excited a flurry of letters to the newspapers. Most of these defended the "Sinhalaya is an Aryan" theory, and many were from citizens well read in the nineteenth-century anthropometric wisdom of the Sarasins, Virchow, and others.[23] In retrospect, one of the salubrious and sobering outcomes of this period of open expression of racism was the opportunity for prejudices that were taken to be scientific, objective, and obviously true to be freely questioned and openly debunked. Within this brief period of less than a decade, racism of this sort had become, if not a proven falsehood, then at least an unfashionable embarrassment.

There are some ironies to the Sri Lankan appropriation of "the lines of face and shades of color," ironies that would have been charming if they had not turned out to be so deadly. In 1983, many a chocolate-colored Sinhala apprehended a chocolate-colored fellow Sinhala and, denying the victim's claim to his "race" on the grounds that his skin was not of the shade that a Sinhala's skin ought to be (like the Sigiriya frescos?) nor his face shape that of an Aryan's (Mr. Jayewardene's? Mrs. Gandhi's?), beat him up and, in one instance known to me, even killed him for being a "Tamil trying to pass as a Sinhala." By the same logic, several Tamils I knew escaped being killed, even when their pronunciation of Sinhala had all the giveaways of misplaced retroflexes and unaspirated *hs*, those distinguishing marks of Dravidian speech. They were excused as understandable speech impediments. Some of these stories constitute the growing collection of "Jokes of the July Riots" told by Tamils. In the following example, a Sinhala rioter, holding up a handkerchief (*lēnsuvə*, in Sinhala) subjects a fair-skinned Tamil to a linguistic test:

RIOTER: *Mēkə mokaddə?* (What is this?)

TAMIL (stammering in fright): *Le-le-le-le . . . lēnji* (the Tamil counterpart of the Sinhala word, *lēnsuvə*).

RIOTER: *Tamusē monə jātidə?* (What "race" are you?)

TAMIL: *Lal-Lal-Lal-Lal . . . Lanji* (the Tamilization of the Sinhala word for "Burgher,"[24] *Lansi*).

RIOTER: *Namə mokaddə?* (What is your name?)

TAMIL: *Jan-Jan-Jan . . . Janji.* (Janz, a Burgher name; in fact the name of the then commissioner of prisons).

The victim is allowed to escape unharmed into an epistemic landscape because he is fair, and because the bully had either not noticed the non-Sinhala accent at all or had excused it as an understandable speech impediment becoming of one in fright (of whom he has by now known many), or of a Burgher, a category of persons he scarcely knows but only knows of. People tell such jokes (morbid as they may be) and—as we shall see in another chapter—compose poems (grim as they might be) so as to dislodge grief and anger from an embodied state of being stuck, to give them a way to move out of its choking stasis.

If Polonnaruwa, the museum town, and Sigiriya, the museum fortress, occupy the epistemic extreme in our typology of orientations toward the past, Kataragama with its ecstatic cult of Murugan or Skanda has until recently[25] occupied the ontological extreme. So has the more arduous southern approach to Sri Pada (also known as Adam's Peak), in a more purely Buddhistic vein. Kataragama and Sri Pada are meaningless without participation. To merely observe is to be alienated at best and, at worst, vulgar. The eye alone is not enough, nor even the ears. The body must be involved in the climb, in the dance, in the singing, in the firewalking, in the trance, in the believing. The myths that energize these places are not stories about their pasts but rather ritual enactments of their pasts. They provide structured contexts in which a people orders its moral life and against which it measures the worth of its endeavors.

The governing myths of Kataragama and Sri Pada draw their believers into conforming to the actualities practiced in the rituals of these places. Whereas the theoretical constructs of history are predominantly referential, providing one with a way of seeing the past in epistemic discourses, mythic constructs are overwhelmingly performative and must be entered into for meaningfulness in ontic experience. The possible objection that theoretical constructs are also, after all, construable as performatives would miss the point of the distinction. Such constructs serve as instruments that inquirers (academic or otherwise) use rather than modes of being into which they enter. Such theoretical constructs perform the normative functions of setting limits to ways of observing and are suggestive of what to look for. They do not provide us with ways of living. For the believer, by contrast, this is what Kataragama and Sri Pada do.

Kandy and its annual Äsələ Perəhärə, the grandest procession of the land, is a curious blend of the two extremes, with the epistemic dimension concealing an active ontic one. Here one finds the reenactment of a once-structured social order with all its attendant obligations of services, prestations and honors, bejeweled elephants, Kandyan dancers, drummers, aristocrats in full regalia, and the casket of the tooth relic. H. L. Seneviratne has argued persuasively for the persistent vitality of the Äsələ Perəhärə and the Temple of the Tooth as political symbol (1978). And it is indeed true that the Kandy ritual complex has provided legitimization to every Sinhala party and politician since independence, including the Trotskyites who, on being elected to office, visited the temple to receive the blessings of the triple gem. To this extent we may concede that many of its discursive constructs are performative rather than predictive and referential (the two distinguishing features of theory). However, these performatives serve as instruments that politicians have used rather than as modes of being into which they enter. It makes one recall Nietzsche's priestly class, which can manipulate the herd only because they themselves do not participate in the drama that makes manipulation possible. As for the "herd," there have not been many in Kandy. In fact, at least as far as concerns the use of the Temple of the Tooth by politicians, the Sri Lankan populace in general have retained a healthy cynicism. If only the politicians could enter into the ritual complex as if it were a mode of being, and if they could be assured that the populace would follow them into it—as it had done in the times of the Kandyan kings—then their conversion of epistemic symbol and pragmatic index into ontic icon[26] would be complete. However, there are ontic forces operating in Kandy and at the Temple of the Tooth. Indeed the tooth relic lies at the center of such centripetalizing ontic forces, yielding myths that require one's participation in their understandings. It is no accident that the months closest to the Äsələ Perəhärə are the ones in which riots of all kinds and ethnic riots in particular have occurred. However, Kandy as a whole remains a spectacle, providing ways of observing the past (in addition to holding out the possibility of using the past), yielding theories that are understandings about "objective" events of the past. It is this "aboutness" of the theoretical coming to terms with the past that has been absent (until recently) in Kataragama and Śrī Pada.

The Äsələ Perəhärə processes through designated streets. That much is not new. It happened this way even in the days of the kings. But of course the British made it more efficient. The ways in which "crowds" (not believers or citizens) are "controlled" are new. The language ("crowd control") is that of a new disciplinary order, a new disciplinary space. The "spectators" are cordoned off onto the sidewalks; the streets are kept free for the "performers." Bleachers are provided for those who can afford them, mainly the tourists and the wealthy. Policemen stand at strategic points to keep the crowds disciplined. Participants and spectators are separated from each other: the one performs; the other looks. Unlike similar ritual processions found all over India, the Äsələ Perəhärə does not draw its spectators in to make them part of the procession (except at the tail end, almost as an afterthought). That would make them believers or citizens, and not spectators. In Peradeniya, the home of the island's prestigious university, I was privy to a discussion about such processions in India—in Puri, in Madurai, and in Trivandrum—among a group of middle-class Sri Lankans. These Sri Lankans found the contrast between the Kandy perehära and its Indian counterparts (if indeed they were comparable at all) quite striking. Some of them were proud of the discipline of their compatriots, which stood in stark contrast to the indiscipline of the Hindu masses of India. Occasional stampedes have occurred in Kandy, but that only when a mad elephant decided to break ranks with its hundred-plus fellow elephants—not because of the people's indiscipline.

The theatrical aspect of Kandy is enhanced by two modern phenomena. The more powerful of the two is the demands of tourism and the cultivated expectations of tourists. The show goes on in July/August, predictably, every year. The second factor is the presence of a museum—an annex of the king's palace and the Temple of the Tooth—where objects of a now extinct royalty lie in labeled glass cases. Theory and theater have epistemicized the past. Thus, despite the presence of the most sacred of relics in this town and the many devoted worshipers who do visit the temple during the perəhärə, there is a characteristic tension in Kandy that makes this city neither Polonnaruwa nor Kataragama, a tension between the contemporaneity of ontic forces and the quaint and distancing picture painted by epistemology. The participation in the myth of Kataragama and Sri Pada is not merely a participation in the performance of their rituals but involves the myth's being somehow enacted for the pilgrim beyond the rituals. It is otherwise in Kandy. There, when the perəhärə ends, the play comes to an end.

Enter Anuradhapura. The Śrī Mahā Bōdhi (believed to be a cutting from the tree at Bodh Gaya in India under which Gautama attained enlightenment), like the tooth relic of Kandy, generates sacred ontic forces that pull the pilgrim toward the conforming-participating center, away from the validating-observing periphery. Until recently, however, the rest of Anuradhapura remained an epistemicized landscape even as its nineteenth century "discoverers" intended it to be. It had been the victim of the archaeologists' and historians' "gaze" (to borrow a Foucaultian concept), a landscape that yielded theories to provide us with a way of seeing the world, a world long past. If we were to once again take note of the shared etymology of theory and theater and extend the play analogy to implicate historical and archaeological theorizing, we would find that observers, however actively they may feel themselves to be a part of the drama, must remain offstage.

Things have begun to change. In 1983 and 1984 I visited the cities of ancient Sri Lanka as tourist, pilgrim, and anthropologist. In Anuradhapura I found a new phenomenon in the person of a Sinhala-speaking tour guide. On the face of it he may appear to be a mere extension of the English-, German-, French-, or Italian-speaking tour guide. The guide whom I followed was bilingual and had learned his craft from English-speaking tour guides and English-speaking tourists whom he had nonchalantly or otherwise followed in their meanderings.[27] Western tourists, after having read synoptic accounts of the ethnic conflict in their newspapers at home or in their tour books in flight, and who, based on these reports, have already assumed that the conflict is based on religion or race, presume to ask "informed" questions.[28] Some of them try to intelligently find out what it is in these two religions or races that is capable of inflaming so much animosity. The guide tries to answer, but only after having already bought into the premise of the question. Our Sinhala tour guide has learned these answers with a vengeance. His goal is to become as good a tour guide as his English-, French-, German-, or Italian-speaking counterpart. But in fact he becomes much more.

In Anuradhapura, our tour guide's focus is not limited to the Śrī Mahā Bōdhi. In fact the Sinhala-Buddhist tourist-pilgrims do not need a tour guide to understand the Śrī Mahā Bōdhi. He becomes irrelevant in its presence. The faithful are drawn into devotion and held in awe by its power and centrality. However, as the pilgrims leave its presence, the tour guide takes over, pointing out its age and the fact that for all the steel props that hold it up, its days are numbered. There is a palpable sadness among the believers, and they resent the intrusion of time, of history. Indeed, the seed of resentment against all intruders is sown. But not much else is said about this sacred place. Instead, our tour guide spends most of his time pointing out other ruins of a glorious past, a Buddhist past, with awesomely elegant stupas that are now in various states of decay and restoration. These restorations have been funded by Western-based international organizations; thus the past glory is an internationally recognized one. He names and describes each one of the *dāgabas*: Thūpārāma, Ruvanvälisāya, Mirisaväti, Abhayagiri, and the largest one of them all, Jetavana. And then there is Lovāmahāpāya, or the Brazen Palace, which had once housed monks. In K. M. de Silva's words, which were quite closely paraphrased by our guide, this structure "is believed to have risen on completion to nine stories in all. . . . All that remains of this early skyscraper are some 1,600 weather-beaten granite pillars which are a haphazard reconstruction of the twelfth century, with some of the pillars upside down and not even on the original site" (1965:53–54). "And who do you think built this?" our guide asks rhetorically. "This great palace was built by that great king who vanquished ("*Guṭi dunnə rajuruvo*" ["The king who gave a beating to"]) the Tamil king, Elara." At this point, our guide repeats a "charter" mythohistory of Sinhala nationalism in its entirety:

> Elara was a Tamil king who invaded this country 350 years after the Buddha attained *nibbana*. It was a time when the Sinhala people had forgotten the Dhamma and began fighting among themselves. Elara ruled the country for forty-four years. The Sinhala king was kāvantissa. He was nowhere to be found in this area. He fled south to Ruhuna. He had two sons, Tissa and Gamani. Tissa, like his father, was a coward. When Gamani was only sixteen—and you tell your sons not to join the army—when he was only sixteen, before he even had whiskers, he attempted to go to war against Elara. Three times he tried and each time his father stood in his way. He preferred to talk, sitting at the round table [an allusion to the all-party amity talks that were taking place in Colombo at that time]. Gamani was

disgusted. So what did he do? He sent his father and brother a cloth and blouse (*redhi-hāṭṭə*) to wear. We must send a few saris to our leaders in Colombo. [Laughter.] One day the prince was very sad. His heart was heavy. He was curled up like a baby in his mother's stomach, on the sofa. "Son, why don't you stretch yourself and sleep in bed?" his mother wanted to know. "How can I stretch myself when there are Tamils in the north and the ocean is to the south?" he replied. Only then did she realize what was happening. She helped him gather soldiers and go to war. He killed one million and thirty thousand Tamils and Elara. Then he united the whole island and ruled it according to the ten kingly qualities laid out in Buddhism (*dasarajadharma*). But our king was still troubled. He could not sleep. He was a good Buddhist and had still killed so many human beings in order to achieve his great purpose. The *arahats* read his thoughts. They came to him in the middle watch of the night, alighted at the palace gates and said, "Oh great and noble king, protector of the Dhamma, do not trouble yourself on account of the dead. Of the million and thirty thousand killed, only one had taken the Three Refuges and only one also observed the Five Precepts. The rest were unbelievers and men of evil life, not more to be esteemed than beasts." Thus it is said in the great history book of Professor K. M. de Silva.

Professor de Silva did not say this, but it is a close rendition of a passage from the *Mahāvaṁsa*. The description of each dagaba and every ruin was followed by an account of how this once great structure was destroyed by Tamils from South India. Given the context of the current Sinhala-Tamil tensions, it was difficult to see how these "closing statements," buttressed by quotations alleged to be from Professor K. M. de Silva's *History of Sri Lanka*, could fail to fan the flames of passion.

Two days prior to my own guided tour of Anuradhapura, I met a family at Mihintale that had been guided by the same retired army sergeant whose acquaintance I was later to make. It was a teenager from this family who informed me of the ex-army sergeant's existence and expertise. What had drawn my attention to this young man was a couple of statements I overheard him make in conversation with other members of his family. He was saying, "The only thing left to do is to send them [the Tamils] back to where they came from." And then he claimed that his school principal (of a leading Buddhist high school in Colombo) had made the following statement during school assembly: "If you see a Tamil and a snake, kill the Tamil first." This is such a ubiquitous pan-Indian formulaic anecdote that it is widely and loosely used by and attributed to ally and foe alike and must in this instance be taken as originating from the boy's fired imagination rather than from his school principal. After having met the guide in question, I found it easy to understand how these pilgrim-tourists had had their fervor and imagination roused in this manner. And furthermore, another interesting process begins to take over. Epistemic history becomes uninteresting and ontic myth begins to move in.

Simultaneously, the affected tourist-pilgrim becomes less a spectator of history and more an actor in myth. For participation in myth involves the myth's somehow being enacted for the person beyond the stage of mere theory, as though the actor, after playing his part in theater, should find the play in a sense continuing when he is offstage. And this indeed was what was happening in Sri Lanka. The act continued beyond the peripheries of Anuradhapura.

The next day, I found in Polonnaruwa a scion of the group I had followed around in Anuradhapura under the guidance of the ex-sergeant. This was the site of the medieval kingdom that survived for over two centuries. I was near the ruins of the Śiva Dēvālaya, labeled by archaeologists as Śiva Dēvālaya No. 1. It was built in the tenth century by the Chōḷās of South India. Its walls were stained and its surroundings reeked of urine. True, there were no signs of worship, no joss sticks or jasmine; the *lingam* had long since lost its oil-anointed sheen. But urine? Just then a young man from the group walked toward me shouting, "Never mind, sir, go ahead and urinate there. Why, it is written there, 'Number One' "—a local euphemism for urinating. An older official in a khaki jacket overheard the remark and came toward me shouting out a warning: "Don't soil (*narakkərandə epā*) that place. It is a *dēvālayə* (temple)." I was getting ready to protest that I did not intend any such thing, but was beat to it by the younger man, who shot back the defiant question to the official, "Did you think that our blood was Tamil blood? The blood that courses through this body is a lion's blood."[29] The young man reached the wall of the ruins and began to urinate. I walked away from the place and passed by the women of the group of pilgrims to which he belonged. The women were untying parcels of food, and the young among them were amused by their male companion's bravado. Our young man may not have quite become a character in the play of the myth, but because he had participated in the play he seemed constrained to act his life out in accordance with the orientation provided by the myth. The myth entered into at Anuradhapura had been carried over into Polonnaruwa and is likely to be carried into other contexts of life as well. As I passed the women, I caught the last few words of an older woman (they called her *ācci*, or grandmother) as she admonished the younger ones with the words, "This is not something to be trifled with. It is madness to play with the powers of the gods." She represented a generation of thought in which Hinduism and Buddhism had not been as demarcated from each other in practice as was beginning to be the case in 1983.[30]

Let us return to our tour guide at Anuradhapura one last time. He is engaged in a double move. On the one hand he brings the epistemicized peripheral ruins of the ancient city under the ontic and centripetalizing forces of the Śrī Mahā Bōdhi. On the other he holds for anxious contemplation the alarming possibility that the ontic center of the Śrī Mahā Bōdhi itself may be epistemicized by history, or more ominously by historical forces let loose by Tamil armies, repeating history, as it were. Eighteen months later, Tamil separatists made their own contribution toward a further onticization of terror by gunning down 146 unarmed Buddhist pilgrims at the Śrī Mahā Bōdhi, fulfilling thereby the worst fears of my fellow pilgrims of 1984. Prior to this event, Tamils were able to claim the higher moral ground vis-à-vis the Sinhalas. Until the 1983 anti-Tamil riots Sinhala citizens who had lived in the heart of the Jaffna Peninsula did so free of harm or harassment even though the state's predominantly Sinhala army and police had persecuted the Tamils of the north and east for over a decade. Even after the July riots of 1983, the Tamils had shown evidence that they did not have the will to harm those Sinhalas in their midst whom they could have harmed. When news of the killing of Tamils and the destruction of Tamil property was brought home to the peninsula by the swelling tide of refugees, warnings had reached some Sinhala bakers residing in Jaffna that their own lives were in peril and that a group of young Tamils were coming to kill them. These Sinhalas fled and took refuge in the School for the Deaf and the Blind at Kaithady, a suburb of the town of Jaffna. The principal of the school, Mr. Jaysingh David (who related this event to me), hid them in a storeroom. The pursuing crowd, however, did find the terrified group of Sinhalas. But after they briefly attempted to pummel them with their fists, their rage was spent; and they told their victims to go back to the south whence they had come. The massacre at the Śrī Mahā Bōdhi changed all that. Some Tamils proved themselves to be every bit as capable of violence as were some Sinhalas, and every bit as morally feeble as their Sinhala counterparts. Tamil militants proved themselves to be every bit as given to the terrorization of noncombatant citizens as had the Sinhala state since the early 1970s.

It may appear, given the last example, that the ontic and the mythic are to be viewed negatively, whereas the epistemicizing craft of theory building and historicizing deserve to be viewed favorably. This need not be so. There are ontic rituals such as Aṅkeliya and Gammaḍuva, described by Obeyesekere (1984) in his massive book *The Cult of the Goddess Pattini*, wherein ritual contains violence, even ethnic violence. I use "contained" in both senses: to possess and to restrain. These two rituals are (about) a host of things, past and present, gods and men, male and female, immigrant and native, outsider and insider. Distinctions are made and differences recognized. There is even a part in one of them for a Muslim. The nineteenth-century discoverers of Anuradhapura and Polonnaruwa were not interested in these unwieldy dramas that kept moving and changing. Static ruins and royal processions were much more comprehensible and therefore manageable. Ethnographers (and Paul Wirz [1954] is no exception) gave summary accounts of these rituals. It took a Sinhala anthropologist, Gananath Obeyesekere, with an interest that spanned twenty-five years, to record them in any detail in his book. And as might be expected, his account of these ritual dramas, even as truncated as they are, have given his book the appearance of unwieldiness and have invited its characterization by one reviewer as "sprawling" (Kapferer 1985). Its fault (the book's, the ritual's) is its lack of self-containedness. For anyone who has participated in these ritual dramas in Sri Lankan villages, even Obeyesekere's *Pattini* would appear to be too self-contained, even though not sufficiently so to satisfy the economy of the ethnographic imagination.

Where the colonial encounter and the ethnographer's interest had failed to reduce the scope and size of these and many other rituals, tourism has succeeded. The healing ritual known as *tovil* is such an example, as is the Kandyan dance, which has been abstracted from its varied contextual manifestations that were primarily ritual. European spectators have been offered, by Europeanized middlemen, abbreviated versions of these rituals, trimmed to just the right size and length so they fit both the auditorium stage of a "five-star" hotel and the average tourist's time schedule and attention span. The choreographer, a man or woman acquainted with Western tastes and patience, in collusion with "middlemen" and "financiers," reduces these rituals to a self-contained sequence such as then seals these rituals into self-congratulation. Reflexively, these rituals (and here I am thinking of tovil) and ritual specialists are mocked by the young.

The Struggle for Recognition

In the opening section of this chapter I suggested that collective violence of the sort found in Sri Lanka in recent years results when the discordance that obtains between epistemic and ontological discursive practices leads to a quest—a quest and a plea for recognition of the new identities constituted by these practices. This point, which has been implicitly developed thus far, needs to be spelled out, even if only briefly, a task to which I shall now turn.

A people's willingness to fight for, kill for, and die for a reality is not a sign of their certainty of that reality but indicates that the reality in question has been brought under the crisis of radical doubt. Doubts can be of a local and parochial kind, academic or otherwise, that do not pose a fundamental threat to a habit-assured way of being-in-the-world. Radical doubt, by contrast, threatens to "swallow up the entire background of perceptual and practical certainties" (Hoffman 1986:31). Heidegger identified the formation of this kind of radical doubt with the emergence of what he specified as "anxiety." For Heidegger, anxiety was no ordinary emotion or mood but one that is experienced in the face of death, one that when rendered positively transforms an inauthentic *Dasein* of everydayness into an authentic one. To invoke the "face of death" in the context of interethnic violence is no mere metaphorical extension of Heidegger's understanding of death and anxiety; it is a vivid and powerful instantiation of these. What is at stake in ethnic conflict and ethnicide in Sri Lanka is more than the mortality of bodies, more than the destruction of life and the demise of security. Rather, what is at stake, especially for those whose bodies have been spared the destruction of death, is the death of a way of being-in-the-world, the death of that which constitutes their identity, honor, and dignity. For each ethnic group in this horrific drama, then, the face of the other is the face of either the affirmation of identity or its denial, potential life or potential death. Which of the two materializes hinges on recognition, the recognition of one's self-assuring identity by the other.[31] An examination of the Sri Lankan ethnic conflict within an extended reading of Hegel's master-slave parable will bring this point home.[32]

Even though there is a line of scholarship (and widely held popular opinion) that maintains the Sinhala-Tamil relationship on the island to have been an antagonistic one for over a thousand years,[33] others who have examined the historical record and the present conflict in light of it reveal the newness of not only the enmity's character but the identities that derive from and depend on it. My own view on the matter happens to coincide with the latter. But what is important is that significant sections of each of the two ethnic groups have displayed a kind of narcissistic self-regard that can only be considered infantile, regardless of whether the animosity in question is recent or old.

Indeed, one way of understanding the current violence on the island is to see it as a check on the narcissistic expansiveness of infantile impulses, impulses that fail to recognize that the whole world is not one's own and that all of being is not encompassed within the boundaries of an ever-expanding identity. As Hoffman puts it, "violence educates [one] to the inescapable reality of others"; it helps one "gain a perspective broader than, and independent of, one's particular self"; it helps one realize that there are values, beliefs, and subjectivities other than one's own (1989:144). The transcendence of narcissistic particularity, along with its corollary, the emergence of a universal/communal being, is the mark of becoming truly human. The threat of violence is the catalyst for this rite of passage.

In the Sri Lankan case, it is not clear whether this recognition of the other has been arrived at, nor whether one group has recognized the other group's recognition of its own. Consequently, the mood surrounding the question of recognition is one of great anxiety, kept alive by a set of contradictions. There are among Sinhalas and Tamils those who have not gone beyond the narcissistic stage of self-expansion and disregard for the other. Others quite clearly have encountered the challenge of their humanity in the threat of violence, wherein not only life and security but, more important, honor and dignity are at stake. The question that faces this second, more evolved, group is how to be assured of the recognition it so desperately desires and needs. One—counterproductive—option is to pursue the path of exclusionary violence in order to annihilate the other qua other, thereby neutralizing, for the time being, the conundrum of recognition, and falling back on the path of narcissistic expansion. This is an option that is available only at the cost of one's refusal to partake of the ongoing process of becoming human or at least renewing one's humanity. And furthermore, this strategy neither solves nor advances the issue of recognition per se, only defers it. The second option is to extend violence until it compels the other into submissive recognition. But then what the "victorious" group gains by this is recognition, not from another that is willing to sacrifice life and security for honor and dignity even as it does, but from a group that has surrendered its honor and dignity for life and security, from a group that has cashed in its human impulses for the concerns of a mere brute. Bluntly stated, the recognition a group gains by this means is not human recognition but a brutal one. It is clearly evident that at more levels than one—interpersonal, intraethnic, interethnic, the armed forces versus civilians, the state versus its citizens—and at one time or another, this is the kind of recognition that has been achieved. Even more poignantly, what the "victorious" group in each of these instances has gained is the recognition of a corpse, which is no recognition at all. Hoffman has this to say regarding recognition and the violence of exclusion:

> When entering the struggle for recognition I must, to be sure, reach out for a freedom and an independence which can come only from my readiness to imperil my (and an other's) life—but I must also stop at the brink, since death (either my own or my adversary's) is incompatible with the very purpose of the struggle. The purpose was from the very beginning, to validate myself (as a free but also living self). Thus the struggle must be carefully staged and controlled; death can only result from an accident. (1989:148)

Thus if a people must survive as a people under conditions of the anxiety of recognition, it must achieve a comportment in its world that entails the recognition of the other as equally and genuinely free, and the awareness that violence is an option as available to the other as to itself. It is far from certain that such a realization has been achieved either epistemically or ontically in Sri Lanka, where violence is neither controlled by ritual nor contained by theory/theater. Rather, it is the option of annihilatory violence that continues to be chosen.

Conclusion

I began this chapter with the proposition that ontological and epistemic realities were significantly different. Specifying their asymmetrical relationship, however, I characterized the latter as an emergent of the former. One of the structural conditions for collective violence, I argued, was to be found in the discordance that obtains between these two discursive practices. The two may coexist with neither friction nor conflagration under two conditions. The first is one wherein the two are consonant with each other; in the second, even though the two may be substantially antithetical to or contradictory of each other, they remain mutually indifferent and irrelevant. The latter has been the case for most Sri Lankans, Sinhalas and Tamils, during the greater part of the colonial period. Neither one of these conditions of equipoise can be guaranteed to endure forever in any social order, especially in one that is caught in the currents of a rapidly modernizing (some may even say, postmodernizing) world. Forces, external and internal, are capable of changing the state of equipoise. In Sri Lanka an incendiary context was created when history was deployed as a time bomb in the midst of a myth, in the midst of a *way of being-in-the-world*. This history was, in many ways, antithetical to the mythic mode of being. Tambiah, in the opening pages of his moving account *Sri Lanka: Ethnic Fratricide and the Dismantling of Democracy*, asks how "Sri Lankans as a people, who, among other things, can laugh at themselves and irreverently tell stories about the foibles of their fellow citizens, especially politicians, are capable of such horrendous riots that exploded in late July and early August of 1983" (1986:1); part of the answer must point a diagnostic finger at history's theoretical/theatrical intrusion.

Heritage as an ontic reality and mythic certainty has been dislodged to one degree or another. Even though the particular manifestations of the ontological and the epistemic that I chose to consider were myth and history, respectively, the latter pair do not exhaust the former. There are other ontic realities, some benign, some malignant, that will flare up sooner or later, with or without the provocation of history. History itself has, as we have seen, begun to settle, in significant measure, into a new ontic state, constituting life on the island. This settling or sedimentation of annihilatory violence in the name of history disregards a more fundamental humanity that needs to be disturbed, its theory revivified and its theatricality interrupted by a countertheater. Such a task can no longer entertain a nostalgia for myth as was once lived, nor can it assume that myth was the only ontic reality of a people's life. Rather, in the exhilaratingly despairing words of Antonin Artaud's hope, we may observe that

> the theater like the plague . . . releases conflicts, disengages powers, liberates possibilities, and if these possibilities and these powers are dark, it is the fault not of the plague nor of the theater, but of life. . . . The plague takes images, a latent disorder, and suddenly extends them into the most extreme gestures; the theater also . . . pushes them as far as they will go: like the plague it forges the chain between what is and what is not, between the virtuality of the possible and what already exists in materialized nature. . . . The plague is a total crisis, but after it has struck and then exhausted itself nothing remains except death or an extreme putrefaction. . . . If it wrecks our present social state, so much the better; that state is iniquitous. (1958:27–32)

The Hegelian parable—even with the Heideggerian insight on "anxiety in the face of death" folded into it—may be correct in the main, but it is also too simple. The existential angst sketched is too neat and antiseptic; so is Heidegger's understanding of individual-centered death. The Sri Lankan situation—like much of the ethnic violence taking place in many quarters of the world today—and the death it spawns are captured more aptly in the words of Artaud. The implications of this quotation are intentionally ambiguous and polyvalent. Is the plague history? Or is the plague the new theoretical perspective—the countertheater—that I have called for? What of the "iniquitous state"? Did it lurk in "prehistorical" ontological realities, mythic or otherwise, or is its formation one with the onticization of modern history itself? The answer is an unanalyzed yes to all the questions, even where the questions called for a choice. Such must be the script of the countertheater that may not *directly* contribute to the dialectic of recognition but will put it in its proper place. For it will expose the theater of sheer cruelty that Sri Lanka has become today and from it extract the lesson that enlightened recognition can come about only under the excruciating brightness of anxiety in which a people (all peoples) come to terms with its (their) ultimate powerlessness and vulnerability.

3

VIOLENT MEASURES, MEASURED VIOLENCE

> If interpretation is the violent or surreptitious appropriation of a system of rules . . . in order to impose direction, to bend it to a new will, to force its participation in a different game, and to subject it to secondary rules, then the development of humanity is a series of interpretations. The role of genealogy is to record its [effective] history, [the history of the event]. [By "event" is meant] the reversal of a relationship of forces, the usurpation of power, [and] the appropriation of a vocabulary turned against those who had once used it.
>
> *(Michel Foucault)*

> Discourse lives . . . beyond itself in a living impulse toward the object; if we detach ourselves completely from this impulse all we have left is the naked corpse of the word, from which we learn nothing at all about the social situation or the fate of a given word in life. To study the word as such, ignoring the impulse that reaches out beyond it, is just as senseless as to study psychological experience outside the context of the real life toward which it was directed and by which it is determined.
>
> *(Mikhail Bakhtin)*

OUR examination of violence continues. By returning to the Estate Tamils, we return from a different direction to the questions of history and heritage, knowing and being, theory and myth; we arrive at the question of the historicity of history itself. We shall see that "there is a structuring power in the living practices of a people that structures the effective aptitudes of every nascent generation, which exercised in its turn, 're-structures' the structuring power of that same people" (Margolis 1993:18). The enabling and disabling structures that we shall consider in this chapter will be located in something unusual: the agricultural and agronomic terminology found in the discourse of Tamil-speaking workers of Sri Lanka's tea estates.

My use of the terms "agricultural" and "agronomic" in this context is admittedly idiosyncratic. The distinction I wish to draw is as follows. In the tea estates of Sri Lanka, two kinds of agricultural (in the unmarked sense) terminology are in use: one belonging to managerial agriculture, the other to folk agriculture. Whereas in village India, folk agriculture prevails, by and large, the tea estate is the regime of managerial agriculture. I call the class of terms belonging to managerial agriculture "agronomic terminology," and I reserve the term "agricultural terminology" for the domain of folk agriculture. By analyzing four communicative events that I observed and recorded on tea estates in Sri Lanka, I attempt to show how these two terminological worlds interact.[1] The nature of the interaction is such that the dominant terminology of agronomy may be seen to be deconstructed by the subdominant terminology of village agriculture.[2]

This chapter is also about several other issues, even if they are expressed only obliquely or implicitly, apart from agro-agri terminology. First—and this is in a sense only briefly attended to—this chapter is about the accident of colonialism in a certain place and time. Much academic writing on colonialism has opted to attend to the history of the colonizer and his doings, the metropolises and their machinations, rather than to focus on the effects that colonialism has had and continues to have, in its own peculiarly transformative fashion, on the people it had once overtly subjugated. This chapter runs counter to that trend.

Second, a theoretical point. This chapter is informed by a semeiotic and is, therefore, concerned about the activity of signs, the signs of an aspect of a people's life in which a distorted and "subalterned" past is being recovered. Perforce, it is a semeiotic that, in contradistinction to much of traditional semiology and semiotics, Francophonic and American, attempts to come to terms with the neglected dimension of power. But how should the activity of signs be conceptualized? Genealogically, as Foucault would have it, or determinedly, as Bakhtin might have preferred? Given the form and content of the ethnographic material, to take sides on this question would be to settle on a metanarrative that would undermine these contradictory impulses which I found to constitute the very "communicative events" I wish to analyze. To recover is not the same as to uncover or to discover. Recovery, in the sense used here, is more akin to regaining one's balance, albeit in a new place and time; it is a coming to terms with contemporary forces that buffet without allowing these forces to overwhelm. Recoveries often do entail radical rearrangement of meanings and forms, but they do not necessarily presume radical ruptures, nor do they deny all continuity, all memory—whether real or imagined—and all familiarity. In this chapter I have attempted to preserve the apparent contradictions of the Bakhtinian and Foucaultian positions as a pervasive backdrop against which is enacted the task of recovering the past in such prosaic linguistic fabrications as agricultural terminology. Words, and even words used as terms, like all symbols, grow. They traverse space and time. They are transformed and transform. They, like all signs, are always on the move. In the topic under examination in this chapter, that which has risen to the surface, that which has transferred itself onto tape and has been transcribed onto ethnographic parchment, bears but a strange resemblance to the agricultural world of village India. These transformations are not passive records of history but active embodiments of the genealogy of power-relations. Third, and returning to the manifest content of the pages that follow, this chapter is not only about certain terms and their link to standards and measures peculiar to the world of tea but also about the manner in which they give expression to contained violence. As in chapter 2, I use "contain" in both senses: "to have" and "to limit." A term may be only a word. But a word is not *merely* a word. As Althusser has observed, "In political, ideological, and philosophical struggle, words are also weapons, explosives, tranquilizers and poisons. Occasionally, the whole class struggle may be summed up in the struggle for one against another. Other words are the site of an ambiguity; the stake in a decisive but undecidable battle."[3]

Let us then make our entry into the discursive practices of Sri Lanka's Estate Tamils through a more detailed examination of these terms and expressions. I shall begin by providing a brief historical sketch of Sri Lanka's Estate Tamils and then move on to explicate two broadly conceived terminological types, the approximate and the precise, as used by these Tamils. Following this, I shall sketch a semeiotic by which the distinction between agriculture and agronomy may be theorized. Next, I shall present and analyze several communicative events in which agricultural and agronomic terminology constitute and are constituted by a people's lived experience, a people's world. In conclusion, I shall attempt to pull together the theoretical threads that weave through this chapter to give its design a measure of tautness as well as greater visibility.

An Abbreviated History of Sri Lanka's Estate Tamils

The first group of Tamil laborers were brought from the villages of South India to the island of Ceylon in 1834. Offices for the sole purpose of recruitment sprang up in Tiruchchirappalli, Madurai, Madras, and other cities of the Madras Presidency in South India. Within a short time, the greater part of the recruiting was done in the villages themselves, by men of some influence. South Indian villagers recall that these recruiters tended to be the younger brothers of a village headman or caste-*panchayāt* headman. As such, they were driven to claim, by other means and in other places, the power they were deprived of in their natal villages.[4] Most of these men accompanied their labor gangs in the migration to Ceylon, and there they became labor-supervisors known as *kaṅkāṇis*.[5]

What these pioneer workers first confronted on the island was not cultivated land ready to be appropriated from the local peasants, but thick, virgin tropical forests. Through the labor of this immigrant group and that of subsequent waves of immigrants, these forests were transformed into coffee and, later, tea estates. The earliest immigrants were exclusively men. In later years, especially after tea began to replace coffee in 1867, women and children joined them.

From the very beginning, the structure of these immigrants' society was to be different from that of South India's villages, re-formed to suit the interests and requirements of a capitalist estate economy. The multiple crops characteristic of villages in India were replaced by a single cash crop. Whereas in their ancestral Indian villages most of what was grown was consumed by the residents, on the estate almost the entire yield of this single crop was to be exported. Caste distinctions that might have been kept clear by distinct residential patterns in village India were threatened and often effaced as all workers were compelled to live in identical, barracks-style line rooms,[6] regardless of caste. Caste-specific occupations became less important, and in some cases even disappeared, because all the residents of an estate had to work toward the rationalized end of manufacturing coffee or tea at a profit. Even though many other cultural changes followed, Estate Tamils never lost their sense of continuity with village India.

One of the most remarkable changes in the lives of these immigrant workers was that, with a few exceptions, they were not allowed to cultivate any land for growing cereals or vegetables for their own consumption, so the land they worked on did not directly yield their subsistence. This was due less to the unavailability of land for personal gardening than to the fact that their labor had been leased for the sole purpose of growing tea. In the agronomy displacing agriculture was found an agency that was committed to the constitution of a "totally useful time," and the elimination of "anything that might disturb or distract" (Foucault 1979:150). The workers' rice, dhal, cereals, spices, vegetables, flour, sugar, and oil were provided for them by the company store, known as the Cooperative Store. A few kaṅkāṇis and some staff members owned one or two milch cows. But cows' milk was beyond the purchasing power of most laborers. Their drink was the dark brew of a heavily sweetened low-grade tea dust.

Forced to give up the old agriculture for the new agronomy, these Tamils were also subjected to the hegemonic pressures of new agronomic terminology and its attendant discursive practices. This new terminology, they learned, belonged to a rationalized system that favored precision over approximation, universal standards and units of measurement over contextualized ones. The island's Tea Research Institute, founded in 1925 on St. Coomb's Estate near the town of Talawakelle, continues to be one of the most prestigious dispensers of these precise terminologies.

The British who owned and operated the tea estates for over a century saw precision as much in terms of fairness as in terms of efficiency. Precise scales were ordered to assure accurate weighing of green leaf and fairness to all the tea pickers. From the point of view of the British superintendent (the title given a tea estate manager), it would have been dreadfully unfair to use two unmatched scales in two different weighing sheds. Similarly, precision was imperative in the measurements used to construct living quarters for the workers. It assured uniformity, and uniformity assured equality, and equality guaranteed fairness. The concern with precision was carried so far that attempts by individual workers to expand their living space or even to reorganize it within the prescribed dimensions incurred the management's instant disapproval. In memoranda and letters that these early planters wrote to their subordinates and to their parent companies in England, the words "fairness," "justness," "precision," and "uniformity" are used as if they meant the same thing.

Nevertheless, the precise by no means displaced the approximate in terminology. Rather, the two have continued to coexist, constituting a contradictory consciousness in Estate Tamil culture and society. In recent times, as we shall soon see, one has begun to deconstruct the other in unexpected and intriguing ways.

The Precise

Writing of another place and another time, Foucault reminds us that "precision and application are, with regularity, the fundamental virtues of disciplinary time" (1979:151).[7] On the side of precision, distance is rendered in feet, yards, and miles;[8] area in square feet, square yards, and acres; weight in ounces and pounds; volume in quarts and gallons; wages in rupees and cents; labor power in number of pounds of tea plucked, feet of trenches dug, number of bushes pruned, acres of field fertilized, and so forth; rainfall in inches or centimeters; and time in minutes, hours, days, weeks, months, and years. Accordingly, a trench should be 1 foot deep, 12 feet long, and 8 feet wide, a line room 100 square feet; the total number of bushes that yield 100 pounds of made tea must be fertilized with 10 percent nitrogen; 5 ounces of pernox (a chemical) are mixed in 1 gallon water; 18 to 24 laborers are needed for each acre of "hard pruning," 14 laborers per acre for "skiffing"; and wages of 12 rupees per day are to be paid for pruning, 7 rupees per day for plucking tea. Prince among the list of precise items is time. For most women, who have to prepare breakfast and a parceled lunch, the 4:30 A.M. gong at the tea factory signals their time to arise from bed; for the men it could be the 5:30 or even the 6:00 bell. *Peraṭṭu*, a word unknown to India's Tamils, dominates their attentions in the morning. None of the laborers with whom I spoke was aware that this word originated from the English word "parade," so thorough has been its assimilation into Estate Tamil. But what is peraṭṭu? Is it the march to the field site? Or is it the lining up at the site in order to receive the day's work order? It is not clear. In either event, it is a review, "an ostentatious examination" (Foucault 1979:188), especially when the superintendent suddenly appears, like a commanding officer before his troops. The workers who rise at the gong of the factory bell gather at muster when the conch blows at 6:30 A.M.; they break for lunch when the conch blows at noon and return to work when the conch blows at 1 P.M., and they quit work when the conch blows at 4:30 P.M. Though the conch is no longer a real conch shell (*caṅku*) but the piercing wail of the tea factory's steam siren, the laborers call it a caṅku anyway. It is only one of the many means by which "time penetrates the body and with it all meticulous controls of power" (Foucault 1979:152). The list of precise measures goes on and on, constituting the tone and texture of this new disciplinary regime, this agronomic world.[9] And clocked time is the herald of this list and this world.

Guards in khaki, parades and musters, troops of workers, rows of bushes, rows of line houses, lines of shirkers, lines in books, names on lines, rows of books, columns in rows, numbers in columns, check-rolls,[10] roll calls, and conch (bugle?) calls, discipline, punctuality, and other discursive units of eighteenth- and nineteenth-century Europe all impel an apparently willing labor force to consent, signifying the militarization and radical remaking of the relations among people as well as between people and land. If the conch announces the beginning of work (or war) for Hindus, it also announces the beginning of prayer. The discipline required in work (and war) finds its "elective affinity," to borrow a phrase from Max Weber (1948:284–285), in the discipline intrinsic to devotion, but one robbed of all dignity. The traditional *namaskāram*, the Hindu greeting of god and fellow man, in which palms are held together in front of the chest, is replaced by *salām*, an Arabic word, and a European gesture. The gesture is a salute, but a docile one, in which shoulders are drawn in and head appropriately lowered.

The Approximate and the "Little Extra"

In the extra-agronomic context, as might be expected, there is a wealth of approximate terms employed. In the kitchen, rice and dhal are measured in *cuṇṭus* (from the Arabic *sunduq*, via the Sinhala *huntuvə*)[11] and *kottus* (a corruption of quart). A cuṇṭu is ideally a cigarette tin, not unusually a condensed milk tin, and sometimes a half of a coconut shell—of the right size, of course. The Sinhala huntuvə, as a token of indigenous agricultural terminology, had always been an approximate measure. The conversion of the precise quart into the approximate kottu is an example of the power of approximation over the precise. In fact, the assimilation of quart in this manner into Estate Tamil is so complete that the primary meaning of kottu is not a unit of measure, per se, but a container of a certain approximate size and shape.

The stores on the estates claim to own a set of the few standardized measuring instruments available. Until about fifteen years ago, the salesmen in these stores used a combination of dry measures, such as cuṇṭus, kottus, and bushels, and weights, such as ounces and pounds, to measure the various kinds of goods they sold. They used dry measures for rice, dhal, and other cereals, and pounds and ounces for such items as sugar, tamarind, and incense.

Since the early 1970s the metric system of weights has replaced both the former dry measures and the measures of weights. The salesman likes this change, not only because the new system is more rational than the old, but because the use of a scale as opposed to a measuring container gives him greater flexibility, which in turn gives him greater power. In the case of the cuṇṭu and kottu the salesman used to scoop up the grain or sugar and fill the measuring container to overflowing, and then, with the help of a stick, level off the excess. The quantity that he was free to play with in this manner was limited, depending on whether he pressed the stick tightly upon the rim of the container or only grazed it gently. With the scale, he has far greater discretionary powers. When a salesman weighs dhal, rice, flour, or sugar, he is more likely to underweigh than to weigh precisely. He does this by pouring the contents of the scale's pan into the newspaper cone before the pointer of the scale has had time to come to rest. But he is free to—and, more often than not, will—throw in a little extra. The customer rarely demands that he reweigh the item already in the cone, for he would not trust the scale anyway. He may, however, ask the salesman to throw in a little more of the extra. The salesman might oblige, especially if the customer is one who belongs to the "he may be needed by us" category (*namakku vēṇṭiyavar*).

One is classified into the "needed" category for reasons that may range from the immediate to the deferred. An example of the immediate would be when a customer is able to oblige the salesman with a few logs of firewood from the estate's store, which he will "lose" during transportation at a point mutually known to him (it is usually a man) and the salesman, to be plucked up by the latter at a specified time after dusk. To the deferred category belongs a case known to me in which the salesman never stinted on the little extra to a certain customer. This customer's son was doing well in school and was considered to have a good chance of becoming a clerk in the estate office who then, it was thought, would be able to wield sufficient clout to find an appropriate bridegroom for the salesman's daughter—then only ten years old. The dynamic involved here entails, to quote Appadurai, "a logic of cross-reference, whereby one set of objects or phenomena is measured by explicit or implicit measures of other objects or phenomena of [this] world of reckoning" (1986:12).

"The little extra"[12] is an important cultural category. At weddings and other occasions where gifts are exchanged, it is important that whenever the gift is in cash, the amount be in odd numbers: 51 or 101 rupees. That extra one is symbolic of generosity as well as prosperity on the part of the giver.[13] When an untouchable places her empty pot at the well to be filled by the woman of a clean *jāti* ("caste") who has access to the well, the latter will invariably pour enough water so that the vessel brims over with that "little extra."

When a man's kinsfolk go to the house of a potential bride to initiate marriage negotiations, they are invariably invited to partake of a feast.[14] This feast is most important, among other reasons, for assessing whether the prospective bride has it in her to be a *Dhaṅalakshmi*, the goddess of wealth. The signs taken note of are kinesic ones, observed especially by the women, as she serves her guests. How does she hold the serving spoon? How much rice does she scoop up (the spoon need not be full)? How many times does she scoop up rice? Does she tap the neck of the spoon on the edge of the container to release the rice that is stuck to the spoon? At which point along the length of the spoon's stem does she tap on the edge of the serving container? (A miserly woman will fail to tap her spoon or will tap it in such a way that the stuck rice does not fall back into the vessel and therefore the amount of rice she scoops up afresh will not be as much as it should be. But sticky rice could be a stickier affair. Too much tapping, indicating excessive glutinousness, could raise questions about the young lady's or her mother's cooking skills.) Most important, does she place that little extra on the guest's leaf, even after the latter has said, "Enough! enough!"?[15] All these signs together—especially the last—indicate whether the girl is blessed with the capacity and the gift of being generous and bountiful—a Dhanalakshmi. All these signs, if they are to be considered auspicious, must reveal absolutely no indications of attempts at measuring, especially measuring precisely.

Agronomic Approximation

Approximate measures have perfused the highly rationalized world of tea estates as well. The factory officer who pays a laborer for tending to his garden on company time (against company rules) will be given a container full of tea (again, against company rules) and a little extra. The gestural language is not unlike that which one finds in village India when the landlord gives his field hands a certain number of *paṭis* (a certain measure) of grain each, as agreed upon by some tacit contract, in return for their services, and then a little extra. The contextually determined measures and standards characteristic of South India's villages are also characteristic of the agronomic tea estates. Ask the kaṅkāṇi how many men he needs for pruning a given field. "Tentwelve," comes the answer. "How many hours will it take?" "Seveneight hours." Ask the pruner how many inches below the surface he should skiff a bush. "At the right level," replies the pruner readily. I say, "The manual says, two inches below the surface."[16] "We don't carry books and measuring sticks," he replies. And any planter knows (having learned from the experienced laborer) that the manual's precision is more a sign of agronomic obsessiveness than one of scientific accuracy. "Some bushes need to be cut two inches below the top, some three inches, some even four," he elaborates. "What about 'cut-across' pruning?" I ask. "At knee level," comes back the reply. What the book says is fifteen inches from the ground, and knees are not high-precision measuring sticks. In practice that matters very little.[17]

When tea pickers bring their baskets full of tea to be weighed by the field supervisor at the weighing shed, the tea is dumped into a gunnysack and hooked onto a spring (salter) scale.[18] The scale faces the supervisor and not the picker. And even if it were to face her, the scale's reading is an average observed between the extreme points of the pointer's oscillations. "Letchumi, twenty-seven pounds!" "No, it cannot be. It must be at least thirty-five," protests Letchumi. "You held your basket in the waterfall on your way here. Too much water here. I have deducted eight pounds for water." "How can you do that? There must be at least three pounds of rainwater, no?" "Well, rain is water too." "Mariyayi, twenty-seven pounds." Mariyayi does not complain. She knows that she is a poorer picker than Letchumi, but her husband makes up for it by carrying firewood to the supervisor's quarters. "Kamatchi, thirty-two pounds"—even though the scale oscillates around thirty, with rainwater and all. But the supervisor knows that she recently lost her kinsman in the communal riots. And so it goes. Fair and unfair, all of them approximations.

There are two quintessential approximations irrevocably built into the manufacture of tea. The first is the standard by which the ripeness of *koṛuntu* is determined (the leaf bud and the two leaves that sprout at its base). "When do you pluck a koṛuntu?" "When it is just right. The bud should not be too closed, nor too open." The second is to decide when the withering of green leaf should be stopped and the rolling of the leaf (in special cones and rollers or, more recently, in retrovane rollers) begun. The answer again is, "When it is just right." And any manual that tries to be more precise than that is wrong.[19] In the third major step in the manufacture of tea, measurement (of humidity and temperature) is nowadays increasingly employed over judgment. This is the step of interrupting the rolling (technically called roll-breaking) every half hour or so for about ten minutes before subjecting the leaf to a second rolling. On the average, five or six rolls can be done, and during each roll-break the *dhool* is extracted for fermentation. The dhool is the rolled tea that does not pass across the roll-breaking sieves. The leaves that pass across the sieves are put back into the roller and rolled again.

A Semeiotic of Agriculture and Agronomy Broadly Conceived

In general, agricultural measures tend to be phenomenological "Seconds," and agronomic measures, phenomenological "Thirds." The semeiosic terminology comes from C. S. Peirce. Briefly, he argues that whatsoever is capable of presenting itself to the mind for contemplation has three aspects to it: Firstness, Secondness, and Thirdness. In this chapter we will be least concerned with Firstness, which is associated with potentiality. Secondness, associated with actuality, is emphasized by existents, the here and the now, the contextually delimited and determined. The universal, the conventional, and the context-free characterize Thirdness, which is associated with generality.

Of the numerous sign-types Peirce wrote about, the best known are the iconic, the indexical, and the symbolic.[20] Each describes the nature of a type of bond, or what Peirce technically calls the ground, that holds together a sign and its object. The iconic sign, which falls under the broad phenomenological category of Firstness, is a sign that signifies by virtue of its resemblance to (or even identity with) the object for which it stands; the indexical sign, which falls under the broad phenomenological category of Secondness, signifies by virtue of its contiguity to the object for which it stands; and the symbolic sign, which falls under the broad phenomenological category of Thirdness, signifies by virtue of a convention that determines that it stand for a certain object in a given way. When the object-sign relationship is prescinded[21] from the triadically constituted sign as a whole, the necessary third correlate of the sign, the interpretant (to whom/what such a representation stands) is provisionally left out of consideration. I shall consider interpretants in a slightly different theoretical context later in this chapter.

Statues and metaphors (iconic conventions) rely on resemblance for their significant import and therefore are iconic. Smoke and fire, lightening and thunder, the rise in temperature and the corresponding rise of mercury in a thermometer are, to one degree or another, indexical. The actual effect of the object on the sign or their invariable contiguity dominates these processes of signification. Even though in nature we most readily find the manifestation of indexical signs, culture provides us with its share of indexical signs as well. In many languages, as is well known, a certain dialect or accent could be indexical of the social status or gender of one or another interlocutor. On tea estates, even when a superintendent is a native Tamil-speaker, he may choose to adopt an Englishman's accent. In doing so, he indexes his status as a manager to plantation workers and his distance from them, whereas in village India such an affectation would be taken for a speech impediment. As for symbols, human existence is perfused with them. Words as signs stand for their objects only by dint of convention. That sixteen ounces make up a pound is a convention and, therefore, symbolic. So is the convention that twelve inches make a foot, much more so now than when the king's foot provided the standard.[22] To be sure, most signs that human beings traffic in are compounds of all three significative modes or sign-types. But what is at issue is emphasis, dominance, and determination.

Let us consider determination, for this is important to the demonstration of the crucial difference between agronomy and agriculture. Let us designate the measuring *implements* the cuṇṭu and the liter—tokens of the agricultural and agronomic domains, respectively—as cuṇṭu^{i} and liter^{i} so as to differentiate them from their corresponding *concepts*, cuṇṭu^{c} and liter^{c}. A semeiosic object is said to *determine* its sign, and the sign *represents* the object to a third, the interpretant. Continuing to bracket out the third correlate, the interpretant, and focusing our attention on the sign and object, we may understand the property of determination as an active one and that of representation as a passive one (Parmentier 1985:27–29). In the case of liter, the semeiosic object is the abstract standard of measure, the liter^{c}, and each actual measuring implement, the liter^{i}, its sign. Stated differently, a liter^{i} is a replica of (i.e., it is an icon of) that semeiosic object, the liter^{c}. This object is none other than a conventional symbol and therefore a semeiosic third, a general idea. Or at least, it is the conventional and the general that are placed in the foreground. In the case of cuṇṭu, matters are turned around. Here, it is the measuring implement—a cuṇṭu^{i}—a cigarette tin, condensed milk tin, or the half-shell of a coconut—that is put forward as the semeiosic object. Here, the abstract idea of a quantity of measure, the cuṇṭu^{c}, is what serves as the sign that is determined by a material object. The cuṇṭu^{c} is an icon or replica of a cuṇṭu^{i} and not vice versa. It is the contextualized material object that is also the determining semeiosic object. Nevertheless, both pairs, the liter^{i} and liter^{c} and the cuṇṭu^{i} and cuṇṭu^{c}, are similar to the extent that they are both ultimately based on iconicity. But the semeiosic object for a liter is a symbolic (conventional) type, while the semeiosic object for the cuṇṭu is an indexical token. Types emphasize generals; tokens emphasize instances.

In determination, the vector of determination for liter moves from the general idea, the conventional liter (liter^{c}), to the actual token, the measuring implement (liter^{i}). The vector of determination for cuṇṭu proceeds from the actual implement (suṇṭu^{i}) to the general convention (suṇṭu^{c}). The convention of the liter is active and the actual liter is passive; but for the cuṇṭu, the actual is active and the convention is passive. This groundedness (pun intended) is seen to operate with the same agricultural insistence in the case of the *vafa* measure, employed in the rice fields of Maharashtra, so astutely explicated by Appadurai (in press).

Measures as abstract standards are located in an environment of other abstract/ideational/general objects and are held together by mutual interrelations. But being conventional, their relationships strive toward a constant and invariable structure. Conventions, by definition, move toward stability and fixity and away from caprice, surprise, and contingency. They invite limitations upon possibilities and lend themselves to the generalities capable of being rendered into conversion tables.

Measuring implements are also located in their own environment of objects, what we commonly call real objects. This is a fluid and variable environment, the variations of which allow for the variability of the instruments as well. Such measuring implements, as objects in and of actualities (or acts), are fraught with surprise and caprice. Acts qua acts are preconventional and highly variable.

The abstract domain of standards and measures is populated with objects that have been normalized and regularized, objects (as concepts) that have been tamed and disciplined. The domain of actualities, by contrast—populated by emergent objects, be these cigarette tins of various sizes or fields of various slopes, or people of various moods—determines representations that are themselves variable and flexible. An object that determines its representation from within a regularized domain determines regular representations. Such is the case of standardized measures, like the liter. An object that determines its representations from within a domain of variables determines variable representations, as in the case of the cuṇṭu.

Implicit in the communicative events that follow and their analyses, we shall see, at varying levels of activity, the interplay among the determining semeiosic vectors discussed above.

Four Communicative Events in Their Ethnographic Settings

Pruning (kavvāttu veṭṭal)

If left unpruned, the tea bush will not be a bush but a tree, producing flowers and seeds instead of a flush of pluckable buds. Pruning stimulates growth yet keeps it in a permanent vegetative state. Finally, pruning maintains the bush at a height that lends itself to efficient and productive plucking.

One prunes with a quick, precise, and powerful stroke of knife, arm, and wrist using a knife called a *kavvāttukkatti*. Because this skill requires considerable muscle strength, it is believed that only adult males can prune (even though wives may be found to surreptitiously help their husbands in this task). A weak stroke will result in the stem's splitting; too ungainly or too free a stroke could damage stems that are not meant to be cut by that stroke; an imprecise hack could result in a poorly angled cut.

There are three types of pruning: skiffing, cut-across pruning, and clean pruning. Skiffing is called *mēcai veṭṭu* in Tamil. In skiffing, according to the

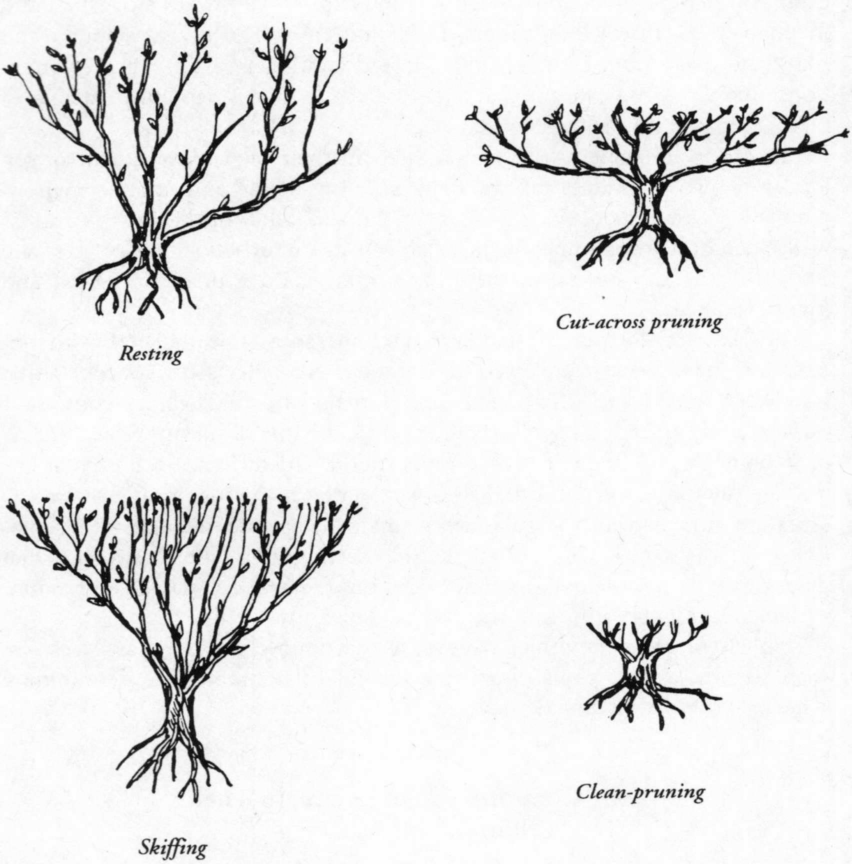

Figure 2. A tea bush in various stages of pruning

manual, the bushes are trimmed two inches from the top with a kavvāttuk-katti. As in all types of pruning, the bush is pruned along the gradient of the hill upon which it grows, and yet each branch pruned is cut at an angle (*cācci veṭṭu*), so that the cut edge faces the center of the bush.

Skiffing allows a bush to be plucked after 35–40 days. Consequently, this form of pruning is often resorted to as an alternative to the more radical types of pruning, which prevent the bushes from being plucked for anywhere from 90 to 150 days. The word *mēcai* means table; thus a mēcai vettu literally is a kind of pruning that makes the surface of a bush like that of a table.

Cutting-across, the second kind of pruning, is called *mēl veṭṭu* in Tamil. The bush is pruned with a kavvāttukkatti, at a height of about 15 inches above the ground, approximately across the middle of the bush. The Tamil laborer describes it as knee level, obviously making ingenious adjustments to varying heights of knee joints and variously dispositioned tea bushes. The tea planter's manual, on the other hand, specifies with agronomic precision that this middle cut should be made 15 inches above the ground. Knee level is admittedly approximate, but its approximation tends to be consistently in the best interest of the healthy growth of each tea bush. As in skiffing, the angle of the cut in cut-across pruning slants inward, toward the center of the bush. Following such a pruning, the bush may not be plucked for at least 90 days.

The third and the most difficult kind of pruning, hard pruning or clean pruning, is called *aṭi veṭṭu* in Tamil. Here, the manual specifies that the bush is pruned with either a kavvāttukkatti or a hand saw (*vāl*), 8 inches above the ground. The laborer measures the height as one and a half spans of the hand (*onnarai jān*). The hard pruning cut is described in the manual as not angled but horizontal. In Tamil this cut is called *poṭṭu veṭṭu*, because the exposed surface of the cut stem resembles a pottu, the auspicious circular mark that Tamil women and sometimes men wear on their foreheads. And any Tamil knows that if a stem is cut at an angle, the pottu will be oblong and not circular as it ought to be.

Formerly, in clean pruning the bush was reduced to leafless stumpy stems. Nowadays, two variations of clean pruning are practiced in the belief that a radical clean pruning might be too severe on the bush. In the first variation, the outermost rim of branches are spared radical pruning. In the second, lung pruning, a single leafy branch is spared. When a bush is hard-pruned, the manual says, it may not be harvested for "125 days." The kaṅkāṇi says, "Hundred'ntwentyhundred'nthirty days."

Communicative Event 1: The Story of the Perumal Cut

Most of the tea estates of Sri Lanka are located at elevations ranging from three thousand to seven thousand feet. The higher reaches of the estate that Poocchi Kaṅkāṇi has worked all his life rise above seven thousand feet. In these higher elevations in particular, the mornings are densely foggy and cold. In the words of Poocchi, one of my principal informants:

> Those who gather at muster, the field supervisors included, especially the field supervisors, would rather be back in their line houses on the cow dung–plastered floor, on mats, under a warm woolen blanket. In those days, only a few supervisors used to sleep on cots. Now all of them do. Therefore, to warm up ourselves, to make our blood flow, and to keep us from thinking about our line houses, we talk a lot, and that too, very loudly. The supervisors yell, swear, curse, and find

fault. "You seeker of vaginas, where did you learn to hold the knife like that? Was it from your wife?" The male worker mutters back a wisecrack or breaks out laughing. To a female worker a supervisor may even say, "You daughter of a harlot, who gave you a name[23] today? Look at her, how she works! Look at her, like a newlywed bride she is." If the laborer is a young woman, she will giggle. An older woman might shoot back, "Why, it was your father who gave me a name." The other women would break into laughter. No one really means what they say. It is all meant to make the blood flow, the sun rise, and the mist disappear.[24] This kind of banter goes back and forth, until they start working like machines, at a constant pace, without speeding up here and slowing down there. The only thought is to finish their assigned acreage as soon as possible so that they could go home or off to a second job. Then they might even start to pluck faster so that they could exceed the minimum poundage and earn additional money for the extra pounds they pluck.

Around noon, the sun gets hot and the workers get hungry. Now when the supervisor wants something done in a certain way, he may shout, but he tempers it with a joke. "Go ahead and work like a tortoise. Both of us are going to be here till seven at night or until we fall dead from hunger."

New superintendents, especially the *cinna dorais* (assistant superintendents—until recently, mostly Britons) are not sensitive to the time of the day and the tempers of the workers. They learn from whoever taught them that the only way to get work out of our people is to shout at them, treat them like dogs, pelt them with obscenities.

Many years ago there was such a cinna dorai. And in those days there was a young lad named Perumal. It was past one o'clock in the afternoon, and Perumal was doing a cut-across prune. The cinna dorai came tearing through the bushes in his khaki shorts, stockings, hat, and boots. They can run that way because of their boots. It is not good for the bushes running through like that. But the cinnai dorais don't care. It shows their power. Their authority. They think it scares us when they come rushing down like that. "Give me that knife, you son of a harlot," this cinna dorai said. "Let me show you how to prune a tea bush." Perumal handed the dorai the knife without saying a word. He watched the dorai swing at the bush, shouting, "Like this, like this. Fifteen inches above the ground. Fifteen inches above the ground." It was clear that the cinna dorai didn't know pruning from shaving off pubic hair. The stems were splitting down the middle, and instead of the slanted cut he was performing the (horizontal) poṭṭu veṭṭu. Perumal felt his blood boil and rise to his head. In his stomach was hunger. He held out his left hand, in a gesture of asking for his knife back, saying, "Here, dorai, please, not like that, not like that. Please, let me show you fifteen inches." The dorai returned the knife to him with contempt, blade-side first, noticing neither the anger in Perumal's eyes, the dangerous sarcasm in his voice, nor that he had asked for the knife with his *left* hand. Like a flash of lightning, Perumal returned the knife's handle to the grip of the other hand, his right hand, and swung at the Englishman

> with the word "*ippaṭi*!"("like this!"). The next thing you saw was the Englishman's arm, severed from below his elbow, writhing in the drain, spouting blood. It was exactly fifteen inches long.

Ever since, this infamous swipe has been known as "the Perumal cut."

Estate life is filled with such recallings and retellings, reminding one of Foucault's distinction between enlightenment historiographies and effective histories. The former are typified by their pretensions to examine things furthest from themselves, whereas "effective history," as in the Perumal story, "shortens its vision to those things nearest to it—especially the body" (1984:89). "The body," Foucault remarks, "is the inscribed surface of events (traced by language and dissolved by ideas). . . . a volume in perpetual disintegration. Genealogy . . . is thus situated within the articulation of the body and history" (1984:83). In "Perumal's cut," the implicated body is that of a white man. As metaphor, it has become the body of a condemned man. But the effect is not only that Perumal, as judge and executioner, left his mark on the Englishman's body and shortened its power, but also that this body has become public property, available for useful appropriation by the collective memory of a subordinated people against future oppression.

Draining (kāṇ veṭṭutal)

Digging drains, like pruning, requires considerable muscle strength and is, therefore, considered to be men's work. The skill required for cutting drains is not as exacting as that required in pruning. This difference is reflected in the difference in wages: pruners are paid twelve or even twelve and a half rupees per day, whereas drain diggers earn only nine. The kaṅkāṇi plays an important role in determining the gradient of the drain and limiting it to a ratio of 1:120 as it follows the contours of the hill. He carries a measuring stick and string to determine this and the distances between the terraced drains. Nevertheless, the most respected kaṅkāṇi is one who is able to plan and direct the digging of perfect drains using no more than eyes, feet, legs, and experience.

Drains check erosion and channel the flow of rainwater during the monsoons. They are cut with a hoelike implement called the *maṇveṭṭis* at 30-foot intervals along the contours of the hills. For those familiar with nineteenth-century sensibilities, the view across the valley of a given hill's drains along its contours might take on the appearance of the flounces of a Victorian gown. These drains are 2.5 feet deep, 2 feet wide, and 12 to 15 feet long. At the end of each drain a 3-foot-long platform or *tiṭṭu* is made, after which the next drain continues. Whenever a drain is dug, the soil is thrown onto the upper slope of the hill; doing otherwise would of course either fill up a lower drain previously dug, make the digging of such a drain extremely difficult, or even gradually cover the tea bushes in the lower slopes.

Communicative Event 2: "Down-Piling"

Behavioral modes motivated by short-term goals or hedonism are often analogized to digging a drain and throwing the soil down the slope of a hill. Initially, it appears to be so easy and only natural to shovel something downhill. But eventually one either brings about destruction or creates for oneself a staggering amount of work. In recent years, down-piling, as this action is called in technical jargon, has come to serve as a general description of the work habits of recently hired Sinhala laborers, and a metaphor of the Sri Lankan government's policies toward Estate Tamils.

Late one morning, I was taken to the field by a Sinhala tea estate manager. He wished to show me how a Sinhala worker was digging a drain. He had been down-piling all morning. "He is the gov'ment," clipped the manager in his quasi-British accent, with overtone diphthongs, glottal stop, and all. "ˀAw the gov'ment does is dompile." Obviously "dompiling," to this Sinhala gentleman planter, was not mere technological terminology: it was a symbol but also an index. Or more precisely it was a "shifter," in Silverstein's terminology, symbolically contributing to the referential content of the discourse as well as indexically implicating aspects of the context of utterance—in this case, the status of the speaker (Silverstein 1976). The accent indicated that he belonged to that proud lineage of planters whose ancestral members were British and whose pedigree he wished to be identified with by virtue of his dialect. Subsequently, I was to learn that this idiom of down-piling, which had its origin in the agricultural terminology of tea estates, has recently gained considerable currency among Tamil workers themselves, used with an ironic twist. More on this shortly.

Down-piling as enunciated by our mimic man,[25] our anglicized but not-quite-English gentleman planter, is a vestige and metonym of colonial discourse. To be sure, not all Sinhala managers resort to "British-English," nor are the Sinhala managers the only ones who do so. Of the proportionately fewer Tamil and Burgher managers as well, there are those who fondly assume such an affectation. Accompanying the assumed dialect is the British style of life: bungalows, men servants who are addressed as boys, scotch, a desire for "English vegetables," khaki shorts, white stockings, safari hat, and rugger. In an earlier day, mimicry had been an ambivalent fetish of the mimic man, who was at once both empowered and disempowered by the condescending validation of the white man; the latter thought he had the last word and could say, "almost as good as an Englishman, but not quite," or could remark on "the slippage, the excess, the difference" (Bhabha 1984:126). However, I have yet to know a white colonialist or a student of colonialism to have remarked, let alone observed, that the subalterns too see these same slippages, excesses, and differences, even though they read them differently. In their view from below, the subalterns had found some comfort and frivolity in seeing the mimic man as one of their kind, who, regardless of what he might have intended, had also ended up reducing the white man's airs to laughable size. If they found him to be the reassuringly ambivalent repository of mimicry, they also found him to be the embodiment of mockery. Even when menacing, his bark had failed to convey the convictions of a beast. Mimicry of this kind was all too human. Now, with the white man gone, mimicry is no longer funny; it is not even human. The simulacrum remains but is abandoned by its original and by the parodic relief it had offered. The shadow has become the demon, the mask the monster. Old metaphors have created new interpretants in new discursive fields. Down-piling itself has acquired currency in a different discourse, a discourse in which the mimic man is top dog; and he bites.

In 1972 and 1974, the Sri Lankan government nationalized its tea estates and introduced several sweeping reforms that had far-reaching consequences for Estate Tamils and for the Sinhala villagers who lived in the peripheries of these estates. Prior to 1970 the privately owned estates, both foreign and local, maintained a ratio of two registered laborers per acre of cultivated land. The available work on all estates invariably exceeded the capacity of the number of registered workers. This state of affairs worked to management's advantage. An army of "nameless" young men, women, and children were available on call to pick up the slack whenever weather conditions or management decisions called for extra labor. The ratio of workers with names to those without names was 60:40. These nameless workers were either paid minimal hourly wages or subcontracted by registered workers afraid of losing their jobs for being unable to complete the amount of work they had been contracted.

Wages thus earned were called *kai kācu*, or small change (lit.: hand cash). At least 75 percent of these seasonal or standby workers were anything but seasonal and did anything but stand by, for most of them worked throughout the year, saving millions of rupees for the management, which would otherwise have had to pay out in regular wages and benefits to workers with names.

When the tea estates were nationalized, the government mandated that the ratio of workers to cultivated land be increased from two to five workers per acre. This policy was enacted with the professed intention of reducing the severe underemployment among Estate Tamil youth, and providing employment for the unemployed Sinhala population of the surrounding villages. In order to assure the latter, the government mandated that two Sinhala workers had to be hired for every Tamil worker employed.

In the case of the Tamils, the purported goal of reducing underemployment was undermined by another government policy, one mandated under its land-reform bill. As a consequence of this bill, parts of many estates were re-colonized by Sinhala villagers, which drove thousands of unemployed and homeless Tamil laborers into the cities of Kandy and Colombo. Many other Tamil estate workers became refugees and fled to the Northern and Eastern Provinces. A number of these displaced persons were transformed into bonded laborers who worked for non-Estate Tamil landowners for wages and in conditions far more deplorable than those on the tea estates. These apparently contradictory effects of government policies—where, for instance, the remedy for homelessness creates only more homeless people—are described by some estate workers as down-piling. At best, the effect of these reforms for Estate Tamils has been to substitute unemployment and homelessness for underemployment and poor housing. Most significant, these reforms have helped transplant a docile and ideologically and experientially parochial youth to the sociocultural environments of the cities and the rural areas of the north and east, where they have become hardened and radicalized.

Recently incorporated Sinhala peasants[26] have devised a work schedule of great convenience for themselves and much inconvenience to the management. But since the management is none other than the government, no single manager need have his reputation on the line with respect to the inconvenience, even though some of the old hands—especially those who were trained under Englishmen and whose habits of thought continue to conform to the "good old days," when profit was all that mattered—are quite troubled by the economically detrimental work habits of most of the newly incorporated Sinhala workers. These work habits range from incompetence, as pointed out to me by the Sinhala gentleman planter, to the more intractable habit of well-timed absenteeism. The latter works in the following manner.

According to the revised set of rules, no worker may lose his or her name (registration) as long as he or she reports to work at least one day a month. Many Sinhala peasants now registered on tea estates choose not to come to work when the weather is bad or when the work is heavy. For the Sinhala worker, bad weather is by definition rainy weather, for work in general picks up its pace when the rains come. For instance, weeds grow far more luxuriantly in foul weather than in fair. The same goes for tea. Rainy weather is also the ideal time for pruning. When the sun is out, the weeds sparse, and the plucking light, Sinhala workers willingly show up. The only heavy work to which an unlucky worker could be assigned during some of these sunny days is cutting drains. There are some sunny days when there is not even an hour's worth of work per laborer per day. These days are everyone's favorite under the new regime, for regardless of the number of hours worked, anyone who shows up in the morning is guaranteed a full day's wages.

Both management and Tamil laborers think that the sole purpose of Sinhala absenteeism is work avoidance. This is only partly true at best. Some peasants have traditionally worked at other jobs in the local towns, as domestic servants, bakers, waiters, vegetable vendors, carpenters, and truck unloaders. Peasants do not live in the estates' line rooms. They live in their own huts and houses, which need repairs, such as roof mending during the heavy rains. But there is work outdoors as well. If weeds grow profusely on tea estates, they also grow in peasants' own gardens of vegetables and cash crops. Some Sinhala laborers have rice fields to tend to, flood waters to channel appropriately, or fields to plow. Whatever the case may be, having a name on the tea estates is a great insurance against hard times. The Tamils, who have few outside options for work and have no choice but to do the hard work in bad weather, are resentful of the new arrangement. Since the early seventies, many young Tamil men too have opted for absenteeism of convenience. Some of these men have found alternative part-time jobs in the local towns; some spend their time at home; others have actively launched into political activities of consciousness-raising and organizing resistance groups in case there is another outbreak of communal violence against them. This brings me to my last example of down-piling.

A forty-five-year-old Tamil man used "down-piling" to describe the work habits of the Tamil youth of the day who were following the work habits of the Sinhalas. His hegemonic logic traced the consequences of these habits from the neglect of tea bushes to the drop in tea prices, to the drop in revenue to the government, to the deprivation of essentials to the Sinhala people, to their taking out their frustrations on the Tamils. His eighteen-year-old son, resentful because his father had ordered him to work regularly on the estate and not keep company with the other "idle young men who waste their time talking politics," retorted indignantly, saying, "It is you [old] people who have been 'down-piling' all these years. You have even buried your children. From the Sinhalas we can learn how not to down-pile." Instead of chastising his son for insubordination, the father's response amounted to admitting the charges. "Why then," he said, "don't we go to the ūr (to our ancestral village in India)? There are no hills there"—that is, one cannot down-pile there.[27]

Tipping (maṭṭam veṭṭutal)

The leaves that are plucked off a tea bush, called koṛuntu, include the tender bud at the very tip of a branch and the two leaves at its base from between which it sprouts. Before plucking koṛuntu off a recently pruned tea bush, the pickers lay a light, eight-foot-long stick known as *maṭṭa kampu* (lit.: leveling stick) atop a row of bushes. Before removing the sticks and moving further down the row of bushes, the workers nip off stemlets that protrude above the level of the sticks, thereby grading the bushes in keeping with the hills' slopes. Tipping is done with a six-inch-long *kōppikkatti*, which has a hooked tip.

From the rim of the crown of a pruned stem, a tuft of fresh stems buds and grows (*kavvāttu vātiliruntu poṭanci varum* means the leaves grow in profusion from the cut stem). The parent stem from which these stemlets grow is called the *poṭai vātu* (*poṭai*, sprout or burst forth; *vātu*, stem or branch). When a stem is not pruned on time, it grows long and erect except for the tip, which angles like the neck and head of a deer. A stem thus grown is called the *tāi vātu* (lit.: the mother branch).

After a tea bush has been tipped, plucking continues every seven days, on the average, until the next pruning cycle. Between cycles, the same bushes are plucked by the same picker. Thus it is in each plucker's interest to tip with care and tend to their bushes.

Communicative Event 3: Betrayal

Of the many jātis represented on estates, the Kaḷḷar and the Parayans are the most numerous and, for this reason, have traditionally competed for leadership. In the 1950s, the Kaḷḷar began to dominate the trade unions and their dominance culminated in the nomination of their leader, Mr. S. Thondaman, as minister of housing and rural development in 1977 by Sri Lanka's president, Mr. J. R. Jayewardene. The unchallenged rise of Kaḷḷar leadership began in the 1950s when the Parayans lost one of their most charismatic leaders, P. Vellayan.

In the communal riots of 1983, when scores of Estate Tamils were killed by Sinhala mobs, many workers saw Thondaman, by his very position as a minister in a Sinhala government, as having betrayed the Tamils. Some remembered Vellayan as a victim of violence, like the many Tamils who were killed in 1983, even though he died of an illness. The following was a song of a *vaḷḷuvan* (a Parayan priest) that I obtained from an estate in the Hatton District:

atiyōṭa veṭṭinānā ācāmi—veḷḷayan
muṭiyōṭa cānjānā enjāmi—
tonṭayanum taivātum vaḷaraṭṭum māmi
poṭṭum poṭanji vaḷarātā collu
kaccāmi?

Even as throated pedigree grows
unpruned with the mother stem,
tell me,
chanter of Buddhist prayers!
Burst forth will it not in gay
profusion,
a crown of buds around the poṭṭu
of my Lord,
Vellayan,
that uncrowned bush,
hewn at the base
by a villain's knife?

(Author's translation)

In Tamil, the poem ends with the words, "tell me kaccāmi"; or rather, "tell me you Buddhists who chant '*Buddham saraṇaṅgaccāmi*,'" or even more expansively, "you who claim to follow a nonviolent religion, tell me." The word *toṇṭayanum* in the third line literally means the throated one (from *toṇṭai* meaning throat). But to any estate worker, it also sounds like part of the minister's name, Thondaman, even though the morpheme *toṇṭai* in the minister's name has nothing to do with throat but means "a great length of time." Thus Thondaman means "chieftain from time immemorial," or "Lord of a long line of chieftains," or "Lord of pedigree." The skill of the poet here is to merge the literal sense of the "throated one" with the minister's name that it evokes through homophony. But no sooner is the name of Thondaman brought into consciousness than he, the "Lord of pedigree," is brought into the foreground and the throated one recedes to lurk in the shadows. From there, however, it does its semeiosic work. It splits the minister's name into two unintended morphemes: *toṇṭai*, meaning throat, and *mān*, which means deer. Once linked to deer, toṇṭai is no longer merely throat but becomes neck. To secure this meaning, the poet yokes it with "the mother stem." To render the first two lines (the third line in the Tamil original) more literally: "Let the throated one and the mother stem grow together (or grow alike)."

As you will recall, the mother stem is an unpruned (uncultured) stem whose posture is like that of a proud deer. But an unpruned stem is useless. One cannot pluck from it the useful koṛuntu. It has been detected and it will soon be cut down. Sound and sense have combined to cast a clearly outlined shadow: a deer, sometimes a pet of the rich, self-absorbed in its pedigree and beauty, with extended neck and veins pulsing, unaware of the rapid shifts in the tones of history. The poet goes on to note that the cutting down of Vellayan did not destroy him even though the villain who wielded the knife might have expected just that. Instead, what we have is a crown of new leaves sprouting from the rim where once a well-crowned bush was supported. He who was cut down then (perhaps prematurely) is beginning to reemerge now, and he who has continued to grow proudly long after he should have been pruned is nearing his end, like a deer that has stood still for too long a time, extending its neck, tempting the knife to do its job.

Tea Plucking (koṛuntu eṭuttal)

Plucking green tea leaves, women's work, constitutes the central and most conspicuous activity on a tea estate. The pickers gather at muster by 6:15 A.M., and by 6:30 they are in the fields among the bushes. As indicated earlier, pickers pluck koṛuntu, the two tender green leaves at the very tip of a branch and the slightly curled leaf bud that grows in between them. This is done with a single nip of the tender stem at the base of the third leaf, held between the thumbnail and forefinger, and a simultaneous slight twist of the wrist. The other fingers tuck the nipped-off koṛuntu into the palms of the hands, where the picker holds the leaves lightly so as not to bruise them. When her hands are too full for the comfort of the leaves, she tosses the handfuls of leaves into the basket (*kūṭai*) that hangs against her back from a rope strung over her head, and the emptied hands return in a flash to pluck more koṛuntu.

A bush may be over- or underplucked. A bush may be overplucked in four ways. In the first two forms of overplucking, the bush may not be harmed, but if caught, the picker will be heavily penalized. The first entails the plucking of the third leaf (*kaṭṭai ilai*), growing at the base of the koṛuntu, along with or in addition to the koṛuntu. The second entails the plucking of mature leaves (*karaṭṭai ilai*). A karaṭṭai ilai is not merely mature but also coarse. If, during inspection, the supervisor finds either a kaṭṭai ilai or a karaṭṭai ilai in a woman's basket, he is likely to penalize her by reducing from her total poundage far more than she might have gained from having plucked the mature leaves. The plucking of a karaṭṭai ilai is seen as a far more serious violation than the plucking of a kaṭṭai ilai. The third and fourth forms of overplucking adversely affect the healthy growth of the bush. In the third, the picker plucks the koṛuntu off the side or peripheral branches (*pakka vātu*). Such plucking curtails the horizontal spread of these branches, thereby depriving the soil underneath the bush of the invaluable shade needed to retard the growth of weeds that compete with the tea bush for the nutrition of the soil. The fourth way of overplucking a bush is to pluck the *arumpu*, or an unopened bud. In an arumpu the two tender base leaves that characterize the koṛuntu are either still barely separated from the terminal bud or are one with it. When an arumpu is plucked, the stem that bore it, being too tender to support the sprouting of a new bud, withers, turns brown, and rolls back on itself. A new bud can sprout from this stem only after the withered stem is nipped with a knife.

The bush can also be underplucked. Underplucking directly affects the plucker's poundage in two ways. First, she plucks less than she might have. Second, if a koṛuntu is not plucked in time, the next time around the sprig will have grown into a mature stem or leaf, unfit for plucking.

While plucking tea leaves, a picker also carries with her a kōppikkatti, the six-inch-long knife with a curved beak that looks like a miniature version of a kavvāttukkatti. This knife is used to nip off bits of stem called *vanki koṛuntu*. A vanki koṛuntu is formed when there is a long space between the two leaves of the koṛuntu and the fourth leaf (kaṭṭai ilai), and when the koṛuntu is nipped so close to the twin leaves that there is left behind a long protrusion of leafless stem. As long as this length of stem remains, a new bud cannot sprout.

The tea bush, upon which so much of a woman's activity is concentrated, has also become the source of a profusion of metaphors for children, most often female children. A Tamil tea worker perceives an obvious similarity between, on the one hand, a child forced to work in the field at a very young age and/or subjected to excessive discipline and deprived of the privileges of childhood freedom and, on the other, a bush whose peripheral branches are plucked. Such discipline and deprivation are seen as misdirected, the actions of selfish, greedy, or shortsighted parents. To paraphrase one of my informants, the nourishing soil of healthy mystery is exposed to the scorching rays of premature knowledge, which in turn encourage the growth of the weeds of bad thoughts and habits capable of retarding, choking, and even destroying the growth of a child and a family with a good name.

The experience of dislocation and displacement suffered by Tamil workers, especially the young, in the wake of the 1974 land reforms and the communal violence since then has been described as "the plucking of koṛuntu from the peripheral branches." In this instance the overplucking is attributed not to the parents but to circumstances of fate. Those who never left the estates see the young raised in urban areas returning to the estates for brief visits as hardened and corrupt and characteristically displaying a thorough disregard for the old ways of deference and respect to elders and authority.

The young men who return to the estates defy the custom of "dressing down," wear long trousers, shoes, and Seiko watches, and above all, refuse to step to the edge of the road when the estate manager rides by on his motorbike or in his car. The same lack of deference is shown toward the staff of the estate, with more immediate and discomforting consequences for the kinsmen who still reside and work on the estates.

The staff constitutes a middle category of estate employees who ingratiate themselves with the estate manager (or superintendent) while behaving with supreme arrogance toward the laborers. These are the mini–mimic men. They include office clerks, field supervisors, factory officers, the cooperative store clerks, and sometimes the truck drivers. Their intermediary position makes them acutely sensitive to the self-assuredness of the youth raised in the cities. The airs of these young people expose the vulnerability of their own position. Unable or afraid to take out their hostility on the visitor, members of the estates' staff make life extremely difficult for the parents, especially the mother of the young man. As a tea picker, the mother is the most vulnerable target of the field supervisors' vindictiveness. Her basket of tea may be underweighed; she may be falsely accused of wetting her load in the local waterfall; or she may be sent to pluck tea on a hill where the bushes are old and are known for their poor yield. The list of possible reprisals could easily be extended and, in practice, is.

The returnees see their parents, especially their fathers, as maṭṭa kampus, the eight-foot-long leveling sticks that are set upon the bushes before tea plucking. The contemptuous connotation is that their fathers are presumably so servile as to be willing even to lie flat on their backs if called upon to substitute for a leveling stick. Throughout their lives, the women are most often compared to the koṛuntu. If the koṛuntu of the peripheral branches ought not to be plucked, the koṛuntu of the central branches must be plucked when they are just right—no sooner, no later. To marry off a girl when she is too young is described as "plucking an arumpu." A virgin in her mid- to late teens is likened to a koṛuntu, ripe for plucking. A woman in her mid-twenties is compared to a kaṭṭai ilai, the third leaf, and an "old maid" is a karaṭṭai ilai, a mature and coarse leaf.

Communicative Event 4: Rage and Hope

A young girl who had departed in 1974 when she was twenty to work as a domestic servant in Colombo returned to the estate of her birth. She was welcomed back by her maternal uncle's wife with the words, "You left us as a koṛuntu and you come back as a kaṭṭai ilai."

Stung by this unkind remark, the girl's mother embarked upon a bitter tirade against the people and life on tea estates and proceeded to proclaim to all her plans for leaving the island for her husband's ancestral village in South India. In the following excerpt from her speech, I have attempted to provide a translation of one of the most eloquent orations of rage I have ever heard in the Tamil language. In addition to revealing the manner in which she summons agricultural and agronomic images to make her point, I have attempted to highlight, for the reader who does not know Tamil, her use of alliteration by providing, wherever possible, italicized Tamil equivalents within brackets. The Tamil original follows the translation.

> Damn the third leaf [*kaṭṭai ilaiyāvatu*] and damn the stemlets [*kāmpāvatu*]. Why don't you who are losing your luster [*mankal*; also means dimming wit] suck [*ūmpu* (obscene)] on the *vanki* stem [sterile and useless protrusion]? This sucking [*ūmpal*] and this hell [*ūṛal*] suits this land just fine. What business does a widow [*kompanaṭṭi*] have with a young virgin [*kumari*] and a tender sprout [*koṛuntu*]. Cursed saturnine coarse leaf [*karaṭṭai ilai*]! Perish here. Go on, eat in silence [also, in secret] kilo loads of squeezed rice from the Sinhala man's [*cinkaḷavan*] hand. The foreign land [*cīmai*] where we [*nāṅka*, first person exclusive plural] are bound for, there are none of these tea sprouts (looks at daughter while she says this) and kilos [*koṛuntāvatu kīlōvāvatu*]. [There], ears of rice [*katir*, also means ray of sun] and grain [*payir*] will pour [be measured out] in *palam*-loads [an Indian unit of measure]. You who weed five acres to earn five rupees in wages [*kūli*], how big you talk! In my grandfather's field of five *kōṭṭais*, for the barber who helps harvest the field for one day they pay him ten *paṭis*. . . . [As for you], you will climb the mountain [*malai*] and look for the level [*maṭṭam* also implies, "lying down like the leveling stick"], I shall be on the level [*maṭṭam*] and look at the mountain [*malai*]. Once I board that ship [*kappal*] I shall not even lift my eyes [*kaṇ*] to look back at these rowdy asses [*kāvāli kaṛutaikaḷ*] or this evil eye of a jungle [*kaṇtiṣṭi kāṭu*].

> *kattai ilaiyāvatu kāmpāvatu. ēn, manki pōra nī vanki koṛuntai ūmpēn. inta ūmpalum ūṛalum inta ūrukku tān cari. komariyōṭeyum koṛuntōṭeyum kompanāṭṭikku enna vēlai?*

cci cani karaṭṭa ilai! nī iṅka keṭa. cinkaḷavankaiyila pecanja cōtta pēcāma kilo kaṇakkā tinnu. nāṅka pōra cīmayila inta koruntum kīlovunkeṭaiyātu. katirum payirum palam palamā koṭṭum. anji rūvā kūlikku anji ēkkar kaḷai puṭunkira onakku enna pēccu. namma tattāṭā anji kōṭṭai vayalila nellarukkira ampaṭṭanukku oru nāḷukku pattu paṭi aḷappānka. nī malaiyila ēri maṭṭatta pāru. . . . nān maṭṭattilayiruntu malaiya pākkirēn. anta kappalila ērunatum inta kāvāḷi karutaikaḷayum kaṇtiṣṭi kāṭṭayum kaṇṇālakkūṭa tirumpikkūṭa pākkamāṭṭēn.

Apart from being impressed by this woman's remarkable ear for reverberating sounds and rhythms, phonemic metonymy, the analysis of which deserves an occasion all its own, I was also struck by the number of agricultural and agronomic images she drew upon. At one level her verbal outrage is directed at her adversary. But at another level it is directed at Sri Lanka in general, and at the agronomic culture of tea in particular. I wish to turn my attention mainly to the latter.

This woman (I shall call her Selvi), like thousands of other Tamils of recent Indian origin, was actively planning her departure to India. When the 1948 Citizenship Act was first passed, almost none of these Estate Tamils wished to return to India. India was, for most of them, as alien as Italy is to most Italian Americans. They knew India as their ancestral home, but they also knew it to be a land of great hardship, harsh climate, and chronic poverty. From the few who had been to village India they learned that even though their lot on the estates was a difficult one, it was luxury compared to life in an Indian village.

By the time the Sirimavo-Shastri Pact[28] had been signed, the Tamils of Sri Lanka had already been the victims of three anti-Tamil riots, and the Sri Lankan government's own attempts to repatriate a section of these Tamils had taken an earnest turn. Yet, year after year, the quota of repatriations was not met. Some who had emigrated to the districts of Ramnadhapuram and Tirunelveli in the late sixties and early seventies reimmigrated to Sri Lanka to escape the severe drought that was consuming southern India during those years. Many of these illicit immigrants, as they are called in Sri Lankan English, were caught while attempting to land on the northern shores of the island and were blackmailed into working for indigenous Tamil landowners as indentured agricultural laborers.

After the events of July 1983, the overwhelming majority of Estate Tamils, including many who had opted for Sri Lankan citizenship under the Sirimavo-Shastri Pact and had thereby given up all claims to Indian citizenship, were attempting to leave for India. For the first time that anyone could remember, India was on the receiving end of illicit immigrants. If we look at Selvi's harangue against this background, we see how she systematically invokes Sri Lankan tea estates' agronomic images in order to present, through them, an entirely tenebrous picture of Sri Lanka, a picture that the greater part of the Estate Tamil community has come to share.

Selvi finds everything about the tea bush damnable. A bush that these Tamils had treated as a deity had now become a vehicle by means of which she could express obscenities. The piece of protruding stem is no longer a test of her care and attention for the tea bush, a blemish that beckons her to trim it away with her knife. Instead, it has become a withered penis that only her worst and most contempt-worthy enemy would suck (ūmpal) on. Then again, by the metonymic juxtaposition of ūṛal (hell) with ūmpal, hell becomes not merely a place of suffering—which indeed Sri Lanka had become—but also one of obscene iniquity. She opens her tirade with the disparaging metaphor that her sister-in-law had used on her daughter. She then follows it with a series of pejoratives such as kampu (plucked pieces of stem) and vanki koṛuntu (unplucked, but protruding pieces of stem). All three are, agronomically speaking, of the same order of undesirables. But she has yoked the last in that series with connotations of obscene immorality on the part of her adversary. In a quick, cutting sentence Selvi reminds her that a widow like her could not possibly know anything about a kumari (young virgin, like her daughter) or its metaphor, koṛuntu, and in so doing indirectly restores her daughter to the status of a koṛuntu. Having done this, she reduces her sister-in-law to *the most* undesirable find in a tea plucker's basket of tea leaves, a karaṭṭai ilai (a coarse, old leaf). Then she moves on to terminology of measures.

Selvi identifies her sister-in-law's state of being condemned to remain in a hell of an island as being condemned to eat kilo-loads of cooked rice, or, more exactly, leavings, from the Sinhala man's hand. The word "kilo" comes to bear connotations of servility, bondage, even immoral concubinage. Before she contrasts this with a positively valued unit of measure found in village India, she interjects a transitional sentence in which she identifies koṛuntu, that most precious product of the tea estate, with the contemptible kilo. In looking (not very happily) at her daughter when she says "koṛuntu" and following it up with the next sentence, in which she speaks of bountiful katir in India, she is indicating that India, unlike Sri Lanka, will give her not daughters (even if they were koṛuntu) but sons. (Her son's name is Kadiresan.)

Selvi refers to India as cīmai. Cīmai has undergone a double-inversion. It is a Tamil word originally used to mean something like homeland, or the place of birth to which one periodically returns. This usage is still prevalent in South India. Once domiciled in Sri Lanka's estate country, the word came to apply meaningfully and conspicuously only to the British superintendents, who were, after all, the only ones who could afford to and did return to their homeland, to spend their furlough there. Despite inconspicuous exceptions, the tea estate laborers were largely confined—first economically and, subsequently, emotionally—to the estates. Thus cīmai came to mean England. Now, in Selvi's vocabulary, the word had taken another turn, spiraling up to a new point in its evolution. She calls India cīmai. By identifying India with England, she is identifying India with England's presumed prosperity. In that land, rice and grain will be measured not in kilos but in palams. Quite clearly, a palam, as far as Selvi is concerned, is a unit of measure found in India and, therefore, a generous one. By contrasting this measure with the kilo of the preceding sentence, she clearly wishes to set this presumed contrast in clear relief. In fact, a palam as a unit of measure is a mere idea, a trace of a tradition, and one that has no practical usage among the Tamils of Sri Lanka. Furthermore, it is, ironically, quite small. More agronomic and agricultural terminology follows. The miserly wages her sister-in-law earns are described as kūli, which also refers to a person of servile status (hence the word "coolie," now naturalized into English).[29] Furthermore, she earns these wages by doing one of the lowliest of jobs on the estate, weeding. Even the barber in India does more honorable work, the harvesting of sun-warmed sheaves of rice. Selvi's adversary weeds acres. The barber in India who works in her grandfather's fields works in kōṭṭais, which is not strictly a measure of area, but of yield of grain (8 *paṭi* = 1 *marakkāl*; 12 *marakkāl* = 1 *kaḷam*; 7/8 *kaḷam* = 1 *kōṭṭai*). It also means "fortress." And the barber is not paid in humiliating kūli, but in patis of grain, the payment in village India that signifies a traditional bond between landlord and field hand.

Then comes the comparison of the terrain: the flat desirable plains of village India against the arduous mountains of Sri Lanka's tea estates. In India, the mountain is only something to look at and enjoy (or perhaps gloat over, in that one does not have to work on it). In Sri Lanka, one labors on the mountains and looks down enviously upon the plains. The sentence also implies that one must prostrate oneself flat on one's back or belly, like a leveling stick, in the most abject servility, if and when management calls upon one to do so. And the final contrast is between India, the *ūr* (home, the civilized village to which one belongs; see Daniel 1984: chap. 2), and Sri Lanka, the *kāṭu*, or jungle, which is inhabited by wild animals and is an immense evil eye.

To say that words change their meaning is to utter a cliché. These transformations are not passive records of history but active embodiments of the genealogy of power relations. The evolution of these terms (even if only by chance, as Foucault would have us see matters) illustrates their embodiment in semeiosic practice in space and time as they came to be articulated as a "metonymical concatenation of deviation from the norm [while concurrently engaging in] a progressive creation of metaphors" (Kristeva 1980:40).

Word has come back that India is not the utopia it was imagined to be. Some have described it as a worse hell than Sri Lanka. Repatriates, the quaint term for those who return and are returned, are swindled and cheated from the time they first disembark from the boat until they reached their "remembered" villages. Many repatriates are destitute. Some have become beggars in the streets of Madurai, Madras, and other cities and towns in South India; some women have turned to prostitution. The minister and labor union leader Thondaman, who was sung of as a villain by the poet in 1983, has survived radical changes in the governing party, played his cards deftly, won pay increases and citizenship for his people, and thereby regained considerable support from them. The view of him as traitor is retained only by a recalcitrant minority. But the poet thinks that something has changed: "The old days are gone. They say the tea bush lives only 120 years. Eighteen sixty-seven to 1967. It's over. We may stay, we may leave. But we won't be tea estate workers for much longer. There is the factory (pointing at the tea factory). Here is the fire (pointing at his chest). Bring the two together. Finished!"

Conclusion

The history of South Indian Tamil workers who migrated to Ceylon (later Sri Lanka) is one of confinement and limitations upon choices. In recent years, under the forces of anti-Tamil ethnic violence, Estate Tamils have been moved to make choices, and in the mid-1980s many of them were choosing to recover, in reality and in their imaginations, what they had lost in their ancestral village-India. An agronomy that had relentlessly imposed limitations upon the variability of the natural environment had also, through its colonial agents, attempted to impose limitations on the variability of the cultural environment—sometimes by force, but more often by consent, subtle and complex—by making available a vocabulary that marked the boundaries of permissible discourse. What may have at first appeared as mere terms, convenient, universal, and neutral in value, turned out to be the very signs that contained and carried forth the hegemony of agronomy and its capitalist concomitants through time as signs in and of history. These terms had become metaphor, metonym, and synecdoche, in Hayden White's sense, of these workers' very existence (1973:31–33).

Consent, so central to Gramsci's understanding of hegemony, is not a simple mental state. Rather, it entails a contradictory consciousness in the subaltern, "mixing approbation and apathy, resistance and resignation" (Lears 1985:568; also see Gramsci 1971:326–327, 333). Counterhegemonic forces find their impulsion in a variety of semeiosic pools. In the case of these estate workers, a recovered past of an agricultural world of approximations provides one such pool.

It is commonplace to note that a past thus recovered is inextricably linked to the present. But such a past cannot and must not be understood in purely temporal terms. Rather, what I wish to mean by past and present is more akin to Walter Benjamin's pairing of the "past" and the "now" in the image.

> It isn't that the past casts its light on the present or the present casts its light on the past; rather, an image is that in which the past and the now flash into a constellation. In other words, image is dialectics at a standstill. For while the relation of the

> present to the past is a purely temporal, continuous one, the relation of the Then to the Now is dialectical—isn't development but image [,] capable of leaping out (*sprunghaft*). Only dialectical images are genuine (i.e., not archaic images); and the place one encounters them is language. (1983–1984:14)

To call these recoveries signs is also to ask what manner of signs they are. They clearly signify many things, some of which, already considered in the body of this chapter, do not need to be recounted. But it is worth considering the manner of their signification, their mode and mood. For this let us briefly return to Peirce, who describes several trichotomous, hierarchically ordered sign-types, including triads of interpretants. By "interpretant" he meant the significant effect of signs upon a third or, more simply, the means by which interpretation is effected. In one of the trichotomies Peirce mentions the production of three hierarchically nested effects: gratification, action, and self-control. He also called these, respectively, the emotional interpretant, the energetic interpretant, and the logical interpretant. As in all genuine hierarchies, each subsequent kind of interpretant subsumes the former, but not vice versa. Thus logical interpretants contain impulses of (physical or mental) effort and emotions; energetic interpretants, nonconceptual effort and emotions; and emotional interpretants, only a welling of feelings before action or thought takes form.[30]

Had Antonio Gramsci had access to Peirce's arcane vocabulary and chosen to use it, he might well have characterized hegemony as actions constituted by logical interpretants, those that contain—in both senses of the term—energetic and emotional interpretants. When Peirce wrote of logical interpretants, he had in mind a world constituted by the repose of habit. Of course, Peirce, the ever-sanguine utopian, attributed to humans the habit of "taking and laying aside habits" (6.101), the "self-analyzing habit" (5.491), or the "habit of self-control" (MS 612,7).[31] In the world of logical interpretants, reason is expected to exert its "gentle force" of reasonableness. There are, of course, lower-order habits, wherein matter is not something apart from mind but is merely "mind whose habits have become fixed so as to lose the power of forming them and losing them" (6.101). Here we have self-control without agency, as it were. In a hegemonic regime à la Gramsci, this lower order of habits constitutes the logical interpretants of the sociocultural domain or a significant part thereof.

In the communicative events considered, we see a deconstruction of the hierarchic encompassment of persuasive reason. In a hegemonic universe, not only do logical interpretants form an intricately linked script that spreads its mantle over underlying layers of emotional and energetic interpretants, concealing and calming them; logical interpretants are also inscribed in the other interpretants in minuscule, though inconspicuously. The conch that sounds for muster sounds for prayer too. In the communicative events we have considered, logical interpretants are dismantled to expose and make viable underlying emotional and energetic interpretants. Words and acts linked together in imperceptible minuscules are disarticulated, thrown asunder, scattered about, and transformed into conspicuously quaint—if not monstrous—majuscules.

In language, metaphors and poetry are privileged repositories of emotional interpretants. Peirce also names gratification and recognition as principal attributes of emotional interpretants. Gratification, though, must be seen not only as the fulfillment of desire, but also, perhaps more important, as the acute realization of its nonfulfillment, as the realization of what deprivation really is. In recent years, thanks to the dismantling of the hegemony of logical interpretants, the Tamils of Sri Lanka's estates have awakened in the grip of such a realization. Recognition is, in Peirce's scheme, an iconic function: literally, cognizing again. As already indicated, an icon is a sign that resembles its object. The recovery of resemblances, then, is at the heart of recognition. But re-cognizing is not only cognizing something that *was* but something that *might be* as well. Such recognitions invoke a past as much as they chart out a future, a future that could subvert and avoid familiar hegemonies. Whether the past in question is real or imagined is of only philosophical interest. Suffice it to note that the objects of iconic signs may be real existents or only imaginary entities. Wherein lies the power of emotional interpretants? Wherein the power to transform?

The word "emotion" brings to mind a welling of feeling, an overflowing of affect. This is certainly true of the communicative events we have considered. Emotional interpretants find their sources in re-cognitions as well as re-memberings, both of which are iconic functions. But the iconic bases of these emotional interpretants provide another insight into the source of their power. As Peirce observed, iconic signs are also diagrammatic. And diagrams select features for representation, disregarding the rest. Mathematical equations are among the most powerful icons. In their very leanness they reveal connections in the object they represent that, without these icons, would have lain concealed in the amplitude of the object. Likewise, the most effective metaphors are lean and can be mean. Metaphors wrench words from their context. But if they destroy, they also reveal. "Fourth leaf!" Mimicry, another iconic function, can turn into mockery, mockery to the undermining of hegemonic conceit. "Dompiling." Metaphors and mimicry employ the iconic function only to index, to point, to throw into clear relief.

The laying bare of energetic interpretants likewise results from the dismantling of the hegemonic dominance of logical interpretants, the world of habit. Uncontained (by logical interpretants) and driven by emotional interpretants they contain, energetic interpretants lead to spontaneous action. Ungoverned by the courtesies of rule-governed behavior, energetic interpretants explode.

Their meanings are precipitated, not before, not after, but *in the act*: "The Perumal cut."

I have not presented these communicative events merely for linguistic show-and-tell or to display the poetic genius of a people. I have presented them as instances of indigenous interpretations, the writing of effective history. I have attempted to capture such interpretation, such writing, in the act. Bearing this in mind, I would like to end where I began, quoting Foucault:

> If interpretation is the violent or surreptitious appropriation of a system of rules . . . in order to impose direction, to bend it to a new will, to force its participation in a different game, and to subject it to secondary rules, then the development of humanity is a series of interpretations. The role of genealogy is to record its [effective] history, [the history of the event]. [By "event" is meant] the reversal of a relationship of forces, the usurpation of power, [and] the appropriation of a vocabulary turned against those who had once used it. (1984:88)

4

MOOD, MOMENT, AND MIND

The future, which [the mind] expects, passes through the present, to which it attends, into the past which it remembers.
(Paul Ricoeur)

The future is available in the present through a feeling of "struggle over what shall be" [Peirce 5.462]. The present is thus the "Nascent State of the Actual" [Peirce 5.462]; that is, the locus where reality becomes actualized and moves towards the determined status of the past.
(Robert S. Corrington)

THIS middle chapter is also a transitional one in that I attempt to make explicit the effort that has in the previous three been implicit: the effort of writing about violence. To mark this transition, I would like to begin by posing the tacit question in the manner of an open query. To what shall I compare the writing of this book? I shall compare it to the lowering of a tetrahedron[1] held by a string attached to its base into a liquid so that the point of the inverted pyramid, where the planes of three triangles meet, enters the liquid first. Alas, an individual "point" of contact is only an illusion. From its very first moment of contact, it is a contact with three sides, each side with three triangular planes. The three corners of the first of these planes are writing, violence, and time; of the second, representation, object, and interpretant; of the third, mood, moment, and mind.

Mood, moment, and mind—the theme of this chapter—are intended to correspond to Peirce's phenomenological triad of Firstness, Secondness, and Thirdness, respectively, a triad that was briefly explicated in the previous chapter. Firstness is the phenomenological category of the possible; Secondness, as you may recall, is the category of actual instantiations of certain possibilities; and Thirdness is the tendency of the universe—including humankind—to adopt and adapt to an evolving "lawfulness" among human beings and between humans and their environment. There is, of course, nothing that is a pure First, a pure Second, or a pure Third, but in certain experiences one category or another might predominate. In considering mood as a relative First, then, I think of its connotations of a state of feeling—usually vague, diffuse, and enduring, a disposition toward the world at any particular time yet with a timeless quality to it. Some of the connotations I wish to associate with "moment" may be drawn from the *Oxford English Dictionary*: a small particle, a moment of time too brief for its duration to be taken into account [I see taking into account as an act that gives meaning to something that lacks meaning], a momentary conjunction of events that afford an opportunity [for change], a determining argument, the smallest detail, and a turning point in a course or event. The "moment," like the category of Secondness under which I have presented it, entails a sense of a unique fact or event, a here-and-nowness, a selective narrowing of possibilities to just one actuality. Reported facts of violence—especially when the informant relives the experience during the telling—are momentous in this sense, with the then-and-there being radically transformed into the here-and-now. "Mind" I bring under the covering category of Thirdness: the tendency to generalize, to reason, to take habit. If a moment, an event, a violent act, say, is a given—to the eye or the ear—it is also a taken. Taking is a mindful act, a phenomenon of Thirdness. But every "taking" of a perceptual fact (a Second) is dependent on its abduction from an indeterminate continuum that arises in humans interacting among themselves and with their environment, providing a "primitive epistemological [and ontological] feel of continuity [that is experienced] as a duration [in contrast to a momentary] present" (Rosenthal 1994:60). This "feel of continuity" experienced as a durational present is a mood, a relative Firstness. To name a mood is to be too specific, to convert a First into a Third. In the case of Sri Lanka, this mood—a primitive feel of continuity—hangs over like a fog of which neither the beginning nor the end can be fathomed. This gray mood has tarried longest with its brooding over the Estate Tamils. How does an anthropographer represent this mood?

The Challenge: Representing the Mood, Moment, and Mind in Violence

More than ten years have gone by since the responsibility of writing an anthropography of violence pierced, like a shriek in the dark, my world of other preoccupations. I distinctly remember the moment of my commission. A daughter who had witnessed her father's murdered body being dragged away by the army Jeep to which it was tied said at one point in her interview with me, "You, a man who has seen the world, please take this story and tell the world of what they did to my father, how they treated him." And at another point, in the same interview, she pleaded: "Please don't tell anyone else this story. My father is such a dignified man. He never comes to dinner without bathing and without wearing a clean white shirt. I don't want anyone to remember him the way I see him, with his clothes torn off his body." Two aspects of this woman's statements are significant to this chapter. The first I shall only mention now and return to later. This concerns her constant and easy drift back into the present or the present continuous while speaking of an event that happened in the past. The second has two parts. One is her construction of me as a "man who has seen the world," presumably a world where the difference between good and evil still holds, but also a world that needs to be told and must not be allowed to forget. The other concerns the ambivalence of her charge to me, to tell and yet not to tell. This same ambivalence was to be expressed by other survivors and witnesses at other moments, in other ways, and for other reasons. Over these twelve years this charge has been further compounded; the task has become one of not only deciding what story to tell and what not to tell, but how to and how not to tell a story. How to tell the truth? With Lacan, I am obliged to say that "I always speak the truth. Not the whole truth, because there is no way to say it all. Saying the whole truth is materially impossible: words fail. Yet it's through this very impossibility that the truth holds onto the real"[2] (1990:3).

Only the extraordinarily gifted or the excessively unmindful (mindless?) can write a book on violence without being troubled by the particular challenge the representational form of writing poses for the task at hand, even if this task be described in the words of my pleading informant, as "a story." Unlike the preceding chapters wherein the problem of writing about violence was, without much ado, relegated to the implicit, in the chapters that follow violence and its representation in language demand explicit acknowledgment. Poets, novelists, and literarily talented writers in general have the privilege of not having to account for why and how they choose to represent their subject in the written form. They, as the cliché goes, "just do it." It is left to the literary critic or reader to determine how well it has been done. For very different reasons, for most social scientists—including, until recently, anthropologists—"writing" was something that we did not have to wrestle with; or if we did, we could not, in deference to protocol and good taste, openly discuss it. In its most "scientistic" form, writing was seen as a medium that, when judiciously employed, provided transparency between writer/reader and reality. To that extent, if there was a problem in writing, it was perceived as being limited to the finding of an objective, neutral vocabulary and analytic framework. More recently, anthropologists have come to acknowledge the fact that ethnography is, among other things, also a literary form. To say that it is a literary form is to admit not only to its aesthetic and rhetorical liabilities but to its political ones as well.[3]

There may come a day when the admission of ethnography's inherent literary burden, and by extension its rhetorical and political ones, will be so commonplace as to warrant neither special comment nor special pleading. That day is not here as yet. Should we, until such a day, belabor the point of such an admission at every possible occasion of writing an ethnography or an anthropography? Heaven forbid! But there are times when and reasons why such a belaboring may be warranted. Writing about violence is such a time, and theorizing about modes of writing provides such a reason. As indicated in the introduction, this book concerns writing about violence as much as it concerns violence itself. I hope the first three chapters have borne this out and the last three will even further. As far as theorizing about writing goes, anthropologists have yet to say much. At the end of this chapter, I shall suggest in prolegomena fashion—and no more—theoretical directions with respect to writing that are worthy of our contemplation. I shall conclude by admitting to a mode of writing as well as a theory of (re)presentation toward which the subject matter of this book, especially as my writing of it progressed, has made me increasingly partial. As I hope to make clear, this partiality has been prompted by the perdurance of the presence (the fact or condition of being present) of violence in the lives of a people among whom I have lived and learned over a great part of my life: Sri Lankans generally, but Estate Tamils in particular.

The Presence of Violence

Greater than the challenge that violence in general poses to writing is the one posed by the presence of violence. My task would have been easier had the violence been a thing of the past, a done deed, or if the future and its hopes, in being attended upon by the present, had better survived the latter's relentless and deforming scourge. Relatively independent of the present, the past and the future[4] are easier to fathom because they can be conceptually seized and positioned for a still-life representation, a representation hovered over by the protective shadow of a coherent narrative. The Sri Lankan experience is overburdened with the present, a present "under (traumatic) erasure," besmudged before the ink on the page is dry. The anthropography at hand is both present-driven and present-stifled. Where the present dominates, the future and the past, because they have to pass through the present, are shaken even as they partake of the present's impermanence. Friends whom one considered to be unshakably like-minded change their opinions on vital matters. Today's good cause turns out to be tomorrow's evil. Yesterday's liberators become today's torturers. Last month's confidants become next month's informers. This week's promise becomes next week's betrayal. There are shifts in the other direction as well: from worse to better. Bigots turn into ardent nondiscriminators, murderers into penitent helpers, avengers into *satyagrahis* (nonviolent activists), hatemongers into compassionate human beings, raving extremists into rational mediators, chauvinists into humanists. Social scientists want the world to hold still or, better yet, to follow the course of their predictions. The world moves on regardless. The Buddhist doctrine of *anicca* (the doctrine of the impermanence of all being) holds.

When the present looms large in this manner, both memory and hope become either emaciated or bloated. In either case, it is the present that determines the past, making the past a mere simulacrum of the present.[5] The future, thanks to the capriciousness of the present, is uncertain and bleak. Neither the vision of a united Sri Lanka nor that of a separate Tamil Eeḷam is clearly defined. In 1990, I spoke with Kamalam in a refugee camp in India. Having lost her son in an army raid five years earlier, and having lost every last photograph of him with her house—it went up in flames when a helicopter gunship dropped a gasoline bomb on it—she confessed that she could no longer remember what her son's face looked like. His features had become vague and confused. She remembered his gait, his school uniform, even his bicycle, but she could not recall his face. All the albums containing his photograph had been burned with the house. This did not prevent her from seeing her son in the face of every young man who came to the camp. Some of them were pacifists, some were seasoned fighters, some were terrorists, some were politicians, some were entrepreneurs, and some were just boys. But traces of her son's face appeared and disappeared in all of them. The more they ruffled the clarity of her memory, the more she longed to be able to see her son again, clearly; but the ever-changing faces of the present got in the way of her enframing the face of her son, in memory or in expectation. In my interview with her in her refugee camp at Mandapam she complained of her eyesight, blaming it for her inability to recall her son's face clearly. Instead of projecting her loss onto her missing son, she introjected the loss of her son to the loss of eyesight. She had just turned thirty-five. As for why her eyes had dimmed, she blamed the sea by which she sat from sunrise to sundown. I asked her why she stared at the sea. She said that at first she did so because she had been told that Jaffna was only twenty miles away and that on a clear day she might be able to see it. When some of her fellow refugees found out what she was doing, they disabused her of that hope. Some other refugees reminded her that even if she could see the shores of Jaffna, her home was not in Jaffna but in Vavuniya, which was farther south. This had reminded her that her home was not even in Vavuniya, for she was born in the hills of the tea country, in the south-central highlands of Sri Lanka.

> May the woman who tells me that I could see Jaffna perish. May those who tell me that I cannot see Jaffna perish. Let them make fun of me. "You are not from Jaffna," they tell me. "You are from Vavuniya." I tell them, "Look here, I am not even from Vavuniya but one who was born on the tea estates." The biggest mistake my father made was to take us to Vavuniya. "Yes," I say, "I am a *tōṭṭakkāṭān*."[6] "She is an Indian Tamil!" they say; as if they have seen a ghost. "But the camp authorities think she is Sri Lankan," says one of these kaṅkāṇis.[7] "Look here," I say, "you are here in Mandapam. This is the same camp from which *my* ancestors left for the tea estates one hundred years ago." He shut his mouth.

And thus she presents the past. She is angry and stares even more determinedly, expecting the tall mountains of the tea country to make their appearance over the horizon and vindicate her anger. She says that of course, she knows that that is not going to happen. "But anger does strange things to your mind. I know that the distance is too far and what is gone is gone, but I don't have to think," she says. Occasionally a wave from the distant past rolls toward her. But most of the time she lives thinking, "What happened, what will happen, who knows." Then she poignantly adds, "I don't say, 'Tomorrow my son might come.' I say, 'Here he comes. Here I see his face.' That is the way I see. That is how my life is."

The vision of and for the future of the nation has undergone a fate similar to this mother's vision of her son's face. Prior to 1983, and even immediately after that summer, both separatists and nonseparatists were able to define the contours of their future nation, as they saw it, with clarity. It is not so today. The moment a glimmer of a clear outline begins to take form, the present, with a bomb, a betrayal, an ambush, or an assassination, shatters the outline and scatters the bits of the nascent image. Scholars gather in person or in their writings, sometimes pooling their thoughts in conferences or edited volumes, attempting to rechart their own visions for the future. It all seems contrived and even hopeless. Only the naive and the innocent pose the straightforward question: "What is the solution?" An embarrassed hush falls upon a room filled with the seasoned, to be broken, after a trying pause, by someone who is willing to offer a polite, even if painfully inadequate, response. There are no clear answers, no clear visions. Bold visions like those of Vijay Kumaratunga and Rajani Thiranagama are few.[8] This lack, however, we are not supposed to admit, and certainly not as social scientists. It is our calling to offer answers, to offer hope, to make the present submit to a (better) future, even if this endeavor calls for a radical remaking of the past.

The Presence of the Past: The Case of the Estate Tamils

That the present bears heavily upon all Sri Lankans today is a truism; and the frantic effort to recover the past either as heritage or as history, by Tamils and by Sinhalas, is but a symptom of the overwhelming presence of the present in their lives. But whereas most Sri Lankans experience the present acutely, the experience of the heaviness of the present by Estate Tamils may be best described as an enduring condition. "How can we think of the future when we don't even know who we are or where we will be tomorrow?" asks a plantation worker, pondering his situation. "We have known nothing different," remarks another. Not only has the existence of these workers been a hand-to-mouth one but their citizenship in a world of nation-states has been equally uncertain. Sri Lankans call them Indians and Indians call them Sri Lankans. "Aliens" in Sri Lanka, they are unwelcome in India. Bilaterally agreed-upon repatriation schemes notwithstanding, on the Indian side those who have been repatriated, and who thought they were "returning to their motherland," are called—much to the displeasure of the repatriates—"refugees." They wish to be called *thāyagam thriumbinōr* (the ones who have returned to their motherland). Most repatriates, especially those who are middle-aged and older, would like to keep the distinction clear because, among many other reasons, they resent being identified with the very group that had held them in such contempt for so long during their sojourn in Sri Lanka, the Jaffna Tamils, who are today the true seekers of refuge in India and elsewhere. Impelled by a certain vindictiveness, they feel that it is time for Jaffna Tamils to be held in contempt for a change, a contempt from which they would for once be excluded. It has not turned out that way, however. The Tamils of South India—those who never left their motherland—call them Sri Lankans and, by extension, refugees.

While the quasi-theoretical focus of this chapter is on representation in writing, the ethnographic focus is on a group of Estate Tamils who were repatriated to India from 1960 onward. Being unwelcome in their ancestral villages is but one fate among several—mostly dismal ones—that may await Selvi, our woman of hope and rage of the previous chapter, and others who have begun to leave the island of their birth. In working with these and other groups of persons displaced from the plantations, one is struck by the burgeoning of the present in their lives. To be sure, neither past nor future is completely extinguished, but they often do appear to be. The group of repatriates of whom I have chosen to write in this chapter are paradigmatic of the burgeoning present that I have just mentioned. The quality of their life seems nothing but an assemblage of instances, disruption their source of possibility, interruption their only reverie, shock their only trance, surprise the basis for their openness to the world, the recalcitrant other the only route to their inner selves, chaos their only community, brute force the main impress of power, action the only manifestation of their feelings, doubt the mark of their innocence, contiguity the ground of their freedom, the timbre of tokens the tone of their lives, suspicion their principal trope, and the moment the determinant of their mood.

In an earlier chapter we came across, in the form of composite oral histories, the deep grievance that Estate Tamils bore against the Sinhala majority and a deeper one against the fully enfranchised northern and eastern "Jaffna" Tamils. The power over their lives seemed to rest in the hands of others: their supervisors, their (mainly) European overlords, the Sinhalas or the Jaffna Tamils, and now the Tamils of southern India. No wonder, then, that their lives are torqued by distrust.

The story of the present chapter begins in 1949–1950, when by two consecutive acts of Parliament—recounted in chapters 1 and 3—a majority of the Estate Tamils (estimated at nearly a million persons) are disenfranchised and made stateless.[9] The Estate Tamil leadership in the late forties and early fifties is made up of two trade unions, the Ceylon Workers' Congress (CWC) and the Democratic Workers' Congress (DWC), and is caught by surprise, without a plan. The government decrees that anyone wishing to lay claim to Ceylonese citizenship has to formally apply to the assigned government agency, which would then determine whether or not the applicant qualifies for citizenship. The criteria for qualification are so stringent as to lead one parliamentarian, Mr. Pieter Keuneman, to observe that "even Dudley Senanayake, who was later to become the prime minister of Ceylon, could not comply with the clauses [of the Citizenship Acts of 1948 and 1949] because according to his own admission in the House of Representatives he could not trace his father's birth certificate" (Devaraj 1985:212). Pieter Keuneman's position is no different from Dudley Senanayake's because the practice of registering births was not current when his father was born.

Ninety-five percent of the vulnerable are plantation workers. The leaders of the trade unions to which these workers belong issue conflicting instructions to members. At first they are instructed not to apply for citizenship so as to collectively undermine the moral, if not the legal, basis of the new decree. Those Sri Lankans of recent Indian origin who are not estate workers, but who belong to a largely successful mercantile class located in the major cities, go ahead and apply for citizenship. Where birth certificates of fathers and grandfathers are unavailable—and this is generally the case—sworn affidavits from leading bona fide citizens and (noncitizen!) Britons, stragglers of the departing empire, are accepted by the appropriately empowered magistrates. Some of Colombo's leading merchants of Indian descent—mainly Borahs and Parsis, but also a few Tamils—whose abiding interests are not in Ceylon but in India, enlist the very same politicians who help pass the Citizenship Act of 1949 in vouching for their qualifying pedigree. Many of the schoolteachers and white-collar workers on the plantations also submit their applications; so do several leaders of the trade unions, even if secretly. Word gets out, and at the eleventh hour instructions spread through rumor and word of mouth that all should apply, only to be contradicted by other rumors that the latest rumor was just that, a rumor. In the confusion, a few more apply for citizenship but most do not. Even among those plantation workers who do request the appropriate application forms, most report that they either never received any or received them after the application deadline had passed. Those who fail to receive the requested forms suspect sabotage by the postal service. Some claim that the highest authorities of government ordered postmasters to delay or entirely refrain from delivering envelopes originating from the government department in question, while others maintain that postmasters made such decisions on their own. Most postmasters who work in the small hill-country towns near the tea estates are Jaffna Tamils, as are a high proportion of all civil servants of the period. This fact makes the charge against postmasters part of a broader suspicion directed against Jaffna Tamils who, it is believed, are against the enfranchisement of Tamils of recent Indian origin. Those estates that happen to fall within the distributive area of post offices manned by Sinhala postmasters, it is claimed, have received their applications without delay or loss. (I had neither the time nor the resources to verify such charges and claims, except to note a pattern in which when and wherever a Sinhala was pitted against a Jaffna Tamil vis-à-vis the interests of the Estate Tamils, justifiably or not, the Sinhala came out the nobler—if more naive—of the two in the opinion of Estate Tamils.)

Mr. Sivaprahasam, a Jaffna Tamil, who had served both as a postal clerk between 1949 and 1953 in one of the post offices of these hill-country towns and, later, as a clerk in a tea estate office, remembers this period somewhat differently. He does not recall any screening of or tampering with mail destined for the tea estates. "The fact is," said Mr. Sivaprahasam,

> very few estate laborers received any mail. They were illiterate. Their relatives in India were illiterate. The only thing they received were wedding cards. These they did not have to read. It was news they already knew, before the cards came. News traveled through messengers. The kaṅkāṇis and a few laborers with money used to come to the post office to send money orders to their relatives in India. That was the only business they ever had with the post office, other than mailing marriage announcements.

In his account, Mr. Sivaprahasam believes that most instances of letters lost, misdirected, or delayed were the result of petty acts of power exercised by the estate office clerks and other white-collar workers on plantations—the literate few, over the mass of laborers, the illiterate many. The laborers depended on those who could read and write well enough to request, receive, and recognize application forms, inform the addressees of their arrival, fill them out, and send them back to the appropriate address. Such favors were rarely done for money in those days, but payment was extracted in the form of labor, loyalty, and acknowledgment of one's lowliness. Who were these empowered literates? Mostly educated Tamils and Malayalees from India, followed by Jaffna Tamils, and a scattering of Sinhalas and Muslims. Many were the laborers who were either incapable or deemed incapable of providing this kind of payment and had their forms sabotaged. In most of their cases their attempt to obtain Sri Lankan citizenship never went beyond the first step of merely having obtained the application forms. Once again, there is no way of verifying Mr. Sivaprahasam's account, but there is reason to believe that there was some truth to it.

Mr. Thomas, a Syrian Christian from Kerala, himself a retired clerk of a tea estate, begs to differ with Mr. Sivaprahasam on several points. His reading of estate intrigue, though at odds with Mr. Sivaprahasam's, is equally insightful:

> Two things were not possible [on plantations]. First, it was not possible to refuse outright, to say no, I cannot, I will not help you by filling out those forms. Because

the laborer can always go to someone [else]. And when that happens? Yes. You will lose respect. You lose authority. Someone else has authority over him, not you. Of course if he is a lazy and useless blackguard, you can tell him to go fishing. But in that case he is the type that everyone he goes to for help will say the same thing. So no loss for you. No loss for anybody. But otherwise we oblige. Any clerk or conductor or tea maker, when asked, helped. Now, sabotaging the forms, misfiling the forms, et cetera, is also not possible. That is too risky. Every clerk watches what the other clerk is doing. If anything is wrong, he will not report it right away. He will save it up and use it at the right time. Because Tamils, all Tamils, especially laborers, never trust. Do you know of a Tamil who asks how to go to someplace from one man only, and believes only that man's advice? No. He will ask again and again, from many people, many times. My own father—he did not know to read or write English very well—used to have me fill out some form or write some letter for him. Then he would slowly take it to my brother, to have him check it to see if it was all right, then to next-door person, to the tea maker, to the schoolteacher. By the time he finished, the whole estate knew everything in his letter. He never trusted one person. Not even his son. So no sabotager of forms could have escaped. Unless several people got together in a plan. But Estate Tamils, unlike Jaffna Tamils, were very bad [at] conspiracy. Secrets are like cash. They don't know how to invest. They only know to spend. That was true then. It is true now. That is why the Jaffna Tamil succeeded in those days, and that is the secret for the Tigers' success today.

While these accounts differ as to what might have taken place in the early part of the 1950s and why, we get a general picture of a climate of suspicion, duplicity, and circumstances in which the illiterate among the plantations' workers feel vulnerable. The net effect on their aspirations for citizenship is disastrous. Most plantation workers are condemned to statelessness. The two estate workers' trade unions subsequently do get their act together and make citizenship for its workers a plank in their platforms. But on the whole these trade unions have little effect on the policies of the government, and they lack the will and the means to bring the appropriate pressure to bear on the tea industry, given the island's dependence on it, so as to push through their wishes on the citizenship question.

There are many other incidents that occasion distrust between the two Tamil groups, but the singularly poignant one occurs when Mr. G. G. Ponnambalam condones the Citizenship Act by accepting a ministry in the United National Party government that has just succeeded in disenfranchising a million Tamil plantation workers. Mr. G. G. Ponnambalam is a Jaffna Tamil, a gifted lawyer and orator, and the founder and head of the Tamil Congress, a party that was formed in 1944, in response to the early signs of Sinhala-Buddhist hegemony. Estate Tamils see G. G. not only as an opportunist who sold the Tamil side for a mess of political pottage but also as the forensic mind behind the two infamous parliamentary acts that rendered these Tamils voteless and stateless. However, this moment of betrayal and rift between the two Tamil groups also yields an opportunity for trust and unity in the figure of another Jaffna Tamil lawyer-politician who soon displaces G. G. from his position of leadership of the Tamils of Ceylon. This is Mr. S.J.V. Chelvanayakam, who becomes the leader of the Federal Party, the party that breaks away from the Tamil Congress in 1949. The fact that G. G. is a Hindu and Mr. Chelvanayakam a Christian does not matter one bit to the Tamil electorates of the north and east. Mr. Chelvanayakam's slow and deliberate speech stands in stark contrast to the specious fluency of G. G. and comes to stand for the contrast between a principled man and an opportunist. One of the reasons for his split with G. G. is the latter's betrayal of the Tamils of the plantations. Most Estate Tamils only vaguely appreciate the stand the Federal Party has taken on their behalf. Rather, the only message of the Federal Party that reaches them loud and clear is its demand for a federated state wherein the predominantly Tamil provinces of the north and the east (not the central highlands where the Estate Tamils live) would be guaranteed a modicum of autonomy and protection from Sinhala-Buddhist majoritarianism. The Estate Tamils, situated as they are in the middle of Sinhala country and with neither vote nor citizenship, see little of interest for them in this prominent item of the Federal Party's platform. They are preoccupied with the politics of the two trade unions, the CWC and the DWC, the one led by a Hindu, Mr. S. Thondaman, and the other by a Muslim, Mr. Aziz. Here again it is noteworthy that religion does not matter at all. (Those were the days.) Ironically, seven years later, when the very article in the Federal Party's platform that contains the potential for the restoration of trust and unity between the two Tamil groups was brought to the Estate Tamils' attention, that potential was shattered in an apparent act of betrayal. This time the betrayal centers on the Bandaranaike-Chelvanayakam Pact of 1957. A year earlier, Mr. S.W.R.D. Bandaranaike has been elected prime minister on the promise that he would make Sinhala the official language within twenty-four hours of his election. His election confirms all the fears entertained by the Tamils—the Jaffna Tamils, in particular—of their systematic demotion to the status of second-class citizens, contravening all earlier assurances, constitutional and otherwise. Those Tamils who engage in acts of civil disobedience and nonviolent protest are set upon by crudely armed Sinhala mobs. As bloodied and wounded parliamentarians, including Mr. S.J.V. Chelvanayakam, arrive at the parliament building, seeking first aid, from the neighboring Galle Face Green where they have been carrying out their nonviolent protests, the pipe-puffing prime minister is supposed to have been garrulous with cruel wit and flippant invectives at the expense of the injured. A senior Tamil politician who had known Mr. Bandaranaike quite well was emphatic in assuring me of Mr. Bandaranaike's racism. A racist Bandaranaike was not. Neither was he even a Sinhala-Buddhist chauvinist. He was a pragmatic politician. On an interpersonal level he is said to have been at greater ease with Tamil politicians of his own class and with similar prestigious high school and university pedigrees than with most of the Sinhala politicians of his party who lacked such pedigrees. When I ask this politician how the prime minister could then have allowed his Tamil friends ("fellow diners and winers," as he called them) to be bloodied up in the Galle Face Green, he replies, "I think the prime minister looked at it more like a ragging in Oxford than an attack by hooligans."

The following year (1957), this pragmatic politician, recognizing his inability to govern without the support and citizenship of a crucial minority, and realizing that the game has taken a far more serious turn than he had thought it would, chooses to be more conciliatory. He invites the leader of the Federal Party to his private residence for deal making. Mr. Chelvanayakam enters the prime minister's residence with four concerns: (a) the recognition of Tamil as an official language and its unimpeded use for official purposes in the predominantly Tamil northern and eastern parts of the country; (b) the reversal of government-promoted Sinhala settlements in areas with Tamil majorities aimed at gradually tipping the balance in favor of the Sinhalas; (c) the creation of regional councils that would result in greater autonomy to the predominantly Tamil regions of the north and the east; and (d) the restoration of citizenship and voting rights to the Tamils of the plantations. After many hours of deliberation he emerges from the prime minister's office with a pact. The pact accommodates the first three of Mr. Chelvanayakam's concerns; the fourth—the one that means most to the Tamils of the plantations, the one that could restore intra-Tamil trust—is sacrificed to politics, the art of the possible. As it turns out, even this pact, such as it is, is dramatically torn up by the prime minister within a year under the pressuring protests of Buddhist monks and in their full view.

The trade unions, for lack of trust or political will and perspicuity, fail to exert any pressure on the Federal Party, the only party that was inclined by virtue of ethnic and linguistic propinquity to represent the interests of these "other Tamils." As things turn out, the Estate Tamils are, as a whole, so thoroughly excluded from the political process that even as late as 1964, when the prime minister of India, Mr. Lal Bhadhur Shastri, and the prime minister of Sri Lanka, Mrs. Sirimavo Bandaranaike, conclude their own pact on the citizenship question, none of the leaders of the Estate Tamils, trade unionists or otherwise, are consulted.

By the terms of the Sirimavo-Shastri Pact, 525,000 of these stateless persons are to be repatriated to India within fifteen years. The fate of 150,000 more and their progeny is to be decided at a later date. This later date comes around in 1974 when a second pact, known as the Sirimavo-Indira Pact, is agreed upon, by which 75,000 are marked for deportation to India. And yet by mid-1984 only 445,588 persons in all have been repatriated to India, most of them against their will. Most of the nearly 112,000 families thus repatriated are, to use the normalizing though ironic terminology of the state, "settled" in their "home state"—another normalizing term—of Tamil Nadu. Of course, as we saw at the end of the previous chapter, the 1983 anti-Tamil riots will suddenly and dramatically alter this state of affairs, and Estate Tamils will flood the Indian High Commissions in Colombo and Kandy to obtain their entry papers to "return" to India. But we are getting ahead of our story. For what I wish to do next is to go back and look at the lives of those Estate Tamils who do opt to return to India well before the trickle turned into the post-1983 flood. Of special interest are those "repatriates" who return to India in the 1970s, for the conditions into which they fall are the most relevant ones against which to measure and understand the hopes and disappointments of post-1983 émigrés like Selvi, introduced in chapter 3. On the whole it cannot be said of most of those who return to India as a result of the various Indo–Sri Lankan accords that they settle successfully in the land of their ancestors. True, the earlier ones fare better than the later ones. The fact that they have had more time to adjust to their new country is only part of the explanation of their relative success. But the resettlement of those who go to India in the 1970s is by far the most distressing. In the following section I wish to focus on one group of these repatriates, a group that ends up in the hills of Kodaikanal, in the vicinity of one of South India's most popular hill resorts.

In the summer of 1987 my own interest descends on one of the most unsettled of these settlements, on an episode that is paradigmatic of the whole story of this immigrant people. I am referring to the three hundred–odd families who live in the state of bondage, confined to what are known as "coupes," in the hills of Kodaikanal. The term "coupe," as understood in the official records, refers to an area of work demarcated by the Forest Department for the commercial purposes of felling, barking, stacking, and transporting forest trees, and where the laborers are settled in temporary sheds. The details of bondage in these coupes have been not so much concealed as deemed irrelevant to the Indian government's democratic concerns for almost twenty years. The whole matter becomes relevant to the various agencies of the government with the "liberation" of forty-four families, brought about by an extraordinary conjunction of events and persons: the accidental discovery of a coupe by a high school class from the local "International School" during a social studies field trip; the presence of a maverick subcollector who happens to be a Sikh (and therefore an outsider in the state of Tamil Nadu); the timely vacation of his boss, the district collector,[10] who doubles as a lackey of a minister in the state government (a vacation that frees the subcollector to push through some papers and petitions beyond the point of retraction); two determined Jesuit priests; an investigative reporter from Poona who manages to convince his southern newspaper colleagues that the story is, if nothing else, potentially sensational; a Supreme Court that is willing to entertain a writ petition filed against two contractors working for Tan India and South India Viscose; and the ambushing of these two giant national corporations when their "what's-so-wrong-about-that" attitude regarding the use of bonded labor is rudely jostled by a series of moves that lands them before the Supreme Court.

The episode develops as follows: The Indian Supreme Court orders the payment of unpaid wages to the heads of the forty-four families in this coupe, that they be liberated, and that they be rehabilitated. Neither Tan India nor South India Viscose is punished, except for being forced to pick up the tab on what it cost the Court Appointed Commission to research and write up its report. As for the contractors who had not paid the laborers, some for as long as fifteen years, their being forced to cough up back pay is deemed punishment enough. A man with "Rajiv Gandhi connections" is appointed to oversee the families' rehabilitation on land made available by the state of Tamil Nadu. At the time of my fieldwork (June 1987), eighteen months have passed since this man was appointed to the job. Over these eighteen months, he visits the "liberated" coupe once and the designated site twice, acquires a Jeep after the first month, a Maruti[11] after the second, and builds himself a two-story bungalow by the tenth. His assistant acquires only a Maruti, but he also buys some real estate in Kodaikanal, the nearby hill resort, and takes to gossiping about how his boss is becoming very rich on the rehabilitation project. The forty-four families are allowed to stay in their shacks until the land has been surveyed and appropriately partitioned. They do not understand why surveying and allocation has to take so long, especially since there are no ecological or potential economic differences among the plots. They are given rice rations and an allowance by the state and are told by the assistant not to try their "*bandhs* [political demonstrations] and such nonsense" with him around.

On the fourth occasion of my collecting narratives of emigration from a middle-aged couple inside one of the coupes, the assistant happens to visit this settlement. "I will have the police skin you alive," I hear him say. A small crowd gathers. I see him from inside the dark coupe, which is lit only by the daylight that comes through the solitary door—now partially obstructed by my informant who has stepped out to see what is happening—and by the light from the fickle flames of the hearth upon which a pot of water has been set to boil for some tea. The assistant cannot see me. His *vēṣṭi* is folded up so as to expose his blue boxer shorts. He arcs an oyster of phlegm, which lands in a puddle of water near the doorway of the dark coupe wherein I squat and watch. As the assistant continues to thunder with threats and abuse, one of the men, cupping his hand behind his ear with an exaggerated gesture signaling deafness shouts, "What did you say?" He has a bark-peeling knife tucked in his waistband. A silence falls upon the crowd. The assistant gently drops his "miniskirt" to the respectful ankle length, acting like a man who for once has been caught without a pose. The women take note. An older member of the coupe, a man with a fatherly manner, gently leads the assistant away and intones in a soothing drone the words, "Now you go along. Go and screw your mother." It is hard to tell whether this advice was intended to fuel or foil the assistant's temper.

No sooner does the assistant leave than I emerge from the darkness and take the shortcut down the hill to intercept his Jeep and hitch a ride to the hill resort town, Kodaikanal. He takes me for a rich tourist from Bombay. But he is even more pleased to know that I am from the United States and that my ancestral village is near the South Indian town of Thenkasi. "An N.R.I.,"[12] he observes with pleasure, and obliges with oily amiability. He considers it quite unwise of me to walk around these parts and tells me that I should have taken the next bus out of the last town even if I had to wait a few hours. "There are Sri Lankans around here. Dangerous people," he warns. He calls them "refugees." I cautiously offer that I have met some "coolies" carrying bundles of wattle along the way. "That's them, that's them," he jumpily interjects. "Dangerous, very dangerous," he keeps repeating. It is obvious that he has been rattled by his recent encounter with the coupe-dwellers, and he proceeds to tell me his version of what has happened: he went to supervise the distribution of payment and food to these refugees and was threatened with a knife for not coming with more. That was the sum of his version. "Refugees! What kind of refugees!" I do not ask him if he thinks there is a difference between Sri Lankan Tamil refugees and the Estate Tamil repatriates who never tire of insisting that they are "returnees to their motherland and not refugees." But I do wedge open the possibility of a retraction or qualification or amendment by remarking that in my conversation with the "coolies" I had heard them speak Indian Tamil and not the Sri Lankan ("Jaffna") dialect of the refugees. "The mostly Sri Lankan Tamil refugees I have met speak such a distinctly different dialect," I observe. "They are all refugees," he insists, and then adds, "they are also Tigers."

On our way we pass the oncoming Jeep of the inspector of police. The assistant stops him to report the impertinence he has just experienced, omitting the bit about taking food and wages to the refugees. He also does me the favor of introducing me to the inspector of police, adding his own elaboration that I am an N.R.I. tourist who likes hiking through the mountains and forests and was on my way to Kodaikanal from Kerala and had misjudged the distance to Kodaikanal from the last town nearest to where he had picked me up, and, thanks to him, I have been saved from the dacoity of the Sri Lankan Tamil refugees. He wants the inspector of police to go to the coupe and give them a good thrashing. The inspector of police tells the assistant to ignore them, that they are dangerous and mad. "These refugees' cheek knows no limit. The more they get, the more they want." Once again, in the South Indian dialect of Tamil, I remark to the inspector that the "coolies" I have met along the road, whom the assistant calls "refugees," did not speak the dialect of Jaffna Tamils. "They are refugees from the tea estates of Ceylon," he observes. "You don't mean those who went from India as laborers and who have been sent back?" I query. "They are all the same. Refugees. The only difference is that those in camps are the ones who have some education and money and connections. These animals here have none. Animals, sir, animals. Just animals."

The laborers I met worry about the 290 other families that are still in bondage. But the contractors of Tan India and South India Viscose have taken measures to assure these other bonded laborers' silence by infecting the labor force with better-paid Indian-born laborers who double as informants. The courageous young subcollector receives transfer orders moving him to a safer and lesser position, getting him out of the way, so that the Supreme Court's orders will get lost and remain unenforced in the deep forests of the Kodai hills. The subcollector finds legal means of resisting the transfer and is reinstated. His brother comes to Tamil Nadu to visit the subcollector but is arrested and tortured under charges of being a Sikh terrorist. Unable to bear the harassment and the plight of his brother, the subcollector gives up the battle and moves out. His brother is released after three years in a maximum security prison; no charges whatsoever have been brought against him. When released, he is insane. The press has moved on to other matters of interest, such as the Liberation Tigers of Tamil Eelam and the state of the chief minister's kidneys.[13] One of the biggest shareholders of the two giant companies happens to be the president of the Republic of India. Alagammal, a "liberated woman," calls him the *Periya Kaṅkāṇi* of *Periya Kaṅkāṇis* (an allusion I shall return to below). She asks me, "Who is this *achārya* of the Kānchi Maṭam?[14] Why does he run away in the stealth of the night from his *maṭam*? And she also wants to know why President Venkataraman has personally gotten involved in the search for His Holiness, why the president's wife herself is so worried about the achārya's whereabouts, and finally, why she or anyone else should care, even though the story about this achārya has been appropriating the front pages of the local newspapers for weeks.

What she wants to know (and does not say) is why and how their own story that had its brief moment of glory in the attention of the press got displaced; why the color photographs that had deservedly made the front page of the glossy newsmagazine *Front Line* are not there any more. Instead, there are pictures of this "holy man" who chose to disappear, abdicating his position of leadership at a famous South Indian "monastery," and pictures of other VIPs, who have been profoundly and visibly affected, in ways quite mysterious to her, by this "holy man"'s willful disappearance. "They [the reporters] took so many pictures of us," she says. "Where are the other pictures?" Neither she nor most of the other residents of the coupe understand or care for the written word, and that the latter no longer embodies their story in the press is something she does not mind. But the photographs she understood and now misses. She turns to me to accuse me of belonging to the "same *jāti* (genus) as those educated people with cameras, pens, and notebooks, who forget us with the first belly-filling meal in their bungalows." Like the woman who told me to tell and yet not to tell of the manner of her father's death, and who constructed me as "a man who has seen the world," Alagammal too sees me as a man who had not only seen a wider world but belonged to it. Alagammal, however, is not sanguine about that world's being one in which good and evil could be told apart. She had been in Sri Lanka, the land of her birth, and now is in India, the land of her ancestors, and has seen only a little of both these countries, never being able to drift too far away from her place of labor. In neither country she is impressed by its people's ability to tell the difference between good and evil. The even wider world that she glimpses through the few issues of *Front Line* gives her no reason to believe that matters are any different elsewhere. Her narrative of events and sketches of her life are never straightforward narratives about her life or events. No narrative, for that matter—mine included—is a straightforward representation, made up of transparently decodable constatives. Alagammal's is not a mere telling; it is a performative. It constructs me as a possible belly-filler, a forgetter, but also as a potential messenger, even as she admonishes me not to forget.

This story that I have chosen to tell you foregrounds the phenomenological moment of Peircean Secondness, albeit in an extended form, as an amplified moment of discordance. This moment is overwhelmed by "the present," the *hic et nunc*, in its capricious, and at times shocking, brutality. The protagonists of this story experience life as a series of interruptions. Power, mostly in its primitive form of force that is neither subtle (as in Foucault's capillary power), reasonable (as in Gramsci's hegemony), nor productive (as in Wartenberg's "coercive power"),[15] raids their lives with frequent irregularity. The moment of discordance, in its sheer momentousness, extends its shock waves into all possible moods and meanings of the lived experience of these displaced and dispossessed people. The here and the now overwhelm and deeply affect mood and meaning. Academic discourse in general and ethnography in particular (whether it is called interpretive or not) tend to privilege what Peirce called Thirdness. In Thirdness, understandings abound, explanations appease, reason holds court, and concordance is king. Such a "concordance is characterized by three features: completeness, wholeness, and an appropriate magnitude" (Ricoeur 1984: 1:38). In writing about a people whose lives have been anything but whole or complete, how does one even determine the appropriate magnitude of one's representation of their lives, let alone presume the possibility of concordance among representations and the correspondence of one's representation with the represented? And yet the anthropologist is asked to tell the world the story. How, in whose voice, or rather, in which of the many available voices, ought an anthropologist to tell such stories? And what does he tell when the most poignant parts of their voices are their silences?

Being Human: Being in Anthroposemeiosis

Anthroposemeiosis is such a cumbersome word. But none other better describes what it is to be human: why it is that the young woman who sees her father being dragged by an army Jeep—and many like her—want their "story" to be told to "the world," and why Alagammal fears that the words she tells me would be forgotten by me and lost to "the world"; why silence is so disconcerting. The universe is perfused with signs, and the activity of signs is what we call semeiosis—with a nod of deference to the Greek *semeion*, "sign." Semeiosis describes the activity of the giving, the receiving, the transforming, and the disseminating of signs. What differentiates anthroposemeiosis from semeiosis in general is that it involving human beings' knowledge or awareness of the relation of signification (Deely 1994:51). In fact, it defines what it is to be human. It is this awareness that separates out anthroposemeiosis from within the larger semeiosic networks of zoösemeiosis, phytosemeiosis, or even the physiosemeiosis that sustains it. "Unlike other animals, we not only know; we know that we know" (Bauman 1992:12). And that is why silence, especially silence that resists its incorporation into semeiosis, is so fundamentally threatening of humanity.

Consider the following excerpt from a dialogue between a sympathetic official from the fact-finding committee appointed by the Indian Supreme Court and a member of the coupe described above:

OFFICIAL: Tell! Tell (me) about your situation.

LABORER: How can I describe it? It won't even come into my mouth (It does not conform to words).

OFFICIAL (After much coaxing by the officer and stubborn silence on the part of the laborer): If you don't say it, it will mean that nothing was the matter.

Throughout Sri Lanka and elsewhere, among Tamil and Sinhala victims of violence, the lasting effect that one often witnesses is a sort of stunned repose settled upon individuals and groups. Whereas silence or speechlessness is one of the main and pervasive effects of violence, the juridical legal apparatus demands words (or other signs) so that justice may be done. The ethnographer, in her turn and in her own way, has come to rely on words (or other signs) so that her ethnography may be done. But in the sympathetic official, whom I later came to know, and his urging the coupe-dwellers to speak, we find not only a desire for justice as an end in itself but also the desire to reestablish the flow of life, human life, in the anthroposemeiosic process. The same would hold true for the sympathetic fieldworker, where the ethnography ought not to be an end in itself, an end to a semeiosic activity begun in the field. Consider again a statement of a laborer from the 22 Beats Coupe—the name given to this particular coupe—as recorded in the Supreme Court Commission's report, who anticipates such a consequence when he observes,

> If the condition of our life goes on this way, then we might soon lose the faculty of speech.

Consider for the last time the struggle of the poet Stefan George whom Heidegger cites (cited in Connolly 1987:143):

> So I renounced and sadly see:
> where the word breaks off
> no thing may be.

In all these instances, however, there is either an implicit or an explicit acknowledgment that language is essential for the being of things, but also for being human. The impasse experienced by all of these persons, where the word struggles to articulate with "the thing," also brings to light the mystery of language, even its essence. At the same time it must be noted that in all these examples (especially in the poem of Stefan George quoted by Heidegger quoted by Connolly—itself a transmission metaphoric of the flow of semeiosis) there is the unwarranted danger of construing language too narrowly. For what defines language is not solely the use of words, or even that of conventional signs; it is the use of any sign whatsoever as involving the knowledge or awareness of the relation of signification. Anthroposemeiosis entails practices that contain an interpretation of what it is to be a human being, to belong to a discursive community, a community with a more or less shared horizon. Thus the "Perumal cut" wielded by the angry young man at the arm of his white overseer—described in chapter 3—indicates as forcefully an awareness of the relation of signification as does the reflexive poet who writes the origin myth of Estate Tamils in chapter 1. And we know through signs, or more precisely through the activity of signs or semeiosis.

Silence or, rather, the unwillingness or inability to partake in anthroposemeiosis of any kind could signify several things. For one, such semeiosic abstinence might conceal a knowledge of its significance. It could be motivated by the desire to bring about a breach between sign and object, words and their customary referents and interpretants, thereby forcing, even shocking, the "world" into taking notice. But it could also, more ominously, indicate the withdrawal from all anthroposemeiosis, as much refusing to be fully human as rejecting others' humanity. Being human is being part of the process of the reception, transformation, and production of meanings, shared and sharable by an indefinitely open community. Silence could spell the cessation of that process. And that would be truly tragic.

Being Human: Being in Time

The highest form of sharing—human sharing—also entails caring. When Alagammal wonders whether I too, like the rest of the photographers and journalists, will forget her people with the first belly-filling meal, she wants to discern whether I care. She wishes to know whether her particular tribulations fall within the compass of things I care about, whether they belong—to be more precise—to my "care-structure."[16] In Heidegger's ontological sense, the "care-structure" is the "structure of disclosedness." Our world, our environment, is disclosed to us by virtue of our familiarity not with particulars but with its referential whole. On so many occasions, after giving me accounts of their trials, victims of violence would say, in despair, "What do they in America care about what happens to us!" or wonder, "Would they understand what is being done?" Questions or rhetorical assertions such as these are the performatives of those whose participation in the ongoing process of being human has been stifled by the threat of silence, by semeiosic paralysis and by the inescapable presence of violence, and who want to be free again. Such performatives are uttered as a means to move the world, even if only by a sort of magical hope, to incorporate their particular condition into the care-structure of a larger humanity and a wider horizon of disclosedness. For it is only within the horizon of our disclosedness that we can *care* about what our fellow human beings care about. And it is through the spread of signs, especially symbols—the carriers of so many of our lives' meanings—that sharing and caring are possible. "Symbols grow and spread among the people. In use and in experience [their] meanings grow" (Peirce 2.302). Furthermore, "for every symbol is a living thing, in a very strict sense that is no mere figure of speech. The body of the symbol changes slowly, but its meaning inevitably grows, incorporates new elements and throws off old ones" (Peirce 2.222). To belong to this growth and this spreading of symbols, to belong to anthroposemeiosis, is to be human.

Growth, however, is a process in time. This is especially true of the growth of signs. Thus, in the words of Santaella Braga, "where there is a sign, there is a temporal process seeing that the action of the sign is to develop itself in time" (1992:313). And growth, especially the growth and spread of symbols, like time, is characterized by continuity. But even though, ontologically, time is continuous, "more like a moving tide rather than a series of discrete atomic moments" (Corrington 1993:182), its continuity is not uniform in its three familiar modes: the past, the present, and the future. This is because the three modes of time are qualitatively different. It is this difference that makes the unfolding of time uneven; and in this "unevening" of time, it is the present that plays the principal agitating role.

In and of itself, the past is closed, and "not a realm of possibility" (Corrington 1993:182). "The Past consists of the sum of *fait accomplis*, and this Accomplishment is the Existential mode of Time"(Peirce 5.459). "It acts upon us in the present as if it were a brute existent" (Corrington 1993:57), and to that extent it is actualized in the present. To illustrate the actualization of the past in the present, let me turn to the story of Palanisamy as an example that is culturally embedded and far more pertinent than the one about the stellar nova given to us by Peirce.[17] Palanisamy is a former estate worker whom I find in the hills of Kodaikanal one evening huddled in his shack in pain, near a dying fire. He is unable to move his arms. The long hours of scraping wattle off trees for Tan India and South India Viscose have almost paralyzed them. He has also fallen and hurt his back. I suspect a pinched nerve at best or a far more serious spinal injury. But he has a different explanation.

His great-great-great-grandfather was the one who left India for Sri Lanka almost 150 years ago. This ancestor's son was born with stumps for hands. His grandson had lost his in a factory accident. His great-grandson, Palanisamy's grandfather, had his arms broken by the police (who were in the estate superintendent's pay) for having dared to write a petition to the police captain against the superintendent regarding his brutality toward laborers on the estate. The punishment, as Palanisamy's wife interjects, was more for his flaunting of his literacy than for the petition itself. His father, who had remarried when Palanisamy's mother died, returned to India with his new family in the early 1950s and died there of leprosy. He, Palanisamy presumes, lost his limbs to leprosy, as all lepers do. When Palanisamy was repatriated to India, he first went to his ancestral village, the village that his great-great-great-grandfather had left. To his surprise, he was not welcome. He was told why. The pioneer ancestor was a teenager when he left. It so happened that his young sister was pounding rice paddy in a *ūṛal* (mortar) with an *ulakkai* (pestle). The wooden mortar was about two and a half feet tall and the heavy wooden pestle was about five feet long. His sister, who was barely four feet tall herself, found it difficult to raise the pestle high enough before dropping it onto the grain in the hollow of the mortar. Deciding to make it easier for herself, she climbed onto the rim of the mortar and began pounding the grain from this more comfortable height. Her elder brother, Palanisamy's pioneer ancestor, seeing his sister desecrate the mortar—considered sacred by Tamils—in this manner, grabbed the pestle from her hand and struck her with it on her back. The little girl's back broke and she died. As punishment, the elders of the village banished him and his parents, forbidding them or their progeny ever to return; they then came to Sri Lanka for refuge and labor. "It is that act of murder that keeps coming back," said Palanisamy. "But my karma is over. I have no sons.

My arms are the last to go. What has happened, has finally happened [i.e., the past is finally past]."

When the past facts return in memory and in experience only to reactualize themselves, the past does not enter the flow of time in the full sense. The past is repeated but is not continuous in and as time. The past's continuity in and as time depends on the possibilities and the generalizability of the future. Expanding on the nature of the future, Peirce wrote, "Future facts are the only facts that we can, in a certain measure, control" (5.461). What did he mean by this assertion and what are its implications? To begin with, a fact is something that one believes to be true. And beliefs are arrived at inferentially, mostly unconsciously. Our—inferentially arrived at—beliefs also determine our conduct, on which Peirce observes that "the only controllable conduct is Future conduct" (5.461). Accomplished facts of the closed past that are *actualized* in the present can be *realized* through beliefs generated by habits and habit taking, these based on inferences that determine how we would conduct ourselves with respect to those facts in the future—what our comportment would be given our belief that certain things are true. Thus we find that continuity is fully realized only in the temporal mode of the future. And the temporal mode of the future is brought into play via elementary forms of inference, be they induction, deduction, or, most important, abduction. Thus even "the 'percept,' that is, the unitary element at the base of experience, is a vague something that is immediately given shape by a perceptual judgment." And "a perceptual judgment, while unconscious and automatic, functions as a kind of primitive abduction" (Corrington 1993:59–60), a mode of inference that disposes one to act toward the world, even if only hypothetically, so as to reduce surprise and shock. To be able to have some control over what would happen (future subjunctive) is to be part of the movement of signs in time, to be part of anthroposemeiosis, to be part of the project of being human. When the future is so uncertain as to be nonexistent, semeiosis is essentially choked off; so is "human" life. For the bonded laborers of the coupes there seemed to be no future but only a present that served as the repository of a deadening past.

It is the presence of violence that concerns us most in this chapter and in this book as a whole. But what is the present? Working through and with Peirce on his struggle with the present does shed light on our own understanding of the presence of violence and of those whose lives are trapped in the violent present. If Peirce was clear about the ontological status of the past and the future, the present turned out to be far more inscrutable. Hence he wonders "whether no skeptic has attacked its reality." And he continues: "I can fancy one of them dipping his pen in his blackest ink to commence the assault, and then suddenly reflecting that his entire life is in the Present—the 'living present,' as we say, that instant when all hopes and fears concerning it come to their end, this Living Death in which we are born anew. It is plainly that nascent state between the Determinate and the Indeterminate" (5.459). And further on, while discussing the nature of introspection too as being wholly a matter of inference, he writes: "One is immediately conscious of his Feelings, no doubt; but not that they are feelings of an *ego*. The *self* is only inferred." And then comes the startling addition: "There is no time in the present for any inference at all, least of all for inference concerning that very instant" (5.462). But if semeiosis is a series of inferences and inferences are possible only in time, how can the absolute present even be a mode of time rather than a mere breach in time? In other words, it would be impossible to tell a percept apart from a perceptual judgment because the percept without a perceptual judgment is not *about* anything; that is, it does *not stand for* anything but itself. As we shall see in the next chapter, in the context of torture, for instance, pain becomes an end in itself, a percept that stands for nothing but itself. It signifies nothing. It is the perceptual judgment that makes introspection and—more generally—inference possible. "Percepts are brought into the structure of time by their mediating judgments. Consequently, thirdness, as ingredient in all perceptual judgments, makes full temporality actual for the realm of percepts" (Corrington 1993:111). The word that Peirce uses for the combined reality of the percept and the perceptual judgment is "percipiuum." Once the percipiuum is born, the present has already lost its unique presence, its characteristic innocence, if you will. Thus Peirce observes that "in a perceptual judgment the mind professes to tell the mind's future self what the character of the present percept is. The percept, on the contrary, stands on its own two legs and makes no professions of any kind" (7.630). "The consciousness of the present is then that of a struggle over what shall be; and thus we emerge from the study with a confirmed belief that it is the Nascent State of the Actual" (5.462). The present qua present is like a tiny bubble in the tide of continuity that, howsoever fleetingly, is an isolated monad, imprisoned in itself, lodged in the heart of time and yet not part of time.

Hidebound with time, semeiosis in general, but anthroposemeiosis in particular, does not always unfold or evolve evenly or smoothly (5.462). And it should be clear now why I said above that it was the present that played the principal agitating role in making the flow of time "uneven." Depending on the agitation of and in the present, time may move tremulously, stochastically, convulsively, and at times even cataclysmically. Life in its everydayness is made unremarkable by the smooth semeiosic activity that bears time along. Strictly speaking, of course, the present qua present, as we have analyzed it, by being only at the threshold of time and not part of it, cannot introduce discontinuities into time. That is, the metaphor of the wave used to describe the flow of time should hold regardless of the present's presence in its conative externality. However, what I wish to argue is that the degree of trauma in the present, within the isolated bubbles that remain unbroken in the midst of the breakers they cause, and the manner of these bubbles' eventual explosion, have a bearing on the shape of time.

To return to our victims of violence, the arrhythmia, the tremors, the convulsions, the cataclysms in their lives are indicative of the continuing presence of the present in their lives, a present that has yet to be inferentially appropriated into the flow of time, a present that—if only it could be redeemed from its self-imprisonment—could play a nonstochastic part in determining future conduct, conduct guided by purpose. The repeated use of or drift into the present tense among my informants and friends who have undergone the trauma of violence I take to be an indication of the persistence of the effects of the presence of violence in their lives, an indication that the foaming, eddying presence of the past has yet to be fully delivered from the present into the flow of the future.

In this chapter, in deference to the presence of violence and the persistence of its effects in the here and now, and in deference to the sustained and predominant use of the present tense to indicate the presence of the not-yet-past in my interviewees' speech and life, I too resort to the rhetorical device of favoring the present tense. I employ, if you will, an iconicity of style. But this rhetorical device alone would fail to do justice, I believe, not only to the stories my informants have told me but, more specifically, to the great number of my informants who are multiply alienated from the master narrative of those in power. Let me explain. What I have called the "iconicity of style" is still, in a certain measure, tethered to the concerns of representation. To that extent, I am more attuned to the concerns of those who either have or wish to possess the master narrative. The master narrative is primarily representational in its presumptions. In other words, its conceit is in its claim that it represents the truth or reality. Even though other functions emerge from or accrue to the master narrative, as those who narrate it see matters, the narrative's main claim is its claim to representational truth. This indeed is the mode of the narrative of "modern history." Those who are multiply distanced or alienated from such narratives teach us not so much that the representational function is only partial and needs to be supplemented and complemented by other functions as that the representational function is not the only function.[18] This compels us to go further, beyond the appropriate tensing of language in the representational spirit, and to attend to the manner of representation's use and the effectiveness of its claims. In order to do this, let us return to Stefan George's problem, expressed in representational terms, as to how language and reality articulate, how "word and thing" come together.

Four Ways of Representing

I shall, adapting a scheme put forth by the political theorist William Connolly, address this problem by reviewing four major modes of relating reality to language. The most common view is that language represents. This view provides the raison d'être of the Supreme Court Commission's report, the newspapermen's stories, and the writ petitions. It stresses the aboutness of language. This representational view of language, in its naive form, has been rightly taken to task by language philosophers, among others. It would be wrong, however, to assert that language is totally unrepresentative. Language does represent whatever object it claims to represent (and more), but only in some respects and not in others, in some capacities and not in others, and to somebody or something and not to others. This modified representational view flows into a second theory of language-object relationship that has been posited. This may be called the constitutive theory of language. Whereas the first affords primacy to the object, the thing referred to, the second vests constitutive powers in the subject or, in the more sophisticated version, in the intersubjective discursive patterns, in a consensual community, or in the system of shared meanings. Some of us call the latter culture.

There is a third theory of language, which, following Charles Taylor, I shall call the expressive theory of language. In this theory is contained the essential critique of the earlier two forms. To quote Taylor: "Our most expressive creations, hence those where we are closest to deploying our expressive power at the fullest, are not self-expressions; . . . they have the power to move us because they manifest our expressive power itself AND its relation to our world. In this kind of expression we are responding to the ways things are, rather than JUST exteriorizing our feelings" (1985:239). This formulation is a corrective to the extreme forms of both representationalism and constitutivism. It brings together, much as Peirce did some one hundred years ago, epistemological idealism and ontological realism in the coconstruction of reality; consensus and correspondence strive toward unity. The consensus is no longer limited to the concordance between what I think and what my fellow human beings think but extends to the concordance between what we think and feel and the world that exists independent of our fancies yet can be known only relative to our fancies.

This theory is very seductive. In my own work on Hindu village India (1984) I have celebrated the cultural value placed on equilibrium and equipoise, the hope that concordance is achievable because it is there to be achieved. My belief is that this concordance should extend to the way of doing ethnography, that the optimal mode for doing such an ethnography is something akin to the expressive mode advocated by Taylor. My own choice of the present tense to be in harmony with the voices of my informants is a form of acquiescing to this theory. There will be, according to this view of the world, a day in the indefinite future when word and object will be perfectly articulated in the *OM*, when event and description will be perfectly attuned. But herein lies the danger: in the seduction, the hope, the illusion that someday there will be the perfect closure. The perfect click in the possible "long run" deafens one to the cacophony of the actual "short run." Connolly highlights the danger thus:

> The rhetoric of articulation, attunement, expression, responsiveness, faithfulness, depth, and self-realization is designed to carry us through interpretation to a closer harmony with the world. But these terms insert a social ontology into discourse which itself might be interrogated. We are led to ask: does the pursuit of attunement draw us to an order in which we can be more at home in the world, or does it insinuate a fictional ideal into discourse which can be actualized only through containment of that which deviates from it? (1987:151)

In other words, the expressive theory of language shares with its representational and constitutive counterparts a vantage point that "consistently gives hegemony to integration" (ibid.). Such a rhetoric may be theoretical, as formulated by the academic and intellectual; it may be commonsensical-juridical, as in the case of the official who wanted the coupe laborer to match words to experience because only such a matching would make his words and his experience real; or it may be cultural, as celebrated in Hindu cultural nondualism. But regardless of which form it takes, it conceals the violence done to life when the recalcitrantly ambiguous character of lived experience is downplayed or swallowed up by ever higher forms of compulsive ordering, an activity in which we intellectuals, in particular, excel.

This brings me to my fourth alternative way of viewing the relationship between word and object. Connolly, with a bow to Nietzsche, calls it the genealogical model. At the very outset let me admit that even though in this chapter I favor the last and fourth view, it is not my intention to deny the appropriateness of the other three in different proportions under conditions of different interests. In this chapter, I make a case for the fourth because (a) this view is in general an excommunicant in social scientific discourse and denied (though ever-present) in commonsensical discourse, and (b) the story of my concern is embedded in a larger social and historical context of discordance, to which this view is most appropriate, not because of its purported consonance with such dissonance, but because it privileges voices that are not in sympathetic vibration with the major channels of history, culture, and power. The representational and the constitutive views of concordance tend to be cognitive and mechanical; this is the view of language that was made and then unmade in the earlier and later Wittgenstein respectively. The expressivist sees this bringing together of word and object as an affective coming together—a coming home, so to speak, with hope and longing, much like the beguiled Sri Lankan tea estate worker who comes to his motherland of India and home state of Tamil Nadu. In contrast to all three, the genealogist does not presuppose either the possibility or the inevitability of concordance. Connolly's, and presumably Nietzsche's, genealogist assumes the world to be fundamentally indifferent to us, the world here being either internal or external nature. My genealogist, if one might still call her that, is too Peircean to go that far. "Peirce ties the meaning of truth and reality to the practices of inquiry in the long run" (Joswick 1995:880). At best, I can only be agnostic about the "long run" and its possibilities for concordance. The states of violence in which and with which one works, the sheer hopelessness this spawns, makes the Nietzschean picture hold, at least in the "short run." My own position on the appropriate stance to take, shaken as it is by the caprice of the present and, at best, by the hopelessness of the "short run," is to strive for congruence—"a notion which I oppose by convention to that of coherence" (Derrida 1978:57).

The genealogist does not seek "attunement with higher unities," be it God, the state, or the world. For Alagammal, the state's symbolic head, the president of the republic, is a kaṅkāṇi, the biggest of them. And who is a kaṅkāṇi? The kaṅkāṇi was the recruiter of labor in the villages of India in the nineteenth and early part of the twentieth centuries. As a fellow villager, he was their self-appointed leader, their proctor and protector, supervisor and solicitor, and often their patriarch and provider. Such was the script. But he works overtime, mostly overtime, and then outside the script. He steals their wages; he squeezes every possible drop of toil out of them; he rapes their daughters and weeps when their sons die; he holds them in bondage; he sells their labor to the white man and builds himself bungalows and buys himself estates; he builds temples and feeds Brahmins; his wife is invariably pious and hankers for holy men. The kaṅkāṇi is that enduring note of discordance in the lives of these immigrant workers, a repository of caprice. The older man who led the assistant away with the words, "Now go along and screw your mother," is, according to Alagammal's daughter, also a kaṅkāṇi. The characterization is part facetious, part earnest. "We are all kaṅkāṇis," Alagammal adds. "This kaṅkāṇi-mentality is born with us and dies with us."

If this were true, then these laborers' agony would be as much the oppression from without as the will to domination from within. Indeed, genealogy does seek out attunement to such discordances within the self. Not just within the individual Cartesian or Jamesian self, that self contained in a "box of flesh and blood" (Peirce 7.591),[19] but within the selfhood of a class, a community, a people. Normalizing discursive practices, practices that employ vocabularies dispensed by the state, welfare organizations, and even trade unions, need to be interrogated by those assertions and asides coming out of the mouths of those like Alagammal, which are ordinarily "deflected, ignored, subordinated, excluded, or destroyed by (normalizing) discursive formations" (Connolly 1987:155).

On a plantation in Sri Lanka, I was once instructed on why the white superintendent was a good man.[20] "He was good because we could laugh at his Tamil." The Sinhala superintendent who took the white man's place when the plantations were nationalized was also seen as good, better than the kaṅkāṇi.

Why? "Because though he is like us (brown), he tries to be like the white man. He makes himself different. He is a dissembler (*vēšakkāran*). We laugh at him." To be able to laugh at someone is to bring him down to size. He is your perfect mimic man:[21] the brown sahib on a motorbike with pith helmet, khaki shorts, boots, and woolen stockings, who speaks Tamil with a cockney accent and English with exaggerated diphthongs and Sinhala syntax. Different and therefore not dangerous.

A kaṅkāṇi, by contrast, is one of them. He is each one of them: their history, their psychic geography, their political economy. He is a Tamil, a recalcitrant force, the embodiment of the "moment," the lord of caprice, not to be laughed at. A genealogical account, then, seeks attunement not with concordance but with its opposite: with the discordance that obtains between the self and the identities established for it by the civil state, civil religion, and civil psychiatry, "between personal identity and the dictates of social identification" (Connolly 1987:155), between metaphors that usher in confluence and those that disrupt and disturb the flow.

How then ought the story to be told in the genealogical mode? In its vocabulary and rhetoric, its own ambiguity must be made overt so as to caution those who read or hear to be wary of doctrines that glorify normalization. This also returns us to the choice of voice. Normalization at its best must be treated as an ambiguous good to be qualified, countered, and politicized. And politics, at its best, calls into question settlements sedimented into moral consensus, economic rationality, psychiatric judgment, academic habit, and ontological necessity. All these are *triangulations* of the moment and mood in meaning, in Thirdness, in semeiosis. But there is a danger in finding meaning before the full effects of discordance are appreciated. For while meanings grow, they are also predisposed to sink into petrified habits, into thinking that the job has been done and questions answered, into solving and forgetting. To be true to discordance, the discordance one detects in the tremulous present tense of Selvi's, Alagammal's, and Kamalam's speech, and—in chapter 7—Nitthi's, one must suspend, not merely hasten to solve; and the triangulation that an ethnography of that discordance must resort to is not one in which meaning dominates but one in which meaning yields to the moment, underwritten by a mood of suspicion turned against readily available normalizing ontologies. It would appear that I contradict myself. If I do, let me do so productively. First, I argued that to be human is to be in anthroposemeiosis. Then I claimed that anthroposemeiosis, the activity of signs in the lives of signifiers who know their significance is an inferential activity. Third, that inference delivers the past and the present into the future. In the successful appropriation of past, present, and future in semeiosis, the necessary triangulation of Firstness, Secondness, and Thirdness, of mood, moment, and mind, is achieved. But now I seem to caution against triangulations of this sort. The caution is against preemptive triangulations of recalcitrant experience, against the premature acceptance of meanings that culture has to offer, or the ready-made solution the social scientist comes up with. The moment cannot be sacrificed to a mind or meaning that will only reproduce the same mood.

With the progression of this chapter, I have drifted toward a mode of writing that I call the genealogical mode. I have already hinted in both the epigraph and the body of the preceding chapter what such a mode or method might be. Despite the singular number in which "mode" and "method" are mentioned, there is no unitary genealogical method or mode. Most specifically, it does not concern the by now tired old distinction between the relative propriety of the first person (reflexive?) account and the third person (nonreflexive?) one—or, as Professor Michael Silverstein once punned over dinner, between "I(eye)-ing" the "it" and "(h)it-(t)ing" the "I(eye)." But genealogy is suspiciously alert to the voice of coherent narratives and their concerns and equally—but sympathetically—alert to those voices that are not in concordance with such narratives and are, at times, in direct discordance with them. This is no claim to questing after a truer "hidden transcript" in the deep recesses of the subaltern (Scott 1990). Nor is it even intended to identify master narratives with centers of power and institutions exclusively. It is to urge the anthropologist fieldworker, who in this one respect has an advantage over his or her fellow social scientists, the economist and political scientist in particular, to tune her ear in the field to statements, claims, accounts, and stories that—in the words of a political scientist friend of mine with whom I shared a sampling from my fieldnotes—"have nothing to do with anything." My friend was at that time working in Colombo with her taped interviews of several leading Sri Lankan politicians; what she meant by her assessment of my gleanings was that there was no way of relating such "fragments" to the master narratives of history, the state, welfare organizations, international relations, international aid organizations, the law, or trade unions. Typically, removed from the centers of power and opinion making, the anthropologist fieldworker is more likely to encounter the "outlandish" and thereby subjects his or her own power and opinion, garnered in the academy and the metropolises, to trial and erosion.

Anthropology and fieldwork notwithstanding, the ideal of writing genealogically is one thing, its realization quite another. True, I chose one of the most marginalized of the ethnic subgroups in Sri Lanka whose perspective I was going to privilege; and among them, true, I turned my attention to the voices of women and children; and true, genealogical writers such as Nietzsche, Foucault, and—more to the point of the task at hand—Allen Feldman (1991) have helped me tune my ear to the genealogical in general. But the gap between my ideal and my achievement is in itself a testimony to the enormity of the challenge of overriding and writing over coherent narratives in general and master narratives in particular. For one, there is, as always, the "background" that needs to be told. It is only natural that the reader who is uninitiated into Sri Lankan matters expects such a telling; equally naturally, the initiated reader also wants it to be told so as to measure the divergences between this telling and the one he or she might have chosen to tell. Background also establishes common ground. And it is the master narrative that serves as the readily available source for such a common ground of understanding, agreement, and disagreement. It makes available prefabricated questions: What is Sri Lanka? Where is Sri Lanka? Who are the Tamils? Who are the Sinhalas? When did the ethnic troubles start? What caused it? Are the Sinhala Buddhists chauvinists? Are the Tamil Tigers terrorists? Who do you think will win this civil war? How do you explain this violence? Does America have anything to do with what is going on? To all these and more, it also has a supply of answers from which one may choose. For another, even the "stateless" plantation worker is a (sovereign) subject of the hegemony of master narratives. The stories that plantation workers tell about themselves and others, about the country of their ancestors and the country of their birth, about goodness and evil, about bad men and kind men, all draw heavily from the text of master narratives, prepared in advance. There is a significant difference, however. Estate Tamils' experience is further removed from the concerns of these master narratives than are those of the Jaffna Tamils and the majority Sinhalas. This distance manifests itself in slippages, contradictions, and lacunae revealed by their stories that serve as potential spaces for genealogical prying. To be sure, such slippages, contradictions, and lacunae appear as such only for those who are at home in little else besides in the unfolding of coherent master narratives. At times Estate Tamil variations of a story are simply wrong. An example would be when a particular member of Parliament is named as having voted against their interest on a major issue when in fact he had voted in its favor. It is easy for me, as a scholar who has access to the facts in the parliamentary Hansards, to say that on this point the master narrative which cites the Hansard to back up its story is correct and the plantation workers' account is incorrect. My task would not be to stop there but to find out the conditions that make the refractory transformation of this "fact" both possible and necessary. The answers may not always be profound; but then again, sometimes they are. And violence, when examined at close range, interrupts the coherence of a master narrative. But to deny the coherence of violence is not the same thing as appreciating the challenge posed by its congruence with time, with semeiosis, and with our responsibility of writing an anthropography.

As indicated in my introduction, my visit to Sri Lanka in 1983 was motivated by a quest to find narratives that were alternatives to the master narrative. Violence revealed far more than I had expected to find. Not only was I inundated by narratives that were alternatives to the expected alternative to the master narrative, but I also found the master narrative itself to be neither singular nor secure but plural and thoroughly vulnerable to the fires it had ignited and then had tried to tame. Although one might be tempted to deem the official story the master narrative, in the context of violence this story was master neither of its own narrative nor of those to whom the story was narrated. There were as many masters as there were narratives, the official source being but one of them. Some masters' narratives were never master narratives, and other masters' narratives were only master narratives some of the time. Violence undermined the narrativity of the master as well as the mastery of the narrative. I was also to realize that the subalterns have their own master narratives, narratives that are—as in the case of E. P. Thompson's English working class (1966)—capable of displacing the official narrative's mastery of itself. The politically dominant institution does not have full control over the master narrative, especially in the context of violence. The kaṅkāṇi's narrative is a subaltern master narrative in its own right, but only to be undermined by the narratives of such persons as Alagammal and Kamalam, narratives that are as disturbing as they are fleeting.

Postscript: In the summer of 1994 I attempted to track down Kamalam. The camp by the sea was being dismantled. Kamalam's batch of refugees had long since left—escaped, died, or returned to live or die. Arrangements for the remaining refugees to be sent back to Sri Lanka were well under way. Where Kamalam had stood the last time I saw her, a russet-colored dog kept watch. The only one to remember Kamalam was an Indian fisherman. According to him, the hours that Kamalam spent looking at the sea began earlier and earlier and lasted later and later until toward the end she spent all night and day by the ocean's edge. She did not know one day from the next. She said that she was waiting for her ancestors who had left to work on the hills of the tea estates. Not for her son—she never mentioned her son—but for her great-grandfather and great-grandmother. "They went for the 'parade' (*peraṭṭu*)," she would say. "Behold, they will come! (*Itō vantiruvāṅka*)." For her, neither death nor distance had consumed them. People who knew her had tried to take her with them when they left, but she had refused to go. "Then," continued the fisherman, "one day, she was gone. Some say soldiers took her away. Some say she went to the hills of Kodaikanal to work on the new potato farms. Others say she went with the sea. My wife thinks she is still around. I think she'll come back." As for me, I still see her

> . . . listening
> to the surf as it falls.
> the power and inexhaustible freshness of the sea,
> the suck and inner boom
> as a wave tears free and crashes back
> in overlapping thunders going away down the beach
> It is the most we know of time
> and it is our undermusic of eternity.
>
> (*Galway Kinnell*)

5

EMBODIED TERROR

Narcotics cannot still the tooth
That nibbles at the soul.
(Emily Dickinson)

Representing the Beautiful

IN their attempts to account for the aesthetic in culture, three semeiotically inclined anthropologists understand the aesthetic as something located in signs that are difficult, if not impossible, to re-present. For this reason, Roy Wagner (1985) writes of "symbols that stand for themselves"; Steven Feld (1982), of "autoreferentiality"; and Nancy Munn (1986), borrowing from Peirce (2.244, 248, 254), of "qualisigns"—that is, of signs that are mere qualitative possibilities in contradistinction to signs that are actualized and/or generalized. Even though all three cultural aesthetes then go on to find ways of representing the unrepresentable in apparent contradiction of their opening premises, the point still holds that any representation of the aesthetic is by its very nature incomplete and vague, and, although richly suggestive, no number of objectifications can exhaust it. In this regard Munn's choice of the Peircean category "qualisign" is instructive. It behooves us to recall Peirce's claim for signs and signification: to wit, that every sign or representation is only a sign in potentia unless and until it stands for a second, its object, and a third, its interpretant, in some respect or capacity (2.228, 2.274). That is, a sign qua sign must be constituted of three correlations: a representation,[1] an object, and an interpretant. Insofar as what Peirce called a "qualisign" is a label for the representation alone, disregarding for the purpose of analytic attention its object and interpretant, it is not a completed sign but a sign of possibility, a pre-sign or hyposign—waiting, as it were, for its appropriate object and interpretant to introduce it into significance. Therefore, Nancy Munn's use of "qualisign" to describe the manner in which "the fame of Gawa" is carried forth from one Melanesian island to another is not a "qualisign" in the strict sense but a qualisign that has broken out of its confinement of mere possibility and found its objects to represent and its interpretants to carry forth these representations into semeiosis. Nevertheless, Munn is justified in highlighting the qualisignificant aspect of "the fame of Gawa," to the extent that neither its objects nor its interpretants are transparent to native or anthropologist, as might be, for instance, an indexical sign such as smoke standing for fire or a symbolic sign such as a word standing for a thing. In other words, a qualisign is a sign that admits to the inexhaustibility of its representational mission; one never gets to the bottom of it. As for its significant effect—technically called the interpretant—in aesthetics, it is rarely logical but mostly immediate and emotional. Thus any given representation of beauty even when interpreted as such, only reveals the profundity of the beautiful. Or to put it differently, beauty is best represented by something that represents beauty's unrepresentability. To return to a more technical formulation, we may say that a sign of beauty bulks large with qualisignification. We shall soon return to beauty and qualisignification, but only after a brief meditation on beauty's relationship to pain.

Beauty and Pain

In the dominant philosophical traditions, or "the great tradition"—to borrow a concept from a Redfieldian anthropology of yesteryear—of the West, the aesthetic has come to be identified with the beautiful, the pleasurable, and the tasteful. This tradition extends from Plato and Aristotle to Burke to Hume and Kant, and to a whole range of neo-Kantians. It is, however, the little traditions of the likes of Maurice Blanchot, George Battaile, Walter Benjamin, some of the surrealists, Freudians such as Julia Kristeva, and of course the Sadians that have explicitly revealed to us, if not the complicity of pain in pleasure, then at least the confusion of pain with pleasure. But rather than invoke the little traditions to illustrate the complicity and confusion in question, let me briefly go to the great tradition itself.

For a start, one would be hard pressed to read Kant's famous definition of beauty as "disinterested delight" without experiencing a twinge of recognition of the torturer brought to our attention by Elaine Scarry and others. Or how can one read Schopenhauer, who, extending Kant's definition, locates the essence of the aesthetic in "the liberation of the will," and not also see the torture victim who has been liberated from his will? Look furthermore at the mirroring of yet another one of Kant's definitions of beauty in the light of what we know about pain in the context of torture and interrogation. "Beauty is," Kant says, "the form of the purposiveness of an object so far as this is perceived in it without any representation of a purpose" (1951:73). To have a purpose is to be suited for some use. In beauty, however, we seem to have an instance in which we say that something is purposive but with no identifiable purpose. But note that Kant does not locate beauty in the purposiveness of an object but in what he calls the *form* of that purposiveness. Ted Cohen parses this definition as follows:

> Because it is purposive in this way: it does suit some use, namely, the use I make of it. . . . The sense that it makes consists entirely in its making sense to me. Its

> purposiveness consists in my finding it purposive. My finding it purposive (which is a finding realized as my feeling of pleasure) takes the place of the genuine purpose that in all other cases accompanies purposiveness. When I engage the object something occurs which Kant calls the harmony of my faculties of cognition. But this harmony (my sense that the object makes sense, is coherent) is achieved without the use of concepts, and without a concept I cannot be regarding the object in terms of any determinate purpose. And yet I find it purposive (for my faculties of cognition). What I encounter is mere sense, mere suitability. Mere suitability of x without any definite y which x is suitable for, is suitability without material content: x displays only the *form* of purposiveness. (1982:231)

Where is the analogue in this to pain in the context of "interrogational" torture? With the appropriate substitutions, Kant's definition would read something like this: "Pain is the form of the informativeness of a victim so far as this is perceived in him without any representation of information." As Scarry, Shue, and other writers on torture have remarked, the vast majority of those on whom the pain of torture is inflicted because of their purported informativeness have nothing to inform about. Shue, who proposes the distinction between interrogational torture and terroristic torture, goes on to admit that "it is hardly necessary to point out that very few actual instances of torture are likely to fall entirely within the category of interrogational torture" (1978:134). To continue with the appropriate substitutions in the quotation from Cohen,

> because pain is informative in this way: it does suit some use, namely, the use the torturer makes of it. . . . The sense that pain makes consists entirely in its making sense to the torturer. Its informativeness consists in the torturer's finding it informative. The torturer's finding it informative (which is a finding realized as a feeling of pleasure) takes the place of the genuine information that in all other cases accompanies informativeness.

"Pleasure" may not be exactly what the torturer is likely to admit to feeling. The three torturers[2] whose accounts I had the dubious privilege of hearing laid claim to a quest for the truth. We may call this the pleasure in "truth." In the words of one of the ex-torturers I interviewed, "You have got to beat them [a generic expression for torture] in such a way until they tell you exactly what happened: no more, no less. Then you know that the beatings [pain] were *just right*" (emphasis mine). This excerpt from my transcription of my fieldnotes merits being read alongside Alberti's celebrated definition of beauty as "a harmony of all the Parts, in whatever Subject it appears, fitted together with such Proportion and Connection, that nothing could be added, diminished or altered, but for the Worse" (1966 [1485]:113). All three torturers interviewed were hard-pressed to come up with a specific instance of "truth" worthy of their efforts. And the circumstances of our conversations were notably such that there was no apparent need for them to conceal any "truthful" information they might have obtained. Their floundering and groping around for something persuasive to offer me when asked seemed to indicate that they were clearly not sitting on anything meriting the label "top secret." Nevertheless, they continued to insist that those who were tortured were deserving embodiments of pain. This leads me to continue with my adaptive appropriation of the quotation from Cohen:

> When the torturer engages the victim something occurs which we may characterize as the harmony of the torturer's faculties of cognition. But this harmony (the torturer's sense that the victim in pain makes sense, is coherent) is achieved without the use of concepts, and without a concept the torturer cannot be regarding the object in terms of any determinate information. And yet the torturer finds the victim-in-pain informative (for the torturer's faculties of cognition). What he or she encounters is mere sense, mere suitability. Mere suitability of x without any definite y which x is suitable for, is suitability without material content: x displays only the *form* of informativeness.

The knowledge of the connection between beauty and pain in "the little tradition" may be commonplace. My detour through the great tradition, rather than summoning this little tradition, is intended to suggest that there is perhaps a stronger case to be made that the sensory mode called the aesthetic ought not to be limited to the beautiful but must be ready to admit a most unwelcome member into its domain, pain. Recalling that signification by definition entails a three-place predication of representation, object, and interpretant, if virtual unsignifiability is what characterizes what we have called the qualisignification of beauty, then what are we to do with the virtual unsignifiability of pain? In short, if unsignifiability (unrepresentability and uninterpretability) were the criterion, then this member's claim to regnancy in the aesthetic domain would be certainly assured, especially in its sheer resistance to language. In *The Body in Pain*, Scarry says of the relationship of pain to language, "Physical pain does not simply resist language but actively destroys it, bringing about an immediate reversion to a state anterior to language, to the sounds and cries a human being makes before language is learned" (1985:4). Insofar as the aesthetic is concerned with the sensory, or rather with throbbing percepts, percepts that push against the conceptual membrane that encloses the world of active semeiosis and articulate speech, pain is one with beauty.

There is, however, one—at least one—difference. While beauty too puts language on trial, it does so in a manner quite different from the way pain does. Beauty finds language wanting because of beauty's profound inexhaustibility; pain finds language wanting in pain's excruciating particularity. If beauty as a qualisign is pregnant with inexhaustible possibilities, pain is a *sinsign*[3] that is exhausted in its simplicity and singularity.

If, as I have indicated, a qualisign is construed to be a pre-sign or a hyposign that contains—in its double sense—significance, its freedom lies in its potential for expansion in semeiosis, in becoming more than a mere qualisign; it "lies" in locating the object for which it stands and an interpretive manner in which it stands. And here I intend the pun in "lie": its situatedness and its mendacity. In finding itself a place or position, it loses a measure of its truth, its integrity. Be that as it may, the manners in which beauty on one hand and pain on the other find their freedom are different. The principal mode of signification in which beauty finds its expression is in iconic signs:[4] in metaphors and in objects that partake of beauty's qualities in different measures.[5] This objectification is generous. It opens out to the world, inviting further signs, objects, and interpretants to partake of its bounty, of its essence. Pain, by contrast, when embodied, closes in on itself. Where beauty extends itself, pain finds affirmation in its intensification. Beauty repressed can be painful; pain expressed is susceptible to incredulity.

Pain is highly localized. Its outermost limit is the boundary of the victim's body. Its inner limit can be as small as a point in one's foot where a nail is being pounded in. And no one pain is like any other. Two examples should help us understand these limits.

The Individual in Terror

In late November 1983, Benedict was rounded up with twenty other young men by the army in Batticaloa in eastern Sri Lanka. He claimed he was innocent then and he claims he is innocent now, saying he had assiduously avoided the militants operating in the area. He was interrogated by a sergeant, then by a captain, and then by a man in civilian clothes, then by one in uniform, then by a corporal, and then by another captain, and soon he lost count of who and how many had interrogated him. They did not believe him. There was another boy who, under torture, named him as one of the militants. The soldiers tortured Benedict repeatedly in order to extract "information" from him. He was beaten with two-foot-long plastic pipes filled with sand. Beatings with sand-filled pipes have an unusual capacity to cause pain without breaking the skin as easily as do other implements. One does cough up blood from the beatings on one's chest and back with one of these pipes, but skilled torturers see to it that the skin does not break. The heaviest beatings are inflicted on the soles of feet, even to the point that the skin actually breaks. But as for the rest of the body, fluid builds up under the skin. The whole body swells up. The face is spared, and above all care is taken not to leave lacerations. The absence of visible wounds is evidence, presentable to the investigating magistrate, that information was not extracted under torture. The victim's greatest certainty, his pain, is paradoxically also the magistrate's locus of doubt. Pain stops at the skin's limit. It is not shareable. Benedict did not give the torturer any "information."

From the local army camp he was transferred to the now infamous Boosa camp in the island's south. In this camp he was handed over to the expert care of the dreaded Special Task Force. There, too, there were numerous torturers; the worst among them was a young woman in uniform. Of the great variety of highly specialized torture techniques he was subjected to, he recalls the swallowing-the-saliva torture as the worst. In this technique one is made to swallow one's own spittle, once every six seconds, as many as two hundred times before a fifteen-minute break. This causes excruciating pain in one's insides: starting with the throat and head, extending through the gullet to the chest and stomach. If he stopped swallowing before it was time, he was beaten with a sand-filled plastic pipe, he was burned with a cigarette on his feet or where the rope handcuffs had already cut through the skin, or a live wire was held to his genitals. "Suddenly one pains all over, inside and out. One single unrelenting (*orē vali*) pain." Finally he was given the option of not providing information but answering "yes" or "no" to a series of questions.

Upon his release in 1987, Benedict showed me black scars on his brown wrist, describing them as marks from rope handcuffs. Pointing to the same area he also tried to show me scars of cigarette burns. I could not tell the difference; he saw them very clearly. He showed me his feet. He could see the stripes caused by the beatings and the burn marks caused by cigarette butts. I could not see these, either. Perhaps the wounds had healed without leaving any traces, or his feet did not scar, or he was never tortured but merely claims that he was. The last was suggested to me by the cook who happened to walk in on my interview. He, too, was a Tamil. But he was not the only one to doubt. Benedict himself doubted the accounts of other torture victims. Nevertheless, three months after his release, he told me: "Even now, sometimes, like the other day when the B.B.C. man was interviewing me, my body feels like a bubbling candle, filled with pain, inside and out, all over the skin and all over inside. One pain."

My second example is based on a torture victim I saw in 1984, in one of the Tamil militant training camps in southern India. The torturer this time was not a member of the Sri Lankan Special Task Force nor a white man from the Keeny Meeny Services—an outfit of British mercenaries, which, it was alleged, trained and assisted members of this unit.

As late as May 1983, the sum total of Tamil militants in the Jaffna Peninsula numbered no more than three hundred, armed with largely primitive weapons. Virtually no citizen of Jaffna was willing to rent his or her home to these ragtag fighters. The anti-Tamil riots of July of that year, however, resulted in a rush of volunteers, and recruiters from the five main militant groups were competing in a field wherein the harvest was plentiful. Most of the enlisted did not know which group they were enlisting in or what difference it made, if any. All they knew was that they would be shipped off to a camp somewhere, most probably in India, where they would be trained in combat; they would return to avenge their kinsfolk, friends, and fellow Tamils who had lost their lives and possessions in the riots, and would help establish the independent state of Eeḷam.

As it turned out, the "training" in the "training camps" was limited to a week's weapons training and months of waiting in a second camp where calisthenics, malnutrition, indoctrination, and despotic intimidation by a twenty-one-year-old camp commander were the daily fare until and unless orders came "from above" that there was a mission to be carried out. At times the commander's intimidation tactics turned to forms of bodily torture. Unlike his counterparts at Boosa, the torturer rarely, if ever, professed the pretense of "information gathering." The torture almost always began as a form of amusement for the commander and a few of his lieutenants. Amusement would switch into fantastic illusions of power on the part of this commander without warning. The more the victim cowered and shrank in pain, the more the commander expanded his swelling power. What began as amusement would often then conclude with the pretense of its having been an attempt at information gathering or punishment for some vague infraction. No two individuals were allowed to carry on a conversation for however brief a moment without a third person's being present. According to one informant, "I am sure most of those in there wanted to escape. But there were a few who were the commander's men. The thing is, no one knew who was and who was not." However, on the basis of my own interviews with ex-inmates of this camp, it was hard to say whether boredom, disenchantment with "comradism," or the commander's sadism was the most unbearable in this camp. There were several daring attempts at escape. If caught, an escapee would face one of two forms of punishment. The more extreme would be execution following the accusation that the escapee was a traitor to the movement, or a spy for one of the rival militant groups or for the Sri Lankan government. The lesser punishment was thirty days' imprisonment in solitary confinement.

One of the residents of the camps, Guhanesan by pseudonym, had been recruited from the Mannar District at a time when his wife was seven months pregnant. On the 270th day after Guhanesan's arrival in the camp, a new recruit arrived from Mannar. He brought Guhanesan the news that his wife had given birth to a son. Guhanesan, a somewhat senior camp member by then, asked the camp commander's permission to make a quick boat trip to see his wife and son, promising to return to camp within seven days. The young commander instantly refused his permission and, furthermore, accused him of harboring "bourgeois feelings." A much touted part of the movement's manifesto was that forsaking family was the true mark of a fighter. In the words of my main informant on matters of this camp, "everybody knew that this was one rule not to be taken seriously, because no Tamil fighter ever forgot his family, not even the camp commander, who visited Tiruchchirappalli or Madras whenever members of his family were passing through these cities." Guhanesan defied the commander's orders and with the help of some of his comrades escaped from the camp. However, as promised, he returned on the seventh day, even though rough seas and the stepped-up surveillance by the Sri Lankan army in the forests in the island's northwest region allowed him only six short nighttime hours to spend with his wife and son. He returned to the camp in order to prove to everyone that he was not a deserter and was willing to undergo the thirty days' solitary confinement, if necessary, to prove this.

Instead of solitary confinement, the camp commander personally tortured him by hammering a nail up the sole of his right foot, leaving it there overnight. The next day, the nail was removed from the swollen (and presumably infected) foot, and Guhanesan was beaten on his back with a heavy baton. "And then," in the words of my informant, "his legs were broken, as a warning to the others of what could happen if orders were disobeyed." In mid-1984, Guhanesan, paralyzed below the hips, was dragging himself around the camp grounds on a tire like a beggar. Orders were that he be described as a beggar to outsiders, but to the residents of the camp he was to serve as a "living example." In this grim environment, where even humor could only be morbid, his condition amused the other militants-in-waiting. Even though the lower half of his body was completely paralyzed, and he could not feel even a live cigarette butt on his foot, he groaned in pain (in "imaginary pain," according to the others), complaining of a nail stuck in his right foot. The excruciating pain was only in this single spot, no larger in circumference than the point of the nail. All attempts by others at locating this spot by feeling and pressing the entire surface of his foot yielded no results. He could not feel a thing except for this single, unidentifiable, excruciating spot of pain. This was a contradiction and an impossibility that some of his more fortunate campmates found hilarious.

I have introduced you to two examples in order to illustrate the limits, the particularity, the unshareability, and the incommunicability of pain in torture. There are dozens of other instances that I could employ to make the same points. The phenomena described are no different from the innumerable accounts that one may find of torture in other parts of the world in reports obtainable from Amnesty International and other human rights abuses monitoring organizations. At this level of experiencing pain it appears that one is unlikely to find any significant effect of culture.

There are, of course, the much more socialized pains: the headache, the toothache, the earache, the back spasm, and the countless other pains that have been given names of recognition in the folklore and diagnostic labels in the medical lore. Their representations are public, available for more than one person to map his or her private experience onto, even though no one pain is like another. And from there sympathy and empathy take over, making the pain in question more or less shareable.

Homo individuum in torture reaches its extreme. Pain's privatization becomes absolute, its *hic et nunc* complete. Indeed, I encountered time and time again torture victims who had been subjected to the same tortures by the same torturers in the same camps and jails, and even at the same time, and who—when they finally were capable of speaking about their experiences—denied that their fellow inmates were tortured and accused them of lying.

Torture perverts all dialogic. For the victim's interlocutor is not that person's parent, friend, or child. The interlocutor is not even a mere stranger but rather the torturer, for whom a scream is not a sign of pain but an insignia of power. And even after the torture victim is set free, regardless of the readiness of friends and kinsfolk who remained free to extend love, understanding, and sympathy, the victim persists in denying that his individuated pain could be shared, contained as it is within the bounds of a private body that is reticent to express itself willingly through any signs in general and incapable of expressing itself in signs of language in particular.

Of course, the newly freed victims did talk. But in interview after interview I found these individuals willing to talk about their capture, their cells, their meals, their fellow prisoners, the weave of their mats and the state of their clothes, food, and furniture. Of these they spoke even with some animation, expecting me to be interested. All these details were believable and therefore understandable. But of torture they volunteered very little.[6] Then gradually—with coaxing, with the purpose of the interview undeniably clear—they began to talk. But the interest that animated the recall of the mundane details of prison life suddenly abandoned the intonation of speech. Of course, brutalities were wearisomely enumerated and details enunciated, first with bored parsimoniousness, then in flat-toned recitations devoid of conviction, the speaker pausing now and then as if to wonder how these details could interest anyone. Cruelties that had lain outside speech and outside reason were recited with such syntactic correctness as to become a routine, a mannerism, a set of clichés. I do not believe that most of the victims I interviewed were unwilling to talk about their experiences because it was too painful to do so. There were no signs of contained passion. Rather, attempts to extract information were met with expressions of utter listlessness. Months later I found out that it was not so much boredom that weighed down on the victim as it was the overwhelming sense of the sheer worthlessness of all attempts to communicate something that was so radically individuated and rendered unshareable. As Scarry describes it, "the narration as a whole has the quality of a sketch: the experience it describes is utterly clear in its outline but all the emotional edges have been eliminated" (1985:32). This disposition of the victim is exploited by the torturers in court to make lies of the victim's claims of having been tortured. The passionless listings of atrocities committed by the torturer leave the judge and the court unconvinced. The unbelievable is also unexplainable and the unexplainable the inexpressible. Thus it would be fair to say that pain does not find its way out of its arrested, sinsignificant state, even when it finds objectification in verbal recitations or in listings of painful experiences. In order for pain to find its freedom in the semeiosis of culture, it must pass through the liminal phases of either terror or beauty, or both.

Of course, it is terror and pain that hyperindividuate the victim in the first place. But the terror I speak of is a second, therapeutic terror, a seismic aftershock. This terror can take many forms. Among the torture victims I came to know whose pain passed into this terror, terror manifested itself in a variety of ways: in uncontrollable sobbing, in rage, in violent shakings of the body, in visible efforts at restructuring a narrative with conscious self-corrections introduced regarding details and their proper sequences—corrections that were far more confusing to the interviewer than the mechanical recitation of the preterrorized torture victim yet carried far greater conviction.

In all its manifestations, therapeutic terror begins the process of the deindividuation of the person, the process of disarticulating a hyperindividualized self that had been compacted in pain. Whether or not in and through terror the victim's pain is reduced, I cannot say. I had no means of measuring pain. On one occasion, in Trincomalee my wife and I witnessed a young man who had just been released by the army as he writhed on the ground with what seemed like uncontrollably violent shivers. When an onlooker described his state to me as a "fit" or "convulsion," the Siddha physician who was treating this young man said, "It is pain coming out. Those who see him are terrified. The boy is also terrified. But that is good, for the pain is coming out." This same physician described this kind of terror as "the trembling and fear that comes through remembering terrible acts." In the original Tamil—"*koṭūrattai ninaittu varum payankaramum naṭunaṭukkamum*"—the description of redemptive terror is made up of a reduplicating consonant-and-vowel series of flaps and trills that onomatopoeically captures and echoes the experience itself,[7] metonymically triggering a veritable shudder of sound-images. *Koṭūram*, *naṭunaṭukkam*, and *payankaram* are all offered as translations of "terror" in the Madras University English-Tamil Dictionary (1963). The terror in question—remembered or relived terror—dislodges pain from its fixed site. In this chapter I suggest that terror shows pain a way out of its static particularity into a domain of inexhaustible virtuality, a domain that is home to beauty as well. But what we do know for certain is that once pain extends into terror, it becomes more understandable to those with whom the victim returns to live, and reflexively, pain becomes more understandable to victims themselves. The mother in whose arms her twenty-four-year-old son is finally able to cry comforts herself as much as her son with the words, "Son, you have returned at last." Not "You are healed at last," but "You have returned at last." Healing, she realizes, will take "as long as it takes to forget what happened."

Pain also finds its exit into semeiosis through works of art. Thirty years ago, the Jaffna Peninsula, which today is the center of the Tamil separatist movement, was a relatively unmusical and unpoetic corner of the island. This is not to deny the few extraordinarily talented artists and art-lovers their due. But such talents were rarely appreciated as ends in themselves, as they often are, for instance, in South India. Art, at best, was seen as a means to other ends. To be sure, a few girls studied the piano for their various certificates in music from the two London schools of music, the Trinity and the Royal Colleges of Music. Every afternoon, in certain villages of Jaffna, among the Christians, one could hear excruciatingly mechanical and earless attempts at thumping out Bach fugues or preludes on untuned pianos. It gave them "culture" and a discount on their dowries. There were also those who learned Karnatic (or South Indian classical) music. The quality of this music as a whole was much better but poor in comparison to what one would find among a comparable class of people in southern India. Students who went into the humanities (or the "arts," as they are still called) in high school and in the university were treated as intellectual rejects. Teachers of Tamil literature were the most frequent targets of jokes. Jaffna liked to think of itself as training sober professionals: physicians, engineers, mathematicians, scientists, and lawyer-politicians. The available poetry and prose were scanty and mostly mediocre.

But since the civil war, street theater has flourished, and such poems are written that make one tremble. It is true that on one hand the people of Jaffna as a whole were experiencing an ever-shrinking perimeter of freedom as if it were a collective body in pain, lost to the wider world as much as the wider world was lost to it. On the other hand, as if to regain the lost world, the voice, especially in its aesthetic mode, provides the needed self-extension as a means of occupying a much larger space than what the pain-inflicting constraints of the military presence allowed.

Since the beginning of the war, throughout the peninsula, blackboards have been nailed to trees near some well-known intersections. On these, every morning, the Tigers wrote the names of those among them who had been killed. Every day for four years, the boards unfailingly bore fresh names. But on the day following the Indian Peace-Keeping Force's arrival in 1987, the blackboards had been wiped clean and stayed clean. In the words of a poem written not long afterward:

ōṭināḷ avaḷ patunki
antru entrum pōl-otunki
pārttāḷ kaṇ kavarntu
māṇṭār pēr attanayum pārttum
pārkkā viṛiyil terittatē
verumpalakai
mutal veruṇṭāḷ
pin amarntāḷ
ēmatramataintāl

tuyaraṅkoṇṭāḷ
naṭu naṭuṅkināḷ
paniyuṇṭa ālamum
tannai maranta noṭiyil
naṭuṅki nimirntatu.

On that day,
unlike on all other days
when having sneaked to the tree
to hide and read with longing
the names of the dead,
she froze as if smitten
by the markless board,
        and settled,
haunches on heels,
        first disappointed,
        then saddened,
to shiver and shiver again
while the great dew-drunk banyan tree too,
in a moment's self-forgetfulness,
shook
and then stood still.

Daniel (after Sitralega Mounaguru)

The poem contains within it both pain and, in its shivers, the ingredient of redeeming terror. Far greater dread is found in a poem written by Thiyagarajah Selvanity (known as Selvi), who was awarded the prestigious Poetry International Award in 1994.

In Search of Sun

        My soul, full of despair
                yearns for life
        where ever I turn
                I see
        primitive humans
yellow toothed, ugly mouthed
thirsting blood, slit flesh
        saliva adribble
cruel nails and horrifying eyes

        Bragging and jubilating
over victories are not new
legs lost from long walks for
        miles and miles

in search of a throne
days wasted waiting for full
moons
only boredom lingers . . .
(*Jaffna, 1988; quoted in de Mel 1994:10*)

The author of this poem was taken into custody by the LTTE on August 30, 1991. That she was tortured is a certainty. She never came back and is believed to have been killed. What seems to have survived are her poems, which are still capable of helping grief move.

In my limited fieldwork I did not find any works of art, in poetry, prose, painting, or sculpture, wrought by survivors of torture. This is not to say that such artists do not exist. However, I have observed such victims moving from a condition of speechlessness or "autistic speech" to the ability to form elementary metaphors. The appearance of the latter is the earliest sign of pain's entry into cultural semeiosis. This process is marked by pain's retreat from its sinsignificant state into pure qualisignification and its reemergence and reexpression through objectification in iconic metaphors. Consider the following excerpts from two separate interviews I had with Benedict, in June 1987 and in September of that same year.

Interview 1

(After lengthy preliminary introductions, and assurances from those who were responsible for his release—therefore those whom he could trust without reservations—that I was all right and that he should tell me everything.)

D: How long were you in Boosa?
B: Twenty-four months.
D: Before then?
B: In Batticaloa.
D: Where in Batticaloa?
B: In the police jail.
D: Tell me a little of what happened.
B (after three minutes' silence): What do you want [to know]?
D: Why did the police arrest you?
B (after a further lengthy silence): The police didn't, the army did.
D: And then?
B (rhetorically): And then what? Then all that happened happened.
D: Is it difficult for you to talk about what happened?
B (flippantly and lightly): What difficulty?
D: Is there any reason why you don't wish to talk about anything? I don't wish to force you to talk.

B: There is nothing like that. (Silence.)

D: Tell me, what were you doing when the army came and arrested you?

B: I was in the shop.

This preliminary bit of dialogue took almost fifteen minutes. After about half an hour more of this pace, we broke for lunch. We continued the interview that afternoon.

D: Tell me about Boosa.

B: What do you want me to tell you?

D: Oh. What time you got up, when you ate, what you did all day, what time you went to bed. Things like that.

B: When they tortured us we would be awakened at different times.

D: How did they wake you up?

B: They poured water on us. They hit us with a stick.

D: So your clothes and bed would be all wet.

B: There was no bed. A grass mat with a single weave, sometimes. Mostly it was the floor. The floor was always wet. There was mud. The room was only so big. At different times different numbers of people would be in it. The first month there were four.

D: The same four people?

B: Never the same four.

A later segment of the same interview:

B: We had to run on our heels so that at all times only one foot was on the ground. While we ran soldiers would hit us on the calves with PVC [polyvinyl chloride] pipes.

D: You said something about cigarettes.

B: Yes, they burned us.

D: Often?

B: Sometimes often. Sometimes not so often.

D: Where did they burn you?

B (Pointing to parts of his body): Here. Here. Here. Everywhere.

D: Not on the face?

B: Not on the face.

D: What did they do to the wounds?

B: Nothing. Sometimes they put chilies in them.

D: Did they ever give you first aid?

B: Yes.

D: How often?

B: Depends.

D: Depends on what?

B: I don't know. . . . Sometimes we would be allowed to do exercises. We always tried to exercise in our cells. The last year it became crowded. Then we would talk. The EPRLF[8] chap used to teach us about Marx and the revolution.

D: Did you learn about Marx?

B: It was a diversion.

D: Was anyone from the other [militant] movements with you?

B: Everybody. Militants, nonmilitants, informers, older men, young boys . . . about twelve.

D: Did these other groups try to teach you, too?

B: Not so much. Some EROS people also did.

D: The Tigers [LTTE]?

B: They did not say much.

D: But there were Tigers?

B: They did not say that they were Tigers. But they did not say much. Tigers don't talk much.

D: TELO?

B: There were some of them, too. Who knows?

D: Were there fights and arguments among the groups in the camp?

B: No. All were happy when soldiers were killed. But then whenever soldiers were killed we would be tortured.

D: Are you going to join a group?

B: I don't know.

D: Which group do you think you'd join if you chose to join a group?

B: Whatever you say.

D (laughing): But I am not recruiting for any group.

B: Or the Lady [the person responsible for his release] says.

D: What does "the Lady" say?

B: I don't know.

D: Was Sudharshan also tortured?

B: I don't know.

D: But you were in the same camp.

B: They all say that they were tortured.

D: But Sudharshan showed me his scars.

B: Lies.

D: How about Nathan?

B: All lies. .

D: But he too showed me scars. He swore.

B: You can get scars from rats biting.

D: Rats?

B: Yes, there were rats sometimes. Here. Look (showing his heels).

D: But now why do you think Nathan, Sudharshan, and all the others would have sworn to me had they not been tortured?

B: The fellow who told the army that I was a militant also swore.

D: So you don't think anyone else was tortured.

B: They might have been. I heard them scream. But who knows if it was for real. Sometimes they have tape recorders, too [i.e., tape-recorded screams]. All I know was they tortured me.

D: But you said that others were tortured with you sometimes in the same room.

B: I don't know. What if they were acting?

In the last part of the interview the paradox of pain—one man's certainty providing the other man's primary model of what it is to doubt—is brought to a pathetic pitch. One even doubts one's fellow sufferer's pain. But what persists in this and many other interviews such as this is the drone of silence—a silence that does not settle for the anthropologist whether it is a silence of a not-being-able-to-speak or of an ought-not-to-speak.

Interview 2 (Discontinuous Quotations)

B: Imagine having to eat where you also have to pass wastes.

B: This woman torturer was the worst. If you just looked at her, she could be your friend's sister. Young. I think she was a Muslim. But when she opened her mouth. Father! I can't even repeat her words. Bad words. Like a sewer (*narakal*).

B: You couldn't find a handful of rice without stones in it. [We] just touched it like that and pushed it aside. You wouldn't even feed your dog rice like that. There was this thing called *coti* [a watery gravy] they served us. It smelled of urine. They used to laugh when they served us that.

B: This one fellow, they beat the bottom of his feet in such a way that the skin from one sole just fell off. Just like that. Like a tire. You have seen these pieces on the road. Like that. And underneath, skin like a baby's.

And finally, to revisit a statement introduced earlier,

B: Even now, sometimes, like the other day when the B.B.C. man was interviewing me, my body feels like a bubbling candle, filled with pain, inside and out, all over the skin and all over inside.

In these quotations one is first struck by the invocation of the domestic. We hear Benedict finding it reasonable to have expected something more like what was true in his home or any civilized home. Eating where one passes bodily waste is unthinkable at home. The outhouse or bathroom is as far removed as possible from the kitchen in a Tamil home. Stones in rice are an acute embarrassment to the women of the home and are often reason enough for the husband or father to stomp in anger or to pick a fight or to berate the wife. It is only reasonable for a domesticated man, a civilized man, to expect stone-free rice. A dog, a domestic animal, is brought in as an illustration. It is not any dog, but "your dog." Perhaps the nucleus of sociality that was torn away in prison and under torture was the reality of belonging to a home and a family. Indeed, kinship is referred to in the second quotation. The torturer is likened, at first glance, to a "friend's sister." In earlier interviews when and if references to home and kin were made, they performed a strictly referential function, as part of a minimally descriptive account. They were never employed in any figurative or extended sense.

Finally, I wish to consider the only torture victim I met who came from among the Estate Tamils. There were not many of them in the camps, but Murugesu was arrested for being in the wrong place at the wrong time. One thing led to another; he was accused, tortured, made to confess, tried, found innocent, and released. The whole process took one year.

Murugesu was much more forthcoming than the others I had interviewed. And in my judgment he was adjusting quite well to his past experiences and his present options. But Murugesu's mother did not think so. I tried to find out what exactly she thought was wrong with her son. All she said was, "He isn't like before." I could get no more details than that, and I had not known him before his ordeal. His father, a retired and sickly plantation laborer, only partly shared his wife's concerns. But the *kōṭaṅki* (the local diviner-healer-priest) seemed to understand the mother's concerns quite clearly. His diagnosis was that Murugesu had a demon in him, a demon that had entered him when he was in Boosa camp. And there was no point in trying to exorcise this demon because he was all tied up inside with rope and was asleep. The kōṭanki's task was to wake up the demon and make him tremble. This was to be done through the offering of blood sacrifices and the singing of mantras to the accompaniment of the *uṭukku*-drum. "In India," he said, "they use a horse-tail-whip to beat the demon into waking up and trembling. My grandfather used to do that. But nobody here knows how." I asked him how big the demon was. He said that it was as big as his fist, "like a swollen boil." Without any further evidence, I hypothesize that this bound, dormant demon is pain that has to be terrorized into wakefulness before being made to move out into the world.

While preparing for the ritual, Murugesu's father, a Hindu, asked me if I was a Christian. I mumbled a brief summary to the effect that my father was a nominal Christian convert from Hinduism, my mother an Anglican Christian, and I a respectful agnostic. My answer seemed to satisfy him, and he asked no further but moved on to tell me tales of life on the plantation during his youth. One sight he said he could never forget. It was that of the Anglican catechist, a dark man from the Nāḍār caste, walking up the hill with his violin in one hand, a magic lantern in the other, and a shoulder bag with a Bible in it. And of all the pictures he showed, the one that they all liked the most, and had asked him to show them over and over again, on every visit, was that of Christ dying on the cross. "How beautiful! What pain! It gave us peace," he said. *(Evvaḷavu vaṭivu! Enna vētanai! Namakkō oru camātānam).*

The next day, Murugesu's father asked me to accompany them to the Roman Catholic church in the town nearby. I told him that I did not quite know how to worship in a Catholic church but that I would like to accompany them. So we went to St. Mary's Church. The mass was taking place. I, knowing only slightly more about what to do in a Catholic church than did my friends, walked up to the first pew and knelt down alongside a few other worshipers. Both Murugesu and his father prayed, with eyes fixed on the icon of Jesus on the cross. Separating us from the priest, the altar, and the icons were scores of candles that had been lit by other worshipers. As the flames cast their flickering light on the statue of the suffering Christ, I also noticed the candles swelling in blisters. In a flash I remembered Benedict, a Catholic, and how he must have come upon the image of the bubbling candle and the body in pain. As Murugesu's father said, "How beautiful! What pain!"

Conclusion

I have argued that beauty and pain are qualisigns and sinsigns respectively. In Peirce's scheme, a qualisign is a semeiosic "first." It is a felt quality of experience in toto—present, immediate, uncategorized, and prereflective. Qualisigns do enter into cultural processes of significance when they are embodied and interpreted and where judgments and evaluations are made. Pain too has a present, immediate, uncategorized, and prereflective aspect to it. But this "Firstness" of pain is overwhelmed by what Peirce calls "Secondness"—the experience of radical otherness in which ego and non-ego are precipitated out against each other in unique and absolute opposition, where the oneness of Firstness is ejaculated into the *hic et nunc* of actuality. Thirdness is Peirce's phenomenological category of mediation, mainly through language and culture. It is in Thirdness that semeiosis resumes its continuity, its movement. Thirdness is the domain of meaning.

The qualisignificant and sinsignificant origins of beauty and pain are such, however, that even when they do become available to language, the traces of their sojourn in Firstness and Secondness, respectively, remain fresh and vivid. Their modes of emergence into general semeiosis differ. In general, beauty unfolds generously and with ease. But even at the brink of language pain lies stuck, individuated and arrested as a sinsign. Nevertheless, pain can be freed. In Sri Lanka, a culturally recognized means of effecting such a freedom entails the experience of remembered terror. Terror remembered disarticulates and "deindividuates." Terror shatters pain and in so doing makes it available for union with beauty. It is as if pain returns to being a qualisign and then, aligning itself with beauty, rides on metaphors and icons of affect into the freedom of the enabling semeiosis of language and culture. Through poetry, theater, art, and other aesthetic forms, beauty is wrung out of terror.

Too easy. For before tuning our ears, lifting our eyes, and opening our hearts to terror turned beauty so as to find therein final redemption and repose, we—the survivors and those among us who find comfort in their recovery into culture—need to ride our consolations between two echoes. The first in time comes from Theodor Adorno's response to poems of the Holocaust's horror written by the Jewish survivor-poet Paul Celan: Adorno judged it barbaric to write a poem after Auschwitz (see Felstiner 1995:188). The other comes in his recantation of his earlier disapproval. "Perennial suffering has as much right to expression as the tortured have to scream," he wrote; "hence it may have been wrong to say that no poem could be written after Auschwitz" (quoted in Felstiner 1995:232). Granted, the horrors of Nazi Germany—and more recently of Uganda, Rwanda, and Bosnia—may appear to dwarf those of Sri Lanka. Regardless of the when, where, and how of horror, to aestheticize at the expense of the fallen, to find in the death-cries of others harmonized verse, or to find vicarious pleasure in those survivors who do transform experience into poetry or narrative is to be trapped in Adorno's ambivalence. Poetry, prose, theater, and painting are not the only aestheticizing agents. The poesis of culture itself is a narcotic, and as such it summons us to respond to Emily Dickinson's charge that

> Narcotics cannot still the tooth
> That nibbles at the soul.

6

SUFFERING NATION AND ALIENATION

Gatherings of exiles and émigrés and refugees,
gathering on the edge of "foreign" cultures; gathering
in the half-life, half-light of foreign tongues, or in the uncanny
fluency of another's language; gathering the signs of approval and
acceptance, degrees, discourses, disciplines; gathering the memories
of underdevelopment, of other worlds lived retroactively;
gathering the past in a ritual of revival; gathering the present.
(Homi Bhabha)

The modes of conspicuousness, obtrusiveness, and obstinacy all have
the function of bringing to the fore the characteristic of
occurrentness in what is available.
(Martin Heidegger)

WHEN violence is transformed into art—or even artful prose, be it reportorial or even analytic—its aestheticization is obvious. Art makes sense out of the senseless. The aestheticizing impulse, however, is less obvious in another creation of culture: the nation-state, that political work of art. The nation-state too promises to bring forth order out of disorder, mold form from that in which form is absent. But even though this order may be posited as a future hope, something to be achieved in the making, this hope is drenched in nostalgia, the imagined glory that once was. In South Asia in particular, the Orientalists' contribution to this nostalgia has been massive. And thus such books as A. L. Basham's *The Wonder That Was India* (1954) or Jawaharlal Nehru's *The Discovery of India* (1960) are found by many South Asians to be highly stirring. Western nations have their own nationalized pasts. The nation-state promises to soothe and heal, but its healing comforts are expressed in the language of recovery and restoration, through an orientation toward the past. The nation-state promises to restore to the chords of collective discontent atunement with a collective consciousness, to recover for its people a moral order where there is only disorder, and to return its nationals to the path of their intended destiny. And above all, as part of its aestheticizing and healing mission, modern nation-states have promised to provide refuge to those whose lives have been rendered chaotic by catastrophic events, be they natural or man-made. This too is claimed to be a legacy from the past, attributed to South Asian generosity or to what a Christian nation ought to do. In short, the nation-state is aestheticized by the nationalization of its past, which is projected onto the future—by which act the present is appeased. In this chapter, I will argue that in the late twentieth century, the nation-state has proved to be a blatant narcotic at least in one respect, and that in this it fails to soothe the soul. I am referring to what nation-states do with their refugees, as revealed in the lives of Tamils who have become refugees within and without their national borders.

This chapter is based mainly on research carried out over the summer of 1993 in London in which I sought to find out how Sri Lankan Tamil immigrants to the United Kingdom are disposed toward the nation, whether they nationalize their past, and, if so, how. These immigrants include asylum-seekers as well as various shades of bona fide British subjects of Ceylonese and (later) Sri Lankan origin. I was interested not only in how these Tamils *imagined* their past but how this past, imagined or otherwise, entered into their way of being-in-the-world, how they folded it into their "background practices." I shall argue that Tamils came to Britain in three phases, and that in each of these three phases came immigrants whose comportment to nationalism in general and a nationalized past in particular took roughly three distinguishable forms.[1] In order to do this I have invoked Homi Bhabha to set the tone, Martin Heidegger to provide the type or template, and I offer the token.[2]

Tamils in Britain

Phase 1: The Elite

By the time Sri Lankan Tamils from Sri Lanka were arriving in Britain in the early 1980s seeking asylum from the civil war, there were Tamils already in Britain who had preceded them under quite different circumstances. The 1980s group indeed represented the third phase of Tamil migration to Britain.

The first generation of Ceylonese (as they were then called) who emigrated to Britain was an odd assortment of Sinhalas, Tamils, and Burghers: women and men who came to Britain in the early years surrounding the island's independence from its colonial power. What most of them had in common was an upper- or upper-middle-class background, an education in the elite high schools of Ceylon, a self-identification as Ceylonese, and a cultivated ease with Western ways and tastes. Many came to Britain to obtain professional degrees in law, medicine, and engineering or to obtain graduate degrees that would ease them into the faculties of the universities and the civil service at home. They cultivated a blend of nostalgia for the colonial days and a sense of national pride for the nation that was theirs. Few had any intention of staying on in Britain, for too many were the comforts of home that they would thereby relinquish. And, more important, to sever the link with Ceylon was to sever the link with a nation, their nation. A survey of this generation's home libraries is a telling revelation: the books they had purchased in the 1950s through the 1960s were, along with those in the fields of their primary interest or specialization, national histories of Ceylon. The standard collection in these home libraries included R. L. Brohier's *Discovering Ceylon*; John Davy's *An Account of the Interior of Ceylon and of Its Inhabitants with Travels in That Island*; Wilhelm Geiger's *The Mahavamsa or The Great Chronicle of Ceylon*; Robert Knox's *An Historical Relation of Ceylon*; H. Parker's *Ancient Ceylon*; and K. M. de Silva's *A History of Sri Lanka*.

For these immigrants, Britain began as a rite of passage. As is true in all such cases, the children who were born in Britain found their parents' vestige of cultural and national loyalties to Ceylon quaint and queer. And yet, provoked by the British context in which emblems of nation were overwhelmingly and insistently present—emblems and a nationhood from which they were alienated—even this generation counteracted British nationalism with an assertion of their own national past. If there was only one fact they could remember and recite, it was that their nation was more than a thousand years older than England and Scotland.

What these immigrants deeply held and tried to inculcate in their children was the belief that they, among South Asians, were special. They were not Indians. They were certainly not "Pakis." They were Ceylonese. They flaunted their "uncanny fluency of another's language," a high-pedigree dialect of British English, far removed from the kind that was spoken by the Indo-Pakistani immigrants of Southhall and Wembley. They had gone to the best of Ceylon's schools and their children went to the better ("public," if possible) schools in Britain; they were professionals, as their children ought to be someday. The Tamils among this first phase of immigrants came largely from the highest Tamil caste in Ceylon, the Veḷḷāḷās. They made sure that their children knew this. There were almost no Estate Tamils among them. The Sinhalas came from the upper classes, even if not all of them came from the uppermost caste of Sinhala society, the Goyigamas. The "cultured" comportment that these immigrants adopted vis-à-vis their fellow Asians as well as white Britons was inscribed with "*national* pride." "We did not want to let down the name of our country," said a retired Tamil surgeon in Nottingham in an interview with me. In spite of the fact that Tamils of this generation had found sufficient cause for being ambivalent about Sri Lankan nationalism and its increasingly Sinhala-Buddhist shading, they chose the company and cultural deportment toward the world, not of South Indian Tamils living in Britain, but of fellow Ceylonese.

Their living room walls sported Sri Lankan "Devil Dancing" masks, nineteenth-century originals or reproductions of paintings of various Ceylonese landscapes or the Kandy Äsələ Perəhärə, and Sri Lankan batik. Brass and silver trays rested on ebony elephant-tripods, all of them made in Ceylon. A few

South Indian touches were to be found in Hindu homes, where a shrine tended to be set up in an inconspicuous corner with an image of Ganesh and/or a picture of Saraswathi, the goddess of learning. Occasionally—in a more recent trend—a picture of the holy man from Karnataka, Satya Sai Baba, looked down from a wall. In dining room cabinets, china (increasingly, china made in Sri Lanka's new free-trade zones by Noritake and others) was the rule, the south Indian "ever-silver" plates and tumblers the exception. As for musical instruments, one was more likely to find a piano, an electric guitar, bongos, and snare drums—instruments of Westernized Ceylonese—than a veena, sitar, tabla, or the South Indian drum, the mṛdangam. Very few among this generation appeared to be connoisseurs of Indian classical music, northern or southern. But there were many who were aficionados of Western classical music and even jazz, another marker of Ceylon's English-educated elite. On the "strictly indigenous side" in their record collections, one was more likely to find "baila" (music of Iberian origin with a 3/4 beat and a melody confined to three chords) than a recording of the classical singer M. S. Subalakshmi singing the "Sri Venkateshwara Subrapadham," a devotional invocation. A number of individuals of this generation and their children still recalled and used the derogatory epithet "thosai kade music" to describe Indian classical music. The epithet derives from Indian-run eateries in Ceylon that served *tōcais* or *dōsas*, which customarily played recordings of Indian classical/devotional music on their radios. There was to be found among these Tamils, however, a countercurrent as well. For while the Sinhalas were actively nationalizing their past, the Tamils were recovering and reasserting a heritage that stressed the cultural over the political, the cultural tending to be Tamil and Hindu. And even though the monuments of this heritage were to be found more richly distributed in South India than in Sri Lanka, these Tamils had come to hold that the best of this heritage was alive in Jaffna, the northernmost peninsula of Sri Lanka, and was to be found in the dialect of Tamil spoken and the kind of Hinduism practiced (Saiva Siddhanta) in their corner of the island. Nevertheless, the overall impression one gets from this generation of Tamils in Britain is that Tamil cultural heritage tended to receive lip service rather than being "transparently"[3] incorporated into their background practices and habits.

At some point in the first half of the twentieth century a nationalized past, and nationalism itself, had progressed from being an instrumental entity employed at the service of national independence to becoming a part of what Heidegger called an "equipmental whole." In his inimitable prose, Heidegger remarks that "equipment—in accordance with its equipmentality—always is *in terms of* its belonging to other equipment: inkstand, pen, ink, paper, blotting pad, table, lamp, furniture, windows, doors, room" (1962:97). Like a piece of furniture, which is only a piece of furniture insofar as it belongs to an equipmental nexus, in Ceylon the national past became part of an equipmental whole called nationalism to which also belonged such entities as development projects, history, archaeology, newspapers, voters, citizens, diplomacy, literature, chronicles, foreign relations, official languages, courts, parliaments, postal stamps, the armed forces, national monuments, national universities, and national costumes. Heidegger saw the way of being of those entities that are defined by their use *in the whole* as being characterized by "availableness." For the Ceylonese of the immediate prewar and postwar years, a national past had not only become available, it had become transparent. For something to become transparent—that is, nonobtrusive—it has to become a fully and genuinely appropriated equipment. Nationalism as well as an increasingly nationalized past became part of a suavely efficient habit of comportment in the world. "In the indifferent imperturbability of our customary commerce with [things surrounding us], they become accessible precisely with regard to their unobtrusive presence. The presupposition for the possible equanimity of our dealing with things is, among others, the uninterrupted quality of that commerce. It must not be held up in progress" (Heidegger 1962:309).

Even during preindependence negotiations with the British, Tamil politicians began to fear the possible tyranny of a Sinhala majority in a new independent nation. But the "availableness" of a nation or a national past itself was never called into question. This was certainly true of the Tamil immigrants of Phase 1 to Britain. All peoples belonged to nations and thereby possessed nationalities. Tamils, like their Sinhala counterparts, belonged to a nation known as Ceylon.

The first clear signs of disturbance of the "availableness" of a nationalized past were to make their presence felt with the passage of the Sinhala Only Act of 1956 whereby Sinhala was made the sole official language. The late leader of the Tamil United Liberation Front Appapillai Amirdhalingam indirectly concurred with this opinion when he told me in an interview in December 1983 that "not until 1956 did we really believe that we were second-class citizens. Until then all we were engaged in were preventive measures, which we thought would hold." Some of the Jaffna Tamils I spoke to said that they began to realize that they had no nation of their own when the Tamils of recent Indian origin who were brought to the island to work on its plantations were disenfranchised and made stateless in two consecutive acts of Ceylon's postindependence Parliament in 1948 and 1949. For many Tamils of this generation who saw signs of Sinhala domination, their claim to a Ceylonese nation and its national past may indeed have run into doubt. However, this did not, as Heidegger might have put it, throw into occurrentness the facticity of nation, nationality, or a nationalized past. "Occurrentness" refers to the presencing of an entity as an isolate, disarticulated from the background practices to which it belongs. They inhabited a world in which the nation was not something alongside which they lived but something that had become part of them and pervaded their relation to other objects of their world. In this respect it is worth noting that "the concept of 'facticity' implies that an 'intraworldly' being has being-in-the-world in such a way that it can understand itself as bound up in its 'destiny' with the being of those beings which it encounters within its own world" (Heidegger 1962:82).

Nationalism itself was such a being. The available options did not consist in the renunciation of a nationalized past but rather in the search for and the discovery of a different nationalized past. In my interviews with over fifty Tamils of this generation only three claimed that they had always—that is, even as early as the 1950s—doubted the very premise of a nationalized past. Such doubts should not be taken in their customary mentalistic sense. Rather, the form in which such a doubt was strikingly expressed was kinesthetic. A statement of a Tamil woman from Wimbledon was typical: "I never *felt* comfortable saying that Ceylon was my country." It is hard to tell how much of this is intelligent hindsight rather than accurate recall of radical doubt or its absence, since my interviews were carried out largely in 1993. At most we may concede that the signs of the "unavailableness" of a nationalized past began to make their faint appearance in the mid-1950s, and possibly earlier in the form of what the Heideggerian scholar Hubert Dreyfus (1991) calls a "malfunction" in the available. When equipment malfunctions, Dreyfus observes, it becomes "conspicuous." "Tradition," when zealously invoked, is one of those noteworthy examples of an equipment that has become conspicuous, thanks to its malfunction. "Conspicuousness presents the available equipment as in a certain unavailableness," wrote Heidegger (1962:102–103). In the case of the nation, as we shall soon see, with time this unavailableness of the nation to Tamils was to disturb the availability of the Sinhalas' own nationalized past. At the very least, it became debatable. For a time these Tamils' cultural past and the Sinhalas' national past found no parallax. For the Tamil, even those aspects of a pointedly Sinhala national past issued forth from a South Indian (ergo, Hindu) cultural past, and minor adjustments brought one in line with the other. For as Dreyfus observes, "for most . . . forms of malfunction we have ready ways of coping, so that after a moment of being startled, and seeing a meaningless object, we shift to a new way of coping and go on. 'Pure occurrentness announces itself in such equipment, but only to withdraw to the availableness of something with which one concerns oneself'" (1991:71–72).

Phase 2: Students

The second phase of Tamil migration to Britain heralded a more serious disturbance of the availableness of the nation, making coping more difficult and the occurrentness of a nationalized past more obdurate. These immigrants represented a wider spectrum of class and caste, for in the 1960s and 1970s the universities and schools back home had opened up to and had educated a more diverse population of students. The opening up of the universities, however, made education a more, rather than a less, precious commodity. The sociopolitical processes that brought about this state of affairs have been well rehearsed. Tamils were bound to face increasing competition from the Sinhalas, whose interest in and access to education were beginning to catch up with the proportion of Sinhalas in the population as a whole. But the competition in, and corresponding value of, education were further intensified by two policies of the Sri Lankan government. The first was the institution of a quota system that adversely affected the Tamils, and the second was the systematic closing up of the civil services and the armed forces to Tamils.[4] Under these conditions, England provided the escape route to many students, and most who migrated in this phase were students. But more to the point of our theoretical concern with nationalizing the past was a realization among educated Tamil youth that their nation's history—a national history—was not theirs. This unavailability deprived them of the privileges that were part of the equipmental whole of which the nationalized past was a part.

There were also class and caste barriers between the first and the second phases of migrants. Many more were choosing to go to the more recent "polytechnics" rather than to Britain's pomp- and tradition-filled older universities that had been the choice of their predecessors. But education and similarities in professional ambitions lessened these differences. The second generation trusted those who had preceded them and accepted their freely given help in the form of guidance, advice, contacts, and tips on how to make it in Britain. Phase 2 immigrants were, on the average, poorer than Phase 1 immigrants because they came from a poorer class, but even when they did have resources at home, the newly imposed exchange controls in Ceylon, renamed Sri Lanka, made it difficult for them to transfer funds out of the country. Exacerbating this financial difficulty, Britain increased the fees it charged its foreign students to three times what domestic students paid. This meant that more of them had to support their studies by working, and most of them chose jobs that were congenial to studying—such as those of night security guards and petrol station attendants. Women found jobs as cashiers in tourist souvenir shops and as clerks in grocery stores. In short, this generation of students was thrown into the rough-and-tumble of their host nation and exposed to its raw bigotries and prejudices in a manner and to an extent not experienced by its predecessor. Furthermore, these immigrants' nostalgia for their home country was qualitatively different from that of the first generation. They had no illusions of belonging to a ruling elite (potential national leaders) or claiming all the comforts and privileges that went with that status. The political climate they had fled soured them on the Sri Lankan state as well as on most aspects of civil society. Unlike their predecessors, they had not gone to school with Sinhala classmates and studied in the English medium[5] but had, as a consequence of the language act of 1956, been schooled in an exclusively Tamil medium and had thereby come to consider their Sinhala compatriots as virtual strangers at best and enemies at worst. Their nostalgia is most aptly described as basic homesickness: the missing of family, temple or church, friends, home-cooked food, and language. In Britain, they gathered in each others' homes to eat and chat rather than in public places because in such places, especially in pubs, they felt that they were being laughed at, talked about, and even stalked by their English neighbors. Both native and stranger have become subjects of "the half-light of foreign tongues." Nonetheless, many in this group who completed their education before the late 1970s found jobs in the United Kingdom or elsewhere in the world and chose not to return to Sri Lanka.

Estate Tamils among Phase 2 Immigrants

In chapter 4, we saw the manner in which the past weighed heavily on the present with no clear signs of future consequences, and how this past, among other things, kept the Estate and non-Estate Tamils of Sri Lanka divided and different. While that account still holds true, mostly for those who left the island before the late 1970s and an older generation of Tamils who still remain in Sri Lanka, there is a new generation both in and outside Sri Lanka, connected to each other by mail, telephone, Tamil militants' publications, faxes, and e-mail; members of this group have begun to see the erasure of at least this dividing aspect of the past. The best place to begin to understand this change is in South India and Sri Lanka.

In South India many young Estate Tamils have begun to feel like "Sri Lankan Tamils" and have begun to form a common bond with non-Estate Tamil refugees in India and the militants who are waging a battle on the island of their birth. Unlike an earlier generation, they know that all Sri Lankan Tamils are not Jaffna Tamils, and feel that they too are more Sri Lankan than Indian. The first erosion of the monolithic categorization of all non-Estate Tamils as Jaffna Tamils, the radical other, began to manifest itself following the Sri Lankan government's land reform policies of the early 1970s. Many Estate Tamils who were displaced from their homes sought refuge and work in the north. True, they worked for and under non–Sri Lankan Tamil landowners. But they worked alongside other non–Sri Lankan Tamils who were not landowners but laborers like themselves. This was a novel experience for the Estate Tamil. Furthermore, the proximity of the two groups spawned friendships and even marriages. True, when crown land was being distributed to the inhabitants of the lower reaches of the Northern Province, many non-Estate Tamil landlords tried their best to keep land away from the hands of the Estate Tamil "immigrant." But in merely living as neighbors, the two groups exchanged many acts of kindness. And with the rise of the Tamil militant movements, these Tamils from the hills found some of their most ardent and belligerent supporters to be young non-Estate Tamil youths. The camps have educated them to this fact and feeling. The second moment in the erosion of the monolithic Jaffna Tamil radical other took place in India, in and outside refugee camps. Here Estate Tamils met Tamils who claimed distinctly different identities of origin, distinct from Jaffna, such as Trincomalee, Vavuniya, Batticaloa, and Mannar. The alienated Estate Tamils who found themselves in a strange "motherland" began to see themselves too as Sri Lankan Tamils. The very realization that there was a whole range of Sri Lankan Tamils other than the English-educated Jaffna Tamil made it possible for the Estate Tamils to retain their own identity of origin on the one hand—even as the Tamils from parts of Sri Lanka other than Jaffna retained theirs—and, on the other, to feel that they (the Estate Tamils included) were all Sri Lankan Tamils. To be sure, the divide has not been completely bridged. Acts of arrogance and contempt on the part of certain Jaffna Tamils are often recalled and (less) frequently experienced, not only by Estate Tamils but also by Tamils from other parts of the island. For example, it is remembered that[6]

> in July of 1983, the Tamils of Colombo who took refuge in some of the schools-turned-refugee-camps found themselves among Tamils of all classes, castes. and regions. They all had one thing in common. They had very narrowly escaped death at the hands of Sinhala mobs and had seen or heard of the killings of some of their fellow Tamil acquaintances and friends. Some still had family members and relatives at large and in danger. On the second day, packets of food were received from well-wishers, including foreign embassies. The divisions began. "Powerful Jaffna Tamils" ordered the food to be taken "upstairs" to where they were housed. After they had picked out the foods of choice (cake from the U.S. embassy seems to have been one of these), the leftovers were sent "down" to the rest. "But not all Jaffna Tamils ate cake." Some of the poorer ones partook of a "more common meal," partly "supplied by the Indian High Commission." "And even some of the elite," finding the segregation, under the circumstances, repugnant, not only refused to join the cohorts upstairs but "raised a rumpus" about it.
>
> In 1983, when refugees from Trincomalee sought refuge in the Jaffna Peninsula, some residents of Jaffna gave them water in coconut shell halves for fear that their possibly lower caste lips would pollute their cups.
>
> A Jaffna Tamil girl lived in the South Indian town of Tiruchchirappalli as a refugee. She attended the local Catholic school. When the Indian Tamil teacher asked her whether she was a "repatriate Tamil," she said, "Chee!"(which translates into something like, "Gross!").

From a different point of view one may see these instances as the last gasps of a dying prejudice, a passing regime. And indeed there is much evidence for this. Admissions and admonishments such as the following, from S. J. Tambiah's first book on the interethnic conflict, have become commonplace among Jaffna Tamils and have gone way beyond the lip service given to such proclamations by an earlier generation of politicians:

> It is a blot on the Sinhalese conscience that considerations of electoral arithmetic have denied the Indian Tamils, large numbers of whom had been in the island for several generations, the rights of citizenship and enfranchisement—a blot all the more dark because for many decades now it is this exploited segment of the population that has made the greatest contribution to the island economy via the tea industry which earns the greater part of the island's export earnings. But the Sinhalese are not alone in this disgrace. The indigenous Sri Lankan Tamils concentrated in the Northern and Eastern provinces for quite other reasons of a social nature have traditionally looked down upon the plantation labor as of low caste and/or tribal status and have not until very recently made an effort to include them within the framework and goals of their politics. (1986:67)

There is another route by which Estate Tamils have come to realize that the Tamils of Jaffna do not form a monolithic group. This is through their knowledge of and dealings with the various Tamil movements as well as their interaction with nonmilitant, upper-caste Tamils. For instance, it is widely held that the Tamil militant movement, especially the LTTE, is composed of young men and women drawn from non-Veḷḷāḷa (lower) castes, the Karayār in particular. This image is favored especially by an older generation of upper- and upper-middle-class Veḷḷāḷas who have lost considerable power and influence in the north and who now live in Colombo. Estate Tamils whose families have been split, with some members living in the north and some in the south, travel between the two zones as frequently as it is safe to do so. They have come to know the upper-caste Tamils of Jaffna who live in Colombo and with whom they interact; and they recognize that this elite group's image of the militants is not quite correct. It is true that Veḷḷāḷas do not dominate these militant groups either in leadership or in ideology. For instance, the martial ideology of the LTTE is drawn more from the folklore and values of the South Indian Kaḷḷar and Maravar castes than from the lore and values of the Veḷḷāḷa and other agricultural South Indian non-Brahmin upper castes. But there is no evidence that there are proportionately fewer Veḷḷāḷas among the militants than there are in the general Tamil population. And if there is one consistent position maintained by all the enchanted and disenchanted militants—and the Estate Tamils who have contact with the militants—whom I have spoken to, it is that in the movement there are no distinctions based on caste. On friendship and loyalty networks, yes. But not on caste. That the days of Veḷḷāḷa hegemony are nearing an end may be observed even from conversation with young Veḷḷāḷa Tamils outside the militant movement. The following should serve as a typical example. When the aunt of a young Veḷḷāḷa man visiting him in the United States in the late 1980s gave him a firsthand account of the state of siege in Jaffna and the ubiquitousness of Sri Lankan army–generated deaths, she also expressed her fear and loathing for the alternative: to be ruled by low castes (i.e., the militants). The nephew, recalling this conversation, remarked to a colleague and me: "These people [the likes of his aunt] should be lined up and shot." This sentiment, even if not expressed so graphically, is shared by a whole generation of Tamils from Jaffna, Veḷḷāḷa or otherwise.

If there is one thing that the rise of Tamil militancy, especially the LTTE and the EPRLF, has done, it has been to make a concerted effort—which, in fact, has now become effortless—to efface these differences (even as they spawn others). One of the differences these movements have gone a long way toward effacing is the split between the non-Estate Tamil and the Estate Tamil. The Sri Lankan state, especially under the United National Party government, has gone to untold lengths to widen the divides among the Tamils. In Batticaloa the government smuggled in well-paid, mostly Muslim, armed thugs from the Sinhala southwest to commit arson and murder and to foment hatred and violence between the Muslim and non-Muslim communities. They have, to a certain degree, succeeded in dividing non-Muslim Tamils from Muslim Tamils in the north and especially the east. But otherwise, on the whole, they have helped all Tamils—particularly the Estate Tamils—share in a common identity to a degree that was not conceivable thirteen years ago. And it must be said in conclusion that the greatest force behind Tamil solidarity and the fusion of divided groups has been the anti-Tamil forces unleashed by the Sri Lankan state. In any case, thanks mostly to the electronic media, this generation has begun to have an effect on their fellow Tamils in countries outside South Asia, especially Britain. Against this background, then, we should return to Britain.

In Phase 2 of Tamil immigration to Britain there was also to be found a trickle of Tamils who originated in the tea estates of Ceylon. However, there were none, to my knowledge, who were the children of ordinary laborers. They were almost exclusively the sons of kaṅkāṇis—the descendants of those who led the gangs of laborers from India to Ceylon and continued to supervise them—or the white-collar workers of the tea estates. Members of the upper non-Brahmin castes, they were, principally, Veḷḷāḷas. Nonetheless, they were keenly aware of themselves as having Estate Tamil origins. This subgroup of Tamils would go almost unnoticed except for the interesting fact that their perspective on Sri Lankan ethnicities reveals how complicated and multiply inflected ethnicity and nationality are. These Sri Lankan Estate Tamils had five significant groups to choose from with whom they could have easy intercourse. These were: (a) fellow Sri Lankan Estate Tamils, (b) Sinhalas, (c) Tamils who came directly from India but belonged to the same or similar castes, (d) non-Estate Sri Lankan Tamils, and (e) other Tamils from India. I have listed them in the rank order of the frequency of Estate Tamils' interaction with them.

What is striking here is that once we go beyond the expected high rate of interaction with fellow Estate Tamils, the next group in order is not those who share their mother tongue or their religion (Hinduism), but those among whom they grew up. This turns out to be the Sinhalas. The much heralded cultural traits of language and religion seemed to take second place to other commonalties. When I asked why this was so, I received the following range of answers, which also indicate the reasons for the others' rankings as well:

1. "We both come from the south."
2. "We understand each other better."
3. "We have the same habits."
4. "We use the same curry powder mixture, most of the time." (Sometimes they use South Indian recipes for curry powder.)
5. "You can trust the Sinhalese. They can be stupid. But they are blunt. They [the Jaffna Tamils] speak a different Tamil, which they think is better than our Tamil."
6. "They [Indian Tamils] are strange. Can't trust them."
7. "You know how Indians eat!" (The South Indians invoked here use the better part of their right palm to mix the rice they eat, whereas Sri Lankans try not to let the rice-line go above the base of the fingers of their right hand.)
8. "Except when we have marriage connections, there is nothing much between us (Estate Tamils and Indian Tamils)."
9. "They [Jaffna Tamils] are very cliquish. Can't trust them."

A finer-grained analysis of these prejudices and preferences must await another occasion when a more systematic questionnaire could be constructed and results better cataloged and correlated. But even from the above statements (and the many like them) culled from interviews carried out with different ends in mind, we see certain general patterns emerging. Nonlinguistic and even nonreligious cultural values (which are, in example 3 above, called "habits") turn out to be more significant than language and religion. These habits include culinary and eating habits, and in this regard Indian Tamils (who speak the same dialect of Tamil as do Estate Tamils) appear the strangest. In fact, here too there is selective emphasis on what matters and what does not. In terms of the kinds of foods eaten (e.g., *idlis*, tōsas, and other steamed, baked, and fried eatables served at breakfast and as snacks), Estate Tamils and Indian Tamils have much more in common than either has with any other group. But what is selected out as being important is the "spicing" of foods—the ingredients that go into making the curry powder. This focus on the spicing itself is salient as a South Indian cultural trait; such traits are by no means essential, but their constructedness is so dense that it takes on obdurate even if not essential qualities. For instance, members of the two major branches of South Indian Tamil Brahmins, the Ayyars and the Ayyangars, can, in the absence of any other evidence, tell each other apart on the basis of the spicing of their *cāmbārs*.[7] In fact, subtle differences in spicing of foods mark one lineage from another, one family from another. Every wife learns the spice combinations most suited for (and presumably, pleasing to) her husband from her mother-in-law. My own Indian Tamil father introduced my Sri Lankan mother to the appropriate spicing of the sambar, *racam*,[8] and vegetables, appropriate to his natal family's tastes.

This selective focus on spices is not as important for the Jaffna Tamils or the Sinhalas. In fact, the Jaffna Tamils and the Sinhalas use spices quite similarly. And for this (and obviously other) reasons, we cannot expect Sinhala or Jaffna Tamil attitudes and prejudices toward Estate Tamils to be reciprocally symmetrical. Their reasons and justifications, their priorities in identifying traits that are significant, will tend to differ. But what is of interest is that these prejudices of Estate Tamils seem to have little correlation with such questions as whether or not there should be a separate Tamil State called Eeḷam, or whether the LTTE or the Sri Lankan army should win, or the Indian army should triumph over everyone else. Opinions on these matters swung widely and wildly. On the one hand, there was little love for the Sri Lankan state and armed forces, and even less tolerance for Sinhala chauvinism, under both of which Estate Tamils suffered. On the other, they prefer to see Sri Lanka intact than broken up. And yet when it came to matters of war, they liked to see the LTTE win because they have not suffered under the LTTE, and because the LTTE's valor is believed to have restored dignity to all Tamils. The Sri Lankan army and police, however, were seen as their persecutors. But a large sector of the Sinhala population sees them thus and for the same reasons, state tyranny having been directed at them during the UNP government's crackdown on Sinhala dissidents. Support for India's role in the civil war was ambivalent: looked upon with approval and pro-Indian pride for reasons of ancestry, as well as with fear and loathing at the thought that Sri Lankans would become like Indians (in some of their habits). Common Tamil pride that brought Jaffna and Estate Tamils together would, the very next moment, be wedged apart by memories of Jaffna Tamils' claims to superiority in rank and status back home. But there was one respect in which this little group of Tamils was experientially in the vanguard of what was to follow for both Jaffna Tamils and the Sinhalas: the crisis of the nation-state. For the Estate Tamils the nation-state had never been available; it was never a transparent and taken-for-granted part of their world's furnishings. In England, this was to become the experience of the Jaffna Tamils and, to a lesser extent, of the Sinhalas as well. It is to this breakup of the nation that we now return.

Great Britain's heavily nationalized past and the racist indignities issuing from it helped throw into clear relief Sri Lanka's own nationalized past and its own forces of comparable exclusion. In the bookshelves of those among these immigrants who are given to reading and collecting books, one is either unlikely to find Ceylonese or Sri Lankan history books in any significant number or likely to find them only as part of a genre of books and pamphlets that reflect a radically new concern with history. In the latter case, the few who allowed themselves to be preoccupied with history were engaged in writing a different history, obsessed with discovering a nationalized past that was distinctively Tamil, with Tamil chieftains and Tamil kings ruling justly over a nation of loyal subjects, if not citizens. For many in this subgroup, Prabhakaran, the leader of the LTTE, was seen as fitting a uniquely Tamil notion of kingship: the king as dispenser of justice, as strong, compassionate, and, if necessary, brutal; not as a negotiating, compromising, vacillating, talk-prone politician. For most Phase 2 Tamils and the asylum-seekers who were to follow, democracy had proven to be a farce and monarchy presented itself as the ideal polity.

Coping with the Unavailableness of the Nation

To the extent that Ceylon's and (later) Sri Lanka's nationalized past presented itself in its unavailableness to the Tamils, and in being precipitated in its occurrentness as isolated and determinate rather than as belonging to an equipmental whole, the experience of the two phases of Tamils was similar. But the difference, one of degree if not kind, also needs to be noted. The two groups coped differently with the disturbances to their world. The earlier generation had, despite its interest in the history of Ceylon, bracketed it away as a thing worthy of curiosity and yet, as they say, as only history.[9] They chose to emphasize the significance of culture, and even a common culture as the basis of their common nationality. To be sure, differences between Tamils and Sinhalas were noted, but so were the differences between Tamils and Burghers or Sinhalas and Muslims. These differences, however, were secondary to the primacy of a common nation based on a common culture. In this respect we may note that the nemesis of a series of Sri Lankan (Sinhala) governments and prime ministers, the founder of the Federal Party and (later) of the Tamil United Liberation Front (TULF), Mr. S.J.V. Chelvanayakam, had not asked for a separate nation-state for the Tamils but only for a federated state, sufficient to accommodate the lesser differences and to acknowledge the greater commonality. The coping employed by this generation of immigrants can best be described as "absorbed coping." In absorbed coping, after a moment of surprise at the disturbance to one's habitual comportment in the world, one shifts to a new way of coping and goes on as if nothing has changed. In such a mode of coping, transparent circumspection—the grasp of one's environment in one's everyday way of getting around—is recovered without any need for a radically new stance in the world. In his passionate "political tract" (1986) the

Sri Lankan Tamil anthropologist S. J. Tambiah recalls his own experience of being caught in the anti-Tamil riots of 1958, the first of their kind in the new nation's history. His recovery from that experience—despite its traumatic quality—is an example of absorbed coping. Indeed, some may argue that his entire book, triggered by the anti-Tamil riots of 1983, in which solutions for reconciliation are offered, continues to exemplify "absorbed coping." (Note that Tambiah belongs to the generation of Phase 1 Tamils.) In the case of the second generation of immigrants we have considered, and among some of those in Phase 3 who were to follow, there is a shift from "absorbed coping" to "deliberate coping" and deliberation. This is especially true of those who were committed to finding the nationalized past of the Tamils in the last king of Jaffna, in the Chōḷās of South India, or in the persons of strongmen such as Prabhakaran. This enterprise entails a deliberate activity with attention paid to what is being done and with an awareness of the consequences of one's actions.

Deliberate coping may also entail deliberation—the act of reflective planning. This was true not only of those who were obsessed with recovering a Tamil nationalized past but also of those who did not care for the distant past but who were deliberative in how they interacted with the Sinhalas they encountered either in Britain or elsewhere. Contrast the following two statements, the first by a Phase 1 barrister and the second by a Phase 2 accountant:

> When I meet my Sinhala friends, I rarely think, "Ah, he is a Sinhala and I am a Tamil; we are different; I better watch out." I can even say I never think that way, and I am sure he does not either. The issue comes up only when we start discussing Sri Lankan politics, the recent stuff. And anyway, my Tamil is only little better than his Sinhala. His is mostly nonexistent.

> Friendships. Yes, there are friendships. It is funny. In the U.K., you know what all Sri Lankans now are called? "Tamils." Even the Sinhalas are called Tamils. Some of them get mad. Feel insulted. Most of those who have been around for some time think it is funny. That is how the whole racism bit is so funny: the anti-Tamil Sinhala racism in Sri Lanka with all the Aryan/non-Aryan talk of Sinhala racists. Some of these Sinhalas are my good friends. But however close we are being friends, I can never forget that he is a Sinhala. And he can never forget that I am a Tamil. That is always there. Fundamental.

To speak of "deliberation," like "imagination" as in Benedict Anderson's *Imagined Communities*, strikes one as succumbing to the kind of Cartesian mentalism I have tried assiduously to avoid. What deliberates is not the mind as distinct from the body—even though "mind" in such a phrase may be used as Peirce used it, as "a sop to Cerberus" (Hardwick 1977:80–81). Deliberation should be more accurately understood as the action of a mindful body or an embodied mind. In deliberation, human beings experience the exercise of their habits' being subjected to habit-change. What habits do we speak of in this instance? The habit of nationhood, of belonging, of being with rather than merely being in or being as. Deliberation is a moment in which such habits are disturbed and rise to the threshold of habit-change. Is intentionality involved in deliberation (even if not in "imagination")? As Heidegger puts it, "intentionality is not an occurrent relation between an occurrent subject and an occurrent object but is constitutive for the relational character of the subject's comportment as such. . . . Intentionality is neither something objective nor something subjective in the traditional sense" (cited in Dreyfus 1991:76).

The wife of a Tamil physician in London told me the following: "I have always put a *poṭṭu*[10] when we go to parties. To me it is as natural as drinking water or wearing my *tālikkoṭi*.[11] But after 1983, I *feel* [her emphasis] my pottu. Even here in England, slightly afraid [when wearing it]. At the same time, slightly proud [of wearing it]." Here we see an example of the "deliberation" of a mindful body: a moment of habit-change.

Phase 3: Refugees

Among the immigrants of this phase, especially in its latter half, we not only find the "national past" as an equipment completely missing; we also find its absence transforming the entire equipmental whole to which it belonged from the available to the occurrent. Of such a transformation Heidegger writes: "The more urgently we need what is missing, and the more authentically it is encountered in its unavailableness, all the more obtrusive does that which is available become—so much so, indeed, that it seems to lose its character of availableness. It reveals itself as something just occurrent and no more" (1962:103). In order to appreciate the manner of the total breakdown of nationalism resulting from the disturbance of the unavailable, the nation, which had once been a part of ongoing activity and a being-in-reality, we need to sift through some of the trials of these immigrants before and upon their entry into Britain.

The third phase of Tamil emigration to Britain and the West in general began with the Sri Lankan government's imposition of the draconian Prevention of Terrorism Act (P.T.A.) in 1979, instituted in response to a certain section of the Tamil population's campaign for a separate state.[12] To appreciate the scale of the government's excessive and indiscriminate use of force, one can only sadly recite that prior to the 1983 anti-Tamil riots, which left thousands of Tamils dead and thousands more homeless, there were no more than a dozen members of the LTTE, the separatist group that was to grow subsequently into one of the most dreaded militant groups in the world. By the late 1970s and early 1980s, for the average Sinhala soldier, every Tamil was not only an anti-Sinhala but an antinationalist. The P.T.A. fell hardest upon the Tamil youth. Every Tamil between the ages of sixteen and forty was considered to be a terrorist whose tactic was surprise. For many young Tamil men (and, later, women) the choice was flight from the atrocity of the Sri Lankan armed forces or flight into membership in one of the many militant separatist groups.

The immigrants of this phase, which extends from the late 1970s up to the present, were not a homogenous lot. Apart from the fact that all Phase 3 Tamils are asylum-seekers, this phase is characterized by its continuously changing social and economic profile. It may be divided into two parts: the first consisting of those who left before the full-fledged civil war of post-1987; the second, of those who left thereafter. It is among the latter that one is likely to find those for whom everything that is national—including a nationalized past—has broken down. Initially, Phase 3 immigrants came as students either because that was the only way they knew how to get to Britain or because they were too embarrassed to seek asylum right away. Once the student-route was choked off by Britain's increasingly restrictive policies, they openly sought asylum. For Phase 2 Tamils this development was something they had feared, expected, and understood. So they went all out to assist these Phase 3 Tamils by serving as sponsors, by providing them with places to stay, and by finding them jobs. Phase 2 Tamils were also more in touch than their Phase 1 counterparts with the constant changes in immigration laws, their interpretation, and enforcement—all set up as obstacles to immigration by the British authorities—and the ways of overcoming or circumventing them. The first generation's advice in these matters was outdated and irrelevant, as indeed the second generation's was soon to become. What these Tamils gained from their acquaintance with Britain's immigration laws and its treatment of refugees was a sense of cynicism toward all things "national," especially national laws and even international laws. They saw, for instance, that international refugee laws did not serve to ameliorate the plight of refugees as much as they did to protect the sovereignty of nation-states and often to protect these nation-states from embarrassment. These nation-states were constituted of nationalized cultures and claims to hoary nationalized pasts that set up barriers to refugees at their borders. When it came to the question of immigrants—especially refugees—Phase 1 Tamils believed in the primacy of national sovereignty, especially the sovereignty of their adopted nation. Phase 3 Tamils, the later arrivals in particular, viewed it with cynicism, dread, or utter disregard. The sentiment of Phase 2 Tamils fell somewhere in between.

Once Phase 3 Tamils had been admitted into the country, Phase 2 and Phase 1 Tamils—especially those of Phase 1[13]—attempted to fit what they saw into a picture that they either knew, remembered, or had heard of. This picture was one of a class/caste-based social order in which the upper castes, when at their best, were helpers and patrons of the lower castes. When advice was extended to these newcomers, it was purportedly done with ultimate democratic intentions—in the words of a Tamil lawyer in Britain, "to help them become fit for a free and equal society." Initially there was even a sense of urgency in their gestures of help because, among other things, they had the "image of the Ceylon Tamil in Britain to protect."[14] If nothing more, they had to preserve their identity as "not 'Pakis,'[15] and certainly not Afro-Caribbean." Before the mid-1980s, much help was given and much received. Phase 1 Tamils expected the newcomers to conform, to continue to take their advice, to move rapidly up in British society (as they had done) by turning to education, and above all to keep a low profile until they were fit to ensure that the dignity of the Ceylon Tamil would not be tarnished by their visibility.

After the "July riots" of 1983, Phase 1 Tamils realized that they were fighting a losing battle against their decimated illusion of the "dignified Ceylon Tamil." For those who were arriving by then were not necessarily young men but older people who were dependents of the post-1979 asylum-seekers. In the beginning, renewed attempts were made to cajole the young men and women of Phase 3 to fall into line with their class/caste-based expectations. The Phase 1 Tamils employed subtle assertions of caste prerogatives on the one hand and overt encouragement of old-country gerontocracy on the other, both being exercises of tradition. What they had not realized is that with the rise of the Tamil militant movements in Sri Lanka, gerontocracy had been overthrown by a generalized neocracy. In the wake of the "July riots" entire families arrived in Britain. When unaccompanied individuals came, their dependents followed them soon after. Marriages were made and in-laws followed spouses. Some Phase 1 immigrants saw the "Paki phenomenon" taking shape in the Tamil community before their very eyes. The character of the Tamil immigrant community in Britain was never to be the same. It did not take long for matters to sour or require radical reframing. Those of Phase 1 who refused to reframe their world withdrew from helping the asylum-seekers, declaring, at least among their own classes, that these "riffraff" were untrustworthy "tree climbers."[16]

Estate Tamils among Phase 3 Migrants

The trickle of Estate Tamils that entered the United Kingdom during Phase 2 continued into Phase 3. But this trickle was both a part of and apart from the bulk of Phase 3 Sri Lankan Tamils flowing into Britain. They were not escaping from a war-torn zone, they were not fleeing from imminent threats of persecution by the state as were the non-Estate Tamils, and they were not as destitute. Like the Estate Tamils who came to England with the second phase of immigrants, they were economically self-sufficient and not children of laborers but of families that had by one means or another made it in economic terms back in Sri Lanka. In fact, most of them had not lived on the estates where their parents and grandparents were born, lived, and worked, but were born and raised in such urban settings as Colombo and Kandy, even though they did have relatives on and links with the estates. What they did bring along with them, however, was a far more sympathetic understanding of the plight of the non-Estate Tamils—those of Phase 3 as well as those who stayed behind—than did the Estate Tamils of Phase 2. Their antipathy toward the Sri Lankan state was total, and any positive sentiments toward the Sinhalas such as those that their predecessors had nurtured were greatly sullied by deep mistrust. They encouraged the Estate Tamils of the previous phase to help, by any means possible, the more destitute non-Estate Tamils of Phase 3 and even to make small contributions to the Tamil war effort back home. Even though Estate Tamils' persecution by the Sri Lankan state in the post-1983 era had not been as severe as that of the non-Estate Tamils or the Sinhala dissidents belonging to the Janatha Vimukthi Peramuna (People's Liberation Front, hereinafter the JVP), there were several anti-Tamil incidents that were executed by the state's armed forces, by the JVP, and by other Sinhala citizens against estate workers in the hill districts of Sri Lanka. Another factor that had brought this generation of Estate Tamils closer to the Sri Lankan Tamils of the north and east was a result of the land-reform policies of the early 1970s discussed in chapter 3. Many estate Tamils who had been ejected from the estates of their birth and ancestors had moved to the relative safety of the Sri Lankan Tamil areas of the near north. In towns such as Vavuniya and Kilinochi, some of them had been partially assimilated into the non-Estate Tamil groups by marriage and dialect switching. But what had united these two groups the most was the common persecution they suffered at the hands of the Sinhala armed forces. They had become brothers and sisters under the trauma of persecution, arrests, torture, and death. Thus even though the Estate Tamils in Britain whom I include under Phase 3 had not directly experienced the kind of persecution regularly meted out to their fellow Tamils of the north and the east—thanks to their being economically better situated—they were better able to empathize with these Tamils' lot because among them were also some of their own Estate Tamils who had been displaced in the early 1970s.

Unlike their predecessors, Phase 3 immigrants (and now I return to the non-Estate Tamil majority) were highly politicized to the brute realities of discrimination and were willing to talk about it openly. Phase 2 immigrants in particular found in this considerable relief. For instance, any Sri Lankan male who works in a London petrol station[17] is regularly on the receiving end of racist remarks from white customers. As one informant put it (with only slight exaggeration, I believe), "There isn't a single night, when you work the graveyard shift, that some white punk doesn't call for your attention by shouting, 'Hey, you black cunt!'" The students found it difficult to convince Phase 1 immigrants that open racial abuse was a reality. The Phase 1 type "tended to blame the victim while they lived in their suburban homes in Surrey and voted for the Tories," one woman observed. Women too were targets of racist epithets but much less frequently than were the men.

Phase 1 Immigrants' Discomfiture

The largely politically conservative and socioeconomically well-to-do Phase 1 immigrants found it extremely discomforting to witness the arrival of Tamils from the lower ends of caste and class, with their poor—even zero—facility with English and their off-the-boat dress and demeanor. But they were most aghast at the "ungentlemanly political tactics they employed": some male asylum-seekers stripped themselves down to their underwear at Heathrow to protest their threatened deportation. Above all, this group found it difficult to come to terms with the fact that they were seeing "Tamils as refugees."

Many of them turned to help instead those young men and women who never left Sri Lanka but had "chosen" to stay behind and fight the Sri Lankan and Indian armies. Ironically, that these fighters were also predominantly drawn from the lower castes of Tamil Sri Lanka did not matter to Phase 1 Tamils, who provided considerable financial and material support to the militant "liberation groups" back home. Some of the wealthiest of this class in Britain and in the United States—more in the United States than in Britain—expected their "boys," as these militants were called, to establish a separate nation-state called Eeḷam in short order, and a few expressed their hope of some day becoming ambassadors of this new nation in some of the leading European and North American capitals. In the meantime they were gallant warriors in a proxy war. One wealthy Tamil physician in America offered me an advance of $60,000 on the condition that I write a book on the ancient Tamil nation. When I told this to a Phase 3 immigrant who had fled both the Sri Lankan state and the militant group to which he briefly belonged, he suggested, only half in jest, that if he were I he would take the money and hire a Buddhist priest for $30,000 to write the same history. He justified his suggestion by noting that only a Buddhist priest could write a convincing history—for was it not a Buddhist priest who wrote the *Mahāvaṁsa*? The remark is one of many indications of the scorn with which many Phase 3 immigrants were willing to regard the national past.

While, on the one hand, fantasies and hopes of nationhood and ambassadorships swelled among some Phase 1 immigrants, on the other, they came to read, witness, and even experience open racism from Britain's whites. Not that Phase 1 Tamils denied British racism before—but they assumed it to kick in only when promotion to upper-level managerial positions in corporations was at issue. "At a day-to-day level the Brits," it was said, "are a decent lot. They keep their prejudices to themselves, we keep ours within us." In short, various forms of equivocation seemed to qualify British racism. But their own trust in the British was shaken when they saw Tamils being called "Pakis," and reports and stories that smarted even more began to reach the self-assured British Tamils. They heard that some young Tamils who, when accused of being Tamil and threatened with physical violence by white youths, claimed that they were Indians or Pakistanis. They heard that in the Netherlands Tamils in trouble tried to pass as British Guyanese or Africans. In Germany, they heard, "Tamil" was the worst insult a German could extend to a swarthy foreigner, from Turk to Vietnamese. Some blamed the asylum-seekers for having robbed them of their dignity. "They cannot even speak proper English. Some cannot even speak a word," complained one of the first-generation Tamils. But others realized that all the while they had imagined that their white fellow Britons knew the difference, the fact was that these whites neither knew nor cared. A sense of identification with all other nonwhites in Britain had begun among some of them, mainly among the children of this generation.

Those Phase 1 immigrants who did not want their habits of body, mind, and heart shaken withdrew either into themselves, their worlds, or the arcane recesses of their fancies. The awkward presence and practices of Phase 3 immigrants appeared to these earlier settlers as mere aberrations, "misfirings of the collective enterprise of inculcation [of what it was to be a Ceylon Tamil in Great Britain] tending to produce habitus that are capable of generating practices regulated without express regulation or any institutionalized call to order" (Bourdieu 1977:17). Phase 2 Tamils, few of whom had the luxury of withdrawal, witnessed the dark fog of their fellow Tamils' suffering gather itself into a thickness that surrounded them without evaporating. Some Phase 1 immigrants continued to insist on playing the part of patron to client vis-à-vis the newcomers: advising, helping, instructing, meddling.

As Phase 3 immigrants saw matters, all Phase 1 types could say was, "Don't do this, *tambi*,[18] don't do that, tambi, and be careful, tambi." The male asylum-seekers found their advice largely a recitation of irrelevant civilities. Many of the female asylum-seekers were invited to work as domestic servants in the homes of Phase 1 immigrants. Surprisingly few female asylum-seekers accepted such offers. Unconfirmed rumors abounded that some Phase 1 immigrants were in collusion with the Home Office, playing the part of loyal British subjects, feeding the latter information that could result in the more recent immigrants' deportation.[19] The following were some of the typical statements gathered from Phase 3 asylum-seekers about their Phase 1 predecessors: "They want us to go back and fight for *their* Eelam." "They want us to take orders from them, be their bearers." "They are jealous that we can drive cars here. Of course they don't know that we drove cars even in Sri Lanka. They remember the days when the only cars in that country belonged to their grandfathers, and their great-grandfathers sucked up to the colonial white man." "They cheated us then, they'll cheat us now."

The only route to dignified settlement that Phase 1 and 2 Tamils had known was education. For Phase 3 Tamils, this was neither their first nor their easiest choice, for several reasons. For one, they were escaping a civil war that had wreaked havoc on their progress in education. Second, they had also spent almost all of their family's resources to come to the United Kingdom. This money had to be replaced. Third, they had to earn and save up more money to bring over their parents, siblings, brides, (in some instances) bridegrooms, and spouses from their strife-torn homeland. Unlike the students who preceded them in Phase 2, there were many married men among these asylum-seekers. Fourth, given the paucity of the earning potential of their fathers and brothers back home under civil war conditions and their consequent inability to save for their sisters' and daughters' marriages, it fell to these refugees to save money for those dowries. Lucky indeed was she whose prospective groom lived in the West and had permanent residency status—but such a man required a higher dowry. In essence, the times were too urgent to permit these immigrants to settle for the deferred gratification education had to offer. They needed cash, and they needed it fast.

The move from a land-centered rural Sri Lanka on a cash-bound quest to a cash-centered urban England seems to have had an effect on the Tamil nation. The nationalized past in which the Tamil nation figured was territorially grounded. Even the current civil war, in which Tamil separatists are fighting for a "traditional homeland," has increasingly become more a war over territory than one over civil rights. For Phase 3 immigrants, the shift from the solidity of land to the liquidity of cash seems, in its small way, to have undermined the land-bound nation as well as a grounded nationalized past. In this regard it is interesting to note that many Phase 1 Tamils had either bought or hoped to buy large English homes with spacious gardens in the exclusive outskirts of London. They called them estates. Those among Phase 2 and 3 Tamils who did invest in real estate in the 1980s preferred to buy flats and referred to them as their "liquid assets." Flats in London were considered liquid, land in Jaffna, a beautiful lodestone. As one asylum-seeker put it, "It is even more important to be solvent than to get asylum in England." He went on to elaborate: "Tomorrow I might get a chance to go to Canada. Then why would I want to be stuck here or miss the chance only because I was not solvent? Even the U.S., I understand, is now giving out green cards for those who have a million dollars." Fluid metaphors such as solvency and liquidity figure prominently in the speech of these immigrants, especially among those who escaped the ravages of the civil war by the skin of their teeth, and those who saw their fellow Tamils stuck in undesirable second countries, abandoned en route to a country of asylum for lack of money. "I am told," another informant announced, "that in Toronto and Montreal there are places called 'Little Jaffna.' That is enough of a Tamil nation for me. Wherever there are enough Tamils, there is a Tamil nation." A far cry indeed from a nationalized past that was determined by solid boundaries! The future is to be fluid, in more respects than one.

Phase 3 and Unexpected Destinations

The early arrivals of Phase 3 had still been those with at least some means: the means to leave before Britain began tightening her laws, before the Immigration Carrier's Liability Act was passed,[20] before racketeers got into the act of facilitating the asylum-seeker's escape with false papers at high cost, before the price for getting to Heathrow went from under four hundred British pounds to more than five thousand. The "success stories" with petrol stations and retail stores that one is likely to hear from asylum-seekers apply mainly to those early arrivals who came to Britain before 1985. For the very poor—increasingly the profile of the average Tamil arriving at Heathrow during the latter part of the 1980s—the new exorbitant passage was bought for only one family member through his or her family's going deeply into debt, in some instances after selling house and possessions. No longer could the one who entered Britain raise enough money to pay back his or her own debt, let alone raise enough to pay the going price for chancy "illegal" exits and entries of other members of the family. And even if and when this was possible, the pits and snares were too many and far too hazardous. There are cases known to the London-based Joint Council for the Welfare of Immigrants in which middlemen—also Tamils—have abandoned groups of Tamils at "transit points" in such faraway places as Bangkok and Nairobi, after these same middlemen absconded with the five thousand plus pounds' "setup money" they received from their charges. Such a middleman takes them to an apartment or a room and tells them to stay put—lest they be caught by the authorities—until he makes arrangements for the next leg of the journey to London or some other Western capital. The room or apartment in question is locked from the outside to ensure double protection. The anxious and frightened group waits, at times for days, until hunger and/or suspicion gets the better of them and they break loose or start screaming for help. Some such desperate and penniless escapees are then offered, by yet another set of racketeers, the opportunity to become drug couriers as a means of buying their way back onto the road to asylum. A refugee who gave me the above account concluded it by saying:

> You ask me about Tamil nationalism. There is only Tamil internationalism. No Tamil nationals. Never was. Never will be. This is Tamil internationalism. Being stuck in a windowless room in Thailand, or a jail in Nairobi or Accra or Lagos or

Cairo or America. Or being a domestic servant in Singapore or Malaysia for a rich Tamil relative. Being part of a credit card racket in London. Crossing Niagara Falls into Canada. I am told there is even a Tamil fisherman on a Norwegian island near the North Pole. All internationals. And don't forget the briefless barrister at Charing Cross who tries to hawk his specialty as an immigration lawyer to anyone who is gullible enough to believe him. He is a Tamil too.

The African destinations were explained to me as follows by yet another informant:

No one plans on ending up in Africa. This happens because of drug-pushing middlemen. Customs in African airports are not that strict. And most of the airport officials are bribed by other agents.

Q. Who are these agents? Tamils?

A. They are. Mainly members of PLOTE.[21] They are caught and deported from European ports back to their last stop, usually Nigeria.

The African connection was widely explained in the following manner: Middlemen in Thailand or Pakistan buy desperate Tamils tickets to African destinations, giving them a package of drugs and a promise of a final European or Canadian destination. The Tamils' only obligation is to hand over the package to an African courier in Africa. Unlike Tamils, Africans are willing to carry their drugs in a form undetectable by European customs: stuffed in a condom that is then swallowed. Because of this method, Africans passed through customs with ease until recently, when a swallowed condom burst in a courier's stomach. The courier was rushed to the hospital where he died, and an autopsy exposed the game. Even though the Tamil role in the Africans' trafficking of drugs has achieved widely held folkloric truth, I have been able neither to confirm nor to disconfirm this story with any Tamil who has directly participated in this dangerous activity. It is known, however, that the use of drugs is strictly prohibited not only by the general Tamil cultural strictures and the opprobrium it could bring upon those who violate them, but also by the moral policing of the LTTE. Drugs are meant for Europeans. The money that is believed to result from the sale of drugs is meant for the war effort in Eelam.

The story of Tamil asylum-seekers' ending up in the United States is a curious one. The number of asylum-seekers who have been granted asylum in the United States over the past decade is around a dozen, more than half of whom are Sinhalas who fled the government's crackdown on dissidents in the south of the island. It is widely known in the Tamil community that it is virtually impossible to get asylum in the United States. Almost none who sought asylum in the United States had intended to do so in the first place, but had been trapped in transit on their way to Canada, where they had hoped to find refuge. The story of Shanmugam is both unique and typical and is worth recalling in some detail.

Shanmugam was a twenty-eight-year-old Tamil whom I came to know in 1989 through a human rights attorney in Seattle, who asked me if I would serve as an expert witness at his hearing before an immigration judge. According to Shanmugam and affidavits sent on his behalf by justices of the peace and other prominent citizens of Jaffna, he was the son of a farmer. He had an older sister and a younger brother. He was unconnected with any of the several Tamil militant groups operating in Jaffna. But he was persecuted by two Tamil militant groups, members of the Indian Peace-Keeping Forces, and the Sri Lankan army. He had bullet marks on his foot and shoulder where he had been shot by an EPRLF[22] guard. He finally fled Sri Lanka in fear of his life. Now let me continue the narrative based on his account to his attorney and me, and to the court.

From 1980 until the riots of 1983 he lived with his married sister in a suburb of Colombo. He had moved from Jaffna to Colombo because he wanted to prepare himself for the G.C.E. (Advanced Level) exams by attending a private "tutory" in Colombo. In 1983, Sinhala mobs attacked his brother-in-law's home by setting fire to it. His sister had left for Jaffna, to deliver, as is customary, her first child in her mother's home. His brother-in-law, who tried to face the mob and dissuade them from attacking his house, was killed. Shanmugam jumped out of a back window and over the garden wall and fled the scene. After spending several weeks in refugee camps in Colombo, he joined an exodus of Tamil refugees and went to Jaffna by boat.

Back in Jaffna, he and his younger brother tried their best to hide from recruiters from the various Tamil militant groups combing Jaffna for volunteers who would be trained to fight the Sri Lankan state. In 1985, his seventeen-year-old brother disappeared, leaving behind a note informing his parents that he was joining the liberation struggle. In 1986, Shanmugam was taken in for questioning by members of the Sri Lankan army. After two weeks of considerable beating and torture, and interventions by the then government agent and his pleading mother, he was released to his parents. Then came the Indo–Sri Lankan Peace Accord by the terms of which the Indian army occupied northern and eastern Sri Lanka so as to restore peace between the Tamils and the Sri Lankan state. A few months after the LTTE had declared its battle against the Indian army, members of the Indian army took him in for questioning. The solitary confinement and beatings lasted for a week. Again, he was released. Again, Shanmugam attributes his release to his mother's indefatigable pleadings with the Indian commander. No sooner was he released than he was captured by the LTTE and taken in for questioning. This time the questions were about what he had told the Indians and what he knew about the whereabouts of his brother. In response to the first question he told them all that he remembered. As for his brother's whereabouts, he said that he knew nothing, not even which militant group he had joined. During the first week of his confinement, he was relentlessly tortured. During the second week, even though the questions continued, he was treated well by the Tigers.

The very day he was released by the Tigers, he was recaptured by the Eelam People's Revolutionary Liberation Front. The EPRLF was a Tamil militant group that came under the good graces of the Indian forces and was given a certain measure of civil and military authority over the citizens of Jaffna. But members of this group also abused their authority, had alienated many Tamils of the north, and came to be seen as the lackeys of the occupying Indians. According to Shanmugam, the torture under the EPRLF was the most severe. First, they were convinced that he had gone voluntarily to the LTTE to divulge details of the interrogation by the Indians, and wanted to know what he had told them. Second, convinced that his younger brother was with the Tigers, they were keen on capturing him for the Indians, who were by now at war with the Tigers. After several weeks of incarceration, torture, and interrogation, Shanmugam managed to escape. He fled Jaffna and after several days of walking through the jungle, he reached Mannar. From there he bought his passage on a speedboat and reached India. From India he informed his parents of his safety and his whereabouts. He knew that it would be only a matter of time before one of the militant groups, if not the Indian authorities, would catch up with him. While in Madras, he learned that he could get a forged passport and a ticket to Canada. Through labyrinthine means he informed his parents of his plans to buy a passport and leave for Canada. A month later, his mother and sister sold all their jewelry, and his father sold most of their land; through equally labyrinthine means they sent him $5,000. With this money he was able to buy a forged passport at a discounted price and to pay a travel agent, who supplied an air ticket, arranged the route of his flight, and provided him with a contact who knew someone in Vancouver, B.C.; the contact would help him learn the ropes for applying for and obtaining asylum in Canada. The only thing he was told he needed to remember was to destroy his passport and flush it down the toilet of the airplane just before landing in Vancouver. His passport was red in color, Malaysian, and was quite worn from considerable use. It seemed as if it had belonged to a Malaysian businessman.

Shanmugam was routed through Hong Kong and, unlike his compatriots who were stranded in Bangkok, did not have to leave any of the airports en route until he reached Seattle. All that he had seen of the countries through which his flight pattern took him were the airports' transit lounges. In Seattle, all passengers had to disembark and go through U.S. customs before continuing on their flight to Vancouver. No one had warned him of this wrinkle in his itinerary. Even before he got to the long line in front of the customs officer's high table with his tin trunk in hand, he was apprehended by another officer and taken in for questioning. He told them his story. He told them that he had no intention of remaining in the United States but wanted to reach Canada.

When given the choice of either being sent back by the next available flight or being incarcerated until he received a hearing where the odds of his repatriation to Sri Lanka were almost assured, Shanmugam chose the latter. This is a short and sweet version of the more detailed, horrendous tale he had told his lawyer and me, and later a court over which a judge by the name of Kahn presided.

A particular episode of the court hearing merits retelling because it illustrates yet another aspect of refugees' predicament that goes unreported: Shanmugam spoke no English and understood almost none. To assist him, the court had hired a South Asian living in Seattle who had been certified by Berlitz as qualified to translate English into Tamil and vice versa. Under cross-examination, Shanmugam had just finished describing the burning of his sister's house in Colombo and the murder of his brother-in-law.

DEFENDANT: And then I ran through the side streets, to avoid the mobs.

PROSECUTOR: Who were these mobs made up of?

TRANSLATOR: (Renders an intelligible translation in a form of Tamil heavily accented by Malayalam.)

DEFENDANT: Sinhalas.

TRANSLATOR: Sinhalas.

JUDGE: Were there policemen on the street?

TRANSLATOR: (Translates the question correctly into Malayalam. The defendant strains to follow him and then answers.)

DEFENDANT: Police and army.

TRANSLATOR: Yes.

JUDGE: Did they help you?

TRANSLATOR: (Translates question into Malayalamized Tamil, but the defendant seems to follow the drift of the question, and responds.)

DEFENDANT: No. They hit me with their rifles. And when I fell down, they kicked me with their boots and said, "Run, Tamil, run."

TRANSLATOR: Yes.

At this point I told the defense attorney that the translation was incorrect, and he conveyed this to the judge.

JUDGE (to defense attorney): Your expert witness is an expert on Sri Lanka. But the translator is an expert in the language spoken and accordingly has been certified by Berlitz. Is your expert witness certified by Berlitz as an expert in . . . Tamil?

DEFENSE ATTORNEY (after seeing me shake my head): No, Your Honor.

Almost immediately after asking the prosecutor to continue, the judge interrupted the prosecutor, asking the court recorder to stop recording the proceedings and turn off the tape recorder. Off the record, the judge asked me to render what I thought was the correct translation of the defendant's response to his question.

EXPERT WITNESS: He said that the police and soldiers did not help him but hit him with the butts of their rifles and, when he fell down, kicked him with their boots and said, "Run, Tamil, run."

JUDGE (to Berlitz translator): Is that correct?

TRANSLATOR (now realizing that there is a native speaker of Tamil in the courtroom): Yes, Your Honor.

At another point in the hearing:

PROSECUTOR: Are you a Malaysian?
TRANSLATOR: (Renders an intelligible translation.)
DEFENDANT: No.
PROSECUTOR: What is your nationality?
TRANSLATOR: Tamil or Sinhala?
DEFENDANT: Tamil.
TRANSLATOR: Tamil.
PROSECUTOR: So you believe in a separate Tamil nation in Sri Lanka?
TRANSLATOR: Do you want a Tamil nation (*tēśam*)?
DEFENDANT: No. I don't even have a country (translatable as "a place to which I belong").
TRANSLATOR: No.

Malayalam is a language spoken in southwest India. Linguists estimate that its breakaway from early Tamil occurred around the thirteenth century. The mutual intelligibility between modern Malayalam and modern Tamil is akin to that between Italian and Spanish. Imagine a monolingual Italian-speaker certified by Berlitz as one who speaks and understands Spanish, and appointed to serve as translator in a court of law between English-speaking attorneys and judge and a monolingual Spanish-speaking defendant. Such was Shanmugam's predicament.

As a postscript to this memorable trial I might add that Judge Kahn rendered his judgment against the defendant. In his judgment he thanked me for my testimony and for educating the court on the recent history of the ethnic tensions in Sri Lanka. But he declared that in the final analysis, he was compelled to take the word of his State Department in meting out his judgment. According to the State Department, "there was no fear of persecution in Sri Lanka."

After two years we learned that Judge Kahn's judgment had been upheld by higher courts. Shanmugam was sent back to Sri Lanka. His family came to meet him at the Colombo airport. They claim to have seen him arrive at customs and then to have waited for him to emerge. But he never came out. After several hours of waiting and inquiries and receiving different kinds of answers, they tried to console themselves by saying that their having seen him briefly must have been only an illusion. Other inquiries pointed toward Sri Lanka's Special Defense Forces, who, it was said, had whisked him off to the notorious Fourth Floor for interrogation. Whatever the case may be, Shanmugam has been neither seen nor heard from since that day.

While waiting for his appeal, Shanmugam had learned Spanish from co-detainees who had come from countries such as El Salvador, Guatemala, and Nicaragua. The detention center was a small international community of card-playing, Ping-Pong batting, story-swapping, language-learning males. Far fewer women were apprehended at the border, and when they were, most of them chose to return to Sri Lanka or managed to get themselves bailed out by relatives in the United States and then found their way to Canada. But there were children who were arrested and detained and whose story needs to be told, if only because of the uniquely dangerous situation into which they are thrown by a well-meaning legal system. Two such cases merit our attention.

And Children

Karunaharan was sixteen years old. He too, like Shanmugam, had his asylum-seeking trip to Canada cut short at the U.S. customs in Seattle. He came from a middle-class family in Jaffna and had, until his escape, attended the prestigious secondary school of Jaffna College along with his older sister. One day when he and his sister were walking back home from school, they were stopped by a Sikh soldier of the Indian Peace-Keeping Forces. He was told to wait on the road while his sister was taken into a house occupied by some Indian army officers. Within minutes of her disappearance behind the closed door of the house, he heard his sister's screams. He ran to the side window of the house, and through a crack he saw his sister "being shamed."[23] Then he ran to the front door, which was being guarded by two grinning Indian soldiers, and tried to get access. He was kicked by one of them, and he fell to the ground unable to breathe. Then he heard his sister's screams become muffled, and grow fainter and fainter, and then he heard her no more. He thought that he was dying. Then he thought that his sister was dead. He sat up and wiped his mouth. There was blood. The place of the two soldiers who were guarding the door had been taken over by two others. And finding them engrossed in their own conversation, he crept back to the window just in time to see his sister being shot in the back. He sneaked back to the main road, and when he reached it, he heard a second shot. He ran home sobbing and screaming. After that incident, his parents managed to get him on a flight to Canada, which brought him into Seattle's detention center instead.

Karunaharan was not an adult and therefore was put in a detention center for children, where his co-detainees were streetwise American teenagers who were incarcerated for crimes that ranged from selling drugs to aggravated assault, to robbery, and even rape. Bright as he was and as much as he tried to adjust to the ethos of the place, his middle-class village background in conservative Jaffna had not prepared him for this. He was gang-raped the very first night and beaten up the next. His attorney succeeded in persuading the judge to release him to the custody of a Tamil citizen in the Seattle area in whose charge he was to be kept until his next hearing. He eventually crossed the border into Canada and was granted asylum there.

Shoba was ten years old when the Indian troops came to Jaffna to keep the peace. When I interviewed her with her attorney in Seattle, she was thirteen. According to her, the Indian soldiers whom the citizens of Jaffna had welcomed with garlands had, within a few months, become enemies of all the people, excepting those who joined the "EP" or supported them. (People in her neighborhood secretly called the EPRLF "EP" and rhymed it with *nāi pī*, "dog shit.") The EPRLF ranked foremost among organizations conceiving of a state based on socialist principles of equality: equality for all castes, both sexes, the Tamils of the various regions, and the Sinhalas. But when given the power of the gun and command by their Indian superiors, low-ranking cadres in particular became drunk with power and patrolled the streets intimidating the citizens. When an EPRLF officer rode in his car, other vehicles had to pull over to the edge of the road; when an EPRLF cadre walked along a street, ordinary citizens had to step to the side, even into a ditch if that was the only side left to the road. Those who refused to grant the respect due were taken in and punished or even beaten on the spot. Schoolchildren whose parents were not open supporters of the EP were especially afraid of running into uniformed members of the movement. They usually rode their bikes and chose side lanes and byways to make their way between home and school. One day Shoba and her friends were returning from school on their bikes laughing over a joke that her friend had cracked, when they suddenly ran into an EP commander with his assistants. They all quickly got off their bikes. The girl who had cracked the joke was her best friend, the class comic and very smart. She was so taken aback by the armed "soldiers" that she just got off her seat, did not have time to wheel the bike to the side of the road, and so stood astride her bike as if in shock—but still had a smile on her face because of her joke. One of the EP men jerked her off her bike. While the other threw the bike to the side of the road and smashed it, the commander ordered the man who had hold of her to take her to the field and made her kneel down. While Shoba and her schoolmates looked on in terror, the commander gave them a lecture about respect and the EPRLF, and then turned toward her kneeling friend and shot her in the head. Then he put his gun in his holster saying, "Let this be a lesson to you." The children pushed their bikes home, sobbing in silence for fear of being heard by the "soldiers," who continued on their promenade.

When she reached home, she broke into hysterical sobs. Her mother and father shook her to make her speak, tell them what had happened. Finally, her father, who had never spanked her, slapped her in order to calm her down. Then she told them what had happened. Her father warned them to expect trouble. "An old woman has shot an Indian officer," he told her. The Indian army had ordered the residents of a neighborhood to vacate their houses, so that they, in response to a tip-off, could carry out a search for Tigers and their weapons. The old woman had refused to leave; she merely huddled in a corner and whimpered in terror. Since the North Indian soldiers did not know Tamil, a compassionate South Indian officer—a Malayalee—went into the woman's low-doored hut and bent down to assure her in the little Tamil he knew that she would be safe under his protection, and pleaded with her to leave with him. The woman pulled out a machine gun that had been concealed by the drape of her sari and shot the officer to death. She in turn was riddled with bullets by the two Indian *jawāns* who had been waiting outside.

Even though the killing of the officer had taken place in another area of the peninsula, it was widely known that whenever a soldier was killed, the army would go on a rampage. This was truer of the Sri Lankan army during their earlier occupation, but it happened with the Indians as well. Shoba's father also had heard that those neighborhoods which "stole electricity" by jerry-rigging connections to the main line were thought to be LTTE sympathizers who were rewarded with LTTE expertise. Shoba maintained that this was not true, that ever since the onset of fuel and electricity rationing, citizens all over Jaffna had resorted to devices for beating the restrictions. As predicted by her father, that afternoon around four o'clock, soldiers came to the neighborhood. Most men had been tipped off to the Indians' arrival and had fled. The soldiers ordered everybody to step out of their homes, and the homes were searched. After the search was finished, the residents, all of them women, were told to go back in. Then a soldier came out of a house dragging a woman and her infant son. Shoba ran into the backyard to peek through the palm-frond fence and see what was happening. The senior officer asked the woman where the man of the house was. She said she did not know. He shot her dead. She fell backwards still holding onto her infant. When her hands let loose of her child and fell to her side, the child, still seated on her stomach, started to scream. The soldiers first left the child and his dead mother on the ground and walked out the front gate. A few moments later, one of the soldiers returned and shot the infant with one bullet. Suddenly there was not a sound to be heard.

That was the night her parents decided to send her out of the country. She had a cousin in Canada, and that would be her destination. But she had no passport. They managed to get her a forged passport, in which her age was recorded as eighteen rather than thirteen. She was too young to travel alone. So they found a naturalized Canadian relative and changed her name to read as if she were his wife; they then traveled to Canada as husband and wife. When they were apprehended in Seattle, it was clear that she was younger than eighteen and much too young to be married. Confessions were wrung out of them with ease. She and her partner were arrested. The partner posted bail and left for Canada. Fortunately for Shoba, there was a guard who, sensing the danger she faced in juvenile detention, pleaded with the judge to release her to the custody of someone—she herself was willing—who would take care of the young girl until her hearing. (In several instances, guards who have seen the danger that these children are in have volunteered to take them into their own homes.) The attorney assigned to defend Shoba got in touch with a Tamil family he knew and asked them if he might request that the judge release her to their custody. The male head of the family said that they would have been only too glad to help but feared to get drawn into anything that could signal their presence to the LTTE members who were operating in Europe and Canada, and who were very aggressive fund-raisers for the cause of Eeḷam. They did not want their name to appear on any LTTE list for fear that this would instigate the Sri Lankan government to harass and persecute family members who still remained on the island. Next, the lawyer contacted an Estate Tamil family that had intermarried with the Ṣinhalas. This family willingly and gladly took in Shoba, saying that Estate Tamils were still Indian Tamils and therefore had nothing to fear from a Sri Lankan movement such as the LTTE. After two weeks, they flew with her to Ithaca, where she was handed over to a Sri Lankan Tamil Catholic priest who took her across the Niagara bridge into Canada; there she applied for asylum and was met by her cousin. Before she crossed over, the priest asked her what she planned to do in Canada. Her answer: "Keep away from anyone who talks about Eeḷam or Sri Lanka or motherland."

Children much younger than Karunaharan and Shoba, as young as five years old, have been put onto planes unaccompanied by any adult and sent to Germany and Switzerland. The German and Swiss news media featured these arrivals in their headline stories. While some kind German and Swiss citizens rushed to adopt them, others described this as a new "wave" and called the children economic refugees. I expressed my puzzlement to a German woman at these children's being called "economic refugees." She saw what was happening as being quite straightforward, based on "confessions" by the children themselves. Most of the children who arrived at one of these country's airports, when asked where their parents were, would say, "Mommy said for me to go and that she will come soon and join me." That was the evidence: a mother's ruse to claim the right to emigrate to the country as a parent, once the child was naturalized! That the child would have to grow up to adulthood before being able to sponsor his or her parent, which would take as many as thirteen more years, did not seem like much of an issue. What this woman told me in an interview in Heidelberg was of course repeated more than once over the German and Swiss media. Many of the kind souls who offered to adopt these children, on the one hand, could not believe the cruelty of their parents, on the other: that they could lie to their children when they knew that they had neither plans nor possibility of following their children. The second group is no closer to the truth than the first.

Unfortunately or otherwise, most South Asian parents choose to hide the truth when the truth, they opine, is likely to cause immediate pain, sorrow, and sadness. This is so with terminally ill patients from whom the nature of their illness is concealed as long as possible by both physician and relatives. This is especially true of parents and children. A mother who is about to administer her child some bitter medicine will not hesitate to lie about its bitterness. The mother who sent off her unaccompanied child to Switzerland or Germany most probably did not have the luxury of reflecting on the long-range psychological trauma that such deceptions would wreak on her child. The story of one woman who had dispatched her child in such a manner and whom I had the opportunity to interview in Sri Lanka is likely to have been a typical variant of the accounts of other mothers (and, in a few instances, fathers) who resorted to such desperate actions.

Punitham lost her father, both brothers, and two of her four children. Left with only a son and a daughter, she decided to somehow or other get at least her son to safety. She knew that it would be only a matter of time before the next shell would fall or the next bullet would hit. She was determined to send her child to any country and have fate take over. Her choice for him was between certain death in Sri Lanka and a chancy life somewhere else. The only country that would not return her child, she had heard, was Germany. So she sold all her possessions and got her son a ticket. She could not get herself to tell her son the truth. How could she be so cruel? How could she tell him that he was never going to see her again, that she would most probably be killed, and that he most likely would be able to live? If she had told him that, how could he have left her behind and gone with the stranger whom he called "uncle," who took him to the airport? The only gift she thought that she could give him was the gift of life. And she is glad that she gave that to him. But otherwise, she says, "there isn't a day that goes by that I don't pray for him, and weep for him. He was my only son. He is my only son. I am glad he did not die for Sri Lanka or for Eeḷam. Maybe he will remember Tamil. That is enough. He will be a German-Tamil. That is enough." Economic refugee, indeed!

The Disaggregation of Identity

Many of the men who, having left their wives and children, came to Great Britain after 1985 came to escape death. Now they hold little hope of seeing their families again. They live in a state of heightened anxiety bounded by a seven-year limit: by the end of the seventh year they must, by law, be notified as to whether their application for asylum has been accepted. Many, unable to bear the strain, have returned home regardless of the consequences awaiting them, some to meet their death there. Others have gone back to Sri Lanka after learning that the reason for their having left that country in the first place no longer exists: their families have been wiped out by one armed group or another. The intransigence of British authorities and the scale of British xenophobia and racism vis-à-vis refugees (as evidenced by the frequent headlines of London's tabloids) are astounding when one realizes that between 1979 and 1989 Great Britain, with a population of almost 58,000,000, admitted only 54,935 refugees, a mere 0.09 percent of the total population. Of these only 7,910 were Sri Lankans (Turner 1996). If white Britain's reluctance to give refuge to asylum-seekers is astounding, Phase 1 Tamils' willingness to share in this sentiment is ironic, but also understandable. They, like the white Britons, believed in a nation and a nationalized past. In the case of Phase 3 refugees, the more urgently they needed a nation or a national past, the more authentically they encountered its unavailableness. The more obtrusively this unavailableness pressed itself upon the lives of these refugees, the more the nation and a national past revealed itself as something just occurrent and nothing more. The national past had been loosened from its hitherto unexpressed inclusion in the background practices of these Tamils. The nationalized past became an isolated property, a cipher.

By the beginning of the 1990s, further changes were observed in the composition of the more recent asylum-seeking cohort. Now, not only did young men and women who had escaped the Sri Lankan and Indian armies seek asylum in Britain, but war-hardened and disenchanted militants, escaping tyrannous militant groups of their own, were arriving in London. This group introduced a climate of suspicion on the one hand and a pervasive cynicism on the other. The most prominent target of this cynicism was the nation. I have witnessed arguments between these Tamils and their fellow Tamils who had embarked upon the project of finding and establishing their national past in which the former thought that the distant past which obsessed their fellow nationalists was irrelevant at best and a sign of derangement at worst. The only past they knew and cared enough not to want to be caught in was the recent past of war, rape, torture, and death that they had just escaped. Phase 3 Tamils have also begun to establish new alliances and to adopt new attitudes toward identity and difference that are now marking them off from Phase 1 Tamils in unprecedented ways. A series of examples will illustrate my point.

A number of Phase 3 Tamils who began at the petrol pump moved up to managing the petrol station and the attached "mini-markets," and then on to acquiring small grocery stores run by Ugandan Indians whose children now have no interest in inheriting their parents' businesses. Along with entailing late hours and hard work, the running of these shops presents a unique problem in customer relations. In Sivapalan's case, for instance, one of his customers is an older English woman who comes to his shop every day to ask him why he sells these nasty-smelling and strange-looking things, and why he does not take it all and go back to where he came from. Sivapalan smiles and checks out the items she buys—because they are inexpensive in his shop—and wishes her a good day. I asked him what he felt. He said, "Hate!" and then added, "But I also know we will win and they will lose." I did not press him to unpack that statement but let it bask in its polyvalence. Sivapalan, and other Tamil shop owners like him, have another interesting customer in the young Afro-Caribbean British male. Some of these young men—"at least one per night"—walk into his shop and pick up a pack or two of beer, presenting, however, only a packet of chewing gum at the cash register. When asked about the beer, the young man boldly declares, knowing full well that everyone knows otherwise, that he brought the beer from outside and owes money only for the gum he bought at this store. Sivapalan takes the money for the chewing gum and lets him go. This practice is so well known that it even piques the sympathetic ire of Phase 1 Tamils, who wonder why the Tamil shopkeeper does not inform the police. Phase 3 Tamils consider this kind of advice a sign of the utter ignorance of Phase 1 Tamils, and of the distance that separates the two groups. For one thing, the policeman is their foremost enemy. In support of these sentiments Phase 3 Tamils supplied me with stories of police racism, injustice, and violence too numerous to recount here. As one Tamil put it, "The policemen of the world should have a country of their own." For another, the shopkeepers find the rage of their "law-abiding" Phase 1 counterparts amusing and out of place. Even I was impressed by the equanimity with which these shopkeepers reacted to these blatant acts of shoplifting. Even though these Tamils did not extend alliances of interpersonal relations to the Afro-Caribbean Britons, they extended them alliances of understanding. They did not see them as breaking the law but as having broken with the law. To this extent their experience was a common one.

Tamils have little to do with the Afro-Caribbean community, a group whose "urban ways" they cannot relate to, people who, in their view, "give the family low priority." However, they find African immigrants much more compatible allies. Not only do many of the latter share Phase 3 Tamils' asylum-seeking status; they also have "rural values." That these new links of affect materialize may be illustrated by the following incident.

Sahitharan was a twenty-nine-year-old asylum-seeker from Sri Lanka. He was waylaid by a group of young whites and bashed to death in London's Eastham. Several of the London-based organizations working for refugees organized a protest march. Over 4,000 people of all ethnic groups joined the march. But there were only 150 Tamils, all from Phase 3. The largest non-Tamil representation at the rally was made up of black Africans. It is of interest that the trustees—all Phase 1 Tamils—of the Wimbledon Hindu temple denied the organizers of the march the right to hang posters on the temple premises. Their reason? "We do not want to antagonize the white community."

Other alliances have been forged among Phase 3 Tamils that have become more vital than any they ever had with their fellow Tamils of the other phases or the separatists/nationalists at home. Most of these alliances span across national boundaries to fellow asylum-seekers in other European countries who have fled both the nationalist Sri Lankan army and the equally nationalist Tamil militant groups. To the immigrant Tamils, the nationalized past that each of these groups is frantically trying to construct is something they have broken away from in the same manner that they feel they have broken with the law. Alliances have also extended to other refugees fleeing other national pasts, and a keen interest is shown in organizations such as Amnesty International whose scrutiny transcends national boundaries.

Displaced Persons and an Agentive Moment

When historians and anthropologists speak of agency, the image that is brought to mind is that of the individual actor, the pioneer, the bold and reflective subject, one who acts, if not from authority and power, then out of determination. Even those who overtly reject such a reduction of agency to the individual do not renounce the covert paradigmatic status of the individual agent in their analysis. This is a testimony to the success of the Cartesianization of much of the modern world in which the myth of the intuiting cogito has been naturalized. From here it is only one step to Cartesian dualism in which the intuiting, self-contained self is set against a radical outside, a radical other. Thus we find formulations of the question of agency rendered in such oppositional terms as agency versus structure or agent versus patient. An agent is seen as one who takes one's future into one's own hands. Such an autonomous and unary self, as I have indicated, can only be intuited and can exist nowhere else but in the impossible world of the Cartesian cogito. And furthermore, as Peirce among others has clearly demonstrated, "because we have no power of intuition, every cognition is necessarily determined logically by previous cognitions" (5.265). Thus historicity is an integral part of the symbol and the self. A semeiotic perspective on the self, on life, and on being human is unavoid ably historic and incorrigibly trinary. The core of Peirce's anti-Cartesianism, at least insofar as it pertains to questions about the individual and agency, is contained in his assertion that "man [*sic*!] is a sign" (or a cluster of signs). An individual is but an illusion, be it the individual person or the individual point in mathematics, even if at times a necessary illusion (see Peirce 3.93n.1). The only thing that is real is process. A sign, as we have already seen, can never be an individual or a monad. It is a triadically constituted process. So is the self.

Self-awareness is not the product of intuition but of inference. Consciousness is a *process* in which "the self becomes aware of itself on becoming aware of what it is not, of the non-self, of the external Other" (Peirce 1.324). Without the precipitation of self against the Other, there is nothing to infer and therefore no reason for self-awareness or self-consciousness to be; and conversely, without self-consciousness, the self remains unrealized, as a mere potential, a pre-self if you will. It is this triadically correlative relationship—among the self, the Other, and the awareness of the relationship of identity/difference that brings the two together—in process that constitutes a self. The triadicity of the self, then, is no different from the triadicity of the sign discussed in a previous chapter. Indeed, the self is a sign, mainly of the order of a symbol. The self and the sign are in time, and like Derrida's signified (1974:49), they are always on the move. And if the self is constantly being inferred, and it can be inferred only in time, then "there is no time in the 'present instant' for an inference, least of all for an inference concerning that very instant" (Merrell 1996:39). What we call a person or limit by calling him or her an "individual" is but an infelicitous shorthand for describing a relatively dense cluster of signs or sign-activities, and whose density is owed to the property of signs to take habits. If a person can take habits, he or she can also lose habits and change habits. But the locus of habit-change is not necessarily confined to an individualized person: "the box of flesh and blood," as James describes the self. It can occur in interpersonal space as well as intrapersonal space. An internal dialogue (which is what Peirce understands a thought to be) could be the locus of the agentive moment. It can occur between two, or among a group or a throng of people. Hence I consider the Gandhian Self-Rule Movement or the civil rights marches of the sixties as loci of agentive moments. Institutions can generate an agentive moment as long as they contain within them the signs of human being. So can any human creation. Thus the U.S. Constitution may be described as agentive, for it carries not only the traces of the authors and signatories of the document but also traces of the human habit of habit-change that is alive in the interstices of that document. Such a semeiotic view of the self positions the question of agency quite differently from what is the case in a Cartesian world. For this reason, the semeiotic perspective is more at home with the notion of an agentive moment than with that of agency per se. What, then, is an agentive moment?

Before answering this question, and bringing the question within the ambit of the substance of this chapter and this book, I must first revisit the semeiotic concept of habit. If the self is part and parcel of semeiosis, and semeiosis is an ongoing process of making inferences from experience, from encounters with the non-self, then inferences also generate expectations, and expectations are of the nature of habit. The more our expectations—conscious and unconscious—are satisfied, the more regularized and ramified our habits become.

Habit describes patterns of feeling, action, and thought. Or as Marjorie Miller puts it: "a habit is a thoughtful mediation between feelings and actions through the development of a meaningful relation: a future imperfect conditional rule for action *in case*. The habit, as a rule, solidifies as it is ramified in mental rehearsal and/or practical action—repetition reveals the antecedents, conditions and implications of the 'associations, "transociations", or . . . dissociations' [see Peirce MS 318,351] established. Meaning *emerges*" (1996:74). Habit describes a relatively settled period or state in semeiosis.

Habits are not confined to "individuals" alone but characterize semeiosic collectivities of various dimensions: a connubial partnership, a family, a department, a discipline, a congregation, an institution, and a society or a culture. And the agentive moment—to anticipate—can be located in any one of these semeiosic configurations as long as there lies in this configuration the human habit of habit-change. To be sure, inorganic matter has habits, plants have habits, and animals have habits. But only humans have the additional habit of or capacity for habit-change.

In our ordinary lives, in our everyday commerce with the world around us, we are, by and large, protected from caprice and shock, from the "bruteness" of Secondness by the Thirdness of habit. Or to put it more precisely, the interruptions of the reverie of the Thirdness of habit by instances of Secondness are but fleeting moments, infinitesimal tests, as it were, to see if semeiosis is active and to determine whether the prevailing "habits" are agentive. That is, are they sufficiently alive (nonpetrified) and capable of activating the habit of habit change if necessary, capable of generating new meaning to life under new circumstances when called upon to do so? Most of the time, they are, and human habits are indeed rife with life, "with things new born," to quote a line from Shakespeare's *Winter's Tale* where life and death are juxtaposed.[24] But these minor events and consequent copings do not merit the term agentive. There are, however, times in life when interruptions of habit or breaches in the order of things are of such magnitude that prevailing habits are not up to the task of providing the inferential appeasement for soothing the resulting shock by providing emergent meanings. The lives of many of those who figure in this book have been held in the grip of such crises of meaning, where existing habits have proved to be unhelpful, where the abyss of a breached moment of Secondness holds its place. Such moments of Secondness are what I call agentive moments. Many Phase 3 Tamils find themselves in an agentive moment.

In the present chapter, the nation has proved to be an inadequate habit, introducing into the lives of many an agentive moment. It is agentive because the only way of escape or resumption of semeiosis and a meaningful life is through the generation of radically new habits that lead in radically new directions. Have new habits emerged under these circumstances? In most cases, the answer is a tentative and timorous yes. But where there have been no redeeming habits, where "deliberate coping" has not given meaning to life, death—corporeal (usually suicide) or psychical—has been the result, the terminus of semeiosis.

If human habit is rife with life—"with things new born"—it is also rife with death. What is the future of the nascent habits of those who, as individuals or as collectivities, have had to choose against familiar habits? They have one of two futures. They may, in time, be reabsorbed into the currents of older habits. For instance, those who have been displaced by the nation-state of Sri Lanka and alienated from the very habit of "nation" may, in new countries, under new assurances, return to being nationals once more by either becoming faithful citizens of their adopted nation-state or by appealing to a nostalgia for the nation of their birth, childhood, and early adulthood, or both simultaneously. In which case we can say that the habit-change was short-lived. Most Tamil students whom I have met in North American universities who continue to be part of the discourse of nation have told me that this is what they expect to happen to their thoroughly alienated fellow Tamils. They may well be proved to be right. On the other hand, it is also possible that the familiar habit of nation is what will have to yield to a thoroughly new constellation of habits. Is this moment in the lives of these displaced Tamils agentive, a moment at the threshold of a new habit-formation? This question can be answered only in retrospect, when the effects of this moment are fully realized and when it can be determined whether or not the habit of nation has undergone a habit-change in order to appease the radical interruption of the agentive moment.

Conclusion

In the modern world we have come to view the nation-state as the ultimate unit of protection. What is it that renders a nation-state legitimate? John Herz's view is typical, combining nostalgic realism and nostalgic idealism: "Legitimacy originates from feelings and attitudes of the people within as well as neighbors and others abroad in regard to the unit, its identity and coherence, its political and general 'way of life'" (1968:24).

He further held that a nation-state's internal politics requires it to be grounded upon a contiguous expanse of territory (1968:25), its "physical corporeal capacity"(1959:40). What Herz failed to add to this is that the physical corporeal capacity in question is a thoroughly temporalized one in the modern nation-state, temporalized with the past. Michael Walzer (1983) in his *Spheres of Justice* subsumes all plurality under the caption of "shared understandings" that make a modern nation-state possible, despite diversity. This, I presume, includes a shared understanding of the past. What political theorists of the modern nation-state such as Walzer and Herz, and Schumpeter before them, failed to appreciate is how problematic a phenomenon "shared understanding" is, and that it has become increasingly so in late modernity.

On the one hand there is the LTTE gallantly and ruthlessly fighting for its Eeḷam, and the Sri Lankan army fighting for its Sri Lanka. On the other hand there is the mother who wishes only for her son to remember Tamil and could not care less for Eelam or Sri Lanka, and the ex-militant who almost lost his or her life for Eelam who comes to share that mother's outlook. The Estate Tamil who never had a nation of his own gives refuge to a Jaffna Tamil who escapes a war being fought for a nation. A child expresses her wish not to be around people who speak of their motherland, even as children who are drafted and who volunteer bear arms for the motherland. One generation of Tamils entertains fantasies of being ambassadors of their victorious nation, while another wants little or nothing to do with their nation. While some fight for solid land and fixed boundaries, others strive for liquid assets and fluid boundaries.

This case study of Tamil immigrants to Britain probes only one instance in which nationalism and the national past have become such contested categories. I am certain that there are many more, and some being spawned at this very moment in other parts of the world. By "contestation" I do not mean the arguments that abound and are abundantly written about as to whose nation a particular territory is and whose nationalized past is a valid one. I do not deny the existence of such debates, but I wish to claim that they conceal a far more radical contestation: a contestation that has been made possible by the unavailableness and occurrentness of the categories in question. Not only are shared understandings of and principles of common membership in nations and national pasts highly ephemeral affairs, but they also deny the reality of counternationalist currents that flow through and over the dikes of the territorial nation and the national imaginary. Refugees—not only Tamil refugees—are one of the many embodiments of this overflow that disturb "established priorities of identity/difference through which social relations are organized" (Connolly 1991:477). The transformation of the Tamil immigrant in Britain is one among many representations of "a social process through which fixed identities and naturalized conventions are pressed . . . to come to terms with their constructed characters, as newly emergent social identities disturb settled conventions and denaturalize social networks of identity and difference" (Connolly 1991:477).

7

CRUSHED GLASS: A COUNTERPOINT TO CULTURE

Only faithless am I true.
(Paul Celan)

Human freedom, . . . as fire, immediately escapes the powers of the guilty party. Fire, an elementary force to which other elementary forces will add themselves, multiplying damages beyond any rational conjecture! The wind adds its whims and violences to it. And yet responsibility is not diminished.
(Emmanuel Levinas)

WHAT is human Being? I cannot think of anything more effective in urgently provoking one to ask this question than violence. This question has served as an undertone in all the chapters so far, but more noticeably in the last three chapters, with some conspicuous help from Peirce and Heidegger. But in our search for human Being in the world, we keep encountering human beings: the result of the pull of an anthropological attitude against that of a purely philosophical one. Anthropology has had an answer to the question, What is a human being? An answer that has, on the whole, served us well, with or without borrowings from philosophers. The answer keeps returning to one form or another of the concept of culture: humans have it; other living beings do not. In this concluding chapter, as a critical tribute to anthropology and the anthropological perspective that I took to the study of violence, I wish to explore further our understandings of and claims to culture and their relationship to violence.

Not long ago it was the privilege of anthropologists to celebrate and take credit for weaning the concept of "culture" from the clutches of literature, philosophy, classical music, and the fine arts—in other words, from the conceit of the Humanities. Our discipline's founding father initiated this emancipatory project, I believe, unbeknownst to himself. He rescued the concept from its joint monopoly by the opera house on the one hand and the petri dish on the other. Sir Edward Burnett Tylor proffered a definition: "Culture or Civilization, taken in its widest ethnographic sense, is that complex whole which includes knowledge, belief, art, morals, law, custom, and any other

This is a modified version of a talk delivered as the Second Wertheim Lecture at the University of Amsterdam in the summer of 1991.

capabilities and habits acquired by man as a member of society" (Tylor 1974 [1878:1]).

For all its unwieldiness, its omnibus character, and despite its embeddedness in the evolutionary paradigm of the day to which Tylor himself paid ample homage, the definition generated the now famous view that culture is relative, that it defines the *human* condition, that all human beings have it, or rather that it has them, and that one human being's culture is no better nor worse than another's. To be fair, it was Franz Boas who, though never offering a definition of his own, breathed life into the implications of the Tylorean definition by putting it into the practice of his craft.[1] Of course, I am sure he did not foresee the silliness into which relativism, freed of its original polemical context, was to degenerate a generation later. And then there was Bronislaw Malinowski, who, though never calling himself a cultural anthropologist, introduced the discipline's methodological sine qua non, participant-observation.

The Humanities, for its part, was vaguely aware of the scandal brewing in anthropology, but, perhaps chalking it up to eccentricity (something many an English anthropologist and a few Americans were guilty of), it was content to continue refining the Arnoldian view of culture in practice if not in theory.

History shared much of the prejudice of the Humanities.[2] To support my argument with an extreme case, take, for instance, that most prestigious of think tanks, the Institute for Advanced Study at Princeton. It has four schools: Mathematics, Physics, History, and the Social Sciences. At "The 'tute,'" as some of the locals call it, "History" means European history. European history is more historical, not in the sense of temporality, but in the sense of an imputed cultural richness: "cultural" in the Arnoldian sense. Even more to the point, historians of classical Greece and Rome are the "real historians" there, and, by the time we get beyond the Renaissance, "History" begins to lose its empyrean dignity. Thus we find the only French social historian, whose work happens to be centered on the eighteenth and nineteenth centuries, housed in the Social Sciences. But even among the "less than sterling" historians who chose to write on the more recent past, the Arnoldian viewpoint persisted in only a slightly different form. Their histories, for the most part, privileged the scripted voices of the powerful and the "cultured." If this bias is true of European historiography, it is even truer of those working on the histories of non-European peoples, up to and including the very latest of historiographies, colonial history. Oral history, even when available, would be suspect and would most likely be relegated to that degenerate form, "folklore."

Speaking of European social historians, however, it is to some of these that the anthropological concept of culture began to make sense and in whose works its implications have been the most profound—more profound, I think, than in anthropology itself. Tylor's name was rarely invoked, and the phenomenon in question was called "social" rather than "cultural." But as was to become clear subsequently, the sense in which "social" was employed was more akin to "culture" than to the concepts of "social" or "society" that were employed by British structural functionalists. It was "social" in the Durkheimian sense that was to influence *L'École Annales* of history, especially through Marcel Mauss. The move beyond the history of the Middle Ages to the creation of a space for what came to be known as early modern history was simultaneously the move from ecclesiastical history to *histoire sériale*.[3] Marc Bloch's two-volume work on feudal society was to become an anthropological canon in the sixties and seventies. Culture found its counterpart in the *longue durée* of history.[4] On the English side, history from below was to find its finest embodiment in E. P. Thompson's classic, *The Making of the English Working Class* (1966). The strikingly similar influence of "culture" on European historian Carlo Ginzburg (1982), on the one hand, and the Americans Robert Darnton (1985) and Natalie Zemon Davis (1975), on the other, is remarkable. What distinguishes all these historians is their ability to "hear" the voices, not of those who were bearers of Culture (with a capital C), but of those who found themselves embedded in culture (with a small *c*), those whose voices were inscribed in minuscule: the witches, the women, the shepherds, the serfs, peasants, the poor, the popular, and the public.

Enter cultural studies and its counterpart, literary study. Scholars in cultural studies, like the anthropologists and the social historians I have referred to, began to take seriously the culture of the neglected. In this case it was the culture, mainly in the West, of the many over that of the privileged few. If the Arnoldian definition was a decanter, students in cultural studies chose to study and appreciate the dregs, not the sublimate. Their topics of interest included, among others, the media, film, billboard advertisements, reggae and rap, potters and punks, gangs and televangelists, wine, beer, and cheese. "Culture," in Raymond Williams's words, became "ordinary" (1983:90).

If cultural studies, paralleling anthropology's turn away from the privileged West, thumbed its nose at the high, the mighty, and the refined, literary study thumbed its nose at conventional literary criticism by emulating anthropology (at least some branches of anthropology) in emphasizing the context in which texts are written and, more important, in which they are read.

The story I have told thus far may make it sound as though all is triumphant in anthropology: its goals reached, its intentions vindicated. Anthropologists teach; others, sooner or later, learn. Alas, it is not so. Allow me to backtrack a bit to Roger Keesing's (1974) review essay of over twenty years ago and, in the interest of convenience, recommit all his sins of slight—of Linton, Lowie, Radin, Kluckhohn, Kroeber, White, and, most regrettably, Sapir. Roger Keesing divided the culture theorists into two broad camps: the adaptationalists and the ideationalists. Marvin Harris and a few archaeologists were the leading spokespersons of the former, while the major subdivisions among the ideationalists were headed by the cognitivists, Lévi-Straussian structuralists, the Schneiderian symbolists, and the Geertzian interpretivists. The adaptationalists de rigueur, who had attempted to define culture as merely adaptation to economic, demographic, technological, and ecological forces, have by now, for all practical purposes, fallen by the wayside. Human beings turned out to be as incorrigibly maladaptive as they were adaptive, and the way they went about being adaptive and maladaptive was as capricious as the proverbial weather in certain temperate zones. As for the cognitivists, their early high hopes of finally making the culture concept scientific—and that too by not having to resort to analogies from the physical or biological sciences but by identifying it as a system of rules along linguistic lines—fell faster than they rose. Brent Berlin and Paul Kay's *Basic Color Terms* (1969) was the last "love story" that came out of those heady days of ethnoscience. Cognitive anthropology survives today in a much more modest but vital form in the fields of ethnobiology, cognitive psychology, and similar subfields. Structuralism, which, in one of its extensions, came paradoxically close to a kind of biologism—with the imputed binary structure of the mind seeking kinship with the bicameral structure of the brain, triune-brain notwithstanding—has been superseded by poststructuralism and postmodernism in intellectual circles. David Schneider's insights, articulated in not-so-clear astronomical terms,[5] were both better stated and overwhelmed by Michel Foucault's writings, where *epistemes* and epochs seemed to displace "culture." Schneiderian anthropology's disregard for history, its essentialism, its unabashed idealism, its hypernominalism, and its absolute disregard of questions of power rendered it parochial and largely irrelevant in the 1980s. This is not to deny that Foucault was guilty of at least some of these apparent drawbacks, but the range of his power and intellect converted them into interestingly defended assets.[6]

For Clifford Geertz too, culture was symbolic. But as against Schneider, however, he played down the *systematicity* of culture. He belittled the cognitivists' emphasis on the rule-governedness of culture. He found structuralism's commitment to universalizing Culture and to locating it in the "human mind" dangerously close to biologism. (I for one am not against making a place for both "Culture" and "culture" but am wary of the structuralist construction of it.) As against all these coideationalists (if we accept Keesing's label in this regard), Geertz was committed to extracting "culture" from the private, especially from within people's minds or heads, and recognizing it as public. And then there is the persistent presence of Geertz's prose style in his brand of interpretive anthropology. This, more than any other single factor—more even than the Weberian and Diltheyan roots of his interpretive anthropology—I believe is responsible for the wide appeal his writings have had, especially in the humanities. What is of lasting significance in this aspect of Geertz's work is the unapologetic incorporation of the ethnographer with and in the ethnography. Once, when asked about ethnographic objectivity by one who still believed that there was an objective/scientific prose, Geertz replied, "I don't want anyone to mistake any of my sentences as having being written by anyone else but by me."[7] Every line bore his signature, so to speak. Thus "culture" was no longer something out there to be discovered, described, and explained, but rather something into which the ethnographer, as interpreter, entered.

"Self-indulgence!" cried the traditionalists. "Not enough reflexivity!" cried the new reflexivists. But culture had become dialogic, less in the much heralded Bakhtinian sense than in the lesser-known Peircean sense, a sense in which the consequences of conversation are shot through with "tychasm":[8] that element of chance contained in the "play of musement"—feeling, sporting here and there in pure arbitrariness (Peirce 6.33), much like Lord Siva's *lilas*, "mindless" eroticisms and asceticisms, acts of wanton love and wanton war, and the cosmic dance that spans it all. Tychasm has been deemed more fundamental than the gentle persuasion of *agapism* and the mechanistic necessity of *anancasm*.

It is *this* dialogic aspect of culture, culture not as a given but as something cocreated anew by anthropologist and informant in a "conversation," that I strived to elaborate in *Fluid Signs* (1984). There I argued for a conversation in which what was generated, exchanged, and transformed consisted not only of words but the world of nonverbal signs as well, not only of symbols—those arbitrary or conventional signs—but also of icons and indexes and a whole array of other, more or less motivated, signs. Built into such a semeiosic conceptualization of culture is an argument against a certain kind of essentialism. Given the silliness of some of the forms of relativism that are on the prowl in anthropologyland and beyond, it behooves me to stress that the antiessentialism I advocate is not directed at what is essentially human—a debatable and refinable list that should include, besides language, a sense of dignity, a need to love and be loved, the capacity to reason, the ability to laugh and to cry, be sad and be happy. My antiessentialism is directed against those who advocate *essential* differences between and among cultures, or rather, against those who believe that the differences are essential and more or less everlasting.[9] The Schneiderians—descendants of a Parsonian-Kroberian anthropology—are most guilty of this kind of essentialism. Antirelativists have charged that this position, best described as essential relativism, is fundamentally irrational and immoral. Others, who believe that the culture concept itself should be jettisoned, employ this formulation of culture and generalize it to all other usages of the concept to create the effigy of a nonexistent object they would like to burn.[10] What galls the antirelativists (chiefly materialists) is the "relativism" part of this position; and what galls the culture-critique group is the essentialism part of this position. What I envisage is a dynamic relativism that does not essentialize differences but believes in the essential humanity of humankind, a humanity that is not merely biological but Cultural (with a new kind of capital *C*), a species of habits that includes the habit of habit-change. Most cultural anthropologists, in focusing their accounts on culture with a small *c*, have been guilty of neglecting, even if not denying, the importance of this kind of "Culture."

At this point allow me to interject what appears to be a radical critique of such a semeiosic view of culture. The charge is that the governing metaphor in such a view, "conversation," exalts consensus at the expense of contestation. One response to this charge is an elementary one. "Conversation" entails communication or even communion in the widest sense of those terms, a sense that includes agreements and disagreements, consensus as well as contestation—but on shared grounds. Such a defense is neither very ingenious nor thoroughly ingenuous. For it is true that most cultural accounts in anthropology have given scant attention to contestations, even if they were only a subset of a larger consensual matrix. Yet the "contestators" must concede the argument in principle. But the critique in question suffers from a more serious infirmity. It suffers from what we may, following Hobbes, diagnose as "bagpipitis," "a going along with the prevailing windy cant, with whatever passes for [radical] *afflatus*, [becoming] indistinguishable from the tamest of *bienséance*" (Hill 1991:17). Contestation itself has become a cliché, a call to combat with phrases "on tap," an obliging mannerism, part of a higher-order consensus. Both consensualists and contestators sleep in the same bed of "complaisance."

Furthermore, regardless of whether we see ourselves as consensus theorists or as contestatory types, and even as we concede that we are culture comaking processualists rather than culture-finding essentialists, we cannot afford to be unaware of our collective logocentric inclinations, our privileging of language over labor, words over acts. True, the culture making that the ethnographer or the poet engages in parallels the culture making of the artisan and the farmer. Both are engaged in trimming or cutting the overluxuriant and in coaxing the stubbornly unproductive to yield. And in both domains, there are the craftsmen and the hacks, both of whom have a bearing on the production of culture. The significant divide, however, is not between the consensus theorists and the contestatory ones but between those who privilege the word—a group to which most academic scholars belong—and those who privilege the deed. I introduce the deed here in order to facilitate our movement to culture's edge, to what I shall call its counterpoint. Words are symbols that, even at the edges, pull one toward culture's center. Deeds, even when culturally centered—"habitus" notwithstanding—threaten to push against culture's limits. The deed I shall employ for making this point clear is the act of violence. But first I must return to my story about the culture concept.

This brief diversion, apart from other matters, was also intended to make the caveat about essentialism clearer. What then do we have? A series of paired terms: culture as given and culture as emergent, culture as reality and culture as realizing, culture as essentially relative and culture as relatively (and dynamically) essential. The second in each of these paired terms could hold its own, even if only by means of various adjustments and equivocations. The first would falter. But for those of us who advocate the second set of terms and thereby think that we are on the winning side, it is too early to gloat. There is a worm in the apple.

The problem lies at the core of the culture concept itself. The problem lies in what Tylor called "that complex whole." For the essentialists, the whole is an existent, a done thing, a thing of the past. For the processualists, "the whole" is something toward which the culture-makers and culture-seekers move. It lies in the future. The movement is toward this realizable entity, a foretaste of which is provided in what the hermeneutician calls "understanding." The dialectic is what guides one toward it. In other words, there is an assumed teleology to the cultural process. You and I may not live long enough to see its completion, its summum bonum, but it is moving toward such an end, however long that end may be deferred. It is this logic and this faith upon which culture—emergent, dynamic, and processual—is built.

Regardless of the difference, both ideas of "culture"—culture as essence and culture as process—partake of a Kantian-cum-Hegelian project. With respect to Kant, I have in mind the implications of his *Critique of Aesthetic Judgment*, whereby we are invited to see the beautiful as against the sublime,[11] and wherein when we contemplate an object and find it beautiful, there is a certain harmony between the imagination and the understanding which leads us to an immediate delight in that object. That whole which we call culture is supposed to end up, in anthropological analysis, having a certain harmony, not unlike the Kantian object of beauty. If we can only make it true, then we will also have made it beautiful. Or is it the other way around? In our monographs, how much time do we spend "rounding it all up," especially through the crafting of a closing statement or conclusion? This ideal is most poignantly captured in W. B. Yeats's description of a poem's reaching this moment of the sublime, in a letter of September 1936 to Dorothy Wellesley: "A poem comes right with a click like a closing box." So would we like our cultural accounts, our monographs, our arguments, to end in a moment of beautiful finality.

Ah beauty! For John Keats, "the aesthetic impulse is encapsulated in the coldness and sterility of his Grecian Urn" (Shaviro 1990:10). The point is made even more effectively by Shaviro's reading of a marvelous poem by Emily Dickinson. First the poem:

> I died for Beauty—but was scarce
> Adjusted in the Tomb

When one who died for Truth, was lain
In an adjoining room—

He questioned softly, "Why I failed"?
"For Beauty," I replied—
"And I—for Truth—Themself are One—
We Brethren, are," He said—

And so, as Kinsmen, met a Night—
We talked between the Rooms—
Until the Moss had reached our lips—
And covered up—our names—

Now to Shaviro's interpretation:

> It is only insofar as they are ironically "Adjusted in the Tomb," assigned their fixed boundaries under the power of death, that beauty and truth are one. "I died for beauty": does this mean that the speaker and her interlocutor died for the sake of beauty and truth (as martyr or witness)? Or, more perversely, did they choose to die *in order that* they might thereby attain truth and beauty? A desire for death is perhaps the hidden *telos* of beauty and truth. (1990:11)

The desire to find culture, either as a present reality or as a deferred ideal, to find it in any case, as a coherent whole, true and beautiful, is the desire to find a corpse. The work of culture becomes the "lifeless residue in which the process of creation is lost," the spark of tychasm denied (Shaviro 1990:10).

The same moral is conveyed in a well-known folktale in South Asia. Its variants probably have a common Indo-European origin. There was once a young man whose quest for truth was insatiable. He crossed the seven seas, climbed every mountain, dared the wildest of jungles, and traversed several deserts until he finally came to a cave where he found a toothless old hag, dressed in rags, with matted hair, holding a chain of beads in gnarled hands with overgrown fingernails. To the young man's surprise and delight, the old woman spoke. She uttered her words with caution and care, pausing to make every syllable true. After a spellbinding session of truth hearing, the young man worshiped the old woman, thanked her profusely, and pleaded with her to allow him to do something for her in return for her having so kindly and so completely slaked his thirst for truth. "Yes," replied this woman, this fount of all truth. "You can do me a favor. When you return to your people, tell them that I am beautiful; will you please?"

You may well object, holding that all this about the sublimation of truth and beauty in an objectified culture may be true enough of the essentialists, but not true of the processualists. You may even be kind enough to count me among those exempt from the charges in question because, in *Fluid Signs*, I described the fixing of culture as something that is forever deferred. And to the heckler who might say, "But where in your book is chance?" my supporters could have chanted, "*Passim, passim, ubique*!" I might have gloated in agreement, had I not confronted the task of writing an ethnography or, rather, an anthropography of violence. So I must demur. The culture concept, even in its processual mode, relies on a unifying metaphysical process called the dialectic. Culture totalizes. Culture is the emergence of higher and increasingly more adequate agreement from less adequate and less developed contradictions. At a more concrete level, a level in which my own fieldwork in Sri Lanka on the anthropology of violence is implicated, we see this Hegelian hope expressed in theories of the state. According to this view of the world, there is a metaphysical process that transforms tribal life, which is primitive and inadequate, into the more adequate and evolved rational nation-state. But the international and intranational strifes of the day and the violence they spawn have made a mockery of this hope. The contradictions inherent in the concept of the nation-state, constructed with the help of an imagined national past, demonstrate most clearly the operation of this exclusionary teleology. In nationalist discourse, the question is not who is a Sri Lankan or who is English, but who is a *true* Sri Lankan and who a *true* Englishman. Mythohistories are invoked to help people recast and relive an idealized past that is "constantly undermined by current and changing realities." And it is in these very imperfections—or, more correctly, in the perception of these "surpluses" or "excesses" as imperfections—that "nationalisms find their succor and sabotage"(Daniel, Dirks, and Prakash 1991:6). Nationalism is a horripilation of culture in insecurity and fright; it is as much the realization of the power in culture as the lack thereof. In either case, culture is not power-neutral.

All this is not to deny the successes of culture's recuperative and appeasing capabilities. Marx's celebrated "opiate" is only one—even if the most poignant—case in point. Marxism itself, like the Hegelianism it turned on its head, is another case in point. Call it cultural or cultured. Culture does make sense, even beauty, and sometimes truth. But its totalizing mission and capacities are what is in question. And to question such capacities is not to invoke their opposite (whatever that may be) as the solution. All of which brings me back to the subtitle of this chapter: Is there a counterpoint to culture?

Let me hasten to warn you, however, that the counterpoint to culture I have in mind undermines Bach—that contrapuntal genius whom the Dutch sociologist Wim Wertheim (1974) extolled as providing a metaphor to enable us to better understand violent revolutions and rebellions required for social change. The counterpoint I speak of is something that resists incorporation into the harmony of a still higher order of sound, sense, or society. It resists the recuperative powers of culture; it runs parallel without ever crossing the dialectic. It resists normalization, in the Foucaultian sense of that term.

Allow me to indicate more clearly what I have called the counterpoint of culture in the only way I know how: by intimation, by example. The example is violence, though violence is not the only event that is constituted of the culturally unrecoverable surplus I speak of. Let me plunge into ethnography and tell you of an event that was described to me by two brothers. It concerns the senseless deaths of two men and the suffering of two survivors. These two brothers narrowly escaped being killed by a gang of Sinhala youth during the 1983 anti-Tamil riots in a northeastern village in Sri Lanka. However, they witnessed the murders of their elder brother and father.[12]

Selvakumar is twenty-two years old and works as a teller in one of the local banks. When arrangements were made for me to interview him on the events that led to his father's and brother's deaths, I was not warned that whenever he recalled these events, he suffered episodes of loss of consciousness. The day of my interview with him was no exception. During our interview, which lasted for over four hours, Selvakumar lost consciousness thrice. The first time was after the first half-hour of the interview, and it took twenty-five minutes for him to recover. On the second and third occasions, he remained unconscious for about ten minutes each time. During these episodes his pulse and temperature fell sharply, his color drained to an ashen gray, he responded neither to pinpricks nor to smelling salts, and he lost control of his bladder. By the physician's orders, a warm poultice of medicinal herbs was applied to his temples and forehead and his lips were moistened with *tippili* tea. When Selvakumar regained consciousness, he did not remember having lost it.

What follows is a partial description of what happened on "that day," as he calls it:

> That day my father and the chairman (of the Urban Council) went to the police and told them that we had heard with our own ears that this Gunasene had collected the other boys on the soccer team and had obtained long knives and sticks and that they were planning to come and beat up all the Tamils in this housing settlement. This Gunasene had already served some time in jail. He is not from this area. He is from Nawalapitiya, from where you come. He has been here for many years, though. This place, this housing colony, was in really bad shape when my father moved in. But he organized the place. He cleaned up the well, cleared the jungle, and cut drains for the rainwater to flow. My brother. Oh, my brother, they killed him. They killed him and I couldn't even help. I was afraid. They beat him to death: "thuk," "thuk." (He passes out.)

Later:

> The police inspector told the chairman that if we had a complaint, we should take it to the navy post. So my father and the chairman went to the navy post. The sentry did not let them through at first. They waited there all morning. Then the commander's car came. He must have been going into town. The chairman waved him to a stop. They asked him if they could talk to him for a moment. The chairman had known him personally. "Say what you have to say. I have a lot of

work." "Can we go into your office?" the chairman wanted to know. "There is no time for that," replied the commander. So my father and the chairman told him what they had heard. The commander told them that they did not have any right to approach him on such matters and that they should have taken their complaint to the police station. They told him that they had already been there and the police inspector had told them to come to him (the commander). "If you are so smart, why don't you control your own people," said the commander to the chairman. My father and the chairman walked back to the police station. On the way, another friend, a Tamil, told us that some Sinhalas from Vavuniya had also joined Gunasene's gang and that he had heard Gunasene say to the boys not to worry, that he had taken care of the police. My father and the chairman walked back to the police station.

We were met there by Nitthi (Selvakumar's younger brother), who came to tell us that all the Sinhala taxi drivers were telling the Tamil taxi drivers that they were going to be killed today. There were no taxis in the Tamil taxi stand. They (the Sinhala taxi drivers) had told my younger brother that the rain had delayed things a little, but when it ceases to be prepared for "Eeḷam."[13] It was raining heavily. The inspector finally came out and said, "So what, the commander did not want to see the Tigers?" The chairman said, "Look, you know all these boys. You know this man. They are good people. They have lived with the Sinhalas in peace. They are neither tigers nor bears. There are rowdies who are threatening to kill them." He said like that. The inspector laughed and said, "Looks like the tigers are afraid. They have become pussycats." The other constables joined in and laughed. "Why don't you go to Appapillai Amirdhalingam.[14] He will take care of you. What do *you* say?" (He was talking to my brother.) "They tell me that you are the big man in the area. What, are you afraid too?" My brother did not say a word. He just clenched his teeth and looked down and walked away. All the constables were laughing. (Then he said,) "Now go home and take care of your women and children. And beware! If any of you dare call a Sinhala a rowdy. I am warning you. That is how you start trouble." Then what was there to do? The chairman went to his home; my father and I came home and shut the doors and put bars against them. Then the rains stopped.

Then they came. About half an hour later. My father was old and not as strong as he used to be. He was not feeling well in his body. But my brother was very strong. He was a big man. He was a good soccer player. That was something else this Gunasene had against him. He used to play soccer with us. We heard this loud noise at a distance. It sounded like one hundred saws were sawing trees at the same time. They were shouting something in Sinhala. Nitthi looked out through the crack in the front door and told us that there were two navy personnel standing on the side of the road. We felt relieved. Our neighbor, she is a Sinhala woman who is married to a Tamil. Her husband works in Anuradhapura. He is a government servant. He used to come once in two weeks. So this little girl, about three years old, used to spend most of her time in our place. This woman treated

> my mother like her own mother, and she used to leave this child with us. That day this child was with us. And the gang started coming closer and closer. My sister and my mother were hiding. Where can they hide? The house has only three rooms. They were in the kitchen behind the firewood. Then suddenly there was silence. All the shouting stopped. Nitthi looked through the crack in the door, and the two navy personnel were talking to Gunasene. Then we saw the navy personnel leave. My father told my younger brother to bar the two windows. But then we heard footsteps in the mud outside. Then they started pushing down the door. My father had fallen to the ground. My brother was still holding the door. But they used crowbars to break it. I ran into the kitchen out of fear. Another gang broke through the kitchen door. They surrounded the house. But the men who entered through the kitchen door didn't look for us in the kitchen; they walked on into the front room. Then I heard the beating. My mother and sister took the child and ran out of the back door into the fields. Then I heard the beating again. I slowly stood up and looked through the kitchen door into the front room. Nobody saw me. They were looking at the ground. I knew it was my brother on the ground. I wanted to help him. There was a knife in the kitchen. I wanted to take it and run and cut them all up. But I was a coward. I was afraid. My brother would have certainly done that for me. (He becomes unconscious. He is laid flat on the floor on a mat. A single tear trickles down his cheek. The man who had arranged this interview tells me, "The boy can't cry. That is the trouble.")

Later:

> Then someone said, "The old man is out there near the well." They looked out and laughed. "He is trying to draw water." They said things like that and were making fun of him. Some of them moved out, and now I could see my brother. They had cut him up. My younger brother had fainted behind the stack of firewood. I left him and ran into the field. Someone shouted, "There, over there, someone is running." I sat down behind some old tires. I must have fainted. When I woke up it was dark. There was smoke coming from where the house was. They had set their torches to it. I went looking for my mother and sister in the dark.

Nitthi is sixteen. He believes that he was in school, waiting for the rains to stop, when his father and brother were killed and his house was set on fire. Most of the time he has total amnesia about the events of that day. There are two exceptions. The first is when he wakes up with a start from a nightmare. From the moment he wakes up, he begins to describe certain events of that awful day in great and minute detail. And then, as suddenly as he awakened, he falls back onto his mat and falls asleep. In the second typical situation, he loses consciousness during the day as his brother does, but he then wakes up, not into his wakeful amnesia but into detailed recall. The recalling and retelling last for about five minutes, and then he falls asleep. He may sleep for several hours before waking up again. What follows are several of Nitthi's accounts taped by his brother for me during several episodes. The statements are all Nitthi's but are drawn from four different "dream episodes" and two separate "postunconsciousness" episodes. I was asked by the family not to play back the tapes to Nitthi. I have, with Selvakumar's help, edited the tapes so as to arrive at a narrative that makes reasonable chronological sense. Apart from rearranging the utterances for such a purpose, I have edited only to omit highly repetitive utterances (ranging from exclamations such as "*Aiyo*" to phrases and full sentences) and those sounds that made no sense to either Selvakumar or me. In this edited version, I mark shifts from utterances drawn from one episode to those drawn from another by rendering the first word of the "new" utterance in boldface type.

> The middle hinge is coming loose. They are pushing the door. Someone is kicking the door. Listen. **He** has put his foot down now. Now he is lifting it out of the mud. Now he is kicking the door. **Kick**, Kick, Kick. Now he is resting his foot again in the mud. It is like a paddy field outside. For all the kicking the door is not loosening. . . . **The** bottom hinge is still holding. The screws in the top hinge have fallen. The wood is splitting. A crowbar is coming through. **It** appears that father has been poked in the back. He can't breathe. He has fallen down. **My** elder brother has turned around and is trying to hold the door back with his hands. **I** see his (Gunasene's) toes from under the door. I know them from seeing him play soccer. He has ugly toes. Mud is being squeezed from in between his toes. **Knives** are cutting through the wood of the window. There is smoke coming through the window. **Gunasene** is shouting, "Not yet, not yet" (*dämmə epā, dämmə epā*). **My** brother's leg is moving. It is moving like the goat's leg. (He is supposed to have witnessed the slaughtering of a goat when he was younger.) **The** front door is open and they are going around to the back. They are going to the back to kill my father. Look through the door. The two navy men are near the *dhobi*'s house (a house at some distance across the main road). My eyes are filling with tears. The navy men look like they are very close. I squeeze my eyes. The navy men are far away again, near the dhobi's house. **Father** is crying. "Give me some water for my son, *Sāmi*.[15] Kill me but give my son some water. Let me give my son some water. The son I bore, the son I bore, the son I bore . . ." **Piyadasa** is asking, "How are you going to draw water like this, lying in the mud. Stand up to draw water from the well, like a man." They are all laughing. **Karunawathi** has come. The tailor boy has come. [The tailor boy is telling her,] "They ran to the field with your child. They are all right. Don't go. They might follow you." **They** are kicking my father. Karunawathi is shouting, "Leave that old man alone. Leave him alone. He is almost dead." "We know your man is a Tamil too. And we'll do the same thing to him if we find him." Karunawathi is crying: "What a shameful tragedy this is" (*monə aparādedə mēkə*). **Someone** is calling the men to the front. They want someone to drag my big brother to the road and leave him there. Listen! Karunawathi drawing water from the well. She tells the tailor boy, "He is dead."

I was not able to meet Gunasene. He was in police custody. However, I was able to find out two things about him. First, he was not from Nawalapitiya, where I had spent part of my childhood, but from a neighboring town called Kotmale. Second, using a police constable as a messenger he had sent Selvakumar Rs.500 and a message, the gist of which (according to Selvakumar) was: "What has happened has happened. Let us forget what has happened. This money is for you to rebuild your house. You can stay in our house if you want until you finish building your house."

Social scientists have tried to understand or even to explain communal violence in Sri Lanka. The grandest, and in many ways the most admirable, attempt so far in this regard is the one put forth by Bruce Kapferer (1988). It sought to understand Sinhala-against-Tamil violence in terms of Sinhala cultural ontology. He argued that Sinhala-Buddhist ontology required that it hierarchically encompass and dominate a subdued antithesis, in this case the Tamils. Insofar as such a contained antithesis might rebel from within, it was seen as demonic, and Sinhala Buddhism was called upon to exorcise this demon by ritual. The available ritual in the context of ethnic rebellion was violence. Such is a rough and shoddy summary of *Legends of People, Myths of State*. The thesis is perfectly Hegelian, except of course for its terminus not in a summum bonum of equipoise but in an ontology condemned to violence. The only problem was that no sooner had this and similar theses been put forth than Tamil violence rose to match Sinhala violence. Furthermore, violence was no longer interethnic but intraethnic, with more Tamils killing Tamils and Sinhalas killing Sinhalas than Sinhalas killing Tamils or Tamils killing Sinhalas; with the Sri Lankan state killing the most, Tamils and Sinhalas.

I must pause to emphasize here that my description of a violent event in which Tamils were victims and Sinhalas the aggressors is fortuitous. Conditions in 1983 and 1984 when I did fieldwork on this topic yielded more tales of Sinhala-on-Tamil violence. Rest assured that there are plenty of equally gory examples of violence in which the Sinhalas were the victims. An altogether separate book needs to be written on behalf of the thousands of Tamils and Sinhalas who watch from afar and from within the violence their own people are capable of and who abhor what they hear and see. Here are two symmetrical statements, one from a Sinhala and one from a Tamil. The first statement was made to me by the nephew of the minister of state at that time, Dr. Anandatissa de Alwis. At a party in Colombo in December 1983, he had this to say: "After I saw what happened that day [July 23, 1983], I am embarrassed to say I am a Sinhalese. I hate the Sinhalese. They are shameless. Cowards. I have never seen so much hate in my life and hope I never will." In 1993, a Tamil gentleman, a retired civil servant and now a refugee in Tamil Nadu had this to say following the assassination of Rajiv Gandhi: "The Tamils are a cursed race. A low race. Those Tamils there [meaning Sri Lanka] and these Tamils here [meaning South India] are both a cursed race. Barely human. Woe unto me who was born a Tamil!" These are strong expressions of self-loathing and frustration, expressions of disbelief that makes the core of their very beings revolt and tremble.

The point is this. Violence is an event in which there is a certain excess: an excess of passion, an excess of evil. The very attempt to label this excess (as indeed I have done) is condemned to fail; it employs what Georges Bataille (1988) called "*mots glissants*" (slippery words). Even had I rendered faithfully, without any editing, the words—both coherent and incoherent—of Nitthi, I would not have seized the event. Everything can be narrated, but what is narrated is no longer what happened.

I have also interviewed young men who were members of various militant movements and who have killed a fellow human being or human beings with rope, knife, pistol, automatic fire, or grenade. "You can tell a new recruit from his eyes. Once he kills, his eyes change. There is an innocence that is gone. They become focused, intense, like in a trance." Such was the account of a veteran militant, who has since left the movement in which he fought. Violence, like ecstasy—and the two at times become one—is an event that is traumatic, and interpretation is an attempt at mastering that trauma. Such an attempt may be made by victim (if she is lucky enough to be alive), villain, or witness. Those of us who are either forced or called upon to witness the event's excess flee in terror or are appeased into believing that this excess can be assimilated into culture, made, in a sense, our own. Regardless of who the witness is—the villain, the surviving victim, or you and I—the violent event persists like crushed glass in one's eyes. The light it generates, rather than helping us see, is blinding. Maurice Blanchot, in *Madness of the Day*, writes thus:

> I nearly lost my sight, because someone crushed glass in my eyes. . . . I had the feeling I was going back into the wall, or straying into a thicket of flint. The worst thing was the sudden, shocking cruelty of the day; I could not look, but I could not help looking. To see was terrifying, and to stop seeing tore me apart from my head to throat. . . . the light was going mad, the brightness had lost all reason; it assailed me irrationally, without control, without purpose. (Quoted in Shaviro 1990:3)

More ethnography.

Piyadasa (a pseudonym) is a Sinhala in his late twenties. I knew him as a young boy who played soccer in the town of Nawalapitiya, where I grew up. He lived in a village near Kotmale and used to ride the bus back and forth to his school with Tamil schoolchildren who came to Nawalapitiya from the tea estates. At times, after a game of soccer, he and his bus-mates would feel so famished that they would pool all their small change, including their bus fares, to buy buns and plantains from the local tea shop. Having eaten, they would start walking up the hill to Kotmale, all of six miles. His village now lies buried under the still waters of a reservoir built by the Swedes as part of the Mahāwāli River damming project.

In 1983, the *paṇṭāram* (the boy who makes garlands) of the local Hindu temple was killed. I was informed by another Sinhala man, a close friend of one of my brothers, that Piyadasa was among those who had killed the paṇṭāram and that he too had wielded a knife. I visited Piyadasa, who has been resettled in the North-Central Province, and asked him to describe to me what had happened. He denied that he had directly participated in the violence but was able to give me a detailed account of the event. The following are a few excerpts:

> He was hiding in the temple when we got there. The priest, he had run away. So they started breaking the gods. This boy, he was hiding behind some god. We caught him. Pulled him out. So he started begging, "Sāmi, don't hit. Sāmi, don't hit." He had urinated. He pleaded, "O gods that you are, why are you breaking the samis?" They pulled him out to the street. The nurses and orderlies were shouting from the hospital balcony. "Kill the Tamils! Kill the Tamils!" No one did anything. They all had these long knives and sticks. This boy was in the middle of the road. We were all going round and round him. For a long time. No one said anything. Then someone flung at him with a sword. Blood started gushing (*Ō gālā lē āvā*). Then everyone started to cut him with their knives and beat him with their sticks. Someone brought a tire from the Brown and Company garage. There was petrol. We thought he was finished. So they piled him on the tire and set it aflame. And can you imagine, this fellow stood up with cut-up arms and all and stood like that, for a little while, then fell back into the fire.

The constant shifting from the including "we" to the excluding "they" is noteworthy. This was in the early days of my horror-story collecting, and I did not know what to say. So I asked him a question of absolute irrelevance to the issue at hand. Heaven knows why I asked it; I must have desperately wanted to change the subject or pretend that we had been talking about something else all along. "What is your goal in life?" I asked. The reply shot right back:

"I want a video [a VCR]."

Two Conclusions

I have struggled to understand this event in which reality overtakes the surreal, to speak *about* it, and thereby to master it. But I have literally been struck "speechless." I am not alone, quite clearly. During my work in 1983–1984 and since, in Sri Lanka, India, Europe, and North America, I have met many witnesses of the excess of violence who have been stricken likewise by abominations that stagger belief. Shaviro puts it eloquently when he describes such a silence as "not a purity before or beyond speech. It does not indicate calm or appeasement. It is rather a violent convulsion, a catastrophe that overwhelms all sound and all speaking" (1990:84).

There are, to be sure, interpretations of such events that friends and "friendly texts" offer me, but no sooner do I seize them than they escape the grasp of my understanding. There are times when I think that I do understand. But, to return in closing to the optic, there remains a blind spot in all such understandings. Georges Bataille considers this blind spot to be

> reminiscent of the structure of the eye. In understanding, as in the eye, one can only reveal it with difficulty. But whereas the blind spot of the eye is inconsequential, the nature of understanding demands that the blind spot within it be more meaningful than understanding itself. To the extent that understanding is auxiliary to action, the spot within it is as negligible as it is within the eye. But to the extent that one views in understanding man himself, by that I mean the exploration of the possibilities of being, the spot absorbs one's attention: it is no longer the spot that loses itself in knowledge, but knowledge which loses itself in it. In this way existence closes the circle, but it couldn't do this without including the night from which it proceeds only in order to enter it again. Since it moved from the unknown to the known, it is necessary that it inverse itself at the summit and go back to the unknown. (1988 [1954]:110–111)

"In this darkness and this silence," there is neither ontology nor epistemology, hermeneutics nor semeiotic, materialism nor idealism, and, most important, neither culture nor Culture. Herein lies (C/c)ulture's counterpoint, a slippery word in its own right. The counterpoint of which Wertheim wrote almost twenty years ago was a counterpoint of hope and human emancipation. He described it as a "tiny and apparently futile beginning", that had the capacity to "evolve into a powerful stream leading humanity, or part of it, toward evolution and, in more extreme cases, revolution" (1974:114). The counterpoint of which I have written today is one that resists all evolutionary streams, be they of action or of thought. It will and should remain outside of all (C/c)ulture, if for no other reasons than to remind us that (a) as scholars, intellectuals, and interpreters we need to be humble in the face of its magnitude; and (b) as *human beings* we need to summon all the vigilance at our command so as never to stray toward it and be swallowed by its vortex into its unaccountable abyss. The first is a sobering point that concerns observation, the second a cautionary one that concerns participation: the twin terms that, hyphenated, constitute the sine qua non of the anthropological method. It is time for cultural anthropology to lose both its Hegelian conceit and its Malinowskian innocence.

But what about understanding, even those little understandings that have no Hegelian pretensions to any grandiose and messianic end of history? "I want a VCR." The statement "gnaws at the soul." Of course it can be explained, or rather explained away. It is a symptom of the growth of materialism. It was his attempt to change the subject. It was just a statement. This is a postmodern world, fractured and refractured. They are simply words. And yet, the will to understand persists. Lacan, for one, tells us that we cannot take words literally; what we must take literally are desires. But he also tells us that the relationship between speech and desire is registered negatively. To become literate in desire, therefore, we need to "read what is inarticulable in cultural statements" (Copjec 1994:14). What is the negative register of the cultural statement "I want a VCR"? What kind of desire does it conceal? Is it merely *a* desire or is it a whole array of desires, a unified field in opposition to the callous disregard or the maddeningly surreal expressed by the statement "I want a VCR"? I am not a psychoanalyst. I am not a competent depth analyst of any sort. But I lurch toward the rustle of hope, wherever it may be heard or found. In so doing, however, I run the risk of arrogating event to word, assimilating brute fact to cultural reality, translating event into language, wringing out of the cries of the boy consumed by an inferno an alibi for his murderers. Do I, in a manner of speaking, run the risk of "writing a poem after Auschwitz," an act that Adorno called "barbaric"? Adorno's charge was directed at Paul Celan, the Romanian Jewish survivor. I am no poet. And yet my riposte will be the same as Celan's to Adorno: "Only faithless am I true." "Which could be translated 'Only apostate am I faithful,' as a bereft survivor might say" (Felstiner 1995:53), an apostate to the suffering of the fallen. Many years later, Adorno came to agree.

It is in this spirit, then, that I would like to close this book with an event that happened in the 1977 anti-Tamil riots. I view this event—which may, in the broadest possible terms, serve as a qualisign, a sign gravid with possibilities—as that negative register or that oppositional field to the verbalized desire "I want a VCR." The incident in question was narrated by Mr. J. D. Immanuel, a retired Tamil school principal. Mr. Immanuel was dark of complexion and in the madness of the times was unlikely to be "mistaken" for a Sinhala. But it was at moments such as these that one hopes for such mistakes, mistakes that are matters of life and death. On this occasion he was dressed in long tussore trousers and a white cotton shirt, in the manner of an English-speaking gentleman. He had boarded the 3:15 up-country-bound train at Kandy. He chose one of the old red train cars, with two long wooden benches, one with its back against the windows and the other, across from it, facing the outside. The only other passenger in this compartment was a Kandyan Sinhala woman.

> She was a typical Kandyan Sinhalese, with the sari worn the Kandyan way. She wore Kandyan jewelry (filigreed silver) and a blouse with puffed-up sleeves that only Kandyan Sinhala women wear. She was seated on the window side; I sat on the bench against the wall, away from the door. She could have been the mother of any of those many Sinhala boys and girls I had taught for fifty years. I knew the riots had started in Kandy town. I knew that the thugs were coming and was

praying that the train would start before they entered the station. But the steam engine gave only one blast and a short whistle, then the mob entered the station and had reached the platform. The guard could have given the signal; and the driver could have pulled out. I don't know what happened. Either they were frightened by the mob or they wanted to see the fun. I was hearing thugs shout in Sinhala, "Get the Tamils out! Kill them! Kill them." I didn't look. I could hear passengers being pulled out and beaten. There was lots of screaming (*aiyo! aiyo!*) but no other words from the victims. All the talking was coming from the rioters. Rioting, cheering. Then I heard screaming in the very next compartment behind ours. The next moment, our door was being opened. As the thugs were climbing the steps to our compartment, this woman suddenly gets up and comes and sits beside me. I have my hands on my legs to stop them from shaking. She puts her hand on my left hand. She does not say a word. I do not say a word. The mob come and stick their heads through the window. Three young men get in. Look at us. Turn around and say, "No Tamils here, go on to the next compartment." Few minutes later, the train pulled out of the station. Tamil passengers from the train were still being chased, beaten, and stabbed. This woman did not let my hand go until we reached Gampola (thirty-five minutes later). She didn't say a word. Not one word. I didn't say anything. I couldn't. Life passed through my head like a reel. All the schoolchildren, all the teachers, all the parents, all the sports meets, all the cricket games, all the prize-givings. Like a reel. At Gampola, she gets off the train and leaves. She doesn't even look at me. I don't even know her name. I reached Nawalapitiya an hour later. Still alive, thanking God. I still hear the screams of those people. I start shivering in my sleep. Pushpa (his wife) here, says, "Wake up! wake up! You are having a bad dream." Then I feel that woman's hand on my hand. I stop shaking.

NOTES

INTRODUCTION

1. This image triggered in me the line from Geoffrey Hill's *Mercian Hymns* (1971) from which the title of this book, *Charred Lullabies*, has been drawn.

2. Even though the bulk of my work is based on events during and since the 1983 anti-Tamil riots and pogroms, I also draw from events recorded or recalled for me by informants of the 1977 anti-Tamil riots. In the body of the text, these events go undated.

3. Peirce's (and my) rationale for this spelling are twofold. "(1) There is no more reason for *semeiotics* or *semiotics* than for *logics* or *rhetorics*, (2) Both the spelling and the pronunciation should (in this case at least) be signs of etymology; that is, should make it e… from Greek *semeion*, sign, not from Latin *semi-* (half). Th… semeiotic; it is all about signs, and it is about all signs. An… e long because it has behind it a Greek omega, not an om…

…on as follows: "Prescission . . . arises from [paying] *at-ten*… *ct* of the other" (1.549).

CHAPTER 1
…HERITAGE AND HISTORY

… critique of these critics of "culture" see Robert Bright-m…

…2) argues that a form of linguistic nationalism in Sri L… egun more than a thousand years ago, not just in the n…

…*etrayed* (1993) and the acrimonious reaction to it in Sri L… nt.

…183) for a discussion of early federalist proposals that v… Sinhala region an identity of its own, distinct from that o…

…ient against the claim that Sinhala (linguistic) national-i… K.N.O. Dharmadasa (1992).

…227–235).

…). The most recent, post-1983 intervention by India in S… nd the justification of protecting Indian or potentially I…

…ion No. 8., 1983.

… denied that all the luminaries involved in the nineteenth- and twentieth-century Tamil cultural revival were concentrated in Jaffna; and it was a remarkable concentration indeed (see Russell 1982:135).

10. To be sure, most of my Jaffna Tamil informants thought "Old" suited them perfectly, and gave the word the same connotation given to it by the Estate Tamils

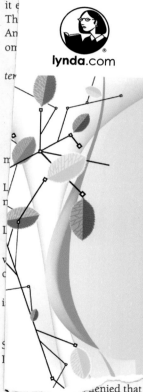

("ancient" rather than "spent"). But the exceptions in this case are more revealing than the rule.

11. I first settled on the name "Estate Tamils" in 1986, when I wrote the earliest draft of this chapter. I continued to stick to this name throughout the subsequently written chapters. In my most recent visit to the tea plantations in 1994, I detected a slight preference, at least in formal and official discourse, for "Hill-Country Tamils." But in everyday discourse among Tamil workers, the term Estate Tamils is what is used with the greatest ease and frequency.

12. *Alberuni's India*, trans. Edward Sachau (London, 1888), 2:10–11, cited in Salomon 1980.

13. The more recent hermeneutic turn, after Dilthey and especially Gadamer, has, by foregrounding the interpretive nature of all historiography, pulled out from under the "objectivist historian" the rug of innocent conceit upon which he or she stood and presumed that what he or she was after were facts qua facts and events qua events, unstained by the subjective presen(t)ce. However, what I have called the "typical historian" continues to exercise his craft much as if hermeneutics had not budged from its "classical" form.

14. See A. K. Warder's *An Introduction to Indian Historiography* (1972) for a general introduction to these various historical traditions.

15. On this point also see Bruce Kapferer (1988). For an excellent account of the amount of passion invested in defending or attacking the "historicity" of the *Mahāvaṁsa* see Serena Tennekoon (1987).

16. A casual count of bibliographic entries of Sri Lankan historians yields a 15:1 (Sinhala:Tamil) ratio of authors. This can be explained only partly by the fact that Jaffna tended to have a higher proportion of schools equipped with science labs than did the Sinhala south—thanks to the early American missionary effort in the north. But that this might not have been the only reason is hinted to us by the fact that a similar "slighting" of history can be found in the educational system of the predominantly Hindu state of Tamil Nadu in India.

17. To be sure, not all that he attributed to K. M. de Silva was said by K. M. de Silva, but some of it was. However, through the surreptitious interspersing of the said with the unsaid, in and out of context, our tour guide was buttressing his speeches with authority. It is telling that our ultranationalist tour guide's historian himself was subsequently to be called a "traitor historian" by a more powerful group of Sinhala nationalists in Colombo because de Silva had claimed that only four Sinhala kings had ruled the entire island (Tennekoon 1987:4, 8).

18. By "vague," I do not mean something insufficiently specific; rather, I use the term in the Peircean philosophical sense of "definitional indeterminacy" (1.204–208). (In keeping with convention of citing from *The Collected Papers of Charles Sanders Peirce*, ed. C. Hartshorne and P. Weiss [vols. 1–6] and A. Burks [vols. 7–8], the number to the left of the decimal point indicates the volume and that to the right indicates paragraph.) "This sort of vagueness . . . signifies only an appropriate level of generality for typological truth and in no way implies a lack of reality" (Haley 1988:26).

19. Semeiosis (following C. S. Peirce's preferred spelling) is the study of the activity of signs.

20. Andrew Lass (1988) uses "concretization" to describe something very similar to what I am trying to describe here. His concerns are with the "concretization" into mon-

uments in the uses of history by nineteenth-century Czech nationalism. However, there are some epistemological differences between Lass's phenomenological framework and my semeiotic one, differences I shall not explore in this study.

21. I have been surprised on more than one occasion when trained Jaffna Tamil sociolinguists have equated the "prestige" of the Jaffna dialect (a prestige, by the way, that is limited only to Sri Lankan Tamil-speakers) with "linguistic purity." If an analogue be needed, one might liken the Jaffna case to the Appalachian community that was discovered some years ago by linguists who found its members to have retained a remarkable number of elements from Elizabethan English, elements that have been lost in contemporary standard English. Imagine these Appalachians' claiming that their English is "pure" and all other versions "corrupt." I consider the Jaffna Tamil presumption to linguistic purity not a mere measure of the degree to which this conceit has been domesticated among these Tamils but as an index of the degree to which *heritage* as a phenomenon has been naturalized in their discourse.

22. Also see Coomaraswamy (1987:84–84).

23. The leader of the biggest trade union of plantation workers, Mr. S. Thondaman, belongs to the Kaḷḷan caste. He was also a cabinet minister in the government of J. R. Jayawardene.

24. I have constructed the oral history that follows by drawing from over twenty-five oral historical accounts gathered in the field. I have rendered this typical oral history in a block quotation because, save for syntactic editorial insertions, the account provided is a composite of actual quotations from informants. All of my "oral historians" are, or were at some time, residents of tea estates or small towns in the Kandy, Nuwara Eliya, and Badulla Districts. Some aspects of these oral accounts do not find redundant corroboration in written accounts, while others do. This does not mean that the former are true only if corroborated by the latter. Unless contrary versions turn up (in which case one may try to find good reasons for choosing one over the other), I take a lack of redundancy as merely indicating indifference on the part of the creators of such documents toward those aspects of laborers' experience that do figure in oral histories. Wherever feasible, however, I have provided references wherein such oral histories are corroborated by documented histories. I do so, not to confirm, but to provide the reader with directions for further research. Furthermore, my failing to provide a documentary counterpart in every instance is not to be taken as evidence of the nonexistence of such documentation. For an admirable overview of Estate Tamils, written by an insider, see S. Nadesan (1993).

25. Estate Tamils never pronounce this last Kandyan king's name the Sinhala way (i.e., sans the terminal *m*), implicitly making the point that he was a Tamil monarch.

26. Whenever calendar years are given in parentheses, this indicates that oral accounts do not, in general, specify such years.

27. In fact, the railways were to come much later, in midcentury.

28. Recall the characterization of these people's ancestors as "drifters," with the implication that people with a deep and connected network of kinfolk could never forget their true identities. Strong identities entailed *kaṭṭuppāṭu*.

29. The following were the years in the nineteenth century when the Madras Presidency was most affected by famine: 1802–1804, 1806–1807, 1823, 1832–1833, 1838–1843, 1853–1855, 1876–1878, 1896–1897 (see Famine Commission Report), and 1899 (See Ludden 1985:194–195).

30. A kaṅkāṇi was a recruiter-cum-leader of labor gangs, a very powerful and important figure in the lives of Estate Tamil workers. At the peak of their powers, both white planters and Tamil laborers were extremely dependent on him. From the white man he could withdraw labor at critical times, and from the laborer he could withhold payment almost at will with impunity (see Wesumperuma 1986, passim).

31. This is contrary to fact. Sinhalas did work on clearing the jungles (see Wesumperuma 1986:9). That the Sinhalas are indolent is a belief widely subscribed to by all Tamils of Sri Lanka, and even by many Sinhalas. This baseless opinion (in my well-studied judgment) is in itself deserving of further study, as a cultural artifact. It is interesting to note, however, that the "indolence" in question occurs in two distinct discursive arrangements. For the Tamil, it occurs within the discourse of hard and efficient work. For the Sinhalas who hold this view, it is a matter of hierarchy and who can and cannot afford such indolence. The Europeans in Sri Lanka and the Europeanized Sri Lankans (such as present-day tea planters) are among the greatest perpetrators of the myth of the indolent Sinhalas.

32. Most probably, the immigration of Indian labor to the island peaked in the late nineteenth century, not in 1827, but in 1889. However, arriving at an accurate figure with the available statistics is extremely difficult (see Wesumperuma 1986, chap. 3).

33. See chapter 4 for a more detailed discussion of the Sirimavo-Shastri and the Sirimavo-Indira Pacts and their effects.

34. The cobbler (Chakkiḷian) is the lowest in the caste hierarchy. A disordered society is compared to a "casteless" society, which is the same as one in which the cobbler is the kaṅkāṇi.

35. I have not located the records for 1903, the year Queen Victoria died. But according to Ferguson's directory, the first decade of the century marks the heaviest net increase of Indian immigrant labor (442,786 individuals), which broadly supports the oral account.

36. Nowadays the women and men of tea estates are embarrassed and resentful about such subservience on the part of their fathers and mothers. The current militant mood does not indulge in any such sentiment toward anybody, including members of the other two ethnic groups who have traditionally held estate workers in bemused contempt.

37. The bhai is a Sindhi moneylender whose reputation for enforcing a verbal contract between his borrower and himself with tactics of terror is legendary in the hill country of Sri Lanka. Moṭṭa Veḷḷāḷas belong to an upper, non-Brahmin cultivating caste from whose ranks many of the supervisors were drawn and many of whom eventually became owners of tea estates. Cheṭṭiars are the very successful merchant-banking class from South India whose interests spanned as far east as Vietnam, as far north as Burma, and south into Sri Lanka (Rudner 1994).

38. Several members of the Moṭṭa Veḷḷāḷa or Āru Nāṭṭu Veḷḷāḷa caste have become wealthy merchants and industrialists in both Sri Lanka and India. The Nāṭṭukkōṭṭai Cheṭṭiārs were the rice merchants and merchant-bankers of Sri Lanka on whom the early English planters depended heavily (see Wesumperuma 1986:165–170, 296–299, and Weerasooriya 1973).

39. Persons of Dutch, Portuguese, or other European ancestry.

40. S. U. Kodikara (1965:79) puts the number of Indian Tamils registered as voters at 143,000 in 1936 and 235,000 in 1939.

41. Indeed, the figure had dropped to 168,000 by 1943.

42. A Jaffna Tamil, professor of mathematics at the University of Ceylon, politician, and adviser to Sri Lanka's first Sinhala prime minister, Mr. D. S. Senanayake.

43. G. G. Ponnambalam, a brilliant Tamil politician-lawyer, founder of the Tamil Congress Party and an eloquent defender of Jaffna Tamils' rights, was subsequently to accept a cabinet portfolio in the Senanayake government. He was seen by Estate Tamils, as well as by many Jaffna Tamils, as having sold his birthright for a mess of pottage (see de Silva 1986:106 for an even more cynical view of Ponnambalam).

44. P. Devaraj (1979), citing H. Wriggins and A. J. Wilson, estimates that seven to twenty leftists' successful election to Parliament was influenced by the Estate Tamil vote in 1947.

45. See R. V. Sagar et al. (1986). More on this in chapter 4.

46. As of the writing of this chapter, I do not know whether this "sketch" was ever developed into a full *purāṇam*. As of now, I have not had access to his papers. The form in which it appears here is an edited version of my fieldnotes and not an exact transcription of a tape recording. Those portions that were written down verbatim appear here within quotation marks.

47. A purāṇam is a legendary mythology. Hence, malayakattamiṛar refers to the legend of the Tamils of the heart of the hill country.

48. This line, "*avaḷukkuttamiṛ entra pēr*," is from a song by a much renowned South Indian poet and songwriter named Bharathithasan, which was made popular in the opening lyrics to a song in a Tamil film. For a fine scholarly account of the rise of Mother Tamil, see Ramaswamy (1993:683–725).

49. Bharathithasan wrote a poem by this title in which Siva is called father (*tantai*). From the lyrics alone it would be difficult to say whether this reference is to Siva as the father of *tamiṛ tāi* as well as of the Tamil people, or if he is to be seen as the father of the Tamil people and the spouse of *tamiṛ tāi*. Of course, in typical mythological fashion, he could be all of these (see Bharathithasan 1985:45).

50. An allusion to Kadirgamam (Sinhala: Kataragama) in the south of Sri Lanka where Hindus and Buddhists go as pilgrims and which is believed to be Skanda or Murugan's main abode on the island.

51. Raymond Williams notes that in English, since the sixteenth century, "labour" has gradually lost its association with pain, except in the context of the labor of childbirth. In C. V. Velupillai's purāṇam, this association seems to be recovered, albeit in Tamil (see Williams 1983:76–77).

52. See Kapferer (1988) for such an ahistorical position and my criticism of it (Daniel 1989). On the Durkheimianism of such *moral orders* see Evens (1982).

53. This is Alfred North Whitehead's term, used to describe the process of coming-to-be.

CHAPTER 2
NATIONALIZING THE PAST

1. I use "modern" or "modernity" to allude not to a stage in the progession of human history but to a certain discursive practice.

2. A recent example would be Gananath Obeyesekere's fascinating essay on Sri Lankan Buddhism's folk and monastic engagement with time and chronology (1991), an essay that, unfortunately, came to my attention at a very late stage of writing this book.

3. Hereafter, when I wish to differentiate the kind of history that originates in a predominantly European discourse, I shall qualify it by the adjective "modern"; and conversely, when I wish to emphasize the sense of history cultivated in precolonial Buddhism, I shall call it "traditional history."

4. "Ground" is a term used by Charles S. Peirce that designates the qualities of a representation or sign that matter for the enabling of signification. Thus it does not matter whether a stop sign is made of steel or wood, but it does matter that it is octagonal and not triangular. Similarly, what *matters* for history is its epistemic qualities, and what *matters* for heritage is its mythic qualities.

5. I ask those familiar with Heidegger's terminology to note that for the purposes of this study I have set aside the distinction that Heidegger draws between the "ontic" and the "ontological." My preference for the term "ontic" over "ontology" is motivated primarily by my desire to emphasize that being-in-the-world is not necessarily beholden to the "word-sign" or logos but has more to do with one's—bodily, spatial, and emotional—comportment with the world.

6. The national dress, which includes a white wraparound lower garment and a loose "Nehru shirt," was widely adopted as a mark of national identity by politicians after the 1956 elections in which the populist Sri Lanka Freedom Party routed the right/elitist United National Party.

7. Though the work is somewhat dated, Gardiner (1959) provides an adequate survey of the plurality of history. For a more recent study of the range in contemporary history and historiography, see the three volumes of Paul Ricoeur's *Time and Narrative* (1984).

8. See especially Ricoeur (1984: vol. 1, chaps. 4–5).

9. See Merquior (1985), Derrida (1981), and Margolis (1993).

10. Compare, for instance, the writings of the great South Indian historian Nilakanta Shastri with those of K. M. de Silva or E.F.C. Ludowyk. Shastri's is a difficult task because the "historical record" he works with lacks the approving stamp of the event.

11. See White (1987:17, 22, 45).

12. For an early construction of this event by eighteenth- and nineteenth-century Orientalists see William Jones (1979 [1788]) and J. R. Harrington (1979 [1809]); for its gradual appropriation for and by Ceylon's view of its past, see Colin McKenzie (1803) and Captain Mahony (1803). Note how also the first attempt to specify an exact date in Indian history by A. L. Basham, in his ambitious Indophilic book *The Wonder That Was India* (1954:259), centers on the death of the Buddha ("between 486 and 437 B.C."). Also see the framing of K. M. de Silva's *A History of Sri Lanka* (1981:9), in which the earliest date of certainty mentioned is the year "around 563 BC" when the Buddha was born.

13. In making the distinction between "myth" and "history" I draw liberally from Thomas Olshewsky (1982).

14. To invoke a logic of cause and effect is not to equate causal explanations, of which there are many, with causal laws in the "covering-law" tradition of Hempel. On this point see Dray (1957).

15. "Single-mindedness" does not imply "simplemindedness." Rather, it implies a form of cultivated selectivity conditioned by certain tropological principles of narrativity in which the clarity of a "story line"is preserved.

16. This sentence was truer when I first wrote it in 1987 than it is today, nine years

later. Even Tamil "heritage" is, as this is being written, becoming increasingly historicized, subjected to epistemic evaluations, and when found wanting has generated defensive and offensive acts of rage.

17. The influence of S. J. Tambiah (1979) on my thinking is acknowledged here.

18. The principal militant group fighting for a separate Tamil state to be established in the island's north and east.

19. This allusive reference is intended to suggest that "onticity" of myth has more than a passing resemblance to what Foucault (1972:50–55) called an "enunciative modality."

20. Considered to be the descendants of the original inhabitants of the island, who predated the Sinhalas and the Tamils.

21. The assertion within quotation marks is a very close paraphrase (if not the exact words) of Mr. Senaratne.

22. See the *Daily News*, October 8, 1983.

23. For a fine contemporary account of the vitality and vituperativeness of scientific racism in Sri Lanka see Serena Tennekoon (1990; especially 214–217). For a witty and devastating review of the Aryanization theory of "philological racism" see Edmund Leach (1990).

24. Persons of Dutch, Portuguese, or other European ancestry.

25. Since the late 1970s, even Kataragama has begun to be nationalized and Sinhalized.

26. "Symbols" are signs of convention, "indexes" are those implicated in the logic of cause and effect (ergo their "manipulatability"), and "icons" are signs determined by the qualities they share with the objects they stand for, a sharing that may range from similarity to identity. A practicing believer whose commitment to his religion is participatory and ontic is drenched with the attributes of his ontic world and is thus an icon of that world.

27. Our guide had served as a sergeant in the Ceylon-British army prior to national independence.

28. Tourists' queries and opinions are amply available for the eavesdropping at the Tourist Information Center in Colombo and the lobbies and coffee shops of tourist hotels all over the island. The company of my American wife, another American couple, and a Canadian friend made this information-gathering method of mine as easy as picking green mangos off the ground following a windstorm in August.

29. Some time later, A. T. Ariyaratne, the founder and leader of the best-known Sinhala-Buddhist grassroots organization, the Sarvōdaya Śramadāna Movement, claimed in public that every last drop of blood in his veins was Sinhala-Buddhist (confidential source).

30. It merits noting that in none of the anti-Tamil riots prior to 1983 had there been deliberate and wanton destruction of Hindu temple images and desecration of Hindu temples. The priest of a Hindu temple in Colombo where the late president of the republic, Mr. Premadasa, worshiped, informed me that he (Mr. Premadasa) "was very troubled by this particular aspect of the riots." Mr. Premadasa was known to fervently beseech various Hindu gods for favors and regularly obtain the advice of at least two Tamil astrologers regarding the disposition of the stars and planets toward him. After 1987, Tamil militants took to vandalizing or destroying Buddhist temples and other sacred items.

31. In strictly Heideggerian terms, the quest for recognition itself may be seen as symptomatic of an inauthentic Dasein. But an authentic Dasein, entirely isolated from everyday life, language, and time, is not possible. On the resolution of this contradiction see Hoffman (1986).

32. In presenting this examination, I liberally draw from Piotr Hoffman's (1989) reading of Hegel.

33. K.N.O. Dharmadasa's book (1992) is the most scholarly defense of this position.

CHAPTER 3
VIOLENT MEASURES, MEASURED VIOLENCE

1. Anthropological fieldwork on which material for this chapter has been drawn was carried out in 1971, 1974, 1976, 1983–1984, and 1987. The most extensive research of 1983–1984 was funded by a grant from the Social Science Research Council, which is gratefully acknowledged.

2. Carol Eastman (personal communication) directed my attention to the "cultural" versus "nomic" distinction in "agriculture" and "agronomy," the former indicating practice-generated behavior and the latter, rule-governed behavior. By extension one may note the nominalist epistemology of "agro*nomy*" and the realist epistemology of "agri*culture*." The former imposes a name (order) on the world; the latter indicates names as real emergents from the world.

3. Cited in Hall (1982:12).

4. Even if primogeniture is not strictly observed in South India, in times of material scarcity, it is known to assert itself.

5. For reasons of simplicity, I have applied to Tamil words the common English form of pluralizing, i.e., the addition of an *s* to the end of a word.

6. On many estates, a line room consists of an open front porch, a middle room, and a kitchen, the total unit measuring ten feet by ten feet. One can find as many as twenty-five such rooms in a single row.

7. What may appear as a liberal use of Foucault in this chapter is in fact a cautious one. I have been cognizant of the inappropriateness of imposing European problematics onto Asian ones. However, the appropriateness of extending Foucault's study of the birth of the disciplinary regime in Europe to facilitate understanding of the social formations of nineteenth-century plantations in Europe's colonies cannot be denied.

8. Since the late 1960s the shift has been gradually made to the metric system of weights and measures. Even though the conversion was officially to have been completed by 1970, the adoption of the metric system is uneven in the manufacture of tea. In the manuals and account books (especially as they near the point of export), the metric system has fully replaced the older imperial system of weights and measures. In the field, however, the English system still persists.

9. For an interesting glimpse into this world see Tea Research Institute (1963, 1966, and 1967).

10. The name given to the huge ledgers in which are recorded the names and productivity (among other matters) of individual workers.

11. Both Sinhalas and Tamils have forgotten the Arabic origin of this word. Most

Sinhalas believe that *huntuvə* came from the Tamil *cuṇṭu*, and the Tamils believe that it came from Sinhala, but both treat it as a thoroughly domesticated "folk-measure."

12. The idea of "a little extra" is not conveyed in a single expression but in a variety of verbal and gestural forms. One of the commoner forms such an expression takes is to be found in the utterance (with appropriate hand gesture, facial expression, and head movement) "*cumma koñcam pāttu pōṭunka*" (literally: "Just or simply / a little / look or take note of / and give").

13. For a more detailed analysis of the symbolic import of the odd-numbered gift, see Daniel 1984:131–135.

14. Material on which this paragraph is based was gathered during my 1973–1974 field research in Tamil Nadu.

15. For a more enhanced understanding of the intricate play of signs in the context of food and feasts in a South Indian community that is unrivaled in its celebration of "gastro-politics," see Arjun Appadurai (1981).

16. For example, see Johnson (1962).

17. The kind of pruning and the length of the pruning cycle vary according to elevation and climate. In the low country (below approximately 2,000 feet) rim-lung pruning or cut-across pruning is carried out every two years, in the middle altitudes (between approximately 2,000 and 4,000 feet) cut-across pruning with lungs; in the up-country (above approximately 4,000 feet) clean pruning with no lungs is the norm (see fig. 2). The branches that are spared the pruner's knife are called lungs, presumably because they help the plant to breathe while the rest of the bush is subjected to radical surgery of sorts.

18. The scale indicates both pounds and kilograms. The weights, which continue to be called out in pounds, may or may not be recorded at this stage in kilograms. Quite often conversions are done at the very end of the bookkeeping process in the estate offices and factories.

19. See G. W. Sanderson (1964:146–156) on how a manual hedges its prescriptions.

20. I use the adjectival forms "iconic," "indexical," and "symbolic" rather than the nominal forms "icon," "index," and "symbol" in order to alert the reader to the fact that the latter misleadingly convey the sense that there can be signs which are exclusively icons, or indexes, or symbols. Not so. All signs partake of mixed signifying modes, with one or another mode tending to dominate in the manner in which significance is effected.

21. "Prescission" is a term used by C. S. Peirce (1.549 and 2.364), the form of the process by which one selectively focuses on certain aspects of a phenomenon to the disregard of other aspects.

22. The origin of the foot as a unit is often said to be traceable to the length of a certain monarch's foot.

23. In Estate Tamil parlance, when a laborer is registered to work, he is said to "have a name," and if he is not, he does not "have a name."

24. If a kaṅkāṇi feels that he has "overabused" someone, he will compensate her by giving her bonus pounds at the day's end at the weighing shed.

25. See Homi Bhabha (1984:127–142), in which mimicry is somewhat differently inflected but which nonetheless considerably influences my own thoughts on the subject.

26. The Sinhala peasant worker who resides in his or her own neighboring village is to be distinguished from the few Sinhala resident workers. What follows applies only to the peasants.

27. Only a few years earlier, the same response could have been read as sarcasm. This was not true in 1984, when I recorded this episode.

28. This refers to the pact reached in October 1964, between the then prime ministers of Sri Lanka and India, Mrs. Sirimavo Bandaranaike and Mr. Lal Bhadur Shastri, respectively. According to this pact, of the estimated 975,000 persons of recent Indian origin in Sri Lanka who were stateless, 525,000 (together with the natural increase in their number) were to be granted Indian citizenship and repatriated to India over fifteen years; 300,000 (together with the natural increase in their number) were to be granted Sri Lankan citizenship over the same period of time; the status and future of the remaining 150,000 (and the natural increase in their number) were to be decided on in a separate, future agreement between the two governments.

29. On the etymology and genealogy of the word "coolie," see Daniel and Breman (1992).

30. See Peirce (5.474–476).

31. "MS" refers to Peirce's unpublished manuscripts, identified in terms of the numbers used by the Houghton Library at Harvard.

CHAPTER 4
MOOD, MOMENT, AND MIND

1. The analogy derives from Peirce (5.263) where he presents the illustration of an inverted triangle ▽ dipping into water in order to argue against the belief in a "first cognition." Cognition arises, he argues, as a *process* of beginning.

2. As a note of caution to the reader who is aware of the difference, I must stress that my understanding of the "real" is Peircean rather than Lacanian. Thus I render the "real" in the quotation from Lacan in Peircean terms.

3. See Daniel and Peck (1995).

4. I am making no claim here regarding whether or not the ontological experience of time in the manner of my treatment of it here is universal. I write only for South Asia and invoke Western notions of time to the extent that they do not contradict South Asian experiences of time.

5. Determination, you may recall from our brief excursus into Peircean semeiotic in the last chapter, is active whereas representation is passive. By "determination" Peirce meant the "delimitation of the possible" rather than "cause" (Peirce 8.177).

6. *Tōṭṭakkāṭṭān* is a derogatory term used by non-Estate Tamils of Sri Lanka to refer to Estate Tamils. It denotes one who labors on plantations and connotes one who is uncivilized and ill-mannered.

7. In this context, the man she refers to is not a real kaṅkāṇi—that is, one who was a labor leader on the plantations and is of Indian Tamil origin—but a Jaffna Tamil man who acts like one. *Kaṅkāṇi* in this context is somewhat like the facetious use of the term "boss."

8. Both Vijay Kumaratunga (a popular movie star of the Sinhala screen and the late husband of the current president, Chandrika Badaranaiake, who campaigned for a truce and an open and unconditional dialogue with the Tamil separatists) and Rajani

Thiranagama (a professor of anatomy who kept the conscience of the Tamil people alive by documenting human rights abuses on all sides) were assassinated in the prime of their political activity.

9. For reasons that will become clear, in this chapter I shall favor the use of the present tense in my narrative. In the translation of interviews I have paid special attention to preserving the tenses used by the interviewee at every point of the interview. This is significant.

10. A collector is an appointee of the Central Government, a man (mostly) who, from the position's inception in the colonial days on, has wielded considerable power and prestige. He is the most powerful government official in a district. His office is comparable to that of the French "prefect."

11. At that time the most fashionable, "sporty," Indian-made car.

12. A Non-Resident Indian, that is, an Indian who has settled in the West, commands a certain measure of respect that the resident Indian citizen does not.

13. The late Mr. M. G. Ramachandran, the chief minister of the state of Tamil Nadu was recuperating from surgery in the United States.

14. An āchārya is, in this context, a kind of Hindu prelate. A maṭam is a monastery. The story that dominated the headlines of all the major newspapers and magazines of Tamil Nadu during this time was about a young Hindu prelate's leaving his maṭam. Ironically, the story had little or no interest for most non-Brahmin Tamils, who constitute 98 percent of the state's population. A story of interest to only 2 percent of the population had taken over the newspapers.

15. Wartenberg observes that force is "predominantly negative in that it can keep an agent from performing certain actions but cannot get an agent to *do* anything. Unlike force, coercive power actually functions by getting an agent to *do* something" (1990:10).

16. For more on the ontology of care see Heidegger (1962:225–273).

17. "For instance, when a *Nova Stella* bursts out in the heavens, it acts upon one's eyes just as a light struck in the dark by one's own hands would; and yet it is an event which happened before the Pyramids were built. . . . The instance (certainly a commonplace enough fact), proves conclusively that the mode of the Past is that of Actuality" (Peirce 5.459).

18. I must thank Webb Kean who helped me appreciate this point (personal communication).

19. Also see Colapietro (1989:27–118).

20. Before the tea plantations of Sri Lanka were nationalized in the early 1970s, most plantation managers, "superintendents," as they were called, were Britons. Since nationalization, the Sinhalas have dominated the rank of planters.

21. See Homi Bhabha (1984).

CHAPTER 5
EMBODIED TERROR

1. I am substituting the more common "representation" for Peirce's more technically precise "representamen." For our purposes, the substitute will do.

2. One was a Tamil militant, the second was a former member of the Special Task Force, and the third was a retired officer of the Sri Lankan army.

3. Peirce defines a sinsign as "an actual existent where the syllable *sin* is taken as meaning 'being only once,' as in *single, simple*, Latin *semel, etc.*"—in short, a sign embodied singularly and uniquely (2.245).

4. Briefly, an iconic sign is a sign in which the representation shares in the quality of the object.

5. This is not the appropriate place for me to develop a theory of aesthetics based on the Peircean notion of iconicity. Suffice it to say that when "beauty" itself is referred to as an "object," what needs to be remembered is that it is an "object" in the semeiosic sense, i.e., not as a thing in itself or an end point. "The object is but the correlate of the sign. It is what the sign aims at reproducing" (Joswick 1995:96). Furthermore, the object has its own constitutive semeiosic genealogy; its semeiosic history is Janus-faced, both representing and being represented. Among other things what distinguishes an iconic sign—say, from an indexical or symbolic sign—is that (a) while all signs are both self-representing and other-representing, iconic signs privilege the former over the latter, (b) iconic signs are not only multivocal but are, contra symbols and indexes, unmotivated toward univocity, (c) iconic signs are paradoxical in that while their constituents may be "composed" into a whole, the harmony thus achieved is a precarious one. Together, (b) and (c) go into creating an aesthetic object that may best be described as throbbing with uncertain potentialities. Also see, for example, Alain Rey (1986).

6. One reader wondered whether this initial reticence was evidence of their defense against reexperiencing pain. In the majority of the fifty or so torture victims I interviewed and reinterviewed several years later in settings of greater acquaintance and trust, this did not seem to have been the case.

7. On the use of language that conforms to Ezra Pound's dictum "The sound must seem an echo to the sense," see Bruce Mannheim's essay of that title (1991); also see Paul Friedrich (1979) and Margaret Egnor (1986).

8. EPRLF, EROS, TELO, PLOTE, and LTTE are either initials or acronyms for the various Sri Lankan Tamil separatist militant groups.

CHAPTER 6
SUFFERING NATION AND ALIENATION

1. The three phases and the Tamils of these phases are herein typified. There are conspicuous exceptions, where Tamils of one phase have acted more like Tamils of a different phase.

2. Tone, token, and type correspond to Peirce's three phenomenological categories of Firstness, Secondness, and Thirdness.

3. A state of being keenly aware of one's action and to be oblivious to that awareness.

4. See C. R.de Silva (1979) and S. Ponnambalam (1983) for a more detailed discussion of facts and figures pertaining to the discrimination against Tamils in these two areas.

5. In an English medium class or school, all the subjects with the exception of the student's mother tongue—if it is different—are taught in English. The case is analogous for the Tamil and Sinhala media.

6. Portions within quotation marks are the actual words of informants recorded in my notes. The rest is paraphrase of what was told to me.

7. A lentil and vegetable dish.

8. A vegetable broth with a tamarind base.

9. The Tamil word for "history" employed in this context is *carittiram*. When Tamils refer to a narrative with "That is a history" (*atu oru carittiram*), the phrase is tinged with sarcasm and is better translated as "Now, that's a story."

10. The vermilion mark that Hindu women who are not widowed wear on their foreheads. During the riots this became an identifying mark of Tamils for Sinhala rioters.

11. The emblem of marriage worn as a pendant on a chain.

12. Among other things, this act provides for arrest without warrant for "unlawful activity" (Articles 2 and 31), detention in "any place," incommunicado and without trial for eighteen months (Sections 6, 7, 11), detention without trial (Section 15A), and the treatment of confessions obtained from a detainee as admissible evidence (Section 16) (Hyndman 1988).

13. There were many among the Phase 1 immigrants, especially barristers and those schooled in the social sciences, who were articulate critics of racism, classicism, and casteism. The most prominent figure among them was the current editor of the journal *Race and Class*: A. Sivanandan. My characterization of Phase 1 immigrants in this essay best fits those who chose the professions of medicine, engineering, and the hard sciences.

14. This and all other statements within quotation marks that occur in this section of this chapter are excerpts from interviews with Phase 1 Tamils obtained during field research in London carried out by either Y. Thangaraj or myself.

15. "Paki" is a common pejorative term applied to South Asians in Britain. It is intended to conjure up an image of poor South Asian Muslims (presumably from Pakistan) who perform menial jobs, speak a strange language, and practice a strange religion that requires them to prostrate themselves toward Mecca during prayer time wherever they happen to be—and whose women dress in strange clothes.

16. This is an allusion to a low caste from northern Sri Lanka whose traditional occupation used to be the tapping of toddy from palm trees. Not all Phase 3 refugees were members of the lower castes. The early ones were of modest means. With the passage of time, however, each month of the late 1980s and early 1990s brought poorer and more desperate refugees. They truly had nothing to return to. They had sold their last goat or brass pot to buy their passage.

17. Since the early days of Phase 2 Tamil immigrants to Britain, employment as petrol station attendants seems to have become the monopoly of freshly arrived non-Estate Sri Lankan Tamils. As the saying goes in this community, "Today at Heathrow, tomorrow at the petrol pump."

18. *Tambi* means "younger brother." It can be used as a term of endearment, but it can also be used patronizingly.

19. Only one individual confided to me his role in informing the Home Office and having a Phase 3 family deported. I was unable to find any documentary confirmation of this claim, and I am not sure whether it reflected fact or misplaced but mendacious bravado.

20. This act made it the responsibility of air and sea carriers to ensure that their passengers carried valid papers. Failure to do so made the carrier liable to heavy fines.

21. The People's Liberation Organization of Tamil Eeḷam is one of the several Tamil liberation movements that were born in the mid-1980s. This group never did engage in

combat either with the Indian or with the Sri Lankan state. But it became quite wealthy through investments made in Bombay and the running of a passport-forging shop in that same city. The drug-pushing charge is quite widely leveled against this group, but I have been able neither to confirm nor to disconfirm it. Its leader, Uma Maheswaran, was killed by a member of the LTTE in 1989, after which the liberation-of-Eelam activities of this group have become extinct for all intents and purposes. The fragmented financial empire, I understand, continues to flourish.

22. The Eelam People's Revolutionary Liberation Front, a millitant separatist group that, since the 1987 pact between India and Sri Lanka, has given up its demand for a separate state and has participated in government-arranged elections.

23. *Kēvalappaṭuttinārkaḷ*, a euphemism for rape.

24. Recall the great pivot line in *The Winter's Tale*, when the shepherd, who has rescued and exposed the infant Perdita, tells the clown, who has just witnessed simultaneous disasters—a shipwreck (by sea) and the bear devouring Antigonus (by land): "thou met'st with things dying, I with things new-born."

CHAPTER 7
CRUSHED GLASS: A COUNTERPOINT TO CULTURE

1. See George Stocking (1968).

2. I owe thanks to Professor Eric Hobsbawm and, especially, to Dr. Miri Rubin for substantive discussions of this and the following paragraph. The responsibility for errors in interpretation is entirely mine.

3. See Emmanuel Leroy-Ladurie (1974 and 1979)

4. See Fernand Braudel (1976).

5. For instance, consider this: "It should be stressed that these concepts rest on the premise that any symbol has many meanings, on the premise that symbols and meanings can be clustered into galaxies, and on the premise that galaxies seem to have core or epitomizing symbols as their foci "; or this: "I am now dealing with a galaxy [American culture] in which coitus is the epitomizing symbol" (Schneider 1976:218 and 216).

6. See, in particular, Michel Foucault (1972, 1973, and 1980).

7. Overheard from a conversation between Geertz and another anthropologist during which I was present.

8. One of C. S. Peirce's several neologisms that he triangulates with anancasm (the force of mechanical necessity) and agapism (loving lawfulness/mindfulness). See Peirce (6.302).

9. If the essentialist treatments of cultures are wanting and deserving of interrogation, so are comparable treatments of "class" and "gender." In this regard, see Joan Scott (1988:2); but see also the back-and-forth between Scott (1993) and Laura Lee Downs (1993).

10. I have discussed proponents of this idea in the first chapter.

11. As for the interesting distinction that Kant draws between the beautiful and the sublime, and insofar as he aligns the former with woman and the latter with man, it is but one step away from the Hindu resolution of the dichotomy in the androgynous divinity of Ardhanarisvarar, except that in the latter, the "male" would be beautiful, the "female" sublime.

12. The killings took place in April 1983. My interview with Selvakumar was in December of the same year.

13. A sarcastic reference to the name that Tamil separatists have given to their hoped for, separate nation-state.

14. Mr. Amirdhalingam was the head of the Tamil United Liberation Front, which was constituted in 1975 of the former (major Tamil) Federal Party and several smaller parties and groups. In its 1976 platform the TULF proclaimed the right of self-determination for the Tamils, even if that were to entail the formation of a separate state. In August of 1983, the constitution was amended so as to outlaw parties advocating secession. Members of Parliament were required to take an oath of allegiance to the new constitution. The elected members of the TULF refused. Consequently the party was outlawed, the members lost their seats in the legislature, and the Tamils were left largely unrepresented.

15. *Sāmi* means god.

GLOSSARY OF FREQUENTLY USED TERMS AND ABBREVIATIONS

abduction — One of three forms of inferring, according to C. S. Peirce. The other two are deduction and induction. It underlies the logic of discovery. In deduction something *must* be the case; in induction something *actually* is the case, in abduction it is suggested that something *might* be the case.

āyutam — Weapon; also tool.

bandh — A political demonstration.

Buddaṁ saraṇaṅ-gaccāmī — The opening line of a Buddhist chant, which means "Lord Buddha my refuge."

Burgher — Persons of Dutch, Portuguese, or other European ancestry.

cinna dorai — The assistant superintendent or, more colloquially, the small boss.

coupe — Originally meaning "a periodic felling of trees or an area that has been thus cleared," the word has come to stand also for the shacks in which the workers employed to fell trees or peel their bark are housed.

cunṭu — A dry measure of about a cup.

CWC — The Ceylon Workers' Congress.

dorai — Lord or, more commonly, boss.

dōśas or *tōsai* — A sourdough pancake.

DWC — The Democratic Workers' Congress.

EPRLF — The Eeḷam People's Revolutionary Liberation Front.

EROS — The Eeḷam Revolutionary Organization of Students.

FP — The Federal Party.

Goyigama — The highest Sinhala caste; members who traditionally saw themselves as cultivators.

idlis — Steamed cakes made of sourdough from rice flour.

interpretant — The significant effect of the relationship between a sign and its object upon a third so that this third itself becomes yet another sign.

- *emotional* — The significant effect of the sign that is affective or results in an emotion.
- *energetic* — The significant effect of the sign that results in action.
- *logical* — The significant effect of the sign that appeals to reason.

jawān — An Indian soldier.

JVP — Janatha Vimukthi Peramuna (People's Liberation Front—a Sinhala nationalist political party committed to the violent overthrow of the government).

Kaḷḷar — A South Indian Tamil caste held to be lower than the Veḷḷāḷas in the caste hierarchy. Believed to have traditionally been a martial caste, given to activities that ranged from robbery (as the term *kaḷḷan* indicates) to protection.

kaṅkāṇi — Leader of a labor gang; also supervisor.

Karāva — Traditionally, a Sinhala fisher caste.

Karayār — Traditionally, a Tamil fisher caste.

karmam — From the Skt. *karma*, roughly translated as the fruits of one's action in previous births, or consequences of present actions in future births; also fate.

kavvāttukkatti — A pruning knife.
kōppikkatti — A six-inch-long knife used for "tipping."
koṛuntu — The tea bud and the two leaves at its base.
kottu — A dry measure of about a quart.
legisign — A sign whose *regularity* serves as a sign vehicle.
LTTE — The Liberation Tigers of Tamil Eeḷam.
Mahāvaṁsa — A Buddhist chronicle.
Malayalee — A speaker of Malayalam and whose home state is the South Indian state of Kerala.
maṇveṭṭi — A hoelike implement used in cultivation.
Paḷḷan — Traditionally, a member of an untouchable caste who served as a hired hand in fields owned by the higher castes.
Panchayat — A council of (usually) five elders of a village.
Parayan — Traditionally, leatherworkers, town criers, and drummers. A member of a low caste.
PLOTE — People's Liberation Organization of Tamil Eeḷam.
poṭṭu — The vermilion mark that Hindu women who are not widowed wear on their foreheads.
purāṇam — Legend.
qualisign — A sign—when considered in relation to itself—whose quality serves as a sign vehicle.
rheme — A term introduced by C. S. Peirce to describe a sign the significant effect of which is a qualitative possibility.
sāmi — God or lord.
semeiosis — A term used to describe sign-activity.
semeiotic — A general theory of signs. Semeiotic is the spelling used by C. S. Peirce; the theory is now generally called semiotics.
sinsign — A sign whose *actualization* serves as a sign vehicle.
skiffing — Describes the manner of pruning a tea bush very near the surface so as to make the surface flat and parallel to the ground.
SLFP — The Sri Lanka Freedom Party.
Śri Mahā Bōdhi — The sacred bo-tree believed to have grown from a sapling of the actual tree under which the Buddha attained enlightenment.
tālikkoṭi — The emblem of marriage worn as a pendant on a chain.
tambi — Younger brother.
tasildhar — A revenue officer of a revenue subdivision.
TC — The Tamil Congress.
TELO — Tamil Eeḷam Liberation Organization.
tipping — The nipping off of stemlets that protrude above the surface of the tea bush.
TULF — The Tamil United Liberation Front.
UNP — The United National Party.
Veḷḷāḷas — The highest Tamil caste who traditionally saw themselves as cultivators.

REFERENCES

Abu-Lughod, Lila. 1991. Writing against Culture. *In* Recapturing Anthropology: Working in the Present, R. Fox, ed., pp. 137–162. Santa Fe: School of American Research Press.

Alberti, Leone Battista. 1966 (1485). Ten Books on Architecture. Trans. by James Leoni. New York: Transatlantic Arts.

Anderson, Benedict. 1983. Imagined Communities. London: Verso.

Appadurai, Arjun. 1981. Gastro-politics in Hindu South Asia. American Ethnologist 8(3):494–511.

———. [In press]. How Does Measurement Mean: Agricultural Terminology in Maharashtra. *In* Improvisation and Experience in an Agricultural Society. Berkeley and Los Angeles: University of California Press.

Arnold, Matthew. 1932. Culture and Anarchy. Cambridge: Cambridge University Press.

Artaud, Antonin. 1958. The Theater and Its Double. New York: Grove Press.

Bakhtin, Mikhail M. 1981. The Dialogical Imagination: Four Chapters by Bakhtin. Ed. by Michael Holquist. Austin: University of Texas Press.

Basham, A. L. 1954. The Wonder That Was India. London: Sidgwick and Jackson.

Basso, Keith M., and Henry N. Selby, eds. 1984. Meaning in Anthropology. Albuquerque: University of New Mexico Press.

Bastian, S. 1987. Plantation Labour in a Changing Context. *In* Facets of Ethnicity in Sri Lanka. Ed. by Charles Abeyesekera and Newton Gunasinghe. Colombo, Sri Lanka: Social Scientists' Association.

Bataille, Georges. 1988 (1954). Inner Experience. Albany: State University of New York Press.

Bauman, Zygmunt. 1992. Mortality, Immortality and Other Life Strategies. Cambridge: Polity Press.

Benjamin, Walter. 1983–1984. N[Theoretics of Knowledge; Theory of Progress. Trans. by Leigh Hafrey and Richard Sieburth. Philosophical Forum 15 (1 and 2):1–40.

Berlin, Brent, and Paul Kay. 1969. Basic Color Terms. Berkeley: University of California Press.

Bhabha, Homi. 1984. Of Mimicry and Man: The Ambivalence of Colonial Discourse. October 28:125–133.

Bharathithasan. 1985. Bharathithasan kavithaikal (in Tamil). Madras: Poompuhar Press.

Blanchot, Maurice. 1977. The Madness of the Day. New York: Station Hill Press.

Bloch, Marc. 1961. Feudal Society. 2 vols. Chicago: University of Chicago Press.

Boas, Franz. 1940 (1896). Race, Language and Culture. New York: Macmillan.

Bourdieu, Pierre. 1977. Outline of a Theory of Practice. Cambridge: Cambridge University Press.

———. 1985. The Genesis of the Concepts of "Habitus" and "Field." Sociocriticism 2(2):11–24.

Braudel, Fernand. 1976. The Mediterranean and the Mediterranean World in the Age of Philip the Second. 2 vols. New York: Harper and Row.

Brightman, Robert. 1995. Forget Culture: Replacement, Transcendence, Relexification. Cultural Anthropology 10(2):509–546.

Brow, James. 1988. In Pursuit of Hegemony: Representations of Justice and Authority in a Sri Lankan Village. American Ethnologist 15(2):311–327.

———. 1990. Nationalist Rhetoric and Local Practice: The Fate of the Village Community in Kukulewa. *In* History and the Roots of Conflict, Jonathan Spencer, ed., pp. 125–144. London: Routledge.

Caldwell, Robert. [1875.] A Comparative Grammar of the Dravidian or South-Indian Family of Languages. 6th ed. 1956. Madras: University of Madras.

Clifford, James. 1986. Introduction: Partial Truths. *In* Writing Culture: The Poetics and Politics of Ethnography, James Clifford and George Marcus, eds., pp. 1–26. Berkeley: University of California Press.

———. 1988. The Predicament of Culture. Cambridge: Harvard University Press.

Codrington, H. W. 1926. A Short History of Ceylon. London: Macmillan.

Cohen, Ted. 1982. Why Beauty Is a Symbol of Morality. *In* Essays in Kant's Aesthetics, Ted Cohen and Paul Guyer, eds., pp. 221–236. Chicago: University of Chicago Press.

Cohn, Bernard S. 1985. The Transformation of Objects into Artifacts, Antiquities and Art in Nineteenth Century India. Paper prepared for the NEH conference, Patronage in Indian Culture.

Colapietro, Vincent. 1989. Peirce's Approach to the Self: A Semiotic Perspective on Human Subjectivity. Albany: State University of New York Press.

Collingwood, R. G. 1946. The Idea of History. New York: Oxford University Press.

Connolly, William E. 1987. Politics and Ambiguity. Madison: University of Wisconsin Press.

———. 1991. Democracy and Territoriality. Millennium: Journal of International Studies 20(3):463–484.

Coomaraswamy, R. 1987. Myths without Conscience: Tamil and Sinhala Nationalist Writings of the 1980s. *In* Facets of Ethnicity in Sri Lanka, Charles Abyesekera and Newton Gunasinghe, eds., pp. 72–99. Colombo, Sri Lanka: Social Scientists' Association.

Copjec, Joan. 1994. Read My Desire. Cambridge: MIT Press.

Corrington, Robert S. 1993. An Introduction to C. S. Peirce: Philosopher, Semiotician, and Ecstatic Naturalist. Lanham, MD: Rowman and Littlefield.

Daniel, E. Valentine. 1984. Fluid Signs: Being a Person the Tamil Way. Berkeley: University of California Press.

———. 1989. Review of Legends of People, Myths of State: Violence, Intolerance, and Political Culture in Sri Lanka and Australia, by Bruce Kapferer. American Anthropologist 91(1):229–231.

Daniel, E. Valentine, and Jan Breman. 1992. Conclusion: The Making of a Coolie. *In* Plantations, Proletarians and Peasants in Colonial Asia, E. Valentine Daniel, Henry Bernstein, and Tom Brass, eds., pp. 268–291. London: Frank Cass.

Daniel, E. Valentine, Nicholas Dirks, and Gyan Prakash, eds. 1991. Nationalizing the Past: A Proposal for a Workshop. MS.

Daniel, E. Valentine, and John Chr. Knudsen. 1995. Mistrusting Refugees. Berkeley and Los Angeles: University of California Press.

Daniel, E. Valentine, and Jeffrey Peck, eds. 1995. Culture/Contexture: Explorations in Anthropology and Literary Study. Berkeley: University of California Press.

Darnton, Robert. 1985. The Great Cat Massacre. New York: Basic Books.

Davis, Natalie Z. 1975. Society and Culture in Early Modern France. Palo Alto: Stanford University Press.

Deely, John N. 1994. New Beginnings: Early Modern Philosophy and Postmodern Thought. Toronto and Buffalo: University of Toronto Press.

de Mel, Leloufer, ed. 1994. *Options* (Colombo, Sri Lanka) 1(1) (August).

Derrida, Jacques. 1974. Of Grammatology. Trans. by G. C. Spivak. Baltimore: Johns Hopkins University Press.

———. 1978. Spurs: Nietzsche's Styles. Chicago: University of Chicago Press.

———. 1981. Positions. Chicago: University of Chicago Press.

de Silva, C. R. 1979. The Impact of Nationalism on Education: The Schools Takeover (1961) and the University Admissions Crisis (1970–1975). *In* Collective Identities, Nationalisms and Protest in Modern Sri Lanka, Michael Roberts, ed., pp. 474–499. Colombo, Sri Lanka: Marga Institute.

de Silva, K. M. 1965. Social Politics and Missionary Organization in Ceylon 1840–1855. London: Longmans.

———. 1981. A History of Sri Lanka. Berkeley: University of California Press.

———. 1986. Managing Ethnic Tensions in Multi-Ethnic Societies: Sri Lanka 1880–1985. Lanham, MD: University Press of America.

Devaraj, P. 1985. Indian Tamils of Sri Lanka. *In* Ethnicity and Social Change in Sri Lanka, pp. 200–219. Colombo, Sri Lanka: Social Scientists' Association.

Dharmadasa, K.N.O. 1992. Language, Religion and Ethnic Assertiveness: The Growth of Sinhala Nationalism in Sri Lanka. Ann Arbor: University of Michigan Press.

Dictionary, English to Tamil. Madras: University of Madras, 1963.

Dirks, Nicholas. 1987. The Hollow Crown: Ethnohistory of an Indian Kingdom. Cambridge: Cambridge University Press.

Downs, Laura Lee. 1993. If "Woman" Is Just an Empty Category, Then Why Am I Afraid to Walk Alone at Night? Identity Politics Meets the Postmodern Subject. Comparative Studies in Society and History 35(2):414–451.

Dray, William H. 1957. Laws and Explanation in History. London: Oxford University Press.

Dreyfus, Hubert L. 1991. Being-in-the-World: A Commentary on Heidegger's Being and Time, Division I. Cambridge: MIT Press.

Dumont, Jean-Paul. 1986. Prologue to Ethnography or Prolegomena to Anthropography. Ethos 4(4):344–367.

Egnor, Margaret T. 1986. Internal Iconicity in Paraiyar "Crying Songs." *In* Another Harmony, Stuart H. Blackburn and A. K. Ramanujan, eds., pp. 294–344. Berkeley: University of California Press.

Evans-Pritchard, E. E. 1937. Witchcraft, Oracles and Magic among the Azande. Oxford: Clarendon Press.

Evens, T.M.S. 1982. Two Concepts of "Society as a Moral System": Evans-Pritchard's Heterodoxy. Man 17:205–218.

Famine Commission Report of 1885 (India). 1990. Microfilm. Vol. 3. London: British Museum Library.

Feld, Steven. 1982. Sound and Sentiment: Birds, Weeping, Poetics, and Song in Kaluli Expression. Berkeley: University of California Press.

Feldman, Allen. 1991. Formations of Violence. Chicago: University of Chicago Press.

Felstiner, John. 1995. Paul Celan: Poet, Survivor, Jew. New Haven: Yale University Press.

Ferguson's Ceylon Handbook and Directory. 1880–1 to 1913–4. London: British Museum Library.

Fisch, Max H. 1978. Peirce's General Theory of Signs. *In* Sight, Sound and Sense, Thomas Sebeok, ed., pp. 31–70. Bloomington: Indiana University Press.

Foucault, Michel. 1972. The Archaeology of Knowledge and the Discourse on Language. New York: Pantheon Books.

———. 1973. The Order of Things: An Archaeology of the Human Sciences. New York: Random House.

———. 1979. Discipline and Punish: The Birth of the Prison. New York: Vintage Books.

———. 1980. Power/Knowledge: Selected Interviews and Other Writings, 1972–77. New York: Pantheon.

———. 1984. Nietzsche, Genealogy, History. *In* Foucault Reader, Paul Rabinow, ed., pp. 76–100. New York: Pantheon Books.

Frege, G. 1960. Translations from the Philosophical Writings of Gottlob Frege. Oxford: Basil Blackwell.

Friedrich, Paul. 1979. The Symbol and Its Relative Non-arbitrariness. *In* Language, Context and the Imagination, pp. 1–61. Palo Alto: Stanford University Press.

Gadamer, Hans Georg. 1975. Truth and Method. New York: Crossroad Publishing Company.

Gallie, W. P. 1964. Philosophy and the Historical Understanding. London: Chatto & Windus.

Gardiner, Patrick, ed. 1959. Theories of History. New York: The Free Press.

Geertz, Clifford. 1966. Person, Time and Conduct in Bali: An Essay in Cultural Analysis. Yale South East Asia Program, Cult. Rep. Series 14.

———. 1967. The Cerebral Savage: On the Work of Claude Lévi-Strauss. Encounter 28:25–32.

Ginzburg, Carlo. 1982. The Cheese and the Worms. New York: Penguin.

Gramsci, Antonio. 1971. Selections from the Prison Notebooks. New York: International Publishers.

Gunawardana, R.A.L.H. 1990. The People of the Lion: The Sinhala Identity and Ideology in History and Historiography. *In* History and the Roots of Conflict, Jonathan Spencer, ed., pp. 45–86. London: Routledge.

Haley, M. C. 1988. The Semeiosis of Poetic Metaphor. Bloomington: Indiana University Press.

Hall, Stuart. 1982. The Battle for Socialist Ideas in the 1980s. *In* The Socialist Register, Ralph Miliband and John Saville, eds., pp. 1–19. London: Merlion Press.

Hardwick, Charles S. 1977. Semiotic and Significs: The Correspondence between Charles S. Peirce and Victoria Lady Welby. Bloomington: Indiana University Press.

Harrington, John R. 1979 (1809). Asiatic Researches 12:52–74. New Delhi: Cosmo Publications.

Harris, Marvin. 1968. The Rise of Cultural Theory. New York: Crowell.

Heidegger, Martin. 1962. Being and Time. New York: Harper and Row.

Hellman-Rajanayagam, Dagmar. 1990. The Politics of the Tamil Past. *In* History and the Roots of Conflict, Jonathan Spencer, ed., pp. 107–122. London: Routledge.

Hempel, Karl. 1959. The Function of General Laws in History. Journal of Philosophy 39:35–48.

Herz, John H. 1959. International Politics in the Atomic Age. New York: Columbia University Press.

———. 1968. The Territorial State Revisited: Reflections on the Future of the Nation-State. Polity 1(1)(Fall): 11–34.

Hill, Geoffrey. 1971. Mercian Hymns. London: André Deutsch.

———. 1991. The Enemy's Country. Stanford: Stanford University Press.

Hoffman, Piotr. 1986. Doubt, Time, Violence. Chicago: University of Chicago Press.

———. 1989. Violence in Modern Philosophy. Chicago: University of Chicago Press.

Hooker, Jeremy. 1985. For the Unfallen: A Sounding. *In* Geoffrey Hill: Essays on his Work, Peter Robinson, ed., pp. 20–30. Philadelphia: Open University Press.

Hoole, Rajan, Daya Somasundaram, K. Sritharan, Rajani Thiranagama, eds. 1988. The Broken Palmyra. Claremont: The Sri Lanka Studies Institute.

Hyndman, Patricia. 1988. Sri Lanka: Serendipity under Siege. Nottingham: Spokesman.

Johnson, R. J. 1962. Johnson's Notebook for Tea Planters. Colombo, Sri Lanka: Lake House Press.

Jones, Sir William. 1979 (1809). Asiatic Researches 2:88–114. New Delhi: Cosmo Publications.

Joswick, Hugh. 1995. Charles Peirce's Pragmatic Pluralism by Sandra B. Rosenthal, A Review. Transactions of the C. S. Peirce Society 31(4):875–886.

Kailasapathy, K. 1985. Cultural and Linguistic Consciousness of the Tamil Community. *In* Ethnicity and Social Change in Sri Lanka, pp. 161–174. Colombo, Sri Lanka: Social Scientists' Association.

Kannangara, E. T. 1984. Jaffna and the Sinhala Heritage. Homagama: E. T. Kannangara.

Kant, Immanuel. 1951 (1799). Critique of Judgment. Trans. by J. H. Bernard. New York: Haffner Publishing Company.

Kapferer, Bruce. 1985. Review of The Cult of the Goddess Pattini, by Gananath Obeyesekere. American Ethnologist 12:176–179.

———. 1988. Legends of People, Myths of State. Washington: Smithsonian Institution Press.

Keesing, Roger. 1974. Theories of Culture. *In* Annual Review of Anthropology, B. J. Siegel, et al., eds., 3:73–98. Palo Alto: Annual Review.

Kemper, Steven. 1990. J. R. Jayawardene: Righteousness and Realpolitic. *In* History and the Roots of Conflict, Jonathan Spencer, ed., pp. 187–204. London: Routledge.

———. 1991. The Presence of the Past: Chronicles, Politics, and Culture in Sinhala Life. Ithaca: Cornell University Press.

Kinnell, Galway. 1982. Selected Poems. Boston: Houghton Mifflin Company.

Knighton, William. 1845. The History of Ceylon from the Earliest Period to the Present Time: With an Appendix, Containing an Account of Its Present Condition. London: Longman, Brown, Green and Longman.

Kodikara, S. U. 1965. Indo-Ceylon Relations since Independence. Colombo, Sri Lanka: Ceylon Institute of World Affairs.

Kristeva, Julia. 1980. Desire in Language. New York: Columbia University Press.

Lacan, Jacques. 1977. Ecrits: A Selection. Trans. by Alan Sheridan. New York: W. W. Norton.

Lacan, Jacques. 1990. Television: A Challenge to the Psychoanalytic Establishment. Trans. by Joan Copjec. New York: W. W. Norton.

Lass, A. 1988. Romantic Documents and Political Monuments: The Meaning-Fulfillment of History in Nineteenth Century Czech Nationalism. American Ethnologist 15:456–471.

Leach, Sir Edmund. 1990. Aryan Invasion over Four Millennia. *In* Culture through Time, Emiko Ohnuki-Tierney, ed., pp. 227–245. Stanford: Stanford University Press.

Lears, T. J. Jackson. 1985. The Concept of Cultural Hegemony: Problems and Possibilities. American Historical Review 90(3):568.

Le Roy-Ladurie, Emmanuel. 1974. The Peasants of Languedoc. Chicago: University of Illinois Press.

———. 1979. Montaillou: The Promised Land of Error. New York: Random House.

Ludden, D. 1985. Peasant History in South India. Princeton: Princeton University Press.

Ludowyk, E.F.C. 1966. The Modern History of Ceylon. London: Weidenfeld and Nicolson.

———. 1967. The Story of Ceylon. London: Faber and Faber.

Mahony, Capt. 1803. On Singhala, or Ceylon, and the Doctrines of Bhooddha. Asiatick Researches 7:32–56.

Mannheim, Bruce. 1991. The Language of the Inka since the European Invasion. Austin: University of Texas Press.

Margolis, Joseph. 1993. The Flux of History and the Flux of Science. Berkeley: University of California Press.

Martin, R. M. 1987. The Meaning of Language. Cambridge: MIT Press.

McKenzie, Capt. Colin. 1803 (1796). Remarks on Some Antiquities on the West and South Coasts of Ceylon. Asiatick Researches 6:425–454.

Merquior, J. G. 1985. Foucault. London: Fontana.

Merrell, Floyd. 1996. Vagueness, Generality, and Undeciding Otherness. *In* Peirce's Doctrine of Signs, Vincent H. Colapietro and Thomas M. Olshewsky, eds., pp. 33–44. Berlin: Mouton de Gruyter.

Miller, Marjorie. 1996. Peirce's Conceptions of Habits. *In* Peirce's Doctrine of Signs, Vincent H. Colapietro and Thomas M. Olshewsky, eds., pp. 71–78. Berlin: Mouton de Gruyter.

Ministry of State Publication No. 8. 1983. Sri Lanka: The Truth about Discrimination against the Tamils. Colombo, Sri Lanka: Department of Information.

Misak, C. J. 1991. Truth and the End of Inquiry. New York: Oxford University Press.

Munn, Nancy. 1986. The Fame of Gawa: A Symbolic Study of Value Transformation in a Massim (Papua New Guinea) Society. Cambridge: Cambridge University Press.

Nadesan, S. 1993. A History of the Upcountry Tamil People. Colombo, Sri Lanka: Nandalala Publication.

Nehru, J. 1960. The Discovery of India. Garden City: Anchor Books.

Nilakanta Sastri, K. A. 1975. A History of South India. 4th ed. Madras: Oxford University Press.

Obeyesekere, Gananath. 1984. The Cult of the Goddess Pattini. Chicago: University of Chicago Press.

———. 1991. The Dating of the Historical Buddha. Symposium zur Buddhismusforchung, 6:1, Gottingen: Vandenhoeck & Ruprecht.

Olshewsky, Thomas. 1982. Between Science and Religion. Journal of Religion 6(62): 242–260.

Parmentier, Richard. 1985. Signs' Place in Medias Res: Peirce's Concept of Semiotic Mediation. *In* Semiotic Mediation, Richard Parmentier and Elizabeth Mertz, eds., pp. 23–48. New York: Academic Press.

Peirce, Charles S. 1938. Collected Papers, vols. 1–6. Ed. by C. Hartshorne and P. Weiss. Cambridge: Harvard University Press.

———. 1958. Collected Papers, vols. 7–8. Ed. by A. Bucks. Cambridge: Harvard University Press.

———. Unpublished manuscripts at the Houghton Library at Harvard University.

Pepper, S. 1942. World Hypotheses. Berkeley: University of California Press.

Ponnambalam, S. 1983. Sri Lanka: The National Question and the Tamil Struggle. London: Zed Books.

Pope, G. U. 1886. Kural. London: Allen & Co.

Ramanujan, A. K. 1986. Two Realms of Kannada Folklore. *In* Another Harmony, A. K. Ramanujan and Stuart Blackburn, eds., pp. 41–75. Berkeley: University of California Press.

Ramaswamy, Sumathi. 1993. En/gendering Language: The Poetics of Tamil Identity. Comparative Studies in Society and History 35(4):683–725.

Rey, Alain. 1986. Mimesis, poétique et iconisme. Pour une relecture d'Aristotle." *In* Iconicity: Essays on the Nature of Culture, Paul Bouissac, Michael Herzfeld, and Roland Posner, eds., pp. 17–27. Tübingen: Stauffenberg-Verlag.

Ricoeur, Paul. 1984. Time and Narrative. 3 vols. Chicago: University of Chicago Press.

Rogers, John D. 1990. Historical Images in the British Period. *In* History and the Roots of Conflict, Jonathan Spencer, ed., pp. 87–106. London: Routledge.

Rosenthal, Sandra. 1994. Charles Peirce's Pragmatic Pluralism. Albany: State University of New York Press.

Rudner, David W. 1994. Caste and Capitalism in Colonial India: The Nattukottai Chettiars. Berkeley and Los Angeles: University of California Press.

Russell, J. 1982. Communal Politics under the Donoughmore Constitution 1931–1947. Dehiwala, Sri Lanka: Tisara Press.

Sagar, R. V., et al. 1986. The Human Cost of Commercial Forestry. A Study of the Conditions of Coupe Labourers in Kodaikanal Hills: A Supreme Court Commission Report. (A typescript copy of this document is available at the Library of the Director, Research and Development, Madurai Province, Beschi College, Dindigul 624-004, India.)

Said, Edward. 1978. Orientalism. New York: Pantheon Books.

Salomon, R. 1980. A New View of the Problem of Ancient Indian History. Unpublished MS.

Sanderson, G. W. 1964. The Theory of Withering in Tea Manufacture. Tea Quarterly 35(3):146–156.

Santaella Braga, Lucia. 1992. Time as the Logical Process of the Sign. Semiotica 88(3/4): 309–326.

Sarasin, C. F. and P. B. 1886. Outlines of Two Years' Scientific Researches in Ceylon. Journal of the Ceylon Branch of the Royal Asiatic Society 9:289–305.

Satyendra, N. 1983. Legitimate Expectation. *In* Ethnic Violence, Developmental and Human Rights, pp. 85–120. Utrecht: Netherlands Institute of Human Rights.

Scarry, Elaine. 1985. The Body in Pain. Oxford: Oxford University Press.

Schneider, David M. 1976. Notes toward a Theory of Culture. *In* Meaning in Anthropology, Keith H. Basso and Henry A. Selby, eds., pp. 197–220. Albuquerque: University of New Mexico Press.

Schumpeter, Joseph. 1942. Capitalism, Socialism and Democracy. New York: Harper and Row.

Scott, James C. 1990. Domination and the Arts of Resistance: Hidden Transcripts. New Haven: Yale University Press.

Scott, Joan W. 1988. Gender and the History of Politics. New York: Columbia University Press.

———. 1993. The Tip of the Volcano. Comparative Studies in Society and History 35(2):438–443.

Seneviratne, H. L. 1978. Rituals of the Kandyan State. Cambridge: Cambridge University Press.

Shaviro, Steven. 1990. Passion and Excess. Gainesville: Florida State University Press.

Shue, Henry. 1978. Torture. Philosophy and Public Affairs 7 (Winter):124–143.

Silverstein, Michael. 1976. Shifters, Linguistic Categories, and Cultural Description. *In* Meaning in Anthropology, Keith H. Basso and Henry A. Selby, eds., pp. 11–55. Albuquerque: University of New Mexico Press.

Siriweera, W. I. 1985. The Dutthagamani-Elara Episode: A Reassessment. *In* Ethnicity and Social Change in Sri Lanka, pp. 108–127. Colombo, Sri Lanka: Social Scientists' Association.

Skagestad, Peter. 1981. The Road of Inquiry. New York: Columbia University Press.

Spencer, Jonathan. 1989. Telling Histories: Nationalism and Nationalists in a Sinhala Village. Unpublished MS.

———. 1990. Introduction: The Power of the Past. *In* History and the Roots of Conflict, Jonathan Spencer, ed., pp. 1–16. London: Routledge, 1990.

Stocking, George. 1968. Race, Culture and Evolution. New York: Free Press.

Tambiah, S. J. 1979. A Performative Approach to Ritual. Proceedings of the British Academy 65:113–169. London: Oxford University Press.

———. 1986. Sri Lanka: Ethnic Fratricide and the Dismantling of Democracy. Chicago: University of Chicago Press.

———. 1992. Buddhism Betrayed? Religion, Politics, and Violence in Sri Lanka. Chicago: University of Chicago Press.

Taylor, Charles. 1985. Language and Human Nature. *In* Philosophical Papers, 1:215–247. Cambridge: Cambridge University Press.

Tea Research Institute. 1963. One Day Course in Tea Production. St. Coombs, Ceylon.

———. 1966 and 1967. Annual Reports. St. Coombs, Ceylon.

Tennekoon, Serena N. 1987. Symbolic Refractions of the Ethnic Crisis: The Divaina Debates on Sinhala Identity. *In* Facets of Ethnicity, C. Abeyesekere and N. Gunasinghe, eds., pp. 1–59. Colombo, Sri Lanka: Social Scientists' Association.

———. 1988. Rituals of Development: The Accelerated Mahavali Development Program of Sri Lanka. American Ethnologist 15(2):294–310.

———. 1990. Newspaper Nationalism: Sinhala Identity as Historical Discourse. *In* History and the Roots of Conflict, Jonathan Spencer, ed., pp. 205–226. London: Routledge.

Tennent, Sir James E. 1859. Ceylon: An Account of the Island—Physical, Historical, and Topographical. 2 vols. London: Longman Green.

Thapar, Romila. 1989. Imagined Religious Communities? Ancient History and the Modern Search for a Hindu Identity. Modern Asian Studies 23(2):209–231.

Thompson, E. P. 1966. The Making of the English Working Class. New York: Vintage.

Turner, Stuart. 1996. Torture, Refugee and Trust. *In* Mistrusting Refugees, E. Valentine Daniel and John Knudsen, eds., pp. 56–72. Berkeley: University of California Press.

Turner, Victor. 1974. Drama, Fields, and Metaphors: A Symbolic Action in Human Society. Cornell: Cornell University Press.

Tylor, Sir Edward B. 1974 (1878). Primitive Culture. New York: Gordon Press.

Velupillai, C. V. 1970. Born to Labour. Colombo, Sri Lanka: M. D. Gunasena and Co.

Virchow, Rudolph. 1886. Ethnological Studies on the Sinhalese Race. Trans. from German and published in Journal of the Ceylon Branch of the Royal Asiatic Society 9:267–268.

Vittachi, Tarzie. 1958. Emergency 58: The Story of the Ceylon Race Riots. London: A. Deutsch.

Wagner, Roy. 1985. Symbols That Stand for Themselves. Chicago: University of Chicago Press.

Walzer, Michael. 1983. Spheres of Justice: A Defense of Pluralism and Equality. New York: Basic Books.

Warder, A. K. 1972. An Introduction to Indian Historiography. Bombay: Popular Prakashan.

Wartenberg, Thomas E. 1990. The Forms of Power. Philadelphia: Temple University Press.

Weber, Max. 1948. From Max Weber: Chapters in Sociology. Trans. and ed. by H. H. Gerth and C. Wright Mills. New York: Oxford University Press.

Weerasooriya, W. S. 1973. The Nattukottai Chettiar Merchant Bankers in Ceylon. Dehiwala, Sri Lanka: Tisara Press.

Wertheim, W. F. 1974. Evolution and Revolution. Baltimore: Penguin.

Wesumperuma, D. 1986. Indian Immigrant Plantation Workers in Sri Lanka: A Historical Perspective, 1880–1910. Kelaniya, Sri Lanka: Vidyalankara Press.

Whitaker, Mark P. 1990. A Compound of Many Histories: The Many Pasts of an East Coast Tamil Community. *In* History and the Roots of Conflict, Jonathan Spencer, ed., pp. 145–163. London: Routledge.

White, Hayden. 1973. Metahistory: The Historical Imagination in Nineteenth Century Europe. Baltimore: Johns Hopkins University Press.

———. 1987. The Content of the Form. Baltimore: Johns Hopkins University Press.

Whitehead, Alfred North. 1978 (1929). Process and Reality: An Essay in Cosmology. New York: Free Press.

Williams, Raymond. 1983. Keywords. New York: Oxford University Press.

Wirz, Paul. 1954. Exorcism and the Art of Healing in Ceylon. Leiden: E. J. Brill.

Woost, Michael D. 1990. Rural Awakenings: Grassroots Development and the Cultivation of a National Past in Rural Sri Lanka. *In* History and the Roots of Conflict, Jonathan Spencer, ed., pp. 164–183. London: Routledge.

Yeats, William B. 1964. Letters on Poetry from W. B. Yeats to Dorothy Wellesley. New York: Oxford University Press.

INDEX

abduction, 105, 125
Abhayagiri, 63
Abu-Lughod, L., 13
Accra, 176
actual, the, 104, 124, 126
Adam's Peak, 56
Adorno, T., 153, 211
aesthetics, 135, 153
Africa, 8, 177
Africans, 174
agency, 189–192; agentive moments, 189–192; and self, 189–190
agriculture, 75, 220n.2; folk, 72–73
agronomy, 75, 220n.2
Alberti, L., 137
Alberuni, 24, 214n.12
Althusser, L., 74
Ambagamuwa, 34
ambivalence, 106, 153
America. *See* United States
Amin, Idi, 8
Amirdhalingam, A., 59, 158, 204, 227n.14
amity talks, 63
Amnesty International, 142
analytic philosophy, 49
Anderson, B., 18, 168
Anglophilia, 48
anicca, 107
Aṅkeliya, 66
anthropography, 4, 5, 106, 107, 133
anthropologist, 12; and voice, 120–121. *See also* ethnographer
anthropology, 4, 14, 48, 132, 194; cognitive, 197; comparative, 11; and cultural studies, 196; interpretive, 197; and Orientalism, 49; physical, 58–59. *See also* ethnography
anthropometry, 58
Anuradhapura, 25, 34, 56, 58, 204; massacre at, 66; ontic and epistemic aspects of, 62–66
anxiety. *See* Heidegger
Appadurai, A., 78, 82, 221n.15
Arabs, 44
Arbuthnot, Sir R., 35
Aristotle, 136
Ariyaratne, A. T., 219n.29
Arnold, M., 195
Artaud, A., 70, 71
Aryanization, 58, 219n.23
Aryans, 55
Äsələ Perəhärə, 56; and ethnic riots, 61; political symbolism of, 60–61
Aśoka, 54
Assam, 24
asylum: application for, 186–187; seeking of, 176–182
Auschwitz, 211
Australia, 38, 48
autoreferentiality, 135
availableness. *See* Heidegger
Ayodhya-Babri Masjid, 47
Ayyangars, 165
Ayyars, 165
Aziz, A., 114

Bach, J. S., 202
Badaranaike, C., 222n.8
Badulla, 34, 215n.24
baila, 49, 157
Bakhtin, M., 72, 73, 198
Bandaranaike, S., 38, 114, 115, 222n.28
Bandarawela, 34
Bangkok, 176, 179
Basham, A.L., 154, 218n.12
Bastian, S., 23
Bataille, G., 135, 208, 210
Batticaloa, 21, 147, 162, 164
Bauman, Z., 121
beauty, 136, 139, 144, 224n.5; and language, 138; and pain, 136–139, 152–153
being: and anthroposemeiosis, 121–123; human, 121–127; mythic nature of, 50–55; ontic nature of, 44, 45, 47, 50; and seeing, 43–71; in time, 123–127; with vs. as, 169
Benjamin, W., 100, 136
Berlin, B., 197
Bhabha, H., 88, 154, 155, 221n.25, 223n.21
Bhais, 37, 216n.37
Bharathithasan, 217nn. 48 and 49
Biller, C. R., 35
Blackwater Estate, 35
Blanchot, M., 136, 208
Boaz, F., 195
body, 87; of the victim, 139. *See also* pain; torture
Boosa, 140, 147, 148, 151

PRINCETON STUDIES IN
CULTURE/POWER/HISTORY

Sherry B. Ortner, Nicholas B. Dirks, and Geoff Eley, eds.

High Religion:
A Cultural and Political History of Sherpa Buddhism
by Sherry B. Ortner

A Place in History:
Social and Monumental Time in a Cretan Town
by Michael Herzfeld

The Textual Condition
by Jerome J. McGann

Regulating the Social:
The Welfare State and Local Politics in Imperial Germany
by George Steinmetz

Hanging without a Rope:
Narrative Experience in Colonial and Postcolonial Karoland
by Mary Margaret Steedly

Modern Greek Lessons:
A Primer in Historical Constructivism
by James Faubion

The Nation and Its Fragments:
Colonial and Postcolonial Histories
by Partha Chatterjee

Culture/Power/History:
A Reader in Contemporary Social Theory
edited by Nicholas B. Dirks, Geoff Eley, and Sherry B. Ortner

After Colonialism:
Imperial Histories and Postcolonial Displacements
edited by Gyan Prakash

Encountering Development:
The Making and Unmaking of the Third World
by Arturo Escobar

Social Bodies:
Science, Reproduction, and Italian Modernity
by David G. Horn

Revisioning History:
Film and the Construction of a New Past
edited by Robert A. Rosenstone

The History of Everyday Life:
Reconstructing Historical Experiences and Ways of Life
edited by Alf Lüdtke

The Savage Freud and Other Essays on Possible
and Retrievable Selves
by Ashis Nandy

Children and the Politics of Culture
edited by Sharon Stephens

Intimacy and Exclusion:
Religious Politics in Pre-Revolutionary Baden
by Dagmar Herzog

What Was Socialism, and What Comes Next?
by Katherine Verdery

Citizen and Subject:
Contemporary Africa and the Legacy of Late Colonialism
by Mahmood Mamdani

Colonialism and Its Forms of Knowledge: The British in India
by Bernard S. Cohn

Charred Lullabies: Chapters in an Anthropography of Violence
by E. Valentine Daniel